Critical Psychotherapy, Psychoan

Also by Del Loewenthal

AGAINST AND FOR CBT: Towards a Constructive Dialogue (*co-author*)

CASE STUDIES IN RELATIONAL RESEARCH: Qualitative Research Methods in Counselling and Psychotherapy

CHILDHOOD, WELL-BEING AND A THERAPEUTIC ETHOS (*co-author*)

CRITICALLY ENGAGING CBT (*co-author*)

PHOTOTHERAPY AND THERAPEUTIC PHOTOGRAPHY IN A DIGITAL AGE

POST-EXISTENTIALISM AND THE PSYCHOLOGICAL THERAPIES: Towards a Therapy without Foundations

POST-MODERNISM FOR PSYCHOTHERAPISTS: A Critical Reader (*co-author*)

RELATIONAL PSYCHOTHERAPY, PSYCHOANALYSIS AND COUNSELLING: Appraisals and Reappraisals (*co-author*)

WHAT IS PSYCHOTHERAPEUTIC RESEARCH? (*co-author*)

Critical Psychotherapy, Psychoanalysis and Counselling

Implications for Practice

Edited by

Del Loewenthal
University of Roehampton, UK

Selection, introduction, conclusion and editorial content
© Del Loewenthal 2015
Individual chapters © Respective authors 2015

Chapter 10 was originally published as 'Everything you always wanted to know about therapy (but were afraid to ask): Social, political, economic and clinical fragments of a critical psychotherapy' by Andrew Samuels in the October 2014 issue of *European Journal of Psychotherapy & Counselling* and is reprinted by permission of the publisher, Taylor & Francis Ltd.

All rights reserved. No reproduction, copy or transmission of this publication may be made without written permission.

No portion of this publication may be reproduced, copied or transmitted save with written permission or in accordance with the provisions of the Copyright, Designs and Patents Act 1988, or under the terms of any licence permitting limited copying issued by the Copyright Licensing Agency, Saffron House, 6–10 Kirby Street, London EC1N 8TS.

Any person who does any unauthorized act in relation to this publication may be liable to criminal prosecution and civil claims for damages.

The authors have asserted their rights to be identified as the authors of this work in accordance with the Copyright, Designs and Patents Act 1988.

First published 2015 by
PALGRAVE MACMILLAN

Palgrave Macmillan in the UK is an imprint of Macmillan Publishers Limited, registered in England, company number 785998, of Houndmills, Basingstoke, Hampshire RG21 6XS.

Palgrave Macmillan in the US is a division of St Martin's Press LLC,
175 Fifth Avenue, New York, NY 10010.

Palgrave Macmillan is the global academic imprint of the above companies and has companies and representatives throughout the world.

Palgrave® and Macmillan® are registered trademarks in the United States, the United Kingdom, Europe and other countries.

ISBN 978–1–137–46056–1 hardback
ISBN 978–1–137–46057–8 paperback

This book is printed on paper suitable for recycling and made from fully managed and sustained forest sources. Logging, pulping and manufacturing processes are expected to conform to the environmental regulations of the country of origin.

A catalogue record for this book is available from the British Library.

A catalog record for this book is available from the Library of Congress.

Contents

List of Tables and Figures viii

Acknowledgements ix

Authors' Biographies, Abstracts and Self-Critiques xi

Part I Introduction

1 Talking Therapies, Culture, the State and Neoliberalism: Is There a Need for Critical Psychotherapy, Psychoanalysis and Counselling?   3
Del Loewenthal

Part II What Can We Learn from Critical Psychiatry and Critical Psychology?

2 The Medical Model: What Is It, Where Did It Come from and How Long Has It Got?   29
Hugh Middleton

3 Towards Critical Psychotherapy and Counselling: What Can We Learn from Critical Psychology (and Political Economy)?   41
Ian Parker

4 The Neurobiological Turn in Therapeutic Treatment: Salvation or Devastation?   53
Kenneth J. Gergen

Part III Users' Perspectives

5 Personal versus Medical Meanings in Breakdown, Treatment and Recovery from 'Schizophrenia'   77
Tom Cotton and Del Loewenthal

Part IV Critiques Coming More from Outside

6 Critical Theory and Psychotherapy 95
   Anastasios Gaitanidis

7 When Love Is Not All We Want: Queers, Singles and the
   Therapeutic Cult of Relationality 108
   Mari Ruti and Adrian Cocking

8 Relating to People as Revolutionaries 125
   Lois Holzman

9 Work in Contemporary Capitalism 138
   Michael Rustin

Part V Critiques Coming More from Inside

10 Everything You Always Wanted to Know about Therapy
    (But Were Afraid to Ask): Fragments of a Critical
    Psychotherapy 159
    Andrew Samuels

11 Critical Priorities for the Psychotherapy and Counselling
    Community 175
    Colin Feltham

12 The Deleuzian Project 189
    Chris Oakley

13 Psychoanalysis and the Event of Resistance 200
    Steven Groarke

14 Psychology, Psychotherapy – Coming
    to Our Senses? 222
    Paul Moloney

Part VI Critiques of Training and Learning

15 Contesting the Curriculum: Counsellor Education in a
    Postmodern and Medicalising Era 241
    *Tom Strong, Karen H. Ross, Konstantinos Chondros and
    Monica Sesma-Vazquez*

16 Systemic Means to Subversive Ends: Maintaining the
    Therapeutic Space as a Unique Encounter 264
    Jay Watts

Part VII Is There an Unfortunate Need for Critical Psychotherapy, Psychoanalysis and Counselling?

17 Psychotherapy, Psychoanalysis and Counselling for Oppressors and Oppressed: Sex, Violence and Ideology in Practice?   285
Del Loewenthal

Index   303

Tables and Figures

Tables

16.1 Sample deconstructionist questions 273
16.2 'Situating professionals' exercise 276

Figures

15.1 Who has something at stake in counsellor education? 246

Acknowledgements

I should first like to thank my parents who, when I was young, for many years had two lodgers, one a *Daily Telegraph*-reading tax inspector and the other a communist shop steward. As a result, I read both the *Daily Telegraph* and such books as William Gallacher's *Revolt on the Clyde*. These two forces of individualism versus social action have taken different guises at different points in my life, varying from facilitating management development for chief executives to helping to develop community enterprises. My own doctorate, which I started over 40 years ago, again looked at how individuals escape from self-awareness and conspire with those who wish to control how they think. Again when I was growing up, my father's best friend, who was an arch capitalist, was particularly worried that the Italian Communist Party would lead Europe into a new renaissance. As a result, he bought Italian newspapers on an almost daily basis, saying that it was vital to understand them if we were to beat them. Unlike most of my contemporaries, therefore, I was not brought up to think that there would be dire consequences as a result of discussing and trying to understand that which one might be opposed to – in fact quite the reverse.

After many years of training counsellors and psychotherapists, in particular regarding the implications of scepticism/continental philosophy for their practices, I have in this book wondered if such approaches are permissible in late capitalism precisely because they avoid the likelihood of anything more radical. How my more recent train of thought came about I am not too sure. What I do remember is having a conversation with my colleague James Davies and writing an editorial for the *European Journal of Psychotherapy & Counselling* entitled 'Is there an unfortunate need for critical psychotherapy and counselling?' As a consequence, I was approached by Nicola Jones from Palgrave Macmillan, who persuaded me to write this book.

My subsequent thanks go to members of the Universities Psychotherapy & Counselling Association Council, who approved my running its, what turned out to be well-attended, annual conference, Critical psychotherapy and counselling – if not now, when? (the phrasing for which I have Andrew Samuels to thank). There are many more people to thank from here. First are the distinguished contributors who so ably met my changing deadlines and coped with my attempts at communication.

I also had the help of Dawn Clark in the early stages and Betty Bertrand throughout, but most importantly, my thanks to Liz Nicholl, for without her abilities and motivation it is quite likely that this book would not have appeared. Last, but not least, my thanks go to both colleagues and students at the Research Centre for Therapeutic Education for our continually evolving conversations, and my wife, Jane, who put up with me again spending at least some of our summer holiday completing yet another book on relationships, albeit a book, I hope, with a difference.

Authors' Biographies, Abstracts and Self-Critiques

Chapter 1: Talking Therapies, Culture, the State and Neoliberalism: Is There a Need for Critical Psychotherapy, Psychoanalysis and Counselling?

Del Loewenthal is Professor of Psychotherapy and Counselling and Director of the Research Centre for Therapeutic Education at the University of Roehampton, UK, where he also convenes doctoral programmes. He is an analytic psychotherapist, chartered psychologist and photographer, and he is the founding editor of the *European Journal of Psychotherapy & Counselling*. He is chair of the Universities Psychotherapy & Counselling Association and former founding chair of the UK Council for Psychotherapy research committee. He also has small private practices in Wimbledon and Brighton. His most recent publications include *Post-existentialism and the Psychological Therapies: Towards a Therapy without Foundations* (2011), *Phototherapy and Therapeutic Photography in a Digital Age* (2013) and *Relational Psychotherapy, Psychoanalysis and Counselling: Appraisals and Reappraisals* (with Andrew Samuels, 2014).

Abstract

The case is presented that the main reason we have critical psychiatry and psychology is that psychiatry and psychology are primarily agents of the state and that this is becoming increasingly true for psychotherapy, psychoanalysis and counselling. An overview is provided of notions of 'critical'; psychotherapy, psychoanalysis and counselling are revisited as cultural practices in the light of both critical psychiatry and psychology; and the apparent paradox of increasing state intervention in a neoliberal world is explored. Questions are raised such as: Is it time for psychotherapists, psychoanalysts and counsellors to start thinking more critically about how much we're caught up with individualism, pseudoscience and the language of medicine and clinical psychology, all of which can be seen as instruments of the status quo?

Preliminary considerations are given as to whether the development of the sceptical tradition, while useful, is also a way through which psychotherapy loses its potential political radicalism through being termed 'critical'. A brief history of the notion of 'critical' is provided with reference to critical theory, psychiatry, psychology, psychotherapy, psychoanalysis and counselling, together with other developments, including the literature on politics and the talking therapies.

The issue is raised: if the state is now controlling the talking therapies, as it cannot risk with the growth of therapeutic provision so many people coming to their senses, then will psychotherapists, psychoanalysts and counsellors need to take a more critical stance if they are to regain their professional independence and intrinsic motivation? This may require them to consider and interpret how individual wretchedness is also caused by external social and economic factors.

The subsequent chapters, providing a range of narratives on critical approaches to questions raised here, are introduced.

Critique

A main criticism of this chapter, and perhaps of the book, is that it starts by raising specific questions as to whether there is a need for 'critical' psychotherapy, psychoanalysis and counselling, with particular reference to increasing state intervention. However, they are not addressed individually. Instead, the editor and contributors take them as a broad indication of the kinds of question that the notion 'critical' might address and then respond according to their interests. However, not directly addressing each question can lead to these questions not being individually explored as much as they might. Also provided is a range of different ways in which the term 'critical' is used in the talking therapies, which is hopefully a strength, but it can also take away from more in-depth exploration of the initial questions. Further criticisms might be around the literature on psychotherapy, counselling and politics, which could have been delved into further as there would appear to be much overlapping interest in the notion of 'critical'. Yet, in defence, the book's focus is on 'critical' talking therapies and not primarily on politics and the talking therapies. Finally, in terms of the structure of the book, the creation of the distinction regarding those contributors who 'come mainly from the inside' or 'mainly from the outside' was perhaps too arbitrary and not helpful because all contributors are practitioners and most refer to varying extents to literature inside and outside psychotherapy, psychoanalysis and counselling.

Chapter 2: The Medical Model: What Is It, Where Did It Come from and How Long Has It Got?

Hugh Middleton is Associate Professor at the School of Sociology and Social Policy at the University of Nottingham, UK, and a National

Health Service (NHS) consultant psychiatrist. Some 20 years' experience of contributing to NHS mental health services has fuelled criticism of their orthodoxies, and between 2000 and 2006 he made specific contributions to mental health policy development and implementation through the work of the National Institute for Mental Health in England/Care Services Improvement Partnership. In more recent years, he has been privileged to supervise several sociology PhDs considering 'mental health' from social sciences and constructivist perspectives. He is co-chair of the UK Critical Psychiatry Network.

Abstract

This chapter is prompted by a recent high-profile publication by the Critical Psychiatry Network. It reviews some of the conclusions and implications of that paper, 'Beyond the current paradigm' (Bracken et al. 2012), as a critique of institutionalised mental healthcare. The paper explicitly challenges the validity of a 'medical' approach to psychological and/or emotional difficulties and it has received little adverse comment from the main readership, fellows and members of the Royal College of Psychiatrists. The background to the development of medicalised approaches to mental health difficulties is considered and set in a Foucauldian perspective of evolving discourse in relation to the 'mad'. Although unsatisfactory and constraining, current provision has to be deemed to be an improvement on the past, but, more significantly, there are signs that a further shift, towards more patient-centred approaches to provision, is under way, and these might be worth following. The chapter also describes the Critical Psychiatry Network, a loose association of some 200 psychiatrists who have developed and promulgate critical appraisal of mental health services and practices, from which such publications come. Consideration is also given to what experiences from the Critical Psychiatry Network might be helpful for critical psychotherapy, psychoanalysis and counselling.

Critique

This chapter is essentially a reflexive comment upon ways in which formal provision for those suffering emotional distress and those concerned by them is organised. Expressions of dissatisfaction with organised mental health services commonly focus upon the shortcomings of co-locating them with other aspects of the medical enterprise, and this commentary is intended as a contribution to that debate. It identifies the wider medical enterprise with an approach to those human difficulties that can be productively conceptualised from a particular ontological position, and it concludes that mental health problems are not sufficiently described in that way. In turn, this identifies formally organised provision for them as insufficient. This is not a novel criticism and neither is its continuing relevance surprising. The need for appropriately sanctioned and supported provision for instances of otherwise uncontrollable emotional distress and instances of concern for public or personal safety can be considered a social universal. Reflexive commentary upon prevailing social arrangements is one way of questioning not the need for them but the form that they take in a particular context. Social sciences' focus upon the forms and activities of social organisation authorises them to define and comment upon interactions between functional social necessities and their contextually defined expressions. Doing so, particularly in the field of mental health difficulties, can make a contribution towards otherwise philanthropically driven change by drawing attention to distinctions between the need for 'something' and the contextual determinants of 'what'.

Chapter 3: Towards Critical Psychotherapy and Counselling: What Can We Learn from Critical Psychology (and Political Economy)?

Ian Parker is Professor of Management in the School of Management at the University of Leicester, Visiting Professor of Psychology at the University of Roehampton, Co-Director of the Discourse Unit and a practising psychoanalyst in Manchester, UK. He is still a Marxist. He is a member of the collective that produces *Asylum: Magazine for Democratic Psychiatry*. His books include *Lacanian Psychoanalysis: Revolutions in Subjectivity* (2011) and six titles in the series 'Psychology after Critique' (2015).

Abstract

This chapter outlines some aspects of contemporary 'critical psychology' which attempt to locate the discipline of psychology in the 'psy complex' and in the context of present-day capitalism and the state. Conceptual resources that critical psychologists draw upon – most notably Marxism and feminism – alert us to the way in which the threat of state regulation of psychotherapy and counselling is complemented by the fantasy that if we were free of the state then we would be free. The chapter uses aspects of critical psychology to develop an account of the political economy of psychotherapy, with a focus on the role of the state. Following an outline of aspects of critical psychology that are relevant to psychotherapy and counselling, it provides a description of the rationale for opting for political economy, which was originally premised on the ideological division between the state and civil society.

Critique

This chapter seems unsure as to whether the political-theoretical framework should be drawn from Foucault or from Marx, and in both cases it is unclear how feminism, and what form of feminism, could be integrated into the analysis. Foucault does seem useful to grapple with 'psychology', 'psychiatry' and 'psychotherapy' because he locates those practices in the psy complex, but this entails an account of power, and a corresponding critique of the notion of 'ideology', which sits uneasily with a Marxist account. Surely, if Foucault were taken seriously, then the conscious collective self-activity of the working class as a privileged agent in the historical process of liberation (from psychotherapy as well here presumably) would be quite impossible. And Foucault's own comments on sexuality and violence (particularly to decouple the two in relation to rape) seem antithetical to feminism, in particular to the kind of socialist feminism that is appealed to here. And if a Marxist account were taken seriously, then surely there would need to be also built into the narrative some redemptive humanist (here, of course, socialist humanist) vision of the creative emancipatory capacities of the human being, which is something that radical psychotherapists have tried to engage with and accentuate. That could then, if the traditional Marxist privileging of the working class as an agent of change (and the fetishisation of the capitalist state as the enemy) were to be questioned, open the way for an alliance with feminism, but this would surely still be an uneasy alliance.

Chapter 4: The Neurobiological Turn in Therapeutic Treatment: Salvation or Devastation?

Kenneth J. Gergen is Senior Research Professor in the Department of Psychology at Swarthmore College, Pennsylvania, USA. He has been awarded honorary doctorates by the University of Athens, Greece; Tilburg University, the Netherlands; and the Saybrook Institute, California, USA. He is a fellow of the Japan Society for the Promotion of Science, the World Academy of Art and Science and the Society of Experimental Social Psychology. He has been the recipient of many awards, the most recent being the Rollo May Award in 2013. His publications include *Social Construction in Context* (2001), *Therapeutic Realities* (2006) and *Horizons in Buddhist Psychology* (2006). His most recent, *Relational Being: Beyond Self and Community* (2009), won both the PROSE Award and the Erving Goffman Award, and it has been translated into Danish, Chinese, Spanish and French.

Abstract

The mental health professions are turning increasingly to a neurobiological conception of human behaviour, and to pharmacological answers to complex problems of living. The movement is largely premised on the assumption that drugs are efficient and effective 'cures' for mental disturbance. This offering, however, touches first on some of the devastating results of this movement. These include not only a meteoric rise in unwarranted drug dependency but also a myopia with regard to the cultural context of 'mental illness', the increase in mechanical care routines, and the erosion of the kind of multi-party dialogue that is essential to the complex challenges that we confront. The chapter goes on to show how brain-based explanations of human behaviour are highly limited. Not only do neuroplasticity studies invite cultural as opposed to drug-based interventions, but the very reading of brain activity is essentially a recapitulation of cultural assumptions. Also, little of the activity that we diagnose as 'mental disturbance' can effectively be reduced to brain states. With these critiques in hand, the chapter briefly considers several proposals of more promising potential.

Critique

There are shortcomings in the present account and they do deserve attention in the following discussion. The first is the one-sided account of the pharmaceutical explosion in mental health. Clearly, for many people such drugs have been very helpful, even if alternatives to drugs have not been explored. When, where and in what ways pharmaceutical applications are useful, and to whom and for how long, are issues worthy of intense exploration. This same broadside critique of neuro-based explanations is also subject to challenge. The relationship between biochemical and cultural factors in determining what we call 'mental disturbance', and in determining the outcomes of both drug and 'talking cures', is enormously complex. The weight we give to these factors and their forms of relationship are also subject to change across history and culture. While I think that in the present context strong critique is needed, the long-term hope is for mutually explorative dialogue.

Chapter 5: Personal versus Medical Meanings in Breakdown, Treatment and Recovery from 'Schizophrenia'

Tom Cotton is a psychotherapist and filmmaker with a special interest in phenomenology and the construction of narrative. Between 2010 and 2012, he managed a residential therapeutic community for clients with a 'schizophrenia' diagnosis. His doctoral research, carried out at the Research Centre for Therapeutic Education at Roehampton University, UK, explores the psychotherapeutic experiences of people who have received a 'schizophrenia' diagnosis. He recently directed a half-hour documentary, *There Is a Fault in Reality* (2010), which explores three people's experiences of 'schizophrenia'.

Del Loewenthal See biographical notes for Chapter 1.

Abstract

This chapter explores some implications of psychotherapy, psychoanalysis and counselling for the treatment of 'schizophrenia'. It is argued that its mainstream treatment is dominated by a medical model, modernist discourse, in which psychiatric and psychological aims have become merged in a psychotherapeutic treatment that is focused on symptom management. These aims have been endorsed by the National Institute for Health and Care Excellence's (NICE) (2014) guidelines for the treatment of 'schizophrenia', despite, by their own measures, yielding a low rate of success.

In his heuristic (Moustakas 1990) doctoral research which explored first-hand experiences of 'schizophrenia' and psychotherapy, Cotton (2014) found that personal meaning – both the loss of and the restoration of – was central to the participants' understanding of their 'schizophrenic' breakdown and subsequent recovery. In speaking about what was both helpful and unhelpful about their experiences of treatment, all participants found that psychotherapy that focused on symptom management was an obstacle to restoring personal meaning, and therefore, unwittingly, an obstacle to recovery. The types of psychotherapy that were most likely to adopt this therapy-as-symptom-management approach tended to be non-critical and non-reflective, and they emphasised technique and theory over relationship and critical thinking. It is argued that a psychotherapy that can maintain critical qualities may be one way of addressing this gap, and facilitating a way of working more closely with the needs of those with the diagnosis, rather than the needs of those giving the diagnosis.

Critique

We explored the significance of personal meaning in the recovery from 'schizophrenia' and were critical of medical meaning and intervening care that seeks to dominate and control. We acknowledge that meaning can, of course, mean many things, and we have chosen to situate our definition of it in one discourse (Heidegger 2008). This reveals something of the wider postmodern and phenomenological psychotherapeutic discourses that we are 'embedded' in (Parker et al. 1995: 4) ourselves. While these discourses offer a way of both critiquing structures of modernist objective knowledge and understanding another's meaning, we should not forget that they carry their own epistemological *a priori* assumptions that offer ample opportunity to get 'caught up'. Similarly, in using the participants' experiences as 'evidence', we acknowledge that we may be imposing our own assumptions of health. In combining these assumptions in the same 'knowledge game' that we are trying to deconstruct, we acknowledge that our critical approach may be no less an 'uncaring violation'. We also acknowledge that the 'conceptual flaccidity and generously inconclusive nature' (Smail 2005: 12) of postmodern thought might appear to offer little comfort to those who are caught up in the anxiety of trying to deliver a mental health service for individuals who may be overwhelmingly distressed and distressing. However, by placing these concerns at the heart of our argument, rather than viewing them as inconvenient obstacles that require circumnavigation, it is hoped that what we are caught up in is more transparent and so can be used as a way of keeping thinking open (about both our anxiety and the anxiety of those whom we attempt to treat), rather than closing it down with totalising arguments. Such thinking seems to be a vitally important way of placing the needs of patients before the needs of the mental health system.

Chapter 6: Critical Theory and Psychotherapy

Anastasios Gaitanidis is Senior Lecturer in Counselling Psychology, Counselling and Psychotherapy and a member of the Research Centre for Therapeutic Education at the University of Roehampton, UK. He is also a psychodynamic psychotherapist in private practice. He is a member of the council of the Site for Contemporary Psychoanalysis and he sits on the editorial board of *Sitegeist: A Journal of Psychoanalysis and*

Philosophy. He has been a regular manuscript reviewer for several journals, including the *European Journal of Psychotherapy & Counselling*. He has published several articles on psychoanalysis and psychotherapy in peer-reviewed journals and he is the editor of two books: *Narcissism – A Critical Reader* (2007) and *The Male in Analysis: Psychoanalytic and Cultural Perspectives* (2011).

Abstract

This chapter critically examines the claim of the Frankfurt School that, in an alienated society, psychotherapy is destined to fail. According to these 'critical theorists', therapeutic 'success' amounts to the 'normalisation' of the patient, their adaptation to the 'normal' functioning of society, whereas the crucial achievement of critical theory is precisely its explanation of how mental distress results from the very structure of the existing social order. Therapy can only succeed in a society that has no need of it – that is, one that does not produce 'mental alienation'. Here we have a special kind of 'failed encounter': psychotherapy is necessary where it is not possible and is only possible where it is no longer necessary. Psychotherapy needs to be neither accepted at face value nor ignored. Instead it should be employed in such a way as to both criticise existing forms of conformist psychotherapeutic practices and promote a form of radical psychotherapy which can provide the means by which patients can retrieve some of their ability to realise the extent of their alienation and fragmentation, recognise a small part of themselves in the fractured social mirror and try to find a way to build on it. It can never aspire to repair the damage done by a society that has seriously undermined the psychological wellbeing of its members.

Critique

In this chapter, I employ Walter Benjamin's and Theodor Adorno's critical analyses of the catastrophic nature of history, the importance of remembrance and redemption, and the destructive character of our post-Holocaust social reality so as to develop certain ideas which could enhance the radical social function of psychotherapeutic practices. However, what is problematic with this kind of cultural and social criticism is that it has become part of the official academic discourse, which is explicit in its very language, in the very gesture of knowledge and understanding of its analytical power of detachment. By attempting to situate itself outside the current social system and its uniformity, this kind of critical discourse participates in the very structures that it claims to attack by its very language patterns and analytical invulnerability.

How can critical theory avoid becoming part of the structures that it criticises? I believe that it should be critical not only of the previous and current philosophical and social systems but also of itself and its logic, of the tendency of any theoretical language to dominate its experiential content. Critical theory should not assume an intellectually superior and invulnerable position, but it should fully embrace its vulnerability when it speaks of the wounds that current society inflicts upon its subjects, the wounds that exploitative systems inflict upon nature, the wounds that we inflict upon each other and the wounds that we inflict on our bodies and minds in the process of civilisation. Critical theory must not only abstractly conceptualise the individual and collective suffering that is generated by our contemporary social system but also test its theories against the individual pain, tears and anger that psychotherapists daily face in their practices.

Chapter 7: When Love Is Not All We Want: Queers, Singles and the Therapeutic Cult of Relationality

Mari Ruti is Professor of Critical Theory and of Sexual Diversity Studies at the University of Toronto, Canada, where she teaches contemporary theory, psychoanalysis, continental philosophy, and feminist and queer theory. She is the author of *Reinventing the Soul: Posthumanist Theory and Psychic Life* (2006), *A World of Fragile Things: Psychoanalysis and the Art of Living* (2009), *The Summons of Love* (2011), *The Singularity of Being: Lacan and the Immortal Within* (2012), *The Call of Character: Living a Life Worth Living* (2013), *The Age of Scientific Sexism: How Evolutionary Psychology Promotes Gender Profiling and Fans the Battle of the Sexes* (2015) and *Between Levinas and Lacan: Self, Other, Ethics* (2015). She has also published a trade book entitled *The Case for Falling in Love: Why We Can't Master the Madness of Love – and Why That's the Best Part* (2011).

Adrian Cocking is a psychotherapist who is currently practising in Toronto, Canada. He holds an MEd in counselling psychology from the Ontario Institute for Studies in Education at the University of Toronto and a BA from the University of Victoria, Canada. He was the recipient of the 2013 Hallam Award of Excellence for his graduate work at the Mark S. Bonham Centre for Sexual Diversity Studies. His interests lie in working with marginalised populations, including the Lesbian, Gay, Bisexual, Transgender and Queer (LGBTQ) and native communities.

Abstract

This chapter mobilises recent work in queer theory to question our society's habitual valorisation of enduring intimate relationships –

particularly marriage – as the pinnacle of human life. Drawing on Sara Ahmed's critique of socially dominant 'happiness scripts', Lauren Berlant's critique of 'cruel optimism' and Michael Cobb's critique of the (heteronormative) culture of coupledom, we ask analysts and therapists to consider the possibility that some patients might prefer alternative relational configurations. For instance, some might deem the enlivening ardency of short-term affairs to be more meaningful than relationship longevity and intersubjective security. Yet others might opt out of relationships altogether in an effort to find non-relational sources of fulfilment. Although our aim is not to denigrate relationality in any global sense, we wish to alert analysts and therapists to the possibility that their propensity to assume that close relational bonds are essential to 'the good life' may feel alienating to some patients. We argue that this attitude may cause some queers and many singles (whether queer or straight) to feel subtly judged for their failure to adhere to the relational norms of our society.

Critique

This chapter relies on recent queer theoretical critiques of social normativisation. As rich as these critiques are, they make it difficult to honour the healing ideals of the analytic and therapeutic process. At the core of this process resides the notion that damaging relational patterns from the past can be broken with the aid of supportive, mutually caring relationships in the present. From this perspective, intimate relationships facilitate intra- and interpsychic growth. One might consequently ask whether such growth becomes stunted in the absence of close relational bonds. Moreover, the so-called 'antisocial thesis' of queer theory – famously articulated by Lee Edelman in *No Future: Queer Theory and the Death Drive* (2004) – sets up a rigid binary between (bad) relationality and (good) anti-relationality, aligning queers with anti-relationality to such an extent that queers who value relationality become ostracised for their failure to be 'properly queer'. Along related lines, the antisocial rejection of relationality can be traced back to a gay male subculture that valorises promiscuous sex at the expense of other relational possibilities, and that often, explicitly or implicitly, flees from 'all things feminine'. Although we are here referring to how femininity has traditionally been constructed in our society rather than to any essential gendered predilection, it might still be possible to argue that in shunning the rewards of emotional intimacy, antisocial queer theory is on some level rejecting the contaminating 'stain' of femininity. Even though this chapter does not endorse the antisocial thesis specifically, the influence of this thesis on the rest of queer theory, and therefore on our analysis, is undeniable. As a result, if we were to develop the arguments that we have advanced, we would need to confront the possibility that misogyny might quietly – but insidiously – nibble at the edges of our analysis.

Chapter 8: Relating to People as Revolutionaries

Lois Holzman is a passionate advocate for conceptual tools and community practices that empower people to transform the alienation and passivity of our culture. As a developmental psychologist and activist scholar, she promotes social therapeutics and other postmodern, culture-change approaches to human development and learning – crossing (and trying to dissolve) the borders that separate clinical, community and educational psychology, and between postmodern, critical and sociocultural theory and practice. She is Director of the East Side Institute, New York, USA, which she founded with the late Fred Newman, and chair of the biennial Performing the World conferences. Her dozen books range from the radically methodological *Unscientific Psychology: A Cultural-Performatory Approach to Understanding Human Life* (with Newman, 2006) to *Vygotsky at Work and Play* (2008), an intellectual-personal history of social therapeutics and its community of human development projects. She is a regular commentator on the website *Psychology Today* ('A Conceptual Revolution') and the blog Psychology of Becoming.

Abstract

This chapter is an invitation to go beyond the critical and to create practical-critical psychotherapy and counselling approaches. The 40-year practice of social therapy serves to illustrate practical-critical psychotherapy. It is a group approach that engages the alienation and authoritarian commodification of contemporary life by relating to people as revolutionaries – that is, as social beings who are engaged in the process of always becoming, as capable of going beyond their societal identities and performing as world-historic in everyday matters. The contributions of Marx and Vygotsky to social therapy as an ontological, and not merely an epistemological, critique of the psychological and psychotherapeutic mainstream are discussed.

Critique

Social therapy has been controversial since its earliest days. It has been attacked from the political and psychological right for mixing politics and therapy and for violating therapeutic boundaries. We have used these attacks as opportunities to raise the assumptions that underlie them, such as that a person automatically becomes vulnerable once they seek therapy. More to the point here, however, is what has caused concern and generated lively dialogue among those with a critical perspective. I will comment on one of these concerns that gets to the heart of our methodology and our politics (and may well have come up for readers of this volume).

As a methodology, social therapy is open-ended, non-objectivist and non-interpretive. If we relate to people as revolutionaries, as always becoming, if our focus is on people developing, and for us development is qualitative transformation of what there is into something new, the question is: Becoming what and developing how? The concern is that 'Development can then go "in the wrong direction" – people could transform into gang members or into right wingers.' Indeed, they might. While that hasn't been our experience, I think what makes critical psychologists and psychotherapists uncomfortable is that our approach is non-ideological. We neither adjust people to the world as 'it is' or is officially described, nor offer an alternative description or interpretation or story. The point, as Marx pointed out, is not to interpret the world but to change it, which is why we relate to all people as revolutionaries – that is, as changemakers.

Chapter 9: Work in Contemporary Capitalism

Michael Rustin is Professor of Sociology at the University of East London, UK, where he was formerly Head of Department of Sociology and Dean of the Social Sciences Faculty. He is Visiting Professor at the Tavistock Clinic, where he has contributed to the development of many university-accredited programmes in the field of psychotherapy and community mental health. He has written about the relations between psychoanalysis and various aspects of society, politics and culture, and about other sociological and political topics. He is the author of *For a Pluralist Socialism* (1985), *The Good Society and the Inner World* (1991) and *Reason and Unreason: Psychoanalysis, Science and Politics* (2002), as well as *Narratives of Love and Loss, Mirror to Nature* (with Margaret Rustin, 2001), *The Inner World of Doctor Who* (with Iain MacRury, 2013) and *Social Defences against Anxiety: Explorations in a Paradigm* (co-edited with David Armstrong, 2014). He is an associate of the British Psychoanalytical Society. He is a founding editor of *Soundings* and an author/editor of the journal *The Kilburn Manifesto*.

Abstract

The argument of this chapter is that work acquired its centrality as a source of value, creativity and entitlement under capitalism. In ancient world and feudal societies, most labour was undertaken by slaves or serfs (or similarly disregarded women) and was assigned little positive significance. Work within capitalism has been defined in two contrasting ways. Within classical economics, it was regarded instrumentally, as a mere 'factor of production'. The 'free' labour contract was deemed to consist of a sacrifice of freedom and happiness in return for a material reward. The pains of work were supposed to be compensated for by the satisfactions of consumption, which became increasingly salient with enhanced prosperity. But in an opposing romantic or expressive tradition, work was regarded as of intrinsic value, as a form of self-expression and self-realisation. Advocates of this conception, such as Marx, Ruskin and Morris, drew on conceptions of medieval craftsmanship in their critiques of degraded forms of industrial labour. During the 1960s and 1970s, vigorous debates took place about the nature and quality of work, within contributions from many sources, from the early Marx to the Tavistock Institute of Human Relations. But instrumental conceptions of labour have been reasserted during the ascendancy of neoliberalism since the 1980s, now with especial force given the prevailing anxieties about the competitive viability of economies. At a time when it would be highly desirable to reorient debate towards more qualitative and expressive conceptions of work and wellbeing, dominant economic concerns are of a different kind. The chapter concludes by asking what space can be found in contemporary society for a renewal of interest in the quality of working lives.

Critique

This chapter is mainly concerned with the ideas and values which frame our understanding of work, and how these have developed historically. It has much less to say about the empirical realities of contemporary labour markets and how they are changing shape. In fact, in recent decades there has been a diminution of the middle levels of the labour force in terms of degrees of skill and remuneration, and in both manual and non-manual forms of employment. Just as machines have reduced the demand for skilled manual workers, so computers have displaced skilled workers in the white collar (and increasingly the professional) sector. Most new employment which becomes available is thus of a minimum wage, low-skill kind (for example in fast food, shelf-stacking or hotel cleaning), while there remains an echelon of highly paid and skilled employment at the top of the labour market. This leads to increasing inequalities and threats to social solidarity, and also to a 'demand deficit' in the economy such as contributed to the 2007–2008 financial crash (through the subprime mortgage crisis) and to the sluggishness of the economic recovery. Rather, as Marx foretold, this tendency embodies an innate contradiction – changes in the system of production – greater capital intensity and the displacement of labour, which are meant to enhance economic wellbeing, in fact lessen it and engender conflict. These developments also have implications for generational inequity (high levels of youth unemployment, especially in southern Europe), and for regional inequality too. Finally, the prospect held out in the chapter, for work in postindustrial societies to acquire greater expressive meaning, is severely undermined when the skilled forms of work, where intrinsic meaning is most often found, are squeezed out in a sometimes desperate quest to maintain competitive advantage.

Chapter 10: Everything You Always Wanted to Know about Therapy (But Were Afraid to Ask): Fragments of a Critical Psychotherapy

Andrew Samuels is Professor of Analytical Psychology at the University of Essex, UK, and he holds visiting chairs at New York, Goldsmiths, Roehampton and Macau. He works internationally as a political consultant. He is a training analyst of the Society of Analytical Psychology and in private practice in London. He was chair of the United Kingdom Council for Psychotherapy (2009–2012), a founder board member of the International Association for Relational Psychoanalysis and Psychotherapy and co-founder of Psychotherapists and Counsellors for Social Responsibility. His books have been translated into 19 languages, including, most recently, *Relational Psychotherapy, Psychoanalysis and Counselling* (co-edited with Del Loewenthal, 2014) and *Persons, Passions, Psychotherapy, Politics* (2014).

Abstract

Three seemingly consensual propositions concerning psychotherapy and counselling are examined critically. All turn out to be unreliable, tendentious and even damaging. First, psychotherapy and counselling can be free and independent professions provided that therapists, acting together, fight for them to be that way. Second, psychotherapy and counselling are private and personal activities, operating in the realms of feelings and emotions – the psyche, the unconscious, affects rooted in the body. Above all other factors, the single most important thing is the therapy relationship between two people. Third, psychotherapy and counselling are vocations, not jobs. Therapists are not simply motivated by money. In developing critiques of these propositions, the chapter utilises social, political and economic perspectives. It reviews new clinical thinking on the active role of the client in therapeutic process and suggests that a turn to the legendary figure of the trickster might be of benefit to the field. The chapter locates its arguments in the author's experience of the politics and practices of psychotherapy and counselling, and engages in self-criticism.

Critique

How 'critical' can an insider be? Can one ever critique the bubble when one is inside it? This is a point that I raised in my chapter. The therapy system has been good to me on the whole. Even the various campaigns that I have led, such as the one to end the discrimination against members of gender and sexual minorities in terms of psychoanalytic training, have, in the end, added a shadowy degree of lustre to my name. So, being self-critical, it is easy for me to kibitz, even to grandstand. Another piece of self-reflection would be that, in what I have written, I am merely pissing in the wind. Numerous developments of a political, economic and regulatory nature mean that psychotherapy and counselling as we know them these days, never mind these critical versions, are completely doomed. It is time to hang up one's interpretations. Then my critics could question my right to be critical. Although I do work in a university for some of my time and also do consultancy work, I am primarily a Jungian analyst in well-paid private practice. A few low-cost clients don't alter this one bit. And I am a white, middle-class, middle-aged heterosexual man (being Jewish is scarcely a disadvantage in this field). What can I possibly know from the inside about other kinds of therapy in quite different situations? Only such a patriarch would propose a 'Hermetic spontaneity' as any kind of solution to the manifold ills from which contemporary counselling and psychotherapy suffer.

Chapter 11: Critical Priorities for the Psychotherapy and Counselling Community

Colin Feltham is Emeritus Professor of Critical Counselling Studies, Sheffield Hallam University, UK, and External Associate Professor of Humanistic Psychology, University of Southern Denmark. He currently teaches, writes, examines and consults in the UK, Ireland and Denmark.

He is on the editorial panels of the *British Journal of Guidance and Counselling*, *Self and Society* and *Irish Journal of Psychology*. His research interests include critiques of psychotherapy and counselling, related human condition topics and depressive realism. His recent publications include *Failure* (2012), *Sage Handbook of Psychotherapy and Counselling*, 3rd edn. (edited with Ian Horton, 2012), *Counselling and Counselling Psychology: A Critical Examination* (2013) and *Keeping Ourselves in the Dark* (forthcoming).

Abstract

This chapter examines what critical thinking is for the field of psychotherapy and counselling by taking a particular, subject-specific position regarding 'thinking and theorising'. It then poses certain questions about the general neglect of critical thinking and possible reasons for this. Subsequently, suggestions are made for what we might consider some critical priorities for the field – aetiologies of distress, competing models, the outcome question, professional issues, training and employment, disciplinary stances and the scope and limits of the field. The author positions himself as a depressive realist with severe reservations about the claims of psychotherapy and counselling, and he attempts to distinguish between accusations of cynicism against his arguments, and fair critique. Problems of class and politics relevant to therapy are surfaced, and the romantic optimism of the field is critiqued. Doubts about the profession's desire and ability make any radical changes are raised. The problematic influences of academia are also focused upon. The critique here extends to those who are perceived as offering somewhat impotent critical analyses of the field from various 'phenomenological silos' and 'critical coteries'.

Critique

Arguments that can be made against my own are these. I am projecting my own unresolved depressive problems in the form of idealisation and disappointment: the profession should be a certain way, just as my mother should have been all that she was not. I fail to appreciate actual gains in the profession due to my all-or-nothing style of thinking. I secretly harbour the belief that if only my opponents would listen to me, and see how perceptive I am, I would be the hero of the piece and rightfully sit alongside Freud or Rogers. I am consumed with envy and cannot feel gratitude. I denigrate the aims and achievements of other reformers because I am unable to be a hopeful team player. I may read extensively and produce some undisciplined intellectual objections but these are all defences against some disowned, devastating feeling locked away inside myself. I fail to understand the realities of gradual professional progress and necessity – how long change takes, what negotiations have to take place – because I am naïve and impatient, incapable of delayed gratification. I do not appreciate what the Enlightenment has done for us, nor what capitalism and anti-capitalism do for us, because nothing can ever compensate for my unloved inner child. I am a cryptomisanthropist, a schizoid outsider. I do not put forward any workable alternatives (although the term 'criticocreative thinking' suggests that critical thinking implicitly prompts new practices). But some will generously concede a few of my arguments and oppose others, in the spirit of leisurely collegial debate. We all see ourselves as reasonable but I suspect that entrenched subjectivities and tribal loyalties inevitably have the last word. When I am being authentic, I have to say that even after this reflection I think I am right.

Chapter 12: The Deleuzian Project

Chris Oakley is a psychoanalyst working in private practice in London. For many years, he was a member of the Philadelphia Association before leaving to join the Site for Contemporary Psychoanalysis. He has contributed to various books and journals, his latest being to *R.D. Laing: 50 Years since The Divided Self* (2012), while his book *Football Delirium* (2007) came third in the 2008 Football Book of the Year.

Abstract

This chapter is an attempt to draw together disparate strands of the Deleuzian project (not to forget Guattari) with particular emphasis on the questions that are raised for psychoanalysis. In so many ways, Deleuze and Guattari propose a fundamental rupture of the transcendental tendencies of Lacan exemplified by his wretched insistence on lack and his fiction of the pure signifier. Deleuze repeatedly upheld the unconscious to be primarily entangled in the production of flows – desire always already being seen as a productive force, while simultaneously being potentially ensnared by the anaesthetising insistencies of our capitalist world. Glimpsed through the prism of our sexual desire, we may explore his unrelenting concern with our predilection for 'deplorable' capture, our subjugation of the multiple possibilities of our being, ultimately 'territorialised' into manageable doses of pleasure. Aided and abetted by psychoanalysis's Oedipal recoding, we submit as the docile body. This is particularly portrayed as the commodification of our desire by pornography, all converging on the valorisation of the 'money shot'. For Deleuze and Guattari, this is a hyperinsistence of our machinic enslavement, underpinned by the demands of representation, whether this is with regard to our pathetic concern with identity or with the form that enjoyment takes. Schizoanalysis becomes emblematic of a countervalence, an attempt to move beyond the stifling production of slavish reproduction, a breaking free from the Oedipal handcuffing of psychoanalysis to facilitate the random, the surprise, the unspeakable. This is the Deleuzian rallying call.

Critique

Any essay that contains within it the suggestion that it might be possible to engage in the emancipation from the very pleasures that enslave runs a veritable risk of being accused of being both an instance of paranoid knowledge and informed by a will to ignorance regarding what psychoanalysis brings to the table: Paranoid knowledge not merely as exemplifying the delights of conspiracy theorists but rather a willingness 'to install oneself at the limit, at a particular horizon, in the desert, the subject of a deterritorialized knowledge that links him (or her) directly to God... (making) it possible to judge life and survey the earth from above'. And who suggests that this is one of the first principles of paranoid knowledge? None other than Deleuze and Guattari. But back to what psychoanalysis brings to the table: Can we really be that surprised that they too have an insistent blind spot with regard to what they just go on enjoying too much? Just like the rest of us really.

Chapter 13: Psychoanalysis and the Event of Resistance

Steven Groarke is Professor of Social Thought at Roehampton University, UK, and a member of the British Psycho-Analytical Society and the International Psychoanalytical Association. He has held honorary appointments with Central and North West London Mental Health NHS Trust at Parkside Clinic and St. Charles Hospital, and he currently works in private practice in London. He is the author of *Managed Lives: Psychoanalysis, Inner Security and the Social Order* (2013) and has recently contributed to a definitive scholarly edition of the *Collected Writings of D.W. Winnicott* (2015).

Abstract

What does psychoanalysis contribute to our understanding of resistance? How far does this provide the possibility of rethinking the politics of psychoanalysis? This chapter argues that the concept of resistance (*Widerstand*) has a wider critical range when it is worked through, rather than pitted against, Freud and psychoanalysis. It presents this argument in the form of a commentary on the three lectures, from the early 1990s, collected in Derrida's *Résistances de la psychanalyse* (1996). Taken together, Derrida's lectures on Freud, Lacan and Foucault highlight various ways in which psychoanalysis may be seen as a resistance to itself, and the chapter links this idea to a series of controversial discussions in the Freudian interpretation. The author's discussion of these controversies focuses in turn on the hermeneutics of reason; being-towards-death (*Sein zum Tode*) and the repetition compulsion; and the ambivalence of unreason. The main argument here is that psychoanalysis's resistance to itself constitutes the conditions of possibility for a critical psychoanalysis.

Critique

I am probably not best placed to comment on my blind spots so will rely on others as always to point these out to me. However, my main argument that Freudian psychoanalysis provides an invaluable critical and political resource is open to criticism on several counts. First, I don't provide a comprehensive overview of critical perspectives, which could leave my account looking very one-sided. Second, I don't mention even the most prominent contributions to Freudian politics, particularly that of the Frankfurt School. Third, while I refer in brief to institutional politics, I don't provide detailed or in-depth examples. Fourth, although I acknowledge the extent to which psychoanalysis has been co-opted onto the side of social administration in the final part of the chapter, once again I don't follow up in any detail on the critique of Freud and psychoanalysis by the likes of Donzelot and others. Finally, I limit my account of Freud's radicalism to the implications of his own thought, whereas a further argument could be made for the relationship between psychoanalysis and other traditions of radical thought.

Chapter 14: Psychology, Psychotherapy – Coming to Our Senses?

Paul Moloney is a counselling psychologist. He has worked for 15 years in the NHS. A former social worker and associate lecturer with the Open University, he is a founder member of the Midlands Psychology Group, a close knit collection of academic and therapeutic psychologists who are dedicated to questioning the assumptions of mainstream therapeutic psychology. He is the author of *The Therapy Industry* (2013), a critical examination of the science, practice and politics of talking therapy in the UK and the USA.

Abstract

Critical scrutiny of the evidence base in support of the practice and theory of the talking therapies shows that it suffers from serious and systematic methodological flaws, to the extent that it is rational to conclude that the vast majority of psychological treatments, including the most popular brands, are indistinguishable from well-designed placebos. Researchers and theorists have ignored this issue because it is professionally inconvenient and because it challenges the neoliberal orthodoxy of our time, which says that if we are miserable or confused then it is we alone rather than our socially noxious surroundings that are to blame. With a little help from an expert, we supposedly have the mental powers to extricate ourselves. This fashionable belief, which the late David Smail called 'magical voluntarism' (Smail 2005), benefits those who gain most from an exploitative social system. However, the talking treatments reflect more than shape the power structures of our world. Neither a more honest recognition of their limitations nor the creation of more thoughtful and rigorous approaches to researching them are likely to flourish until those power structures themselves begin to change.

Critique

Perhaps the most obvious critique would be to cite the reams of research which claim to show that talking therapy is effective, a reliable technology of personal change. This is a familiar rhetorical manoeuvre: the heaping-up of marginal, contradictory and questionable findings to create a mountain of conviction that – upon closer scrutiny – becomes a pile of bric-a-brac. A more interesting criticism might be to focus upon the drawbacks of the randomised control trial (RCT) approach. The interactions between clients, therapists, techniques and treatment settings are perhaps dynamic, subtle and complex enough to elude the coarse net of the standardised medical research trial – a method suited to the evaluation of inert and easily administered physical treatments, such as pills. On this view, I have been attacking a straw man. However, within Western culture (and increasingly many others), this man wields far too much power and authority. He is worth demolishing. Moreover, the key conclusions – that talking therapy cannot free people from the burden of their own biography, nor from the grip of a noxious environment – remain, supported by a large epidemiological literature on the causes of distress, and by the accounts of those therapists and clients who have courageously confronted the limitations of the therapy trade. As far as the academic world is concerned, critical voices are few, and unwelcome. Epstein's work, for example, has been largely ignored for the last 25 years, and few have followed in his footsteps. Much of the university sector has become a commercial industry, increasingly closed to anyone who questions the business values that dominate it. To the extent that talking therapy is itself a business and shares the values (or illusions) of consumer capitalism, the signs are not encouraging.

Chapter 15: Contesting the Curriculum: Counsellor Education in a Postmodern and Medicalising Era?

Tom Strong is Professor and Counsellor-educator at the University of Calgary, Canada, who researches and writes about the collaborative, critically informed and practical potentials of discursive approaches to psychotherapy. He is the author or co-author of over 100 articles and chapters, he is the co-author of *Discursive Perspectives on Therapeutic Practice* (with Andy Lock, 2012) and of *Social Constructionism: Sources and Stirrings in Theory and Practice* (with David Paré, 2010) and *Furthering Talk: Advances in the Discursive Therapies* (2012). His most recent co-edited book is *Patterns in Interpersonal Interactions: Inviting Relational Understandings for Therapeutic Change* (with Karl Tomm, Sally St. George and Dan Wulff, 2014). His current research focuses on medicalising tensions in counsellor education.

Karen H. Ross is a doctoral student in counselling psychology at the University of Calgary, Canada. Her research explores how different discourses of 'mental health', such as those found in public health campaigns, institutional policies and popular culture, shape options for problem-solving and identity construction, particularly among young people. She is also interested in the intersection of self-help, governmentality and technology in modern neoliberal societies. She completed her master's degree at the University of Toronto, with a thesis focusing on the experience of losing faith in fundamentalist Christianity. She volunteers with community-building initiatives and cultural arts programmes in Calgary, and she is a strong believer in making academic scholarship accessible and relevant to the general public. She was recently awarded a Scholarship for Creative Marketing and Communications and she received funding for her doctoral research from the Social Sciences and Humanities Research Council of Canada.

Konstantinos Chondros is a native of Greece and has lived in Calgary, Canada, since 2011. After completing his Bachelor of Arts Honours in psychology at the University of Crete, Greece, he went on to receive his Master of Science in counselling psychology from the University of Calgary. During his undergraduate and graduate studies, he received numerous scholarships and awards for his strong academic performance, including the State Scholarships Foundation award for graduating at the top of his undergraduate class and the Lilian Voudouri Foundation scholarship for pursuing a graduate degree abroad. His academic interests revolve around the areas of community psychology, multiculturalism and social justice, human sexuality, feminist-informed research and qualitative inquiry. In terms of his professional interests, he identifies as a pluralistic counsellor who is highly influenced by postmodern ideas. He began his doctorate in counselling psychology at the University of Calgary in September 2014.

Monica Sesma-Vazquez is a social constructionist psychotherapist and supervisor. She was born in Mexico City where she pursued studies (bachelor's, master's and PhD) in psychology and several specialisations as an individual, couple and systemic family therapist. She was a professor in three universities in Mexico City (Universidad de Londres, Universidad de las Americas and Alliant International University) where she supervised and taught postmodern therapies in graduate programmes. Currently, she is a postdoctoral fellow at Werklund School of Education, University of Calgary, Canada. Her research projects focus on examining discourses around psychiatric diagnosis and medicalisation as these occur between individuals/families and professionals within the therapeutic space. Her research interests include how families and their children perform 'psychiatric' meanings and understandings in social interactions, and how these performances shape their relationships and experiences. She is a Taos Institute associate and a Houston Galveston Institute faculty member.

Abstract

The psychiatric classification system of DSM-5 (*Diagnostic and Statistical Manual of Mental Disorders*, version 5) has become a default commercial and scientific language for helping professionals, especially when it is coupled with evidence-based interventions for addressing human concerns that are understood as diagnosed disorders. Counsellors, however, have traditionally responded – conversationally – to their clients' concerns by drawing from diverse discourses of practice. This is even more the case now that the field of counselling offers popular new postmodern approaches. Tensions between these medicalising developments, pluralistic traditions and postmodern sensitivities in counselling make counsellor education an interesting context of study. From critical document and website reviews, the authors use situational analysis to map medicalising tensions to shape contemporary counsellor education. Their aim is to draw attention to how curricular tensions associated with DSM-5 use may challenge the pluralism that has long been associated with counselling and counsellor education.

Critique

Negatives

- We have been selective in researching our archival documents, focusing on medicalising while not contrasting it with the broader literature. While we have aimed to capture a growing (medicalising, or diagnose and treat) phenomenon in the publicly documented literature and media associated with counsellor education, the general counselling literature has also been growing.
- We have questioned the scientific basis for counselling and counsellor education, because that basis has largely been undertaken in medical ways, but we have offered no alternative way of assuring public/student confidence in what constitutes good or effective counselling.
- We approach systematising counselling into manuals based on pre-defined client concerns/pre-specified interventions as reducing or obscuring the complexity and generative possibilities of counselling when many regard this as essential for good practice and teaching good practice.

Positives

- We raise awareness of how counsellors and counsellor educators face a narrowing of ways in which they can be helpful while possibly being complicit in an expanding medicalisation of counselling and counsellor education. This medicalising direction plays into pharmaceutical concerns that date back to Aldous Huxley and carry forward to Robert Whitaker's *Anatomy of an Epidemic*.
- We contest a medical focus on vulnerabilities and symptoms as a good thing. In counselling and counsellor education, this can lead to failing to attend to clients' preferences and resourcefulness. There is a related iatrogenic effect that all of this has in furthering what Furedi has called a therapy culture.

- We accept a medicalising discourse as one discourse of practice, being concerned that it could dominate counsellor practice and education, and compromise the pluralistic traditions and creative growth of new approaches in counselling. Counsellors and counsellor trainees are further off, in our view, when they can draw on multiple theoretical approaches.

Chapter 16: Systemic Means to Subversive Ends: Maintaining the Therapeutic Space as a Unique Encounter

Jay Watts is a clinical psychologist and psychotherapist working from systemic and Lacanian orientations. She is an honorary senior research fellow at Queen Mary University of London, UK, as well as being in full-time private practice. She has held a number of senior academic and NHS posts, including leading early intervention in psychosis and integrative psychotherapy teams, heading research for an NHS Trust and developing teaching modules as Senior Lecturer in Counselling Psychology at City University. She continues to teach on a number of clinical and counselling psychology courses and has published widely. She is the Practice Editor for the *European Journal for Counselling & Psychotherapy* and is foreign correspondent for the website *Mad in America*.

Abstract

Psychotherapy has become a marketplace for an increasing number of approaches, many with wildly different perspectives on what it means to suffer, or even whether an approach focused on cure is possible. This chapter argues that within this marketplace the growth of an ideology that privileges notions of 'illness', 'cure' and 'evidence-based treatment' can be problematic for the critical practitioner who wishes to maintain space for more subversive approaches. There is also concern that with academic training programmes being increasingly subject to external pressure, there is a move to the mainstream and away from critical thinking. The author describes how she incorporated systemic techniques and ideas into a doctoral training programme in order to help to maintain a space for practice-driven psychotherapy to flourish. These include facilitating a tolerance of uncertainty, of challenging trainees' mindsets and of connecting with the psychiatric survivor movement. The author suggests that we either see ourselves as trapped and excluded by the dominant culture, or we recognise the extraordinary work that is going on in the survivor movement and in cyberspace and draw these into our everyday psy interactions. If we choose the latter, we can produce spaces that may incorporate multiple stories on 'evidence', 'illness' and the other signifiers that otherwise threaten to colonise us.

Critique

This chapter reflects a belief that critical practitioners must retain a thinking, questioning presence in training and state-influenced institutions such as academia and the NHS to reach the most disenfranchised in society whose suffering appears in police cells, acute psychiatric wards and GPs' surgeries. My aim here is to encourage trainees to use their considerable social power to connect such patients to emancipatory movements such as the Hearing Voices Network, which, situated outside the state and regulatory movements, can act from a more radical perspective. Yet I also wonder if we should 'give up the ghost' of what is possible in professions that are either regulated by the New Public Management agenda or willing to become complicit with it and the power/money/status that it brings. I have a deep suspicion of the hypertheoretical nature of critical thinking in the UK, worried that we can fall into just writing papers to one another, but I wonder if the position that I take in my chapter and work is too much of a compromise.

Is the attack on thinking space within academia a good opportunity, actually, to kick ourselves out of that safety and radicalise again? I wonder if we shouldn't renew interest in community therapy movements and their links to community-based social movements. Is it not the legacies of Freire, Martín-Baró and others from the South American liberation psychology movements that are the most alive examples of living critical practice? Do we not hear the whispers of possibility here in recent movements such as OCCUPY? Given that we know that formal training can hinder as well as help the formation of critical practitioners, is the future not rather in considering formations in talking sites away from the mainstream that connect the individual and social? And will social media allow us to connect the most disenfranchised to our new locations, side-stepping involvement in the mainstream entirely? These questions I debate with myself most weeks.

Chapter 17: Psychotherapy, Psychoanalysis and Counselling for Oppressors and Oppressed: Sex, Violence and Ideology in Practice?
Del Loewenthal Please see biographical notes for Chapter 1.

Abstract
It is concluded that threats to our providing a therapeutic confidential space must be resisted; the training of talking therapists should

include sociology, anthropology and political economy; we should not be seduced by either a medical model or neurobiology; RCTs are an absurdity; state intervention and DSM-5 threaten the pluralism of our approaches; we need multiple stories of signifiers that otherwise threaten to colonise us; clients need the option to explore personal meaning; talking therapists need to recognise their and others' sexuality and violence, and question values, such as the need for close relational bonds; our approaches need to affect our and others' being and the quality of our working lives; we need to disobey normal rules and conventional behaviour and not merely talk in rarified jargon; psychotherapy and our sexual desire are interwoven with capitalism; state regulation may give new capacities for resistance; talking therapists can be more the problem than the solution; to be critical we need theories outside the talking therapies, yet to give primacy to our work as cultural practices; and in using 'critical' rather than 'radical', politics can get replaced by scepticism, and capitalism by modernity.

Overall, there are two key forces for psychotherapists to interpret in order to help to release clients from their bonds. The first involves the individual's denial of uncomfortable thoughts, fantasies and dreams. The second concerns the ideologies of those who do not want the managed to understand how this is done. These forces are explored in terms of individual responsibility versus social and economic contexts with regard to sex, violence and ideology through case study vignettes. There is an unfortunate need for critical psychotherapy, psychoanalysis and counselling as this is probably the best that can be permitted in neoliberal capitalism on the understanding that it allows some possibilities so long as it doesn't change the world.

Critique

With regard to the final chapter, perhaps a main criticism here is that a conclusion is reached which could possibly have been stated in Chapter 1 and then developed from there. Also, implications for practice lack much in the way of substantial case studies, although this might be the basis of a subsequent book. Perhaps a more fundamental criticism is that this volume doesn't really go into depth regarding Marxist and related philosophical texts, yet it is hoped that my more introductory approach to such areas will help interested practitioners and students to gain some insight into areas such as capital governance, power and social inequalities that weren't, and aren't, being covered in most trainings. A further criticism is that the book focuses on very traditional Western approaches to the talking therapies and does not cover approaches from other cultures including the effects of race and religion.

References

Bracken, P., Thomas, P., Timimi, S., Asen, E., Behr, G., Beuster, C., Bhunnoo, S., Browne, I., Chhina, N., Double, D., Downer, S., Evans, C., Fernando, S., Garland, M.R., Hopkins, W., Huws, R., Johnson, B., Martindale, B., Middleton, H., Moldavsky, D., Moncrieff, J., Mullins, S., Nelki, J., Pizzo, M., Rodger, J., Smyth, M., Summerfield, D., Wallace, J. and Yeomans, D. (2012) 'Psychiatry beyond the current paradigm', *British Journal of Psychiatry*, 201: 430–434.

Cotton, T. (2015) 'Schizophrenia' and the Crisis of Meaning: A Heuristic Exploration of the Psychotherapeutic Experiences of Those Who Have a 'Schizophrenia', Diagnosis, Research Centre for Therapeutic Education, Roehampton University. Unpublished doctoral thesis.

Derrida, J. (1996) *Résistances de la psychanalyse* trans. Kamuf, P., Brault, P.-A. and Naas, M. (1998) *Resistance of Psychoanalysis*. Stanford, CA: Stanford University Press.

Edelman, L. (2004) *No Future: Queer Theory and the Death Drive*. Durham, NC: Duke University Press.

Heidegger, M. (2008) *Being and Time* trans. Macquarrie, J. and Robinson, E. London: Harper Perennial Modern Classics.

Moustakas, C. (1990) *Heuristic Research: Design, Methodology, and Applications*. Newbury Park, CA: Sage.

NICE (2014) 'Psychosis and schizophrenia in adults: Treatment and management', guidance.nice.org.uk/cg178. Accessed 12 September 2014.

Parker, I., Georgaca, E., Harper, D., McLaughlin, T. and Stowell-Smith, M. (1995) *Deconstructing Psychopathology*. London: Sage.

Smail, D. (2005) *Power, Interest and Psychology. Elements of a Social-Materialist Understanding of Distress*. Ross-on-Wye: PCCS Books Ltd.

Part I
Introduction

1
Talking Therapies, Culture, the State and Neoliberalism: Is There a Need for Critical Psychotherapy, Psychoanalysis and Counselling?

Del Loewenthal

Introduction

We already have critical psychiatry and critical psychology. In this book we explore whether there is now an unfortunate need for critical psychotherapy, psychoanalysis and counselling. The proposition will be considered that the main reason we have critical psychiatry and psychology is that they are primarily agents of the state, and that this is becoming increasingly true for psychotherapy, psychoanalysis and counselling.

In this chapter, I attempt to provide an overview of notions of 'critical', revisit psychotherapy, psychoanalysis and counselling as cultural practices in the light of both critical psychiatry and psychology and consider the apparent paradox of increasing state intervention in a neoliberal world. In the subsequent chapters, space is given to a range of narratives about 'critical' approaches where authors have been commissioned to help with such questions as:

- Can there be a 'critical' approach to practice from inside the psychotherapeutic modalities?
- Can psychotherapeutic practice be theorised or researched as it is fundamentally different when one is in it?
- Do critical theory, critical psychiatry and critical psychology limit or further the potential development of 'critical' psychotherapy, psychoanalysis and counselling?
- Should we as talking therapists be able to explore how our practices may legitimise various power structures?

4 *Introduction*

- Should we be more aware of how we are engaging politically with issues around mental health?
- Do we need to revisit how madness and distress are experienced and to what extent our debates are constrained by state and other interests, including professional?
- How much are we still caught up with modernism attempting to separate an individual's wellbeing from social contexts which may be the prime cause of 'psychosis' and other forms of distress?
- To what extent are our modalities, whether they be psychoanalysis or cognitive behavioural therapy (CBT), primarily exercises in power?
- Will the rise of the service-user movement make a beneficial difference to service users?
- Is it time for psychotherapists, psychoanalysts and counsellors to start thinking more critically about how much we're caught up with individualism, pseudoscience, and the language of medicine and clinical psychology, all of which can be seen as instruments of the status quo?
- Is it possible for us to be able to be thoughtful about where our knowledge comes from and yet not be banished or incorporated by dominant choices in our culture?
- What sort of political agency do we as practitioners (and our clients/patients) have?
- How possible is it for us to consider the abuses stemming from our own personal and professional position, as well as of related managers and their audit cultures, and even of users, as well as how their voices are managed?

Such questions are interrogated here with reference to the talking therapies in a climate of increasing state-regulated practice (Mace et al. 2009; Parker and Revelli 2008) with its growth of manualisation, the training of technicians and approaches that favour taking clients' minds off their concerns. The contributors to this book are practitioners from North America and the UK who are known for their engagement, from a range of perspectives, with the various notions of 'critical' in the context of therapeutic practice. Their abstracts, critiques of their own work and brief biographical details are given separately before Part I. In editing this book the question has emerged as to whether the potential need for being 'critical' applies at least as much to what appears to be the state-sanctioned talking therapies' greater propensity to help us to deny our own violence and sexuality as it does to our unwillingness to think politically. This potential need to be critical of the personal as well as the political is also returned to in my concluding contribution (Chapter 17, 'Psychotherapy, psychoanalysis and counselling for oppressors and oppressed: Sex, violence and ideology in practice?').

It is hoped that one outcome will be to encourage readers to consider their modality, whatever it is, as also an exercise of power, and wonder about the use of, often so-called, 'science' in the pursuit of vested interests' notions of progress and authority. Throughout this book the terms 'psychotherapy', 'psychoanalysis' and 'counselling' are collectively referred to as 'the talking therapies'. It is intended that with both sets of terms this includes 'counselling psychology'. At other times the term 'psychological therapist' is used, and this is intended to include those that I have just mentioned, together with arts and play therapists. There are, however, some occasions when the term 'psychotherapist' is used to include all of the above.

This book arises therefore following increasing concern about the growing state influences on talking therapies' practices. As one commentator has put it, there has been a transformation in practice in recent years, moving from a 'cottage industry to a factory-based production line' (Parry et al. 2010) with equally disruptive effects for practitioners. There would appear to have been a significant shift from accepting talking therapies as essentially both confidential and subversive, and inevitably being located on the edges of our society, to such confidentiality (Loewenthal 2014a) being constantly risk assessed together with practices and trainings being increasingly registered, regulated and incorporated into mainstream society. Much of this change has been legitimised through an increasingly pervasive audit culture, coupled with a narrow notion of evidence-based practice involving some very dubious claims to being 'scientific'. Yet isn't this more to do with those in power at a particular time attempting to determine what is and is not science? As Foucault states, 'if we ask what is, in its very general form, the kind of division governing our will to knowledge – then we may well discern something like a system of exclusion (historical, modifiable, institutionally constraining)' (Foucault 1971). Andrew Samuels, in Chapter Ten, is one who argues that we are fooling ourselves if we think that the talking therapies were ever free and independent. Certainly it appears that most trainings do train people with regard to their particular guru, leading perhaps to less rather than more thoughtful practice. Yet previously, didn't seeing a talking therapist lead to far fewer possibilities that what one said would be reported to the 'authorities'? This increasing role of the state in the training provision and so-called 'quality assurance' of the talking therapies, in parallel with what is being described as an era of neoliberalism, where market-based economies, we are told, promote efficiency and value for money, is regarded here as the essential new development. As a consequence I wrote an editorial for *European Journal of Psychotherapy & Counselling* entitled 'Is there an unfortunate need for critical psychotherapy and counselling?' (Loewenthal 2013). My concern there was, and still is, that once the field of critical psychotherapy, psychoanalysis and counselling is established it will become a minority module on mainstream programmes with the implication that (as with psychiatry and psychology) mainstream psychotherapy, psychoanalysis and counselling become by definition primarily 'uncritical'. The 'critical' add-on is then there to allow for a notion of democracy and what is increasingly becoming perhaps the illusion of academic freedom. The above mentioned editorial led to three further activities: a London conference (Critical psychotherapy and counselling – if not now, when?, Universities Psychotherapy & Counselling Association/Research Centre for Therapeutic Education Conference 2014), a special issue of *European Journal of Psychotherapy & Counselling* (Loewenthal 2014b) with the same title as the conference and a request to edit this book.

Some preliminary considerations

There is the question of what we might mean by 'critical'? In this chapter I will look, albeit briefly, at the history of this question in psychiatry, psychotherapy and counselling. There are several traditions in the notion 'critical'. There is 'critical theory' coming from the Frankfurt School of Adorno, Horkheimer et al. with one of their assumptions being that we will need to make some fundamental changes to the language we use in order to think outside the ideology that has imprisoned us. Another notion is a more libertarian view of those such as Thomas Szasz, where freedom of expression and confidentiality would be given primacy. Another notion of 'critical' is the sceptical tradition from the Greeks through to continental philosophy, with more recently such figures as Heidegger (who in contrast with the Frankfurt School stresses the importance of ordinary, non-technical language), Levinas, Derrida, Wittgenstein and so forth. Another possibility of being 'critical' is from other ways of thinking that are currently outside the dominant discourses in the talking therapies – for example, queer theory, literary criticism, and cultural and emotional critiques. John Heaton (2006), who was involved with Ronnie Laing and David Cooper in developing the Philadelphia Association in London (where I am also a member), argues against the notion of 'radical' and in favour of 'critical', pointing to the sceptical tradition. While I am very much influenced by this sceptical tradition, in writing this book I have become increasingly concerned that this can too easily become a process of watering down political/ideological implications.

Hence, one important question appears to be whether practitioners can be critical through just reconsidering the literature in their field or whether different external theoretical ideas need to be introduced in order for 'critical' perspectives to be adopted. In Chapter 13, 'Psychoanalysis and the event of resistance', Steven Groarke, drawing particularly on Derrida, is one of our contributors who does both in exploring whether the concept of resistance can both help us to be and prevent us from being critical.

Questions about the role of the talking therapies in capitalism have been raised at the start of this chapter, and this is developed further later, particularly through Ian Parker's Chapter 3, 'Toward critical psychotherapy and counselling: What can we learn from critical psychology (and political economy)?', Lois Holzman's Chapter 8, 'Relating to people as revolutionaries', Michael Rustin's Chapter 9, 'Work in contemporary capitalism' and Chris Oakley's Chapter 12, 'The Deleuzian project'.

What is new is the extent to which the state's involvement in purchasing/providing specific psychological therapies has been introduced, alongside our new era of neoliberalism with its audit culture, and in the UK what is referred to as New Public Management (Barzelay 2001; Gruening 2001). Thus while we might question whether the talking therapies have ever been free and the extent to which many previous trainings have discouraged rather than encouraged thoughtful practice (see for example Kernberg (1996), 'Thirty methods to destroy the creativity of psychoanalytic candidates'), what we have now is something else besides.

Other preliminary considerations include whether we see the talking therapies and the way in which they are researched/evidenced as primarily cultural practices. We might then critique any theory or regulation in terms of implications for our practice at any moment with any specific client/patient rather than starting with theory (Loewenthal 2011).

There is the perhaps fundamentally important consideration, and ever-relevant notion, of Plato's defining *therapeia* by urging us to attempt to regard science and technology as important but always secondary to the resources of the human soul (Cushman 2002). Plato, however, was not very optimistic about our succeeding in this and, disturbingly, we seem increasingly to have not only 'technology' pretending to be 'science', but also less interest in what we might mean by the 'human soul'.

Perhaps a related aspect is the question of what we regard as human values. For example: Are we fundamentally good or evil? Are we rational or irrational? Are we free or determined? Such questions are not uncommon (Coleman 1979). However, in response, are the usual 'bit of both' answers more part of a deluding smokescreen in order to attempt to not stay with thoughts of our evilness, irrationality and relative lack of agency? In particular, if we are all not only at least potentially evil but also increasingly alienated, what can we best hope for through the psychological therapies? Perhaps to realise just this. But how long can we stay with that?

In Chapter 6, 'Critical theory and psychotherapy', Anastasios Gaitanidis reminds us of our ability to do violence to each other. Also, the history of psychotherapy, psychoanalysis and counselling would seem to be a watering-down of the recognition of not only our potential violence but all of us as sexual beings. Furthermore, sociologists such as Etzioni (1961) attempt to offer us an escape route by suggesting that 'moral involvement' can be experienced rather than alienation. But wouldn't the best we might come closest to be 'calculative alienation' (Loewenthal 2002a)? Also, those particularly stemming from Levinas (1999) have increased our awareness of our responsibility to be open to the Other's Otherness. Yet to what extent is our awareness of our and Others' evilness really avoided through such religiosity?

Again, if we consider being critical of texts outside the talking therapies, Donna Orange (Frie and Orange 2009: 126) suggests a particular distinction between the perspectives of Gadamer and Derrida, which could also be helpful in considering critical psychotherapy, psychoanalysis and counselling. For her, Gadamer (2004) might be seen as arguing that the precondition for dialogue is the trust in the goodwill of the Other. Whereas Derrida suggests 'not only that this good-will should never be trusted, but even that we will be blinded by our desire to trust the other'. In an interesting footnote, Orange proposes that this attitude possibly represents the hermeneutics of suspicion that Paul Ricoeur attributed to Marx, Nietzsche and Freud. So to what extent do psychotherapy, psychoanalysis and counselling texts provide a surface level meaning as 'a method to conceal the political interests which are served by the texts?' (Ricoeur 1970: 27). So as talking therapists are we set up through our training to fail if 'The purpose of interpretation is to strip off the concealment, unmasking those interests'? (Ricoeur 1970: 27).

Orange further suggests that postmodernism can be seen within those involved in the tradition of scepticism who have over the centuries 'protested against exaggerated claims to knowledge, unmasked dogmatism and relativist totalizing world views'. 'The resulting skepticism has ranged from a refusal to make any truth claims to holding theory lightly and suspending judgment, perhaps following more closely, Aristotle's injunction to seek in every domain, the head of knowledge and degree of certainty appropriate to it.' However, what these authors have in common is that they 'abhor the reductionist assumptions of enlightenment claims to objective knowledge present in both past and present forms of psychotherapy and counselling'. Orange does, however, acknowledge 'that the deconstructive tools developed to combating, what is seen as for example, Freudian and Kleinian essentialism could themselves result in new reductionisms' (Frie and Orange 2009: 126).

I will argue here that psychotherapy, psychoanalysis and counselling are cultural practices, and the way that both oppressors and oppressed provide smokescreens for others and themselves also changes, and part of this is what is taken as evidence at any one time. More generally, one example of our changing values regarding what we view as sexually and gender appropriate is provided in Chapter 7, 'When love is not all we want: Queers, singles and the therapeutic cult of relationality', by Mari Ruti and Adrian Cocking.

Neoliberalism and the role of the state

In the talking therapies we seem subject to two parallel developments. On the one hand we have neoliberalism encouraging 'the privatisation of everything public and the commercialisation of all things private' (Barber 2000) affecting our relationships (Verhaeghe 2014a), including what is meant by the notion of public service and how we attempt to educate. It can be argued that the introduction of New Public Management, referred to below, provides a smokescreen for such privatisation. However, simultaneously the state is tightening its grip on the psychological therapies in the name of safeguarding the public. There is the argument that neoliberalism has brought out the worst in us (Verhaeghe 2014a). In that case, where do psychotherapy, psychoanalysis and counselling place themselves in relation to these cultural changes? If the talking therapies are becoming too much agents of social control within neoliberalism, could 'critical' psychotherapy, psychoanalysis and counselling provide an alternative space? Or will the talking therapies only be allowed to survive if we don't rock the neoliberalist boat too much? George Monbiot, in reviewing Paul Verhaeghe's (2014b) *What About*

Me? The Struggle for Identity in a Market-Based Society, suggests that those proponents of a market-based society claim that 'unrestricted competition, driven by self-interest, leads to innovation and economic growth, enhancing the welfare of all'. Monbiot continues in his excellent summary by saying that the notion of succeeding through merit – that is, that people succeed through talent and hard work – has led us to believe that the free market 'breaks down hierarchies and creates a world of opportunity and mobility...'. This is not necessarily the case.

> Even at the beginning of the process, when markets are first deregulated, we do not start with equal opportunities... Even when outcomes are based on talent and hard work, they don't stay that way for long. Once the first generation of liberated entrepreneurs has made its money, the initial meritocracy is replaced by a new elite, which insulates its children from competition by inheritance and the best education money can buy.

Monbiot continues in what some readers may consider harsh tones, stating we have been sold the notion that a free market offers us 'autonomy and freedom', but that instead we are caught up in a self-serving system where the very richest people in society fund the think-tanks and gurus that perpetuate the status quo. So where is 'the common good' in both this and our work as talking therapists? Furthermore, while there was a time when we as talking therapists only saw people whose work was alienating and mainly had extrinsic rewards for them, isn't even our own work becoming one where 'The workplace has been overwhelmed by a mad, Kafkaesque infrastructure of assessments, monitoring, measuring, surveillance and audits, centrally directed and rigidly planned...' (Monbiot 2014).

So what in our audit culture of the independence of the psychotherapist and counsellor? Surely, as shown, for example, by so many contributors to this book, we cannot rely on those dependent on a medical model or increasingly the independence of the academic. Can we at least still have in our society a place where an individual can be free to speak of whatever comes to mind? Perhaps many of us have got too used to saying that what is said in the consulting room is confidential so long as the client/patient will not harm themselves or others. But, in practice, couldn't this include just about anything? And isn't this becoming increasingly successfully sold along with the monitoring of our emails and telephone calls in order to counter through 'internal security' such threats as terrorism? Furthermore, we have professional bodies reducing standards whereby a psychotherapist can now advertise as such after a two-year part-time course with no therapy. Aren't such psychotherapists more likely to willingly report to the authorities things that those benefiting from longer training might have been more usefully able to stay and work through with their patients/clients?

In the UK, what has probably had the greatest effect on psychotherapy, psychoanalysis and counselling are the Layard report (2005) and the recommendations for the talking therapies from the National Institute for Health and Care Excellence (NICE 2009). One view is that the Layard report has been influential in that, first, in the case for the talking therapies, in contrast with pharmaceutical interventions, it has convinced successive governments. Second, governments are increasingly taking mental health needs seriously. However, in providing for mental health using a population-based approach with the Improving Access to Psychological Therapies (IAPT) national programme, the government's role becomes central to the training, provision and delivery of talking therapies, with a focus on what many see as narrowly defined evidence-based practice. What then become favoured are approaches that meet the imposed measurement systems, which seem to be those that take clients' minds off their problems rather than attempting to help them work through what is bothering them. Meanwhile the public are encouraged to have those talking therapies where the evidence base has been established through randomised control trials (RCTs). Yet given the questions regarding how appropriate, if not scientifically absurd, RCTs are for investigating therapeutic approaches (Guy et al. 2012) even when manualised, we can only hopefully imagine the incredulity of future generations at our attempts to do so.

Education and training

Again in the UK, while there is a growing university presence, counselling and psychotherapy are frequently taught through private or charitable institutions with students being 'trained' rather than 'educated'. This results in the danger that thoughtfulness about theory and practice is sidelined in favour of students promoting the theories of their particular 'guru'. It might be hoped, though not necessarily warranted, that university-based trainings might offer the opportunity for less biased and more thoughtful questioning of psychotherapy and counselling practice, but there has always been the issue about whether it is appropriate to offer trainings via an academy (see for example the Special Issue of *European Journal of Psychotherapy & Counselling*, Loewenthal 2002b; Parker 2002). The effects of neoliberalism are radically changing what were regarded as universities (Lorenz 2012). Furthermore, more recently, with the New Public Management of universities where academics' five-year research plans are subject to managers who also determine the individuals' terms and conditions of employment, universities can even more be seen as places that are more driven by state and commercial pressures to commodify knowledge rather than independent quests for knowledge for its own sake.

The predominant audit culture, combined with a shift whereby education has come to be seen as a marketable commodity, has also led to the academy being increasingly seen as an agent of, and subject to, the state. This growing dominant role of the state has had two consequences. First, private trainings, at least in the UK, are now often validated by universities and can therefore result in a degree. In counselling, psychotherapy and, in particular, counselling psychology, the aim of many students upon graduating is to achieve state-sanctioned competences required by publicly funded jobs. Second, the public are being advised to seek out such evidence-based therapies when looking for therapists in private practice. This has resulted in most approaches and professional bodies attempting to demonstrate that they meet these state-endorsed criteria. This further reduces the possibility of thoughtful practice and the questioning of assumptions that underlie that practice. Although it was hoped that university-based trainings would provide a space for such enquiry, what has happened instead is that young people who are interested in counselling and psychotherapy are primarily encouraged to focus on the future job prospects that their degree may offer them. In conjunction with this, trainings tend to be shifting from university departments of education where, for example, the influence of Carl Rogers' (1969) approach to learning was predominant, to psychology departments, which are generally far more informed by a scientific, medical model paradigm. Regarding critical talking therapies and education and training, Tom Strong et al. in Chapter 15, 'Contesting the curriculum: Counsellor education in a postmodern and medicalizing era', provide a very helpful overview with specific reference to issues that stem from the dominance of the medical model. Then in, Chapter 16, 'Systemic means to subversive ends: Maintaining the therapeutic space as a unique encounter', Jay Watts usefully explores some of the issues in attempting to keep a counselling psychology programme alive and not stultified by such increasing external pressures as the state and audit cultures.

A brief history of the notion 'critical'

In psychotherapy, psychoanalysis and counselling

Since at least the 1970s, critical thinking in the social sciences has been seen as particularly influenced by the Frankfurt School (see Chapter 6, 'Critical theory and psychotherapy'). As is described later, the Frankfurt School highlights our alienation and the horrors we seem to so ably inflict on each other. Subsequently, those such as Eakin et al. (1996) and Rubin and Babbie (2009) have attempted to develop critical theory in the social sciences with the hope of critiquing and changing society rather than just explaining it. However, the notion of critical psychotherapy, psychoanalysis or counselling seems to have taken off only at the start of the twenty-first century with Ian Craib's (2001) *Psychoanalysis: A Critical Introduction*. Here he argues that psychoanalysis is less about curing people or making them happy and more about understanding individuals' lives. (This could be more akin to what users of the talking therapies who have a psychiatric diagnosis describe as being important in terms of allowing the personal development of meaning, as in Cotton and Loewenthal's Chapter 5, 'Personal versus medical meanings in breakdown, treatment and recovery from "schizophrenia"'.) Then Lisa Hoshmand edited *Culture, Psychotherapy and Counseling: Critical and Integrative Perspectives* (2005). This book, to which I contributed, attempted to examine social and moral implications in psychotherapy and counselling, positioning culture as a central determinant in healing. A few years later, Colin Feltham produced a textbook entitled *Critical Thinking in Counselling and Psychotherapy* (2010), which set about examining what are considered to be critical debates around key topics, with particular attention being given to person-centred approaches. He followed with *Counselling and Counselling Psychology: A Critical Examination* (2013), also with a focus on counselling psychology, which provides socioeconomic and philosophical critiques. In Chapter 11, 'Critical priorities for the psychotherapy and counselling community', Feltham provides an overview of where he has got to with such critical examinations. Also in 2012 the journal *Changes* became *The Journal of Critical Psychology, Counselling & Psychotherapy* under the editorship of Craig Newnes. Additionally there have been related books claiming to look critically at aspects such as race and culture (Moodley and Palmer 2006), psychotherapy research (Roth et al. 2006) and concepts (Smith et al. 2012).

In psychiatry

However, preceding this there have been, and continue to be, publications about critical psychiatry and psychology. In the UK, with regard to psychiatry, the term anti-psychiatry was used by David Cooper in his *Psychiatry and Anti-Psychiatry* (1967) and also *The Dialectics of Liberation* (1968), where psychiatry is seen as an agent of capitalism, with the hope that psychiatric patients could challenge their oppressors and start a revolution for all. Could it be that once psychotherapy, psychoanalysis and particularly counselling become available, if indeed not a necessity, for more than a privileged minority, such freer thinking forms a potential problem for the state in terms of social control, thus requiring state intervention in controlling (through, for example, taking responsibility for so-called 'quality assurance' and safeguarding the public) the psychological therapies? Otherwise, with so many receiving therapy (over 1 million per year in the UK; Chunn 2013), might this lead to a different type of society away from the current status quo? In the 1960s and 1970s there was great interest in the UK and North America in Cooper's colleague Ronald Laing (see for example *Sanity, Madness and the Family: Families of Schizophrenics* (1970, with Aaron Esterson), *The Divided Self* (1965) and *The Politics of Experience* (1967)) – though Laing distanced himself from the term 'anti psychiatry'. In North America the Harvard psychiatrist and anthropologist Arthur Kleinman (1989) wrote *Illness Narratives: Suffering, Healing and the Human Condition*. Here he argued that interpreting the illness experience is an art that is tragically neglected by modern medical training. In critical psychiatry, an important book is Philip Thomas' (1997) *The Dialectics of Schizophrenia*. Here he argues that an individual's experiences need to be understood in the context of their personal history as well as social and cultural factors. The need to continue this argument seems ever present, as shown by the work done, for example, by Robert Whitaker (2002) and Kenneth Gergen (2011). Gergen continues to stress the importance of culture in Chapter 4, 'The neurobiological turn in therapeutic treatment: Salvation or devastation?', where he also warns us not to be seduced away from this by so-called advances in neuroscience. Back to the UK, in 2004, David Ingleby brought out a second edition of his book *Critical Psychiatry*, which first appeared in 1980. Here he questions both what mental illness is and the adequacy of conventional psychiatric responses to it. In 2006, two further important books in this field were published.

Del Loewenthal 15

One was Duncan Double's (2006) *Critical Psychiatry: The Limits of Madness*, which challenged the polarisation created by the anti-psychiatry movement and instead encouraged critical thinking about the theories that form the basis of psychiatry. Also that year, Patrick Bracken and Philip Thomas' (2006) *Postpsychiatry: Mental Health in a Postmodern World* examined both the power of psychiatry in shaping our understanding of ourselves and the limitations of psychiatry as science. More recently has been the work of Joanna Moncrieff: *The Myth of the Chemical Cure: A Critique of Psychiatric Drug Treatment* (2009), *The Bitterest Pills: The Troubling Story of Antipsychotic Drugs* (2013), *De-Medicalizing Misery: Psychiatry, Psychology and the Human Condition* (Moncrieff et al. 2011) and *De-medicalizing Misery II: Society, Politics and the Mental Health Industry* (Rapley et al. 2014). In these publications she attempts to re-evaluate the nature and efficacy of psychiatry, together with the history and politics of psychiatry. Moncrieff campaigns, with service user groups, against the dominance of the biomedical approach to psychiatry, which is seen as psychiatric coercion and the influence of the pharmaceutical industry. In Chapter 2, 'The Medical Model; What is it, where did it come from and how long has it got?', Hugh Middleton reviews these developments from Joanna Moncrieff and others of the UK's Critical Psychiatry Network. Through this he challenges the validity of the 'medical' approach to psychological/emotional difficulties and suggests that there are now signs towards more patient-centred approaches.

In psychology

With regard to psychology, in 1991, Ian Parker published *Discourse Dynamics: Critical Analysis for Social and Individual Psychology* in which he defended a realist position (which involves what we can know and how we know it, as well as questions of morals/concerns in knowledge and practice). Then we saw the publication of Fox and Prilleltensky's (1997) *Critical Psychology: An Introduction*, in which they explored such influences as feminism, critical theory, postmodernism, hermeneutics and discursive psychology. There have also been numerous authors referring to aspects of critical psychology. These include Lucy Johnstone (1989, 2000), who argues as a clinical psychologist that traditional ways of treating mental distress can make peoples' difficulties worse. There is also Richard Bentall (2010) who in *Doctoring the Mind: Why Psychiatric Treatments Fail*, for example, again as a clinical psychologist, claims that psychiatry relies on misunderstandings of mental illness. Ian Parker was also editor of *Radical Psychology* and then editor of the *Annual Review of Critical Psychology*. Is the trend here that what was radical, as in the case of David Cooper, makes way for critical, which may reach a broader audience but in so doing becomes weakened as it becomes incorporated by precisely that mainstream capitalism? In the often quoted first issue of *Radical Psychology*, Parker (1999) concludes that such critical activity needs journals and organisations, and that such critical psychology 'should be more theoretically intense as well as being a more thoroughly practical endeavour'. He argues that the importance of challenging ideology and power in order to 'link the variety of radical activities... in and against the discipline and to construct a field of debate where different theoretical positions and practical initiatives' can evolve. In Chapter 3, 'Towards critical psychotherapy and counselling: What can we learn from critical psychology (and political economy)?', Parker provides us with his recent thinking about the implications of critical psychology for critical psychotherapy, psychoanalysis and counselling.

More recently, several publications have appeared, including *Critical Social Psychology: An Introduction*, by Gough et al. (2001, 2013), who describe the field as complex and fast moving. While many of these authors have much to offer us by introducing such aspects as feminism and postmodernism to clinicians, it also appears that there is the constant danger that the word 'critical', rather like postmodernism previously, becomes incorporated and killed by those whom it originally attacked.

Other developments

There have also been other developments which may help in our exploration of 'critical' psychotherapy, psychoanalysis and counselling. Taking just the UK, as mentioned there is the Philadelphia Association and, connected with Ian Parker, the Discourse Unit. I would also like to take this opportunity to describe some of the work of the Research Centre for Therapeutic Education (RCTE) – previously at the University of Surrey and now at the University of Roehampton, which I direct – as an indication of critical work taking place. In *Post-Existentialism and the Psychological Therapies: Towards a Therapy without Foundations* (Loewenthal 2011), I am critical of the theories and research which attempt to justify what was discovered by Freud, Klein and others as a practice. It is argued therefore that theories may have implications but not applications. Other books include *Against and for CBT: Towards a Constructive Dialogue?* (House and Loewenthal 2008), *Childhood, Well-Being and a Therapeutic Ethos* (House and Loewenthal 2009) and *Critically Engaging*

CBT (Loewenthal and House 2010). Also, *In, against and beyond Therapy: Critical Essays towards a Post-Professional Era* (2010) is a collection of Richard House's writings within the therapy field.

Another member of the RCTE is Anastasios Gaitanidis, who has made a particularly significant contribution to this volume (Chapter 6, 'Critical theory and psychotherapy') on the Frankfurt School, and whose other publications include *The Male in Analysis* (2011). Of importance to the subject of this book is the anthropologist and psychotherapist James Davies, whose publications include *Cracked: Why Psychiatry Is Doing More Harm than Good* (2013). Here he reveals how the *Diagnostic and Statistical Manual of Mental Disorders* (DSM-5) is built far more on personal politics than on any scientific basis. He is currently involved with the RCTE as well as with the Council for Evidence-Based Psychiatry, which is arguing for long-term research into the effects of psychotropic medication. Another RCTE member is Rosie Rizq, whose various publications include *Perversion, Neoliberalism and Therapy: The Audit Culture in Mental Health Services* (2014) and *IAPT and Thoughtcrime: Language, Bureaucracy and the Evidence-Based Regime* (2013).

Julia Cayne, another member of the RCTE, writes about practitioners staying with unknowns (Cayne 2014; Cayne and Loewenthal 2011), and how they might achieve this despite the dogma of some training institutes and the ever-growing requirements of professional bodies to make their members toe state provision and guidelines.

Contributors Tom Cotton, Andrew Samuels and Ian Parker are also members of the RCTE, the latter two as visiting professors. Former member Dennis Greenwood's publications include *On Learning to Work with Someone with a Label: Some Post-Existential Implications for Practice, Theory and Research* (Greenwood and Loewenthal 2011). Onel Brooks, another member, contributed to the recent special issue of the *European Journal of Psychotherapy & Counselling*, 'Critical psychotherapy and counselling – if not now, when?' (2014). In 'Critical psychotherapy, post-psychotherapy and the cult of technicism' (2014), he argues that what is most important is not the case for using these terms but what they might be taken to refer to – an argument which is of particular importance if we are to show some resistance to neoliberalism. It is also worth mentioning, in order to further elucidate the current 'critical' field, the other articles which appear in that special issue. In John Lees, Jane Macaskie and Dawn Freshwater's 'Social and political perspectives on the psychotherapy and counselling profession: Returning caravelles' (2014), they suggest that for the first time there is substantial UK government funding, coupled with the principles of evidenced-based practice and the policies of the New Public Management systems, for the talking therapies. They draw on the experiences of Latin American and Indian practitioners, which suggest that we should engage with the social and political contexts of peoples' lives. There are also papers here that suggest different ways in which psychotherapy should be externally influenced, as in Nic Bayley's 'Who dares, speaks: Critical psychotherapy and the poetics of suffering' (2014) and Martin Jordan's 'Moving beyond counselling and psychotherapy as it currently is – taking therapy outside' (2014). Andrew Samuels in his paper, which is reproduced in this volume (Chapter 10, 'Everything you always wanted to know about therapy (but were afraid to ask): Fragments of a critical psychotherapy'), suggests that what are often regarded as consensual propositions in psychotherapy and counselling, including that they can be free and independent professionals, 'are unreliable, tendentious and even damaging' (in 1995 he co-founded the organisation Psychotherapists for Social Responsibility). Also in the special issue are two critical reviews, one by Keith Tudor, which will be referred to shortly, and the other by Colin Feltham, who, as mentioned, provides an overview of his thoughts on critical therapies in Chapter 11, 'Critical priorities for the psychotherapy and counselling community'. Of particular importance in the UK in attempting to limit the powers of the state is a group of talking therapists, under the banner of the Alliance for Counselling and Psychotherapy (which includes several members of the RCTE, including Darian Leader, who is a visiting professor). It instigated a judicial review in 2009, successfully preventing talking therapists, other than counselling psychologists, from being forced to join the government's Health Professions Council (now the Health and Care Professions Council). This led instead to the establishment of a voluntary register (the Professional Standards Authority). In doing so the Alliance claims that it helped to maintain 'the diversity and independence of psychotherapy and counselling' (2009).

And what of politics?

Additionally, there has been a relatively limited amount of literature on aspects of psychotherapy, psychoanalysis and/or counselling and politics. Even though in 1929 in *Dialectical Materialism and Psychoanalysis* Wilhelm Reich pointed out that psychoanalysis, like Marxism, is a product of capitalism, Reich also attempted to show how the bourgeoisie had to defend itself against 'the people' by devising its own double standards regarding sexual morality. For Reich, 'just as Marxism was sociologically the expression of man becoming conscious of the laws of economics and the exploitation of a majority by a minority, so psychoanalysis is the expression of [individuals] becoming conscious of the social repression of sex' (Brinton 1972). In the UK, Stephen Frosh wrote *The Politics of Psychoanalysis: An Introduction to Freudian and Post-Freudian Theory* (1999). The focus of this book was more on the influence of psychoanalysis on such areas as psychiatry, sociology, literature, feminism and politics, with particular reference to the relationship between individual subjectivity and social relations. There is a tendency to privilege psychoanalysis – for example, in Hinshelwood's interesting article 'Projective identification and Marx's concept of man' (1983). However, Nick Totton in *Psychotherapy and Politics* (2000) argued that from its inception, psychotherapy has had a political face. He explores not only how ideas from psychotherapy have become incorporated into the political agenda but how psychotherapy can be an instigator of social and political change. Again, Andrew Samuels in his *Politics on the Couch: Citizenship and the Internal Life* (2001) focuses on both 'the hidden psychology of politics and the hidden politics of the psyche'. It was in 1996 that Ann Kearney in *Counselling, Class and Politics: Undeclared Influences in Therapy* attempted to show how the notion of ideology was vital to the talking therapies. In North America, Layton et al. (2006) wrote what is closest to the aims of this book in their *Psychoanalysis, Class and Politics: Encounters in the Clinical Setting*. They argue that the ideologically enforced split between the political order and personal life has become more difficult to sustain. They are particularly interested in how issues of class and politics emerge in the clinical setting, how unconscious defences are employed to deny reality, how unconsciously ideology is enacted, and how psychotherapists might address rather than deny their significance. This can be seen as following on from Slavoj Zizek's earlier attempts to bring to our attention the complexities of contemporary ideology for the talking therapies in his *The Sublime Object of Ideology* (1989).

As I write this there is the news of the death of David Smail, a clinical psychologist who attempted to 'expose the damaging psychological effects of an increasingly competitive and unequal society' in his *Power, Interest and Psychology: Elements of a Social Materialist Understanding of Distress* (2005). For his obituary, Moloney and Faulconbridge (2014) describe how he outlined 'what he called a social-materialist psychology. This places distress firmly in a material context, recognising the extent to which our feelings, thoughts and behaviour are shaped by our economic and social circumstances.' He 'proposed that if we want to understand why we are unhappy, rather than insight, we must cultivate what he termed "outsight" into the world around us. It is a perspective that encourages personal modesty, appreciation of luck, compassion, and recognition of our common humanity.'

There is now at least some interest from the talking therapies in how our individual wellbeing is affected by the political order and not just how the theories of these therapies can help to explain social and economic forces. This is witnessed by the creation in 2002 of the journal *Psychotherapy and Politics International*, currently edited by Keith Tudor, with the stated aim of exploring 'the connections and interactions between politics and psychotherapy, both in theory and in practice'. Also, Proctor, Cooper, Saunders and Malcolm produced *Politicizing the Person-Centred Approach: An Agenda for Social Change* (2006). Here they look not only at how person-centred theory can contribute to an understanding of sociopolitical therapy but, importantly, at the contribution that a critical analysis of social and political factors can make to the practice of person-centred therapy. It would seem that if we explore what is being written in terms of the talking therapies, in terms of the political it can potentially open up much for those who are interested in critical perspectives, particularly when the focus is on the external effects on the lives of our clients/patients rather than how our theories can explain these external effects.

Another relatively recent development is the interest in potentially critical voices from actual users of psychotherapy, psychoanalysis and counselling. This is a long overdue development for the good but also a problematic area. On the one hand we have the abuses that can and do take place from the power positions of the talking therapist, and on the other we have consumerist developments. These are coupled with the audit culture and consumer legislation, which bring in a new elite, including managers whose own power base in turn becomes potentially abusive and self-sustaining, potentially at the expense of the service that it purports to protect. Thus the state and, for example, the New Public Management can use consumers rather than hearing them as people, albeit not always without justification, to reduce the talking therapies' professional abuse. In Chapter 5, 'Personal versus medical meanings in breakdown, treatment and recovery for "schizophrenia"', Tom Cotton and I explore an aspect of Tom's doctoral research which attempts to consider some service users' experiences. Finally, as already mentioned, what will also be explored in this book is the extent to which it is possible to be critical within the talking therapies, or is this really more of the same with someone being critical of what exists in order to develop yet another new school? There is a strong case that we should have started this chapter, and the book, with users' views. Again, in reviewing the notion of 'critical', I could have started rather than ended with the case put forward by those who are against the talking therapies per se. There has for some time been those who argue against the talking therapies, including Masson (1992) and Morrall (2008). In Chapter 14, 'Psychology, psychotherapy – coming to our senses?', Paul Moloney presents such an argument.

There are criticisms which combine various elements of the above strands. However there is a danger of developing a new school, and what is attempted in this volume is to avoid the type of schoolism where one modality, new or otherwise, is critical of another.

The chapters

It is hoped, therefore, that this book can provide a start to the questioning of how useful it is, and to whom, to develop the notion of critical psychotherapy, psychoanalysis and counselling by bringing together, particularly from the UK and North America, those who are currently writing about this area. As with the conference that preceded this book, interest in contributing far exceeded expectations and there has been the difficult question of what to include.

There was also the question of how to organise the book. Should it be, for example, in terms of 'political, economic, social and technological' criticisms? Should it be along the lines that my co-editor, Richard House, and I adopted for our book *Against and for CBT*, namely 'paradigmatic, clinical, epistemological and research, and political and cultural' perspectives? There again, in the previously mentioned special issue of *European Journal of Psychotherapy & Counselling* that I edited, Keith Tudor (2014) used Mingers' (2000) critiques of 'rhetoric, tradition, authority and objectivity'. Instead, it seemed better for any classification to emerge from the chapters themselves. It was also decided not to make a distinction between theory-orientated and practitioner-informed sections because all contributors are practitioners. We do, though, have contributions from psychotherapists, psychoanalysts and counsellors, as well as counselling psychologists.

So after this introduction and overview we look at what we might learn from critical psychiatry and critical psychology. This is followed by an exploration of some clients' experiences, after which critiques are considered which are more external, followed by critiques more from within psychotherapy, psychoanalysis and counselling. (This distinction is attempted on the basis of whether the author's critical stance is seen

22 Introduction

as more or less from psychotherapeutic, psychoanalytic or counselling theory.) We then offer critiques of teaching and learning. In the last contribution (Chapter 17, 'Psychotherapy, psychoanalysis and counselling for oppressors and oppressed: Sex, violence and ideology in practice?'), I return to whether there is an unfortunate need for critical psychotherapy, psychoanalysis and counselling. Initially I comment on the forthcoming chapters in the light of the questions raised here. Then I conclude exploring how we – both individually and through the state – and other interested parties attempt to dilute both our own sexuality and violence, and conspire not to step outside the ideology that contains us.

References

Alliance for Counselling and Psychotherapy (2009) 'Against state regulation: Statement'. www.allianceforpandc.org. Accessed 14 September 2014.
Barber, B. (2000) 'Ballots versus bullets', *Financial Times*, 20 October 2000.
Barzelay, M. (2001) *The New Public Management: Improving Research and Policy Dialogue*. Berkeley, LA and London: University of California Press.
Bayley, N. (2014) 'Who dares, speaks: Critical psychotherapy and the poetics of suffering', *European Journal of Psychotherapy & Counselling*, 16(4): 348–360.
Bentall, R. (2010) *Doctoring the Mind: Why Psychiatric Treatments Fail*. London: Penguin Books.
Bracken, P.J. and Thomas, P. (2006) *Postpsychiatry: Mental Health in a Postmodern World*. Oxford: Oxford University Press.
Brinton, M. (1972) 'Review: Dialectical materialism and psychoanalysis', *Solidarity*, VII (3). http://www.connexions.org/CxArchive/MIA/brinton/1972/reich2.htm. Accessed 31 July 2014.
Brooks, O. (2014) 'Critical psychotherapy, post-psychotherapy and the cult of technicism', *European Journal of Psychotherapy & Counselling*, 16(4): 331–347.
Cayne, J. (2014) 'Learning beyond the known', *European Journal of Psychotherapy & Counselling*, 16(3): 212–227.
Cayne, J. and Loewenthal, D. (2011) 'Post-phenomenology and the between as unknown', in D. Loewenthal (ed.) *Post-Existentialism and the Psychological Therapies: Towards a Therapy without Foundations*. London: Karnac, 31–52.
Chunn, L. (2013) 'Britain on the couch: UK therapists share our biggest worries', *Guardian*, 7 December 2013.
Coleman, J.C. (1979) *Contemporary Psychology and Effective Behaviour*. Glenview, IL: Scott Foresman.
Cooper, D. (1967) *Psychiatry and Antipsychiatry*. London: Paladin.
Cooper, D. (1980) *The Dialectics of Liberation*. London: Pelican.
Craib, I. (2001) *Psychoanalysis: A Critical Introduction*. Cambridge: Polity Press.
Cushman, R. (2002) *Therapeia: Plato's Conception of Philosophy*. New Brunswick and London: Transaction Publishers.

Davies, J. (2013) *Cracked: Why Psychiatry Is Doing More Harm than Good*. London: Icon Books.
Double, D.B. (ed.) (2006) *Critical Psychiatry: The Limits of Madness*. Basingstoke: Palgrave Macmillan.
Eakin, J., Robertson, S., Poland, B., Coburn, D. and Edwards, R. (1996) 'Towards a critical social science perspective on health promotion research', *Health Promotion International*, 11(2): 157–165.
Etzioni, A. (1961) *A Comparative Analysis of Complex Organizations*. Glencoe, IL: The Free Press.
Feltham, C. (2010) *Critical Thinking in Counselling and Psychotherapy*. London: Sage.
Feltham, C. (2013) *Counselling and Counselling Psychology: A Critical Examination*. Ross-on-Wye: PCCS Books.
Foucault, M. (1971) 'The discourse on language' trans. Swyre, R., *Social Science Information*, April 1971, 7–30.
Fox, D.R. and Prilleltensky, I. (1997) *Critical Psychology: An Introduction*. London: Sage.
Fox, D.R. and Prilleltensky, I. (2009) *Critical Psychology: An Introduction* 2nd ed. London: Sage.
Frie, R. and Orange, D. (eds.) (2009) *Beyond Postmodernism: New Dimensions in Clinical Theory and Practice*. New York: Routledge.
Frosh, S. (1999) *The Politics of Psychoanalysis: An Introduction to Freudian and Post-Freudian Theory*. Basingstoke: Palgrave Macmillan.
Gadamer, H.-G. (2004) *Truth and Method* new ed. London: Continuum.
Gaitanidis, A. (2011) *The Male in Analysis: Psychoanalytic and Cultural Perspectives*. Basingstoke: Palgrave Macmillan.
Gergen, K.J. (2011) *Relational Being: Beyond Self and Community*. Oxford: Oxford University Press.
Gough, B., McFadden, M. and McDonald, M. (2001) *Critical Social Psychology: An Introduction*. Basingstoke: Palgrave Macmillan.
Gough, B., McFadden, M. and McDonald, M. (2013) *Critical Social Psychology: An Introduction* 2nd ed. Basingstoke: Palgrave Macmillan.
Greenwood, D. and Loewenthal, D. (2011) 'On learning to work with someone with a label: Some post-existential implications for practice, theory and research', in D. Loewenthal (ed.) *Post-Existentialism and the Psychological Therapies: Towards a Therapy without Foundations*. London: Karnac, 53–72.
Gruening, G. (2001) 'Origin and theoretical basis of New Public Management', *International Public Management Journal*, 4: 1–25.
Guy, A., Loewenthal, D., Thomas, R. and Stephenson, S. (2012) 'Scrutinising NICE: The impact of the National Institute for Health and Clinical Excellence Guidelines on the provision of counselling and psychotherapy in primary care in the UK', *Psychodynamic Practice*, 18(1): 25–50.
Heaton, J.M. (2006) 'From anti-psychiatry to critical psychiatry', in D. Double (ed.) *Critical Psychiatry: The Limits of Madness*. Basingstoke: Palgrave Macmillan, 41–59.
Hinshelwood, R.D. (1983) 'Projective identification and Marx's concept of man', *International Review of Psycho-Analysis*, 10: 221–226.
Hoshmand, L.T. (2005) *Culture, Psychotherapy and Counseling: Critical and Integrative Perspectives*. London: Sage.

House, R. (2010) *In, against and beyond Therapy: Critical Essays towards a Post-Professional Era*. Ross-on-Wye: PCCS Books.
House, R. and Loewenthal, D. (eds.) (2008) *Against and for CBT: Towards a Constructive Dialogue?* Ross-on-Wye: PCCS Books.
House, R. and Loewenthal, D. (eds.) (2009) *Childhood, Wellbeing and a Therapeutic Ethos*. London: Karnac.
Ingleby, D. (2004) *Critical Psychiatry*. London: Free Association Books.
Johnstone, L. (1989) *Users and Abusers of Psychiatry: A Critical Look at Psychiatric Practice*. Hove: Routledge.
Johnstone, L. (2000) *Users and Abusers of Psychiatry: A Critical Look at Psychiatric Practice* 2nd ed. Hove: Routledge.
Jordan, M. (2014) 'Moving beyond counselling and psychotherapy as it currently is – taking therapy outside', *European Journal of Psychotherapy & Counselling* 16(4): 361–375.
Kearney, A. (1996) *Counselling, Class and Politics: Undeclared Influences in Therapy*. Manchester: PCCS Books.
Kernberg, O.F. (1996) 'Thirty methods to destroy the creativity of psychoanalytic candidates', *International Journal of Psychoanalysis*, 77: 1031–1040.
Kleinman, A. (1989) *Illness Narratives: Suffering, Healing and the Human Condition*. New York: Basic Books.
Laing, R.D. (1965) *The Divided Self*. London: Penguin Books.
Laing, R.D. (1967) *The Politics of Experience and the Bird of Paradise*. London: Penguin Books.
Laing, R.D. and Esterson, A. (1970) *Sanity, Madness and the Family: Families of Schizophrenics*. London: Pelican.
Layard, R. (2005) 'Mental health: Britain's biggest social problem?', Paper presented at the No. 10 Strategy Unit Seminar on Mental Health, LSE, 20 January 2005. http://www.cep.lse.ac.uk/textonly/research/mentalhealth/RL414d.pdf. Accessed 31 December 2012.
Layton, L., Hollander, N.C. and Gutwill, S. (2006) *Psychoanalysis, Class and Politics: Encounters in the Clinical Setting*. Hove: Routledge.
Lees, J., Macaskie, J. and Freshwater, D. (2014) 'Social and political perspectives on the psychotherapy and counselling profession: Returning caravelles', *European Journal of Psychotherapy & Counselling*, 16(4): 298–314.
Levinas, E. (1999) *Totality and Infinity: An Essay on Exteriority*. Dordrecht: Kluwer Academic Publishers.
Loewenthal, D. (2002a) 'Involvement and Emotional Labour', *Soundings*, 20: 151–162.
Loewenthal, D. (2002b) 'Special issue on counselling and psychotherapy in the universities: The nature of psychotherapeutic knowledge: psychotherapy and counselling in universities', *European Journal of Psychotherapy & Counselling*, 5(4): 329–418.
Loewenthal, D. (2011) *Post-Existentialism and the Psychological Therapies: Towards a Therapy without Foundations*. London: Karnac.
Loewenthal, D. (2013) 'The unfortunate need for critical psychotherapy and counselling', *European Journal of Psychotherapy & Counselling*, 15(1): 1–4.
Loewenthal, D. (2014a) 'Are psychological therapists less trustworthy than they used to be?', *European Journal of Psychotherapy & Counselling*, 16(2): 97–100.

Loewenthal, D. (2014b) 'Special issue: "Critical psychotherapy and counselling – if not now, when?"', *European Journal of Psychotherapy & Counselling*, 16(4): 295–297.

Loewenthal, D. and House, R. (2010) *Critically Engaging CBT*. Maidenhead: Open University Press.

Lorenz, C. (2012) 'If you think you're so smart, why are you under surveillance? Universities, Neoliberalism and New Public Management', *Critical Inquiry*, 38: 599–629.

Mace, C., Rowland, N., Evans, C., Schroder, T. and Halstead, J. (2009) 'Psychotherapy professionals in Europe: Expansion and experiment', *European Journal of Psychotherapy & Counselling*, 11(2): 131–140.

Masson, J.M. (1992) *Against Therapy*. London: Fontana.

Mingers, J. (2000). 'What it is to be critical? Teaching a critical approach to management undergraduates', *Management Learning*, 31(2): 219–237.

Moloney, P. and Faulconbridge, J. (2014) 'David Smail obituary', *Guardian*, 17 August 2014.

Monbiot, G. (2014) 'Sick of this market-driven world? You should be', *Guardian*, 5 August 2014.

Moncrieff, J. (2009) *The Myth of the Chemical Cure: A Critique of Psychiatric Drug Treatment*. Basingstoke: Palgrave Macmillan.

Moncrieff, J. (2013) *The Bitterest Pills: The Troubling Story of Antipsychotic Drugs*. Basingstoke: Palgrave Macmillan.

Moncrieff, J., Rapley, M. and Speed, E. (2014) *De-Medicalizing Misery II: Society, Politics and the Mental Health Industry*. Basingstoke: Palgrave Macmillan.

Moodley, R. and Palmer, S. (2006) *Race, Culture and Psychotherapy: Critical Perspectives in Multicultural Practice*. Hove: Routledge.

Morrall, P. (2008) *The Trouble with Therapy: Sociology and Psychotherapy*. Maidenhead: Open University Press.

NICE (2009) 'Treatment and management of depression in adults (CG90). National Collaborating Centre for Mental Health', published by the British Psychological Society 2010. http://www.guidance.nice.org.uk/CG90/Guidance/pdf/English.

Parker, I. (1991) *Discourse Dynamics: Critical Analysis for Social and Individual Psychology*. Hove: Routledge.

Parker, I. (1999) 'Critical psychology: Critical links', *Radical Psychology*, 1(1): 3–18.

Parker, I. (2002) 'Universities are not a good place for psychotherapy and counselling training', *European Journal of Psychotherapy and Counselling*, 5(4): 331–346.

Parker, I. and Revelli, S. (2008) *Psychoanalytic Practice and State Regulation*. London: Karnac.

Parry, G., Blackmore, C., Beecroft, C. and Booth, A. (2010) *A Systematic Review of the Efficacy and Clinical Effectiveness of Group Analysis and Analytic/Dynamic Group Psychotherapy*. www.academia.edu/2723418/A_systematic_review_of_the_efficacy_and_clinical_effectiveness_of_group_analysis_and_analytic_and_dynamic_group_psychotherapy. Accessed 17 August 2014.

Proctor, G., Cooper, M., Sanders, P. and Malcolm, B. (2006) *Politicizing the Person-Centred Approach: An Agenda for Social Change*. Ross-on-Wye: PCCS Books.

Rapley, M., Moncrieff, J. and Dillon, J. (2011) *De-medicalizing Misery: Psychiatry, Psychology and the Human Condition*. Basingstoke: Palgrave Macmillan.
Reich, W. (1929) *Dialectical Materialism and Psychoanalysis*. Cambridge: Socialist Reproduction.
Ricoeur, P. (1970) *Freud and Philosophy: An Essay on Interpretation* trans. Savage, D. New Haven, CT: Yale University Press.
Rizq, R. (2013) 'IAPT and thoughtcrime: Language, bureaucracy and the evidence-based regime', *Counselling Psychology Review*, 28(4): 111–115.
Rizq, R. (2014) 'Perversion, neoliberalism and therapy: The audit culture in mental health services', *Psychoanalysis, Culture and Society*, 19(2): 209–218.
Rogers, C.R. (1969) *Freedom to Learn (Studies of the Person)*. New York: Charles Merrill.
Roth, A., Fonagy, P., Parry, G., Target, M. and Woods, R. (2006) *What Works for Whom? A Critical Review of Psychotherapy Research* 2nd ed. New York: Guilford Press.
Rubin, A. and Babbie, E.R. (2009) *Research Methods for Social Work*. Stamford, CT: Cengage Learning.
Samuels, A. (2001) *Politics on the Couch: Citizenship and the Internal Life*. London: Karnac Books.
Smail, D. (2005) *Power, Interest and Psychology: Elements of a Social Materialist Understanding of Distress*. Ross-on-Wye: PCCS Books.
Smith, V., Collard, P., Nicolson, P. and Bayne, R. (2012) *Key Concepts in Counselling and Psychotherapy: A Critical A-Z Guide to Theory*. Maidenhead: Open University Press.
Thomas, P. (1997) *The Dialectics of Schizophrenia*. London: Free Association Books.
Totton, N. (2000) *Psychotherapy and Politics*. London: Sage.
Tudor, K. (2014) 'What do we want? Critical psychotherapy and counselling! When do we want it? Now, now, now! A critical review of a critical issue', *European Journal of Psychotherapy & Counselling*, 16(4): 388–395.
Universities Psychotherapy and Counselling Association/Research Centre for Therapeutic Education Conference Critical Psychotherapy and Counselling – If Not Now, When? 22 November 2013, Whitelands College, University of Roehampton.
Verhaeghe, P. (2014a) 'Neoliberalism has brought out the worst in us', *Guardian*, 29 September 2014.
Verhaeghe, P. (2014b) *What about Me? The Struggle for Identity in a Market-Based Society*, trans. Hedley-Prole, J. London: Scribe Publications.
Whitaker, R. (2002) *Mad in America: Bad Science, Bad Medicine, and the Enduring Mistreatment of the Mentally Ill*. New York: Basic Books.
Zizek, S. (1989) *The Sublime Object of Ideology*. London: Verso Books.

Part II

What Can We Learn from Critical Psychiatry and Critical Psychology?

Part II

2
The Medical Model: What Is It, Where Did It Come from and How Long Has It Got?

Hugh Middleton

This chapter takes 'Beyond the current paradigm' – a paper published in the *British Journal of Psychiatry* by members of the UK Critical Psychiatry Network (Bracken et al. 2012) – as a starting point. The essence of the paper was a reiteration of critical reviews of clinical research, which conclude that the evidence base upon which psychopharmaceuticals are promoted is seriously flawed (Moncrieff 2008, 2013), and that the so-called Dodo bird verdict concerning psychological therapies remains as supportable now as it was when it was first conceived (Budd and Hughes 2009; Rosenzweig 1936; Stiles et al. 2008). Fully realised, these criticisms of the evidence supporting professionalised mental health services and practices have profound implications. At face value they can be read as: 'There is no conclusive science supporting claims that any of the psychopharmaceuticals work as claimed, and when they do help, it is as likely as not that "help" is the result of complex phenomena not indistinguishable from placebo' and 'Useful outcomes of a psychological therapy are primarily the result of a helpful relationship, rather than the result of any identifiable psychotherapeutic technique.' If these conclusions were to be widely acknowledged, then much of what conventional mental health services are commissioned to do would have to be seen as acts of faith rather than fact. In the event, few have reacted to 'Beyond the current paradigm' with any rebuttal of these underpinning conclusions, despite the fact that it was published in the house journal of the Royal College of Psychiatrists. On the other hand, neither is there evidence of revolutionary deconstruction of conventional mental health services which such conclusions should suggest. From this starting point the chapter goes on to reflect upon why that may be.

Madness and civilisation

A helpful place to do this is to draw upon Michel Foucault. *Folie et déraison: Histoire de la folie à l'âge classique*, his first major book and doctoral thesis, was initially published in 1961. It examines ideas, practices and institutional responses to 'madness' from the early enlightenment to the modern era. *Folie et déraison* describes ways in which across time a variety of metaphors have been used to describe social exclusion and confinement of the disturbing, the threatening or the merely inconvenient. Its historical narrative ends with Sigmund Freud and medically administered psychoanalysis. It outlines how Tuke's and Pinel's work, which is generally presented as liberating, can be seen to have ushered in our most modern form of alienation and oppression whereby 'madness' becomes an affliction to be treated and the 'mad', aliens to be acted upon.

> To the doctor, Freud transferred all the structures Pinel and Tuke had set up within confinement. He did deliver the patient from the existence of the asylum within which his 'liberators' had alienated him; but he did not deliver him from what was essential in this existence; he regrouped its powers, extended them to the maximum by uniting them in the doctor's hands; he created the psychoanalytical situation where, by an inspired short-circuit, alienation becomes disalienating because, in the doctor, it becomes a subject.
>
> (Foucault trans. Howard 2007: 264)

As Foucault's historical account ends in the 1950s it does not, and could not, include an account of the last half-century during which, in Euro-American settings, a discourse identifying 'madness' as an illness to be treated by experts in specialised settings and facilities has become dominant. Landmarks of this period include a shift in emphasis to networked provision and the proliferation of psychopharmacological treatments. They also include changes in mental health legislation which oblige even those who are not considered sufficiently 'at risk' to require detention in hospital, to submit themselves to medical treatment and supervision. In parallel, the view that 'madness' is a collection of illnesses to be treated by professionals, as in any other field of medical endeavour, has been consolidated. This modern development can be seen as one which provides as robust a defence against unreason and discomfiting deviance as any of its seemingly more brutal antecedents, such as certification or incarceration. It is not, however, without its shortcomings.

The classic sick role

To consider a state of affairs an 'illness' is a very specific and influential step, identifying it as a particular form of deviance and defining associated power relations. Although frequently criticised, Parsons' outline of the sick role (Parsons 1951) has stood the test of time and remains an effective summary of this process. Simon Williams provides a contemporary outline of the balance of rights and responsibilities entailed in the classic sick role:

> From the point of view of the social system, too low a level of health and too high an incidence of illness is dysfunctional. Illness, in other words, given its interference with normal role capacity, becomes a form of social deviance that needs channelling therefore in an appropriate fashion through an institutionalized role or niche. The sick role, for Parsons, fulfils precisely these goals through a series of rights and obligations that its incumbents must recognize and respect. On the rights side of the equation, the patient (according to the severity of the illness) is exempt from normal role obligations, and is not deemed responsible for falling ill. On the obligations side of the equation, the patient must seek technically competent help and must want to get well. The doctor, for his part, must apply these technically competent skills in order to facilitate (a swift) recovery, guided as he is by the professional constellation of achievement, universalism, functional specificity, affective neutrality and collectivity... The sick role, therefore, serves to discourage the secondary gains of illness and prevent what Parsons, rightly or wrongly, sees as a deviant subculture of sickness from forming through this reciprocal cluster of rights and obligations, the aim of which is to reintegrate the individual back into society through a return to normal role capacity (or an approximation thereof) as quickly as possible.
>
> (Williams 2005: 124)

'Illness' is considered to be a form of deviance, but by providing an institutional response to it the social system negotiates a highly specific contract. The 'ill' person enjoys relief from responsibilities and access to care in exchange for a resignation of authority, submission to expertly defined treatment and dependency upon others. The ill person may resign command over most of their affairs but they still have power over others in the form of expectations of care and support. They also give up their right to assumptions of full competence and are at risk of assumptions of incapacity or incompetence. Despite criticisms, Williams argues, this combination of structural and relational features provides a good explanation of many interactions between individuals and healthcare practitioners. Substantive shortcomings only come to light when the arrangement is applied to circumstances that do not conform to a particularly formed pattern of illness.

Before the widespread introduction of sterile surgical techniques, effective antibiotics and immunisation during the second half of the nineteenth and the first half of the twentieth centuries, life-threatening illness commonly took the form of an acutely debilitating fever due to bacterial infection, such as pneumonia, puerperal sepsis or septicaemia from a gangrenous wound. Until very recently, common experience of illness was a fever that either 'broke' – in other words, resolved as the body's natural defences prevailed – or resulted in death. During the fever the victim would be incapacitated by pain and weakness, and personal hygiene, nutrition and fluid intake would have to be supported by others. Under these circumstances it is adaptive to employ an institutionalised interaction between 'patient' and 'carers', in which the 'patient' temporarily surrenders autonomy in return for professional care and support which are realistically likely to improve their outcome, perhaps even save their life. This may have even greater antiquity, reflecting the biological efficiencies of intensively caring for a relatively small number of dependent young that is characteristic of mammals, or a parent–child relationship if viewed from a psychodynamic perspective. Clearly, however well validated the classic sick role might be from an historical perspective, it loses validity when applied to situations that do not match this historical stereotype.

Limitations of the classic sick role

With the development of sterile surgical techniques and the availability of antibiotics, survival after serious injury, such as spinal transection causing paralysis, loss of a limb or a brain-damaging head injury, have become much more likely than was the case. Mortality following surgical amputation of a limb stood at around 60% in the early nineteenth century. By 1910, it had fallen to some 10% (Alexander 1985). The need to accommodate the 'disabled but no longer ill' is a relatively new development that has only recently found full expression in the form of disability rights legislation, and progress towards this occupied much of the last century. It includes redeeming the disabled from a status of 'patronised and dependent person' that is characteristic of a patient inhabiting the classic sick role, to that of 'autonomous and independent person' with full expectations of rights and responsibilities. Other developments in medical technology have altered the prognosis of many conditions from 'certainly very disabling and commonly life-threatening' to 'manageable provided certain regimes are followed'. Examples include diabetes, hypertension, asthma and epilepsy. Over a period of little more than 150 years the everyday experience of serious illness has widened from that of a time-limited episode resulting in either recovery or death to include chronic physical disability; the presence of a persistent threat of life-endangering recurrence despite ongoing wellbeing, as in cancer in remission; steadily declining health beyond the reach of professional skills, such as the experience of progressive arthritis; and continuing wellbeing contingent upon a programme of professionalised intervention, such as controlled diabetes, asthma, hypertension or epilepsy. None of these is adequately accommodated by the classic sick role and all of them present challenges to the oversimplification that it represents. Nevertheless, the role has deep historical roots and it is a resilient social structure. It orders and legitimises influential institutions and power relations. When it is applied to situations that do not match its historical template, these may be unhelpful. Related power relations lose their legitimacy and the scene is set for tensions and dissatisfactions. Although these have begun to influence practice and have stimulated the introduction of supportive legislation in relation to physical conditions, the same has yet to happen with any measure in the mental health field. Thus mental health service users experience institutions, practices and power relations that commonly reflect the ill-suited application of social arrangements derived from an illness ideology. In parallel, mental health service practitioners persist in holding expectations of conformity to the classic sick role upon individuals and situations where it may not be appropriate.

Mental 'illness'?

These limitations of the classic sick role resonate with Foucault's criticism of its application to 'madness'. He suggests that adoption of an illness metaphor for 'mental disorder' was not the humanitarian advance it has generally been considered. In his view, before this, 'the mad' had been viewed as inherently flawed persons in need of paternalistically provided care in segregated settings. Adoption of the illness metaphor during the first half of the twentieth century, for Foucault in the form of psychoanalytic psychotherapy, but at the same time also in the form of shock therapy and leucotomy, did not deny the notion of a flawed person any more than 'heart failure' denies the perception of a flawed body. What it did do is unhelpfully introduce the dynamics of the classic sick role into understandings of the social arrangements that are available to accommodate 'the mad'. As these are historically deep rooted and carry considerable residual influence, they have played a major part in shaping mental health services and power relations among those participating in them. They legitimise and encourage certain interests, and they oblige actors to conform to particular roles and expectations. As 'mental health difficulties' only occasionally fit specifications of situations that suit the classic sick role, these can be experienced as oppressive, constraining or exploitative by one or more of the participating actors.

This is illustrated by a paper published in 1982 and charmingly entitled 'Chancers, pests and poor wee souls: problems of legitimation in psychiatric nursing' (May and Kelly 1982). Relationships between inpatient psychiatric nurses and their charges are used to comment upon the occupation of psychiatric nursing. As commonly happens, certain people are identified as 'problem patients'. May and Kelly were able to show that such individuals were those who challenged the validity of nurses' therapeutic authority. They were those whose needs and behaviours were not readily accommodated by specifications of the classic sick role. Such patients' reasons for being in hospital were not readily attributable to a clearly defined diagnosis. Their expectations of staff went beyond the limits of what might be expected of a professional working in that context. They were unwilling to accept the submissive role that is usually expected of a 'patient'. They made practical or emotional demands that could not be fulfilled within the conceptual framework of an incapacitated person in legitimate need of assistance. They challenged the applicability of the classic sick role to their needs. Such patients experienced a reluctance to acknowledge their concerns on the part of staff, and providers experienced unjustified or seemingly inappropriate expectations of entitlement normally associated with the sick role. Satisfactory relations between mental health service users and mental health service providers depend upon both parties adhering to a particular code of conduct. The 'rules' of conduct are set by longstanding and widely accepted conventions. The identities of 'service user' and 'service provider' are functions of these conventions. Their validity is no greater than the applicability of the sick role to the purpose of their interaction. In the many contested situations where 'users' experience inappropriate paternalism, and 'providers' experience unwelcome intrusion, this happens because the situation is one in which the identities of 'user' and 'provider' are being forced upon a situation that does not suit them. The role of 'user' or 'patient' comes with expectations of privileged access to resources, and the role of 'provider' or 'professional' comes with expectations of power and authority. This supports productive collaboration when the task is the provision of expert care for one who is temporarily limited in their ability to care for themselves. It becomes a source of conflict if the task is otherwise, such as the facilitation of personal growth and autonomy. Under these circumstances the relationship is different. The professional's contribution is not so much to act upon the recipient of their services but more to join with them in co-constructing a developed understanding. The recipient's role is equally altered – from passive submission to the professional's ministrations to active participation in a joint enterprise. The need for such shifts is widely acknowledged in the form of language that is associated with 'recovery' and with person-centred counselling, but there are widespread challenges to this. Provision for people with emotional and/or psychological difficulties is institutionally located in a healthcare system which continues to be framed by dynamics of the classic sick role.

Investment in the sick role framework

Considered as a whole, mental 'health' care is a large and institutionalised activity. Within the UK it is the fourth largest hospital speciality after medicine, surgery and anaesthetics. The mental health services of the National Health Service (NHS) mental health services employ some 5,500 full-time consultants and associate specialists, roughly 3,000 medical trainees, 48,000 nurses, 30,000 healthcare assistants, 10,000 clinical psychologists and a significant number of other clinicians, such as occupational therapists and pharmacists (Health and Social Care Information Centre 2013).

This is a major enterprise which has developed over the last half-century as the ideology of provision for people with emotional and/or psychological difficulties has evolved into one that is much more closely aligned to that of medicine as a whole, framed as it is by the configuration of the classic sick role. This is not the place to go into that evolution in fine detail but landmarks include (in the UK) the foundation of the NHS, with expectations of consultant status among psychiatrists; the progressive closure of the large asylums with transfers to settings associated with the general hospital; the introduction and subsequently energetic promotion and profiting from psychopharmacotherapeutics; the establishing of chairs in psychiatry in medical schools; the associated growth in psychiatric biomedical research and its support by the pharmaceutical industry; and the development of reliable but entirely descriptive sets of diagnostic criteria, such as DSM-III. As Foucault may have predicted, the development of a medical approach to 'mental health difficulties' has flourished, it provides a livelihood for a great number of people, it has supported many eminent careers and it is a source of massive profit to the pharmaceutical industry. These developments may be seen as more profiteering than philanthropic but unfortunately the need to govern the 'mad' remains a powerful social pressure. Foucault recounts the evolution of alienation – from the casting out of devils, through incarceration of the inconvenient and the certification of defectives to 'medical' treatment – as a continuous process whereby one and then another dominant discourse and related set of institutions has taken on a seemingly essential task. It remains inescapable that there will be those whose despair and hopelessness offer no other way forward than to contemplate suicide, situations where anger and confusion lead to violence, and relationships so tortured by misunderstanding that third parties find them intolerable and seek assistance. It is unthinkable to walk away from such circumstances, leaving individuals, their associates and the law to clear up the mess in the way that other critics of medical involvement in these matters have advocated (Szasz 1974). People are fallible and our humanity insists that we do reach out to others who are in need. Furthermore, and possibly more significantly, challenges to rationality and social order are profoundly disturbing. It is barely surprising that history offers an uninterrupted narrative of institutional arrangements to address these matters. The last century saw medicine step forward to take up this baton, grasping both the privileges and the responsibilities that come with it. Critical scrutiny of the success and suitability of this is beginning to reveal some of its shortcomings.

Shortcomings of applying the sick role framework to 'mental health difficulties'

Foucault felt that espousal of the illness metaphor by those who are concerned with the 'mad' was not the humanitarian advance that it is generally considered to have been. Certainly it has shortcomings, and more than 50 years on it is salutary to consider how well 'mental illnesses' are usefully served by the classic sick role, and the power relations that come with it.

Conventionally, 'mental illnesses' are not considered to be periods of temporary incapacity. Levels of disability might fluctuate, but most if not all are considered to be evidence of enduring vulnerability. The classic sick role presupposes that 'illness' is a time-limited state of affairs from which the individual will return to full competence, provided they conform to treatment.

'Mental illnesses' are not stable entities that are similarly apparent to lay and professional observers alike. The 1970s and 1980s saw considerable investment in developing detailed diagnostic criteria. These have proved unstable and of limited clinical value (Middleton 2008). The classic sick role is predicated upon the fact that the 'illness' is an identifiable, externally verifiable phenomenon whose presence or absence can be formally determined by an authority, such as a doctor, in ways that lay observers can respect and agree with. 'Mental illnesses' are irreducibly subjective phenomena whose presence is only detectable in the form of patients' reports of their experiences. In order to present their craft as a negotiation with 'objective reality', doctors make diagnoses of 'mental illness' on the basis of diagnostic criteria that are founded upon more or less contestable phenomena. These judgements are commonly contested by their patients and only rarely do they provide a sufficient explanation of the difficulties under consideration.

There is little agreement about how any one 'mental illness' might be understood. Someone suffering the common affliction of recurrent panic attacks might be considered to have disturbed brain chemistry, catastrophic misinterpretations, psychodevelopmental issues or stress, depending upon the professionals' theoretical leanings. Thus there is no authoritative view shared by all concerned, and derived from an agreed and authoritative body of professional opinion. Medical authority as it is exercised in the application of the classic sick role is legitimised because it reflects an agreed body of specialised knowledge.

Finally, there is equally little consensus regarding treatment, and this is the point made in 'Beyond the current paradigm': 'There is no conclusive science supporting claims that any of the psycho-pharmaceuticals work as claimed, and when they do help it is as likely as not that is the result of complex phenomena not indistinguishable from placebo' and 'Helpful outcomes of a psychological therapy are primarily the result of a helpful relationship, rather than the result of any identifiable psychotherapeutic technique.' Despite these challenging conclusions, and to reiterate, it is striking that the psychiatric establishment has not contested them. Nevertheless, medical psychiatry retains its grip upon the resources and opportunities that are offered by a need to provide for the 'mad'. As it exercises particularly strong and hegemonic rule in places where that is experienced as most pressing, such as in the provision for the dangerous or most vulnerable, the model it frames influences practices and discourse much more widely. Psychological therapists are obliged to demonstrate that their treatments are 'evidence based'. Measureable outcomes are sought and recorded. Interventions are identified as 'courses of treatment' and are remunerated on that basis, and access to the privilege of being paid to provide such assistance is regulated by a plethora of professional organisations and qualifications. Some of this may be necessary and appropriate governance of situations and interactions that can develop in relation to vulnerable people, but much of it has to be understood as accommodation to the wider, medical framework in which a significant proportion of psychological therapies are embedded.

These tensions are apparent to many but are seemingly difficult to resolve in the context of highly institutionalised arrangements which make up public care provision in the UK. Against a background of funding cuts, tight corporate governance, commissioned targets and accreditation, it is hard to see the light, but a broader historical perspective does emphasise the fact that 'mental health care' is an evolving subject and that, overall, progress is being made. Foucault may have roundly criticised medicine (in the form of Dr Freud) as another and more insidious form of oppression than its antecedents. If alive he might well have said 'I told you so' a few years ago. However, in terms of whether or not all of the contemporary mental health services can and should be damned as oppressive, the glass might now be half full rather than half empty. DSM-5 has been widely criticised and cut adrift by the neuroscience fraternity. In name at least, 'recovery' is the zeitgeist among senior mental health service managers and policy-makers. Even those who market them agree that newer antidepressants and antipsychotic agents are no more helpful than the originals, which were introduced some 60 years ago; it is just that the side-effects have changed. The bulk of mainstream mental health service provision is by multidisciplinary teams. Except perhaps in very esoteric circles, it would be considered quite improper to denigrate 'person-centred' approaches or therapies. Insofar as it was published in the house magazine of the Royal College of Psychiatrists, 'Beyond the current paradigm' was presented to the full membership of the College. It made some challenging assertions and the result has been a stunning silence. Polite dismissal or grudging acknowledgment? Thomas Kuhn (1996) reminds us that paradigm shift is a very real but complex social phenomenon. On the one hand, '"Closely examined, whether historically or in the contemporary laboratory, that enterprise [normal science] seems an attempt to force nature into the preformed and relatively inflexible box that the paradigm supplies' (1996: 24), and on the other, 'scientific revolutions are inaugurated by a growing sense, again often restricted to a narrow subdivision of the scientific community, that an existing paradigm has ceased to function adequately in the exploration of an aspect of nature to which that paradigm itself had previously led the way' (1996: 92). One of those corners may be opening up. Very recently the newly appointed president of the World Psychiatric Association said, in public, that he 'wants all medical, psychiatric and nursing students to be trained first in sociology and anthropology so they understand the culture in which they will practice' (*Guardian* 2013). People are listening as far as the applicability of medical techniques is concerned, but Foucault identified a seemingly more intractable problem: our reactions to deviance, and to distressing and anxiety-provoking behaviour. Do we have a new paradigm for this?

References

Alexander, J.W. (1985) 'The contributions of infection control to a century of surgical progress', *Annals of Surgery*, 201(4): 423–428.
Bracken, P., Thomas, P., Timimi, S., Asen, E., Behr, G., Beuster, C., Bhunnoo, S., Browne, I., Chhina, N. Double, D., Downer, S., Evans, C., Fernando, S., Garland, M.R., Hopkins, W., Huws, R., Johnson, B., Martindale, B., Middleton, H., Moldavsky, D., Moncrieff, J., Mullins, S., Nelki, J., Pizzo, M., Rodger, J., Smyth, M., Summerfield, D., Wallace, J. and Yeomans, D. (2012) 'Psychiatry beyond the current paradigm', *British Journal of Psychiatry*, 201: 430–434.
Budd, R. and Hughes, I. (2009) 'The dodo bird verdict – Controversial, inevitable and important: A commentary on 30 years meta-analysis', *Clinical Psychology and Psychotherapy*, 16: 510–522.
Foucault, M. (1964) trans. Howard, R. (2007) *Madness and Civilisation*. Abingdon: Routledge Classics.
Guardian (2013) http://www.theguardian.com/society (/2013/nov/27/dinesh-bhugra-psychiatry-mental-illness. Accessed 28 November 2013.
Health and Social Care Information Centre (2013) http://www.hscic.gov.uk/searchcatalogue?productid=12545&topics=1%2fWorkforce%2fStaff+numbers&sort=Relevance&size=10&page=1#top. Accessed 28 November 2013.
Kuhn, T.S. (1996) *The Structure of Scientific Revolutions* 3rd ed. London: University of Chicago Press.
May, D. and Kelly, M.P. (1982) 'Chancers, pests and poor wee souls: Problems of legitimation in psychiatric nursing', *Sociology of Health and Illness*, 4: 279–301.
Middleton, H. (2008) 'Whither DSM and ICD, chapter V?', *Mental Health Review Journal*, 13(4): 4–15.

Moncrieff, J. (2008) *The Myth of the Chemical Cure: A Critique of Psychiatrc Drug Treatment*. Basingstoke: Palgrave Macmillan.

Moncrieff, J. (2013) *The Bitterest Pills. The Troubling Story of Antipsychotic Drugs*. Basingstoke: Palgrave Macmillan.

Parsons, T. (1951) *The Social System*. London: Routledge and Kegan Paul.

Rosenzweig, S. (1936) 'Some implicit common factors in diverse methods of psychotherapy', *American Journal of Orthopsychiatry*, 6: 412–415.

Stiles, W.B., Barkham, M., Mellor-Cark, J. and Connell, J. (2008) 'Effectiveness of cognitive-behavioural, person-centred, and psychodynamic therapies in UK primary-care routine practice: Replication in a larger sample', *Psychological Medicine*, 38: 77–88.

Szasz, T. (1974) *The Myth of Mental Illness: Foundations of a Theory of Personal Conduct*. New York: Harper and Row.

Williams, S.J. (2005) 'Parsons revisited: From the sick role to...?', *Health*, 9: 123–144.

3
Towards Critical Psychotherapy and Counselling: What Can We Learn from Critical Psychology (and Political Economy)?

Ian Parker

Critical psychology is now a massive expanding field of work that encompasses many different traditions of research around the world, and it is all the more diverse because it is tackling a host discipline – psychology – that is a sprawling contradictory mass of approaches to understanding individuals. We have learnt a lot from critical psychiatry, and many of us have allied ourselves with the anti-psychiatry and democratic psychiatry movements. We are, of course, against the medicalisation of distress, and there have been particular lessons from psychiatry about how not to do clinical psychology – lessons which then impact on how we think about the place of psychotherapy and counselling (Parker 2011a).

Sometimes we have thought of psychotherapy and counselling as such as part of the alternative – as an alternative to mainstream psychology because psychotherapy and counselling value subjectivity and are not intent on the prediction and control of behaviour. The earlier forms of 'radical psychology' that were a precursor to contemporary critical psychology looked, in particular, to humanistic perspectives on understanding and caring for others. We are a little more suspicious of those perspectives now, and the scope of critical psychology today is much broader and perhaps a bit less tolerant of attempts to patch things up, to make people feel better.

One of the dimensions of debate that structures critical psychology today is precisely about the possible 'positive' role of some form of alternative psychology. So, on the one hand there are those who would see psychology as such – as so complicit in exploitation and oppression that our task must always and only be relentless critique. On the other hand there are those who argue that participatory research, for example, opens up a space for reconfiguring psychology, and that way of attending to subjectivity and action is crucial if we really want to bring about social change. I am stretching apart the two poles of the debate to make clear what the stakes of the argument are. There are many positions somewhere between the two. One way of opening up the specific question of how the debates in critical psychology might be useful now for some kind of 'critical psychotherapy and counselling' is to look at four aspects of critical psychology. Let us take them in turn, and think about what they might mean for therapeutic work.

Four aspects of critical psychology

First, we question the way in which psychologists spend their time studying other people outside the discipline whom they assume to be 'non-psychologists', and we turn the gaze of the discipline back on psychology itself. We study how psychology has developed and what psychologists do. This means, of course, that we do not buy in to the assumption that psychology is neutral about what it studies, and we argue that the observation and measurement of thinking and behaviour have profound consequences for those who do the observing and measuring as well as those whom they turn into objects of their research.

There is, at least, a question here for psychotherapists and counsellors about how their own field of work emerged, and why it is that they feel so strongly about their own specific identity as a professional. We have seen how important this question is recently with the development of 'counselling psychology' and the way in which claims are staked for distinctive expertise tied to professional identity. And we know that when moral weight is given to the position of the therapist it is all too easy for therapy itself to turn into a process of induction and then into the notion that the ideal endpoint would be that the client themselves should become a counsellor or therapist (Rowan and Dryden 1988). That is, there is a reproduction of a hierarchy of knowledge and insight in which psychotherapy and counselling are higher up the pyramid, and psychotherapists often like to think that they are higher up than counsellors. So historical analysis is necessary to dismantle this pyramid of enlightened souls.

Second, we question the attempt to stitch the variety of theories and methodologies in psychology together in order to arrive at one complete watertight covering explanation for why people do what they do.

We work at the contradictions in psychology to give more space for resistance to the power of the discipline. This means that we do not buy in to the assumption that there must be a correct or universal account of psychology, either in any of the particular approaches or as a combination of them, for elements of psychology to be useful. Any positive engagement with any aspect of psychology is relativist, opportunistic and pragmatic.

The question for psychotherapists and counsellors, then, is how their techniques might be useful in enabling people to have some better understanding of themselves, but in such a way as to avoid endorsing the complete package of any theory that houses the technique or the complete package of therapy as a cure-all. There is a general problem in that psychotherapy and counselling coexist with psychology and psychiatry in a constellation of theories and practices – which we term the 'psy complex' – which prescribe good behaviour, and even correct thinking and feeling (Ingleby 1985; Rose 1985). A specific problem with psychotherapeutic practice is that local domains of the psy complex are sometimes governed by charismatic individuals who then provide moral examples for those whom they treat. So attention to contradictions is necessary to unravel those particular regimes of truth and power.

Third, we question the expansion and ambitions of psychology as a framework, or set of frameworks, with a reach and appeal way beyond the colleges and the clinics. We attend to the increasing psychologisation of contemporary society, and the way in which psychological models of the person facilitate the globalisation of ways of being and reflecting on ourselves. This means that we are just as critical of pop-psychology and self-help approaches that operate as informal and ostensibly homegrown alternatives as we are of the theories and methods that are peddled by those who are paid to develop and test them out. Any form of psychology that claims to describe how we develop and learn, for example, tends to end up proscribing and then pathologising other ways that people do actually think and learn.

Psychotherapists and counsellors will respond to this problem, perhaps, by claiming that the more intensively reflexive nature of their practice means that they would always already encourage critique and self-critique. Their understanding of other rival theories and of their own chosen modality is more sophisticated than that of psychologists and, of course, psychiatrists. And the therapeutic process, it is true, encourages such reflexive work as crucial to the cure. The problem, however, is that the appeal to reflexive mindful activity, to the disentangling of feelings and thoughts from each other and the attempt to find a better way to live, is exactly how psychologisation works today (De Vos 2012). So a focus on the way in which useful frameworks congeal into psychologised systems of thought is necessary to good critical reflexive practice.

Fourth, critical psychologists question the way in which our colleagues construct their favourite theories, and most of the time they do that by correcting, refining and systematising what the less canny non-psychologists already think about themselves. Psychology is grounded in actually existing practices of prediction and control, and it has been so successful because it formalises everyday ideological explanation and sells it back to our managers and to us. This means that the issue here is that we are concerned not only with where incorrect ideas come from but also with where some of the good ideas might be. When we look critically at mainstream academic and professional psychology we ask ourselves why some of it seems to make sense, and when we look critically at pop-psychology and alternative psychology we explore what the appeal of those approaches are, not only how they mislead.

Psychotherapists and counsellors do, of course, build their own sense of what it means to help someone and what their own ethical investment is in the theoretical frameworks that they use in their clinical practice. And as they do that they piece together facets of theory and of everyday understanding. Much more than psychology, and with important lessons for mainstream psychological research practice here, therapeutic work involves careful listening, witnessing and honouring of the strategies and hypotheses that people bring to the task of making sense of their lives. Now the question is how the institutional frame of 'therapy' channels that understanding into what the therapist or counsellor will be able to recognise as useful, and how we might break that frame so that we can appreciate the many different forms of practice that are just as effectively 'therapeutic'. So exploring non-therapy could be a way of deconstructing the frameworks that privilege an apparently real therapy (Parker 1999).

The fantasy that there might be a domain of 'real therapy' against which the various components of the psy complex conspire to inhibit brings us to the even more powerful fantasy that the state presses down on the potentially free activities of the individual presupposed in most psychological theory. The aspects of critical psychology that I have described so far are informed by an analysis of structures of power given by Michel Foucault and his followers, whence comes the use of the conceptual device the psy complex (Rose 1985). However, there is another conceptual framework that is useful in describing the place of psychotherapy and counselling in contemporary society and in addressing the vexed question of their relation to the state. This is the critique of political economy (Marx 1867).

Psychotherapy and the state

There have been interminable analyses of state regulation of psychotherapy in the UK in recent years. Humanist-inflected objections to regulation have railed against the reduction of personal and relational phenomena to procedures and outcomes that can be evaluated and monitored according to positivist criteria (for example Mowbray 1995). Psychoanalytic studies have emphasised the way in which one generalised standard, bureaucratised ethics and a discourse of the university blot out the particularity of the subject and facilitate adjustment of the individual to the social (Parker and Revelli 2008). Across the spectrum of debate – humanist to psychoanalytic – some other arguments have been mobilised to draw attention to disciplinary mechanisms, surveillance of the apparatus of therapeutic confession and the malign effects of the psy complex in governing who should speak to whom, where and about what (House 2002).

I want to take a different tack – one which accompanies these existing critiques but focuses on the political economy of state regulation. This is designed to take a critical distance from the historical moment we are living through so that we can perhaps find some new coordinates to get through this. It draws on some of the analysis developed in 'critical psychology', but by applying it to the particular question of psychotherapy, counselling and state regulation we can see implications for the way we better grasp the nature of the psy complex in contemporary political economy. This analysis involves some necessary level of abstraction to grasp what is happening, so that we are not trapped in the immediately intuitive nature of the problem, and it combines this abstraction with an account of us inside it as something contradictory, as something we can change. Even the shift to an analysis of political economy already pits us against a context in which certain assumptions about the individual and the social are naturalised, taken for granted, and it pits us against the specific ideological mutations which reflect, warrant and support life under contemporary neoliberal capitalism. Those assumptions and mutations provide the conceptual ground for much psychotherapy and counselling, so it is worth starting by briefly reviewing them now.

The work of individual reflection, clarification and empowerment that most psychotherapy concerns itself with, as well as being part of the wider project of the Western Enlightenment, rests upon conceptions of the productive citizen in a free-market economy that followers of Adam Smith still look to today. For Smith (2008), self-interest gives rise to the collective good, and both blossom in civil society when left unhindered by the state. The separation of civil society from the state is therefore a precondition for the self-regulation of individuals acting in commerce with each other. One can already hear echoes of the reassurances given by some existing registration bodies to government that statutory self-regulation is quite sufficient, and that it promises the best measure of good behaviour. This is not to say that judicial review of the threat of regulation by the Health Professions Council (HPC) was not tactically the right course of action, but it does mean that this tactic chimes with calls for the free-market 'big society' to be free of 'red tape'. And the defeat of the HPC was quickly followed by what is now an attempt to get the registration bodies to regulate themselves, overseen by the Professional Standards Authority for Health and Social Care (previously known as the Council for Healthcare Regulatory Excellence). The issue here is not so much the shuffling around of signifiers of 'health' as an ideal against which psychotherapy should measure itself as the attempt to enrol each collective body as an obedient and adapted 'self-regulatory' mechanism (Reeves and Mollon 2009).

One way beyond this idealisation of civil society and the contradiction between it and the political state was to try to resolve the contradiction by appealing to broader historically transcendent agencies. This was the way of Hegel (1991), for whom such agencies eventually resolved once again into some kind of state apparatus. Another way out of the contradiction was to understand the ostensibly autonomous operation of civil society as a fictional arrangement which obscured the conflict between labour and capital, and to work towards the dialectical resolution of the contradiction and the withering away of the state. Far from being a realm of harmonious exchange, 'civil society' in emerging critique referred to the place in which 'the individual's relations with others are governed by selfish needs and individual interests' (Marx 1843: 59). This approach, which is that of Marx, brings us to critique of political economy of the relationship between the state and civil society under capitalism (Mandel 1971).

This approach entails not merely the analysis of economic forms – production, consumption, commodities, exchange value and so forth – but also the political processes in which they are embedded. Class, which is central to Marx's analysis, of course, is but one instance of a social relation that is reified under capitalism such that it becomes a social position tied to a form of identity, but it is itself a process (Bensaïd 2002). It is a function of the labour process, a relation to the state which guarantees capital accumulation, and conditions of life in civil society which include political representation and self-exploration that occurs in, among other places, the consulting room (Samuels 1993). Civil society, separated from the state, still shapes the state as a political apparatus, and it calls upon the state to regulate it, whether that is to ensure the smooth running of the supposedly 'free' market or to provide welfare support so that producers and consumers will themselves be free to participate in it. The state thereby also 'protects the *imaginary* universality of particular interests' (Marx 1843: 107) as if it were the universal interest.

Political economy of psychotherapy

The political economy of psychotherapy is a necessary starting point for thinking more generally about the domain of psychological health under capitalism (Singer 2007), and a critique of that political economy therefore attends to at least the following two aspects of the practice. First, it attends to the production and circulation of value, and how the sedimentation of this value in things bought and sold divides exchange value realised in commodities from another apparently more fundamental use value that seems to be hidden within those commodities. The labour of the psychotherapist is at issue here, as is the labour of the patient, as something of value might be produced and circulated as if it were a commodity and perhaps accumulated as a form of capital. (I will return to this form of capital later.) The conditions in which the psychotherapist works will determine the production of 'surplus value' and the estrangement of the worker from their creative labour. I leave open the question as to whether the patient is also alienated as a worker producing value for the moment, partly because the psychotherapist does also assume the function of patient at points in the history of the practice. It is not immediately clear whether the psychotherapist is always only a worker or consumer or petit bourgeois with their own particular exploitative function. This is a question that requires further work.

If the first aspect concerns the specific political economic arrangements of the individual psychotherapist's practice, the second aspect of the political economy of psychotherapy we need to attend to is its societal function. Here we turn to the production and circulation of abstract value in a society where psychotherapy in its various guises becomes important, where its place in the process of capital accumulation must come under the purview of the state. There are a variety of accidental and idiosyncratic reasons why some legislators are interested in the regulation of psychotherapy, and it is not unimportant to keep track of them for lobbying purposes, but the question that underpins this second aspect of the political economy is independent of the intentions of any particular state agent; rather, we need to ask what is produced and consumed by psychotherapy such that its form of value becomes included in calculations that pertain to investment and growth.

Historical trajectories: Class and gender

To the first and second questions raised by these two aspects of the political economy of psychotherapy – the class position of the psychotherapist and what of value is produced by psychotherapy in society – I will add a third question, which arises from our analysis as a critique of political economy rather than as a disinterested description; only as something 'partly as it exists in reality and partly as it exists in its own view of itself' (Marx 1843: 106). If the analysis is Marxist, then the question that drives the analysis is what the point of view of the working class is as an historical agent in relation to these issues. This is, needless to say, an extremely difficult question, and its complexity flows from the history of modes of production that coexist under capitalism today and from the transformations that the working class has undergone with the emergence of contemporary globalised neoliberalism (Went 2000). Let us briefly take each of these historical processes in turn. (The first bears primarily on the class character of the psychotherapist, and the second more on the societal function of psychotherapy as such.)

With respect to modes of production and psychotherapy, it is still possible to find residues of pre-capitalist forms in the networks of privilege and patronage which made it possible for some members of the aristocracy, the haute bourgeoisie and associated artistic circles to develop an interest in psychotherapy (Hinshelwood 1995). In some cases, medicine – specifically psychiatry – was the arena in which a dilettante involvement in psychotherapy developed. These individuals have always been quite marginal to their class, but those class networks have facilitated personal contacts between the House of Lords and the Royal College of Psychiatrists. They become more significant in relation to the mercantile bourgeoisie, which is more interested in what use psychotherapy might serve, and there is usually little direct evidence that it is useful at all. Together, they (aristocratic and bourgeois elements) tended to exclude and disdain working-class involvement in training until the advent of the NHS, when the provision of psychotherapy opened up access not only to patients but also to a new layer of professionals (Miller and Rose 1988). Then we can see the class differentiation of psychotherapy reconfigured to some extent around professional titles, with British-tradition psychoanalysis tied more closely to the older patrician psychiatric practice (for example around 1,450 registrants with the British Psychoanalytic Council), psychotherapy opening up a space to the middle class (with about 7,000 registered through the UK Council for Psychotherapy) and counselling drawing in more lower-middle-class and working-class practitioners (with over 37,000 members of the British Association for Counselling and Psychotherapy). These are broad-brush characterisations that do not do justice to the internal contradictions of each distinctive class involvement in psychotherapy. The impact of immigration from continental Europe with the rise of fascism is an important factor that complicates the picture, as is the involvement of women in psychotherapy, and that issue leads us to transformations of the labour force under capitalism in recent years (Mandel 1974).

The overwhelming majority of psychotherapists in the UK are women, a preponderance that is mirrored across most countries of the world. The analysis that we need must therefore be as much feminist as it is Marxist, and so must connect the two traditions of work while acknowledging the contradictions between them (Arruzza 2013). The proportion of women practitioners varies across different modalities, with large numbers working in what is usually perceived as lower-status 'counselling'. One of the peculiarities of British-tradition psychoanalysis is also that, apart from its organisations being open fairly early on to non-medics, women have been visible as leaders, which may partly be an effect of prominent figures who were not medically trained arriving in the 1920s and 1930s as immigrants from central Europe and gathering other women around them (Frosh 2003). Even so, the overall pattern of the distribution of gender in psychotherapy organisations has been that while most practitioners are women, the higher levels of management are populated by disproportionate numbers of men. There is an issue here to do with the image of psychotherapy as a 'caring profession' (which applies more to counselling and less to some forms of psychoanalysis, which are then as a result sometimes accused of being more stereotypically masculine), as a profession that has to some extent operated as a 'feminised' domain of work and labour process.

What is important now for our understanding of psychotherapy is that a certain kind of labour in the home was carried out by women.

When many women in the UK re-entered the workforce with the rapid expansion of the service sector after the Second World War, labour in that sector was reconfigured such that women's work, at one time undervalued (including in Marxist analysis), now assumed a significant role. The segregation of men labouring outside the home from women labouring inside it meant that it was women who then brought to the service sector (and to many organs of the welfare state) what has been termed 'emotional labour', no less creative and alienating when it produces surplus value than men's manual labour (Hochschild 1983). The 'feminisation' of work, then, does not so much mean that it is women per se who are the workers – and men have been adept at developing stereotypically 'feminine' skills to keep managerial positions in the caring professions – but that empathic and interpretative qualities that were historically assigned to women's roles become valued as commodities.

It is evidently profitable for an organisation to buy this kind labour power, this labour as a commodity, and then it makes sense for a state that is sensitised to the importance of this form of labour to guarantee it as a source of surplus value. Abstract value, which it is the function of the state in capitalist society to ensure the production and circulation of, now includes as one component the kind of value that is realised in a constellation of practices that are concerned with personal growth and wellbeing, and so it includes 'psychotherapeutic labour'.

Conclusions

In place of a conspiracy theory of attempts to regulate psychotherapy, political economy provides us with an analysis of how it is that this regulative process should appear to be a conspiracy in the first place. On the terrain of economic self-interest that capitalism bases itself on, and that the capitalist state facilitates, cluster a number of forms of capital. These include 'cultural capital' that those already with sufficient resources can accumulate from their unpaid labour in psychotherapy services – for example, a form of capital that reaps dividends when an administrative position is obtained that calls for psychotherapeutic emotional labour (Bourdieu and Passeron 1977). There is also a distinctive 'psychotherapeutic capital' accrued through training and supervision, and then in committee work that may or may not be part of paid employment, in educational settings that value the circulation of this kind of knowledge (Parker 2011b).

These political-economic questions are preliminary to an analysis of the relationship between Marxism and psychotherapy as such (Cohen 1986). What underpins this analysis is an attention to this work as productive labour that gives rise to value that then operates as a form of capital. It is at that point that it becomes of interest to the state. Political economy of psychotherapy that is also a critique of this political economy would attend to the separation between civil society and the state without romanticising civil society, and thereby imagining that the state is an unnecessary impediment to good practice. The state already enters into everyday economic transactions, shaping what we understand as a contract and the value produced from psychotherapeutic labour. A wish to be rid of the state is a fantasy formation that functions ideologically, in the service of capital and so eventually in the service of the state as well.

This is important not only for psychotherapists and counsellors but also for psychologists and 'critical psychologists'. Psychology is necessarily entangled with therapeutic work, with many of the more radical psychologists who express the same hope that is voiced by most undergraduates beginning a psychology course who want to eventually be 'clinical psychologists' because they want to care for others. The hope is that some good can come out of psychology, and that psychotherapeutic and counselling practice might show the way forward. If we are to learn lessons from critical psychology for psychotherapy and counselling, however, we need also to be critical of psychotherapy, and one way of being critical that then has implications for the contemporary practice of all of those working in the psy complex is to look carefully at what the psy complex is part of – that is, capitalism and the operations of the capitalist state.

References

Arruzza, C. (2013) *Dangerous Liaisons: The Marriages and Divorces of Marxism and Feminism*. London: Resistance Books.
Bensaïd, D. (2002) *Marx for Our Times: Adventures and Misadventures of a Critique*. London: Verso.
Bourdieu, P. and Passeron, J.-C. (1977) *Reproduction in Education, Society and Culture*. London: Sage.
Cohen, C.I. (1986) 'Marxism and psychotherapy', *Science and Society*, 1(1): 4–24.
De Vos, J. (2012) *Psychologisation in Times of Globalisation*. London: Routledge.
Frosh, S. (2003) 'Psychoanalysis in Britain', in D. Bradshaw (ed.) *A Concise Companion to Modernism*. Oxford: Blackwell, 116–137.

Hegel, G.W.F. (1991) *Elements of the Philosophy of Right*. Cambridge: Cambridge University Press.

Hinshelwood, R.D. (1995) 'Psychoanalysis in Britain: Points of cultural access, 1893–1918', *International Journal of Psychoanalysis*, 76, 135–151.

Hochschild, A.R. (1983) *The Managed Heart: Commercialisation of Human Feeling*. Berkeley: University of California Press.

House, R. (2002) *Therapy beyond Modernity: Deconstructing and Transcending Profession-Centred Therapy*. London: Karnac Books.

Ingleby, D. (1985) 'Professionals as socializers: The "psy complex"', in I. Parker (ed.) (2011) *Critical Psychology: Critical Concepts in Psychology, Volume 1, Dominant Models of Psychology and Their Limits*. London and New York: Routledge, 279–307.

Mandel, E. (1971) *The Formation of the Economic Thought of Karl Marx*. London: New Left Books.

Mandel, E. (1974) *Late Capitalism*. London: New Left Books.

Marx, K. (1843) 'Critique of Hegel's doctrine of the state', in K. Marx (ed.) (1975) *Karl Marx: Early Writings*. Harmondsworth: Pelican, 57–198.

Marx, K. (1867) *Capital: A Critique of Political Economy Volume I*. https://www.marxists.org/archive/marx/works/1867-c1/. Accessed 18 September 2013.

Miller, P. and Rose, N. (1988) 'The Tavistock programme: Governing subjectivity and social life', *Sociology*, 22, 171–192.

Mowbray, R. (1995) *The Case against Psychotherapy Registration: A Conservation Issue for the Human Potential Movement*. London: Transmarginal Press.

Parker, I. (ed.) (1999) *Deconstructing Psychotherapy*. London: Sage.

Parker, I. (ed.) (2011a) *Critical Psychology: Critical Concepts in Psychology*. London and New York: Routledge.

Parker, I. (2011b) *Lacanian Psychoanalysis: Revolutions in Subjectivity*. London: Routledge.

Parker, I. and Revelli, S. (eds.) (2008) *Psychoanalytic Practice and State Regulation*. London: Karnac.

Reeves, R. and Mollon, P. (2009) 'The state regulation of psychotherapy: From self-regulation to self-mutilation?', *Attachment: New Directions in Psychotherapy and Relational Psychoanalysis*, 3, 1–19.

Rose, N. (1985) *The Psychological Complex: Psychology, Politics and Society in England 1869–1939*. London: Routledge and Kegan Paul.

Rowan, J. and Dryden, W. (eds.) (1988) *Innovative Therapy in Britain*. Buckingham: Open University Press.

Samuels, A. (1993) *The Political Psyche*. London and New York: Routledge.

Singer, D. (2007) 'The political economy of psychotherapy', *New Politics*, 11(2). http://newpol.org/content/political-economy-psychotherapy. Accessed 18 September 2013.

Smith, A. (2008) *Wealth of Nations: A Selected Edition*. Oxford: Oxford University Press.

Went, R. (2000) *Globalization: Neoliberal Challenge, Radical Responses*. London: Pluto.

4
The Neurobiological Turn in Therapeutic Treatment: Salvation or Devastation?

Kenneth J. Gergen

> Most Americans, and even many doctors, have never heard of social anxiety disorder, and it affects more than 5 million Americans, according to the National Institute of Mental Health. Drug companies, eager to expand their markets, are now spotlighting the disorder – and advertising medications to treat it... Technology is now helping to pinpoint changes in socially anxious brains.
>
> (*Newsweek*, July 2003)

If there is one hallmark of the mental health professions since their very beginnings, it is conflict. Not only was conflict a dominant motif within Freud's privileged circle of colleagues, but since that time the professions have come to resemble a virtual battlefield of competing schools, practices, ideals and truths. Yet there is now a gathering of forces into two major camps, and far more hangs in the balance than the survival of one orientation as opposed to another. At the broadest level I am speaking here of a competition between two major ways of understanding human functioning, their resulting forms of practice and policy, and their impact on the culture more broadly. On the one side are professionals who emphasise the natural or biological roots of human behaviour, and on the other are those who are concerned with the cultural constitution of human action. From the former standpoint, rigorous diagnostics, neurological research, managed care and pharmacology are favoured routes to 'curing mental illness'. From the latter standpoint, not only are there enormous dangers inherent in this naturalist orientation but there is rampant blindness to the cultural process in which human suffering is embedded, and to the kinds of therapeutic process that are essential to bringing about change. How are we to respond to this conflict? Much hangs in the balance.

In what follows I first wish to consider some of the negative repercussions of the neurobiological movement in today's world of therapeutic practice. This discussion will give way to an examination of neurological inquiry into psychological processes. To what extent does such research warrant or support a shift towards a biological orientation in mental health practices? Is there sufficient support for the neurological orientation to offset the various costs? Finding such support quite negligible, I will explore several important implications for policy and practice. The reader should be sensitised in advance to two aspects of this analysis. First, while there are many who not unwisely conclude that both biological and cultural factors play a part in 'mental illness', in what follows I will place the two positions in an antagonistic relationship. It is important at this juncture to gain clarity on what is taking place in the neurobiological movement. Simply fusing the positions leaves many issues unaddressed. Second, in this analysis I do not ultimately mean to objectify either the neurobiological or the cultural orientations. That is, both construct the world in their own particular ways. However, much hangs on these constructions in terms of their impact on cultural life. It is the consequences that concern me most.

The emerging tragedy

While resistance to the biomedical model of mental suffering has long been robust, recent decades have dramatically shifted the momentum. Relying on various developments in brain-scanning technology, research consistently reveals what appear to be the neural bases of wide-ranging behaviour. To the extent that such research can pinpoint the neural basis of what are commonly viewed as psychological disorders, strong support is provided for (1) the diagnostic categorisation of mental illness; (2) the development of pharmacological treatments for such illnesses; and (3) the efficient dispensing of treatment to the afflicted. If 'mental problems' are essentially biological problems in disguise, then the same diagnostic precision pursued by the medical profession should be installed in the therapeutic professions. If abnormal behaviour can be traced to particular brain states, then treatment of abnormality must primarily focus on the alteration of neural conditions. Such alterations can be achieved least intrusively and most dependably through biochemistry. And, if problems in human behaviour are essentially biological, then any form of treatment that is non-biological fails to be cost-effective. To effectively manage care, pharmacological treatment should ultimately replace the more expensive and less relevant forms of 'talk therapy'.

In earlier work I have examined the societally injurious consequences of the trend towards unwarranted and unbridled psychodiagnostics (Gergen 2006). Here I shall confine myself to the societal repercussions of the neurobiological programme more specifically, and its alliance with pharmacological treatment and managed care programmes.

Towards a drug-dependent culture

Perhaps the most dramatic cultural transformation favoured by the biologising of human suffering is the shift from 'talking cures' to psychopharmacology. Some 30 years ago there were relatively few antipsychotic drugs available, and drug treatments were typically limited to the severely impaired. In 1970, there were approximately 150,000 mental health cases treated pharmacologically in the USA. By 2000, the number had jumped to 9–10 million. More than half of the cases treated by psychotropic drugs were schoolchildren. At the time of writing, Amazon lists more than 3,000 books on the subject of psychopharmacology. The browser of this list will have a difficult time locating more than a handful of books that are critical – or even cautious – about the use of drugs in psychiatric practice.

Putting aside the increasingly vast literature on the failure of such drugs to promote positive change (see for example Kirsch 2011; Moncrieff 2009), the cultural impact of this movement is dramatically demonstrated in this account of a Florida therapist, Phillip Sinaikin:

> A 60 year old divorced female was referred to me by a fellow psychiatrist who was leaving private practice. The frazzled looking woman informed me that she is diagnosed as a rapid-cycling bipolar and then presented me with a list of her current medications. She was being treated with Lamictal [an anticonvulsant] 100 mg three times a day, Alpazolam [a tranquilizer] 1 mg three times a day, Celexa [an antidepressant] 40 mg per day, Wellbutrin (an antidepressant) 150 mg twice a day, Seroquel [an antipsychotic] 300 mg at bedtime, Fiorinol [a barbiturate containing a pain pill] up to 4 a day and finally Ritalin [an amphetamine stimulant] 20 mg three times a day. That is 17 pills a day!... Asked about her current supply of medications, she didn't know what she had or needed. All she knew for certain was that she

was out of Ritalin and needed a refill. By that time, the hour allotted for her intake was up. So, do I give her a refill and further legitimize what I view as an irrational and dangerous diagnostic conceptualization and treatment plan by her previous psychiatrist? And if I choose not to, what do I do?

(Sinaikin 2004: 38)

There is more to the pharmacological turn than its impact on the suffering client. There are also economic and cultural implications of enormous proportions. In economic terms, consider the growth of the major antidepressant, Prozac. According to a *Newsweek* (26 March 1990) report, a year after the drug was introduced to the market, sales reached $125 million. A year later (1989) the sales had almost tripled to $350 million. By 2002, Prozac was a $12 billion industry. At present there are over 25 million prescriptions for Prozac (or its generic equivalent) in the USA alone. A similar number of prescriptions are written for Zoloft, a close cousin, and another 25 million for a combination of other competitors (*New York Times* 30 June 2002). In terms of the number of users, the figures have also soared. In 1998 some 11.2 million Americans used these drugs. By 2010 it was 23.3 million. Consider that, at the turn of the century, depression was virtually non-existent as a cultural concern.

One may read such figures in three equally unsettling ways. In the first case, they represent increased expenditures on mental health. Given the unwarranted practices of diagnosis, we must confront the possibility that as a culture we are needlessly constructing the population in ways that increasingly expand public expenditures. In this sense, drug cures are not enabling managed care programmes to reduce healthcare costs as anticipated, but are working cooperatively to produce exponentially increasing expenditures. Second, one may also read these economic figures in terms of profits to the pharmaceutical industry. Given the unfettered expansion of psychodiagnostic categories and the willingness of a society to 'trust the experts', future profits are almost guaranteed. The availability of profit also means the launching of additional research and the availability of still further drugs, and the marketing of these drugs to both mental health professionals and the public. Again we confront an unending spiral. Finally, one may see these figures in terms of the capacity of the pharmaceutical industry to discourage or block any legislation that would threaten profitability. With the enormous funds that are available to the industry, the power of the lobbies also increases. Help from the government becomes ever less likely.

One must ultimately inquire into the message which the routinising of drug treatment sends to the culture at large. Essentially the culture is informed by professional authorities that drugs are the answer to common problems of human living.[1] If one is deeply grieving, anxious about work, distressed by failure, frightened of social life, unable to stop working, worried about homoerotic tendencies or is growing too thin, drugs are the answer. In previous times we human beings acquired individual coping strategies or relied upon one another. These cultural resources for resiliency are increasingly under threat. In effect, the neurobiological shift increases dependence of the culture on artificial supports for normal life. Psychopharmacology takes its place alongside drugs for sleeping, sexual arousal, increasing athletic prowess and euphoric pleasure. A recent cartoon depicted a little leaguer asking a druggist if he had something that could help him to hit home runs. We are approaching a condition in which we will turn to the medicine cabinet in order to 'get through' a normal day.[2]

Cultural myopia

To the extent that we attribute the problems of the individual to neurobiological conditions, concern for the cultural context fades from view. In certain degree, the medical model of illness, of which the neurobiological orientation to human suffering is a descendent, shares in this problem. The medical profession is deeply engaged in searching for a cure for various diseases, but it is the task of other professions (for example public health and epidemiology) to consider means of changing social practices to reduce, for example, the spread of a virus. But in the case of what passes for mental illness, the case for neglecting application is far more serious. There are two major issues to consider, as described below.

Of primary importance, there is substantial reason to believe that much of what we call mental illness is sociogenic in origin. This is so in two important ways. First, the origins of most human suffering are lodged within traditions of cultural meaning. Experiences of personal failure, loss of control, deficient self-confidence, shame, humiliation, loss of love, the death of an intimate and fear of evaluation, for example, are all common topics that are addressed to therapists by suffering patients. Yet all of these exist within traditions of meaning. For example, there is nothing about personal failure that itself demands anguish. One could see a failure as an important and valued signal for means of improvement. Second, it is only in a culture that places a value on autonomy or the personal control of outcomes that losing control is a reason for depression. Even in many Western subcultures there is a strong value conferred on placing one's destiny in the hands of a deity. To the extent that personal problems are embedded within processes of cultural meaning, the primary therapeutic emphasis should be placed on movement within these processes. Neurobiology is largely irrelevant.

This emphasis on culture is also important because it opens up consideration of the social conditions in which we live our lives. As Karen Horney (1950) once proposed, many of our institutions are themselves sources of anxiety. Conditions of intense competition, high professional insecurity, information overload, poverty and oppression will all be reflected in degrees of human suffering. To treat such suffering as biological in nature is not only to blind oneself to the proper origins but to insure that therapists are left only to treat the effects of our problems and never the cause.

Such arguments have long been fortified by cross-cultural, historical and demographic studies of mental illness. In the cultural case we find broad and significant differences in what is counted as deviant in cultural life, how it is understood and the cultural practices in which it is embedded (see for example Al-Issa 1995). The fact that some forms of 'mental illness' in the US cultural setting scarcely occur in others is a strong argument against a biological disease model. Coupled with significant cultural differences are significant accounts of historical changes in what is constructed or defined as mental illness (Greenberg 2013; Hacking 1995; Hepworth 1999; Lerman 1996). And in terms of demographics, the fact that depression is most disproportionately located in lower-class populations, in women and in the aged is difficult to justify in terms of a disease model of depression. For example, people in the lowest economic strata in the USA are three times as likely to be diagnosed with a mental disorder. Strong arguments for the contagiousness of mental disease have never been put forward, and why such groups should be more genetically prone to mental illness remains a mystery. However, the fact that all such groups live under circumstances of high stress provides a ready explanation in terms of a cultural genesis.

There is a second way in which the attribution of anguish to neurobiological issues suppresses concern with sociocultural issues. In this case attention turns to the very definition of 'mental illness'. As impressively documented by Whitaker (2011) and others, there has been an exponential expansion in the diagnosis of undesirable behaviour as 'mental illness'. If our definitional systems were otherwise, such behaviour would not count as illness and new questions could be asked about the source of its undesirability. For example, there is nothing inherently 'ill' about a highly active child, and the primary reason for the diagnosis of attention deficit hyperactivity disorder (ADHD) resides in the inability of teachers to effectively carry out their task. In effect, the teacher's suffering is redirected towards the child, and labelled as an illness for which pharmacology is the answer. Virtually no attention is thus directed to practices of teaching more optimally suited for highly varied student proclivities, or the cultural conditions that favour a need for stimulation (for example video games, Facebook, television).

Emily Martin argues that, indeed, some forms of activity that were at one time defined as mentally ill are now becoming valued:

> Mania is becoming highly valued in the workplace. If concepts of the ideal person are changing in such contexts as work, life and value, demanding restless change and development of the person at all times, in all realms, then manic depression might readily come to be regarded as normal – even ideal – for the human condition under these historically specific circumstances.
>
> (2000: 190)

Closely related to the cultural construction of illness is the impact of disease diagnosis on those who are treated. The individual who is labelled as mentally ill takes on a dimension of self-doubt for which there is no ultimate termination. Unlike physical illnesses, in which one can typically identify the onset and termination, the label of mental illness essentially remains forever. Because there are no unambiguous indicators of beginning or end, there is no way in which one can be certain that the 'illness' is not influencing their actions in some devious way or is there hovering in the wings. A strong case can be made for much that counts as mental illness being iatrogenic in character – that is, a form of suffering created through the very practices of diagnosis and treatment. At least 41,000 websites now attest to this possibility. Inquiry into all of these matters is pushed aside in the turn to the neurobiological model.

Mechanical care

To the extent that problems of human suffering can be attributed to biological causes, then the medical model of treatment is invited. Among the traditional criteria for medical treatment are rapidity, efficacy and efficiency. The most effective treatment of the body should be provided as rapidly as possible for the least cost. Although we are beginning to understand the limits of medical care that is bereft of concern for the human conditions of illness (Bolen 1996; Murphy 1997), the medical model is deeply problematic when applied to problems of unspecified biological origin. In the case of physical illness, the patient's anguish typically originates in the illness itself (for example pain or incapacity in physical functioning); personal problems are secondary. When people ask for psychotherapeutic help, their problems are almost invariably personal and physical pain is infrequent. To treat the personal problems as secondary, if not irrelevant, is a virtual negation of human being as such. Critical issues of human social existence are trivialised in favour of drug treatments that effectively render the individual insensitive to such issues. Donald (2001) describes the 'Wal-Marting' of US psychiatry, the movement towards mindless cost-control measures, and the associated vision of human beings as generic and interchangeable. In the same vein, Cushman and Guilford (2000) see the managed care of mental suffering as negating the significance of human experience, and replacing a concern with individual meaning with impersonal quantification. As they see it, the move towards managed care brings with it a fundamental change in our definition of what it is to be human. The humanistic vision gives way to a materialist instrumentalism.

The erosion of multiparty dialogue

In his pivotal volume *Legitimation Crisis*, Jurgen Habermas brought critical attention to the limitations of instrumental reasoning. Such reasoning is centrally concerned with how various ends can most practically be achieved. How can we build a faster computer, improve law enforcement or combat terrorism more effectively? And yet, argues Habermas, the headlong thrust towards implementing ends typically subverts debate over the values underlying such efforts. Focusing on products, we jettison reflective deliberation on the process. In fighting terrorism, for example, we neglect inquiry into underlying issues of cultural differences, value relativism and our own contribution to the phenomenon.

The mental health professions have a long tradition of instrumental reasoning. The neurobiological turn serves only to intensify such an orientation. The purported identification of brain-state indicators of mental illness, and the accompanying expansion of pharmaceutical cures, constitutes a strong invitation for more experimentation, more facts and greater efficacy. Yet, as we launch inquiry into effective practices, removed from consciousness are significant differences in views and values about such issues as defining illness, who gains and loses from such definitions, and the broad societal implications of drug prescriptions. In the quest for the goal, we no longer ask about the value of the goal and its potential for injury. Thus to launch broad-scale inquiry into the neurological basis of mental illness or optimal drug dosages for cure is not simply the quest for scientifically neutral knowledge. Rather, the very presumption that non-normal behaviour or various forms of human suffering constitute 'illnesses' is already value saturated. As Sadler's (2002) important effort makes quite clear, the DSM illness categories are themselves implicit statements of what constitutes the 'good society'. When Peter Kramer (2005) rails against those who would romanticise depression by seeing it as a route to creativity and deeper understanding, he is essentially making a moral claim: those who find value in 'feeling down' do not contribute to the good society as he defines it. This is not to argue against the values that are inherent in the DSM or to privilege happiness over the blues. However, what is essential is to bring these biases to light, and to project them into the broader cultural dialogues on the nature of the good society. The failure to acknowledge and debate is little short of an oppressive silencing of the diverse subcultures making up the society.

The limits of neuroscience

The perils outlined here are unsettling primarily to the extent that the neurobiological orientation is inadequate in either explaining or treating what we commonly term 'mental illness'. If indeed there was outstanding evidence in support of the orientation, we might simply have to reconcile ourselves to a certain degree of collateral damage. We might have to content ourselves with dramatic increases in drug use, less humane healthcare, inattention to the cultural context of human suffering and questions of the common good. So we may well wish to ask: What is the evidence?

While a full review of all of the biological evidence is beyond the scope of this chapter, I do wish to take up the recent spate of neurologically centred research.[3] It is this work that has come to provide the most dramatic support for the biological orientation. As indicated earlier, such research has been spurred particularly by the development of various technologies (for example magnetic resonance imaging, positron emission tomography, electroencephalography, magnetoencephalography) for scanning brain activity. Thus, as subjects are engaged in various activities – problem-solving, remembering, bargaining, watching films, meditating, and so on – measurements can be taken of heightened neurochemical activity in various areas of the brain. The typical approach is to locate those areas of the brain that are specific to a given psychological state or behaviour, or a given group (for example schizophrenic, bipolar) is singled out and compared with a 'normal' sample in terms of brain activity.

Such research is dramatic in implication because it seems to reveal the neural basis of the state or activity in question. In the field of mental health, the drama is particularly powerful. Rather than relying on the highly ambiguous diagnostic criteria outlined in DSM-5, brain scans can supposedly reveal the different locations in the brain implicated in various pathological states. Differences in brain functioning – let's say between normal samples in comparison with those diagnosed as schizophrenic or bipolar – directly demonstrate the locus of pathology. The guess work is finished.

Given this general logic, and the resulting cornucopia of research findings, what reasons are there for pause? On what grounds, if any, should we resist what appear to be reasonable and empirically grounded proposals? In my remarks I will put aside the notorious methodological problems that inhabit such research. There are enormous problems, for example, in isolating from the continuous flow of neurological change a singular state to which a given behaviour can legitimately be attributed. And, given the differing ways in which human brains can react to the same external conditions, locating an identical state across populations of any kind is hazardous. Further, brains of various groups may differ, not because of a supposed psychopathology but because of different forms of life in which they have been engaged, or the different drugs to which they have been exposed. One might assume, for example, that athletes might exhibit a different pattern of brain activity than accountants, but this may say nothing at all about differences in their hard wiring. Finally, one can only imagine the theory-invested sorting and sifting of visual data that must occur. Rather, my concern here is with major flaws in the logic underlying the attempt to locate neural bases of human problems.

Plasticity and the return of culture

To say that a given brain state is the underlying basis of a given problem is to specify the brain as the causal source. Thus, if the source of the problem is fixed within the nervous system, therapeutic intervention must focus on the alteration of the nervous system. By analogy, if one's automobile fails to function properly, engine repair may be required. However, this argument is reasonable only to the extent that it is the structure of the machinery in itself that is at fault. If the failure of the machinery can be traced to a prior cause – falling outside its confines – then correcting the machinery is only a temporary and possibly futile effort. If one's engine does not function properly because one has failed to replenish its oil, then attention must be directed to the oil supply and not the properties of the engine.

This latter possibility is most obviously relevant in those brain studies that attempt to isolate a singular process from an ongoing stream. Here, for example, researchers focus on the neural processes that are 'responsible for' memory, problem-solving, trust, meditation, prayer, political preferences and the like. In all such cases, however, various experimental manipulations or instructions are required to bring the state of the brain into its condition. To create a brain state that is indicative of 'distrust', for example, requires that circumstances of distrust are established in the laboratory. Thus the circumstances, it may be said, bring the state into existence. It is not the brain condition that is the basis of distrust but the conditions of distrust that bring about the brain state.

A more compelling case for neural origins is found in research that compares brain scans of people who are chronically ill with those who are deemed normal. Here, as mentioned, researchers might compare schizophrenic, depressed, ADHD or obsessive compulsive samples with 'normals'. Yet, while such research often reveals differences, the question of cause still remains. To what extent is it the brain condition that gives rise to the symptoms, as opposed to a preceding condition that brings about the brain condition? If one lives for many years under oppressive, stressful, hopeless or anxiety-provoking conditions, it is possible that cortical connections are altered. However, we may ask, could we not be more effective by attending to the precipitating conditions as opposed to their results?

It is at this point that an enormous body of evidence for neural plasticity becomes relevant. As wide-ranging research has demonstrated, the brain continues to reorganise itself by forming new neural connections throughout life. For one, neurons can be developed to compensate for injury. Existing neural pathways that are inactive or used for other purposes show the ability to take over and carry out functions that have been lost to degeneration. Further, neurogenesis (the development of new nerve cells) enables the individual to adjust to new situations or changes in the environment. Although accelerated in the pre-natal period, neurogenesis continues into old age. To the extent that plasticity prevails, we may abandon the view that the brain serves as the chief determinant of cultural action; rather, it is the cultural context that determines how the brain will function.

To the extent that the plasticity explanation is reasonable, then the reliance on pharmacological 'cures to mental illness' is also thrown into significant question. If states of what we call 'depression' (along with associated neural markers) are not inherent in biology, but are created culturally, then pharmacological cure is akin to tinkering with the engine to cure the problems of oil depletion. To be sure, medications may enable one to cope with oppressive or stressful conditions. If properly sedated, the conditions are less arousing. However, without intervention into the conditions, or enhancement of the person's resiliency skills, we succeed only in contributing to a culture of zombies.

Interpretation bias: The cultural reading of the brain

Brain-scan studies have been welcomed with enthusiasm by many mental health professionals because they seem to provide an answer to the plaguing problem of inference. This is the problem of inferring the existence of a psychological condition (for example depression) from behaviour (for example inability to sleep). Traditionally, we guess about the nature of 'mental illness' by its symptoms, and we attempt to validate our inferences through multiple expressions. For example, while inability to sleep may not guarantee that a person is depressed, that the person says that they think about suicide strengthens the inference. However, such apparent validations are ultimately problematic because they too remain inferential. Thus an individual may feel suicidal precisely because they are so exhausted from lack of sleep that they cannot cope. Depression may be irrelevant. Any interpretation remains suspended, then, on a network of ultimately unwarranted and hypothetical interpretations.

Do brain-scan data solve this notorious problem of inference? Let us take a closer look. Consider again the dilemma of psychological diagnosis. We are presented with a collection of expressions that we classify as symptoms of an underlying condition, but we have no access to the causal condition itself. In effect, we have been forced to speculate that loss of appetite, lack of sleep and feelings of hopelessness are symptoms of an underlying state of depression. We now observe the neural condition of the person whom we have shakily diagnosed as depressed. We succeed in locating a neural condition that is unique to this population. Yet, we may ask, how can we determine that the observed state of the brain is in fact 'depression'? Why is it not simply a neural correlate of sleeplessness, appetite loss or feelings of helplessness? Or, for that matter, how could we determine that the neural state is not one of 'spiritual malaise', 'anger', 'withdrawal from oppressive conditions' or 'cognitive integration and regrouping'?

In effect, brain-scan data do not solve the problem of inference but simply remove it from one site of ignorance to another. Brain scans do not speak for themselves. To read them as evidence of depression, deceit, trust, empathy, political preferences and so on is little more than exercising a subcultural bias. It is precisely the reading of the mind in terms of 'mental illness' that contributes to the massive diseasing of the population.

Winks and blinks: The impossibility of reductionism

Neurological description is optimally employed in giving accounts of specific observations of the brain. Brain-state terms may legitimately be employed to explain various behavioural movements of the body, when neurological conditions are constituents of the movements themselves. Thus, to the extent that there are lesions in the motor cortex, I may not be able to move my arms or fingers. The condition of the brain is neurologically linked to the bodily movements; I am physically constrained in what I can do. It is thus that the study of the neural mechanisms involved in aphasia, Down's syndrome or brain tumours may serve vitally useful purposes. We are speaking in each case of a contiguous neurological system.

Yet we encounter severe problems when we attempt to apply the neural model to what we might call 'meaningful actions' within the culture. In carrying out cultural life, it is useful to describe various people as 'aggressive', 'moral', 'helpful', 'dishonest', 'humorous' and the like. We may usefully describe our emotional expressions as 'anger', 'happiness', 'love' or 'anxious'. Yet, while such discourse is critical to living an effective life within the culture, none of these descriptors is linked to determinate movements of the body. To illustrate, consider the following bodily movement: my hand takes the shape of a fist, and I move my index finger back and forth. To be sure, there is a neurological basis for the spatiotemporal movements of the finger. But our cultural descriptors are linked only partially and contestably to movements of the body. If the movement of the finger is pulling the trigger or a gun aimed at another person, our description is far different than if the finger is used to beckon us to the bedroom. And it is crucial for effective cultural life to make a distinction between 'murder' and 'seduction'. The scope of neurological expertise ends with the account of the bodily movement; it is mute with respect to cultural meaning. Neurology can tell us much about the blink of the eye but nothing about the wink.

On this account, neurological accounts are highly limited with respect to most activity that we describe as mentally ill. Consider an eight-year-old boy walking about the classroom while the teacher is talking. We may account for the specific movements of his body neurologically. But these movements are not themselves significant in the diagnosis of ADHD. The boy could have walked slowly or rapidly, haltingly or smoothly, stamping his feet or not. The precise movements are not at all important. What is important in labelling the behaviour as a symptom of ADHD is that the movements are inappropriate in the classroom setting. In the same way, activities that are described as compulsive, phobic or masochistic have no determinate neural correlates. More broadly we may say that most of the behavioural descriptions employed in the DSM cannot be described in neural terms. The behaviours in question may be infinite in their variation; it is the cultural meaning that enables us to identify them, and it is by working within these systems of meaning that change may effectively be accomplished.

Proposals for a more promising future

To be sure, my arguments here are dedicated to illuminating the shortcomings of the neurobiological movement in mental health. In my view, the claims made for the movement – both professionally and in the public media – are virtually without critical self-reflection. Perhaps the present account can contribute to a much needed dialogue. In spite of my critique, however, I am not at all proposing a termination of neurobiological inquiry into problems of human suffering or the pharmacological treatments with which such inquiry is identified. However, if the current trajectory in our understanding of human problems and their treatment is continued, we are collectively bringing about a cultural disaster. In my view it is first essential to slow the pace of the neurobiological juggernaut, and as we do so to nurture the kinds of careful assessment that can yield more reasonable and culturally protective policies and practices. Three initiatives seem especially demanding of attention, as discussed in the following three sections.

Restrict the pharmacological alternative

At the present time we are witnessing an exponential increment in drug prescriptions for therapeutic clients. Under the continuing influence of the pharmacological industry and managed care programmes to expand profit margins, there is little reason to suspect a decrease. Indeed, given the attempts of other professions, such as clinical psychology, to gain prescription privileges, we might anticipate an expansion in drug usage. And, given the steadily increasing conversion of common problems in living to diagnostic categories, there is no upward limit in sight.

It seems to me that of immediate importance are initiatives that would place significant restrictions on drug prescriptions. Policies might be developed that would place medication as a form of final-resort treatment, essential only in serious conditions. I would like to think that the psychiatric profession harbours a sufficient sense of dedication to the public good that movements towards responsible treatment would originate there. At the same time, such a movement is not likely to be successful without involving both the institutions of managed care and the insurance companies. There are not only complex financial problems to address but also issues of malpractice litigation attendant upon failure to administer drugs.

Awaiting major shifts in policy, two additional ends are more easily in reached. First, policies of full disclosure are essential before clients are placed on medication. The side-effects of pharmacological 'cures' are notorious (see for example Breggin 2009). It is not only the range and seriousness of these side-effects that should be clarified but also the trajectories of drug use that are possible. The likely failure, readjustments and compounding of drugs over time should be clarified. That one may soon find themselves taking 17 pills a day is a fact that might well deter many from embarking on the pharmaceutical journey. Highly recommended in this case would be the development of websites that spell out for therapy clients the impact of medications on their lives. The increment in superficial mood or coping capacity is always purchased at a cost to wellbeing. These costs should become matters of public knowledge.

Second, coupled with responsible warning practices, programmes of drug reduction are vitally needed. While drug prescriptions can be obtained with the virtual ease of over-the-counter purchasing, means of exiting regimens of drug usage are not well developed (Breggin and Breggin 1995). On the contrary, in many quarters of psychiatry the presumption prevails that psychiatric illness is a lifetime affair. When we consider the inability to locate a medical infirmity, such a presumption invites accusations of gross irresponsibility. Again, we find a condemning contrast with traditional medical practice. To cure a medical condition and leave the patient with a life-long prescription for the condition would be unconscionable. Inventive programmes are needed for reducing and ultimately eliminating drug dependency. At present, most 'patients' must find their own way of eliminating this dependency. Many are heroic in this respect; others suffer greatly and fail (Lehmann 2004). The professional challenge – both practical and moral – is clear.

Prioritise cultural meaning

To be sure, it is essential to explore more thoroughly the nexus of cultural and biological processes that give rise to what we commonly classify as 'mental illness'. I have little doubt that there are numerous cases of suffering for which a clearly identifiable physical cause may be located and for which drugs are appropriate. However, the mere location of neurological correlates to suffering provides no basis at all for presuming a medical illness. Certainly, pharmaceuticals can sedate those who are suffering and thus provide a temporary 'time out'. Yet the ultimate cause of the suffering remains unexplored. In the medical case one would scarcely consider reducing conscious suffering at the expense of determining the cause. Indeed, such a practice would typically prove fatal for the patient as the disease would intensify. If one could eliminate all symptoms in the case of what we call 'mental illness' there would be little remaining to treat.

In my view, strong investments should be made into forms of therapy and related practices that are (1) maximally sensitive to cultural meaning systems and/or (2) engender skills in navigating a world of conflict, oppression and threat. In the first instance, the tradition of talking therapies, from Freud through cognitive behavioural, do engage the client in meaningful conversation and provide a supporting relationship. However, these traditional therapies are also circumscribed in terms of their focus. The more recent therapies, often labelled as postmodern, are more directly concerned with transformations in meaning. Narrative- and solution-oriented therapies, for example, are more concerned with the process of creating viable meaning than with changing what is traditionally viewed as 'mental process'. At this juncture, I find especially promising a range of collaborative therapies (see for example Anderson and Gerhart 2006; Håkansson 2009; Seikkula and Arnkil 2006). Here the emphasis is on developing meaning within ongoing relationships, with special sensitivity to multiply constructed worlds, and to the action patterns in which language functions. With respect to engendering skills of resilience, I fear that we are only at the beginning. So much attention has been given to talk alone that attention to other forms of action has been neglected. Most promising at present is the development of meditation skills, a form of action that can furnish relief from the intense stresses of daily life. Much needed, however, are means of enhancing skills in conflict reduction, detoxing personal failure, avoiding overcommitment, acting collaboratively and moving improvisationally across complex contexts. Traditions of cultural life furnish numerous avenues to suffering; the challenge is to develop resources for moving through cultural life effectively as opposed to sedating ourselves for the journey.

Research: Nothing about us without us

Virtually all mental health research, treatment practices and policy formation is in the hands of professionals. While reasonable in many respects, it is also fair to say that decisions that affect the lives of millions – often in dramatic ways – are made by a small number of people, few of whom have ever experienced the problems that they confront, or have themselves lived with a diagnosis of 'mentally ill'. In effect, those who have the most extensive and intimate experience of suffering, therapy and pharmaceuticals have virtually no voice in the decisions that affect their lives.

In the area of human disability there has been a lively resistance movement. Those who are labelled 'disabled' find the ways in which they have been defined, segregated and dismissed highly abusive. James Charlton provides a glimpse into the mounting passions:

> The dehumanization of people with disabilities through language... has a profound influence on consciousness. They, like other oppressed peoples, are constantly told by the dominant culture what they cannot do and what their place is in society. The fact that the most oppressed people accept their place (read: oppression) is not hard to comprehend when we consider all the ideological powers at work... In the case of disability, domination is organized and reproduced principally by a circuitry of power and ideology that constantly amplifies in the normality of domination and compresses difference into classification norms (through symbols and categories) of superiority and normality against inferiority and abnormality.
>
> (1998: 35–36)

As is clear, those who are affected by the profession should be systematically included in developing research policies and practices, in evaluating therapeutic procedures, and generating more promising pharmaceutical treatment.

Towards generative dialogue

At present there is precious little dialogue about how we might move ahead towards more mutually acceptable practices and outcomes. It is evident that the anti-psychiatry movement of the 1960s has new wind in its sails. Both regional and worldwide movements of ex-mental patients have now sprung to life. Resistance groups are challenging the pathologising of hearing voices (www.hearing-voices.org), autism (www.autisticadvocacy.org) and virtually every other way in which individuals may be different (www.mindfreedom.org). As commonly proposed, human difference does not equal pathology. Numerous academic journals, international conferences and books for the reading public give voice to these issues. National research institutions reject the diagnostic labels. In effect, we are witnessing the formation of two combatant camps – the majority of mental health professionals on the one side and those who reject the 'therapeutic state' for its problematic diagnoses, faulty research and injurious drugging. Productive dialogue is rare. In my view it is essential that such dialogue ensues. It should include not only mental health professionals and their critics but also pharmaceutical companies, insurance companies and the government. The dialogue should move beyond mutual recrimination to considering the future wellbeing of the societies of which we are all a part.

In conclusion

The preceding remarks represent a critical confrontation with the burgeoning movement towards understanding and treating problems that are traditionally understood as 'psychological' from a neurobiological standpoint. I first outlined a number of major costs that are incurred by presuming the neurobiological bases of human problems. I have touched on the spiralling and costly trajectory of 'cultural drugging', the emerging myopia with respect to the cultural context of human suffering, the dehumanisation of treatment forms and the deterioration in value-centred deliberation about our cultural future. I have turned attention to the rapidly expanding domain of brain research, which has provided strong support for the neurobiological movement. Here we confronted important problems inhering in the isolation of relevant brain states, the responsivity of the brain to cultural conditions, cultural biases in the interpretation of brain-state data and the ultimate inability of neuroscience to account for meaningful behaviour.

Given the immense costs of the neurobiological orientation and the problematic grounds on which it rests, I put forward four proposals to slow the current momentum and open up broad deliberation on a more promising future. My specific concerns are with imposing restrictions on the prescription of pharmacological treatment, prioritising treatment forms specifically engaged in transforming cultural meaning, drawing those affected by research into the process as partners and opening up multiparty dialogue.

In the end, however, I must admit to a certain degree of scepticism regarding the future. The pharmaceutical industry has enormous wealth and highly effective organisation. The power of the pharmaceutical lobbies almost ensures that there will be no governmental intervention. And the managed care industry has thus far proved more invested in profitable outcomes for itself than grappling with the complex challenges that are confronted here. Further, the insurance companies profit by reducing coverage for 'talking cures'. Finally, the psychiatric profession stands to gain financially from the current trend, and prescribing drugs provides a certain degree of security against malpractice litigation. Therapists from outside the medical profession – clinical psychologists, social workers, family therapists, counselling psychologists, nurses and the like – have largely buckled under the demands of the insurance companies for psychiatric diagnosis.

Ultimately, the most powerful lever of change may be legal. There is one significant point of vulnerability in the current rage towards pharmacological treatment. Psychiatrists are essentially using a disease model of diagnosis, and prescribing medication with virtually no basis for either the diagnostic categories or evidence of neurobiological malfunction. The side-effects of these prescriptions – both biological and psychological – along with the disinterest in terminating prescriptions, are injurious to clients. Perhaps it is in the 'return of the repressed' that class-action litigation will take place. I would count this as a victory for human wellbeing.

Notes

1. The role of the drug companies in the active and unwarranted advertising of drugs must also be noted. See, for example, Peterson (2009).
2. See also Timimi (2014) on the medicalisation of childhood.
3. For a more extended account of the shortcomings of neurological explanations of human action, see Gergen (2010).

References

Al-Issa, I. (ed.) (1995) *Handbook of Culture and Mental Illness: An International Perspective*. Washington, DC: International Universities Press.

Anderson, H. and Gerhart, D. (eds.) (2006) *Collaborative Therapy: Relationships and Conversations That Make a Difference*. New York: Routledge.
Breggin, P. (2009) *Medication Madness: The Role of Psychiatric Drugs in Cases of Violence, Suicide, and Crime*. New York: St. Martins.
Breggin, P. and Breggin, G.R. (1995) *Talking Back to Prozac: What Doctors Won't Tell You about Today's Most Controversial Drug*. New York: St. Martins.
Bolen, J. (1996) *Close to the Bone: Life-threatening Illness and the Search for Meaning*. New York: Scribner.
Charlton, J.I. (1998) *Nothing about Us without Us, Disability Oppression and Empowerment*. Berkeley: University of California Press.
Cushman, P. and Guilford, P. (2000) 'Will managed care change our way of being?', *American Psychologist*, 55, 985–996.
Donald, A. (2001) 'The Wal-Marting of American psychiatry: An ethnography of psychiatric practice in the late 20th century', *Culture, Medicine, and Psychiatry*, 25, 427–439.
Gergen, K.J. (2006) *Therapeutic Realities, Collaboration, Oppression and Relational Flow*. Chagrin Falls, OH: Taos Institute Publications.
Gergen, K.J. (2010) 'The acculturated brain', *Theory and Psychology*, 20, 795–816.
Greenberg, G. (2013) *The Book of Woe: The DSM and the Unmasking of Psychiatry*. New York: Blue Rider Press.
Hacking, I. (1995) *Rewriting the Soul: Multiple Personality and the Science of Memory*. Princeton: Princeton University Press.
Håkansson, C. (2009) *Ordinary Life Therapy: Experiences from a Collaborative Systemic Practice*. Chagrin Falls, OH: Taos Institute Publications.
Hepworth, J. (1999) *The Social Construction of Anorexia Nervosa*. London: Sage.
Horney, K. (1950) *Neurosis and Human Growth*. New York: Norton.
Kirsch, I. (2011) *The Emperor's New Drugs: Exploding the Anti-Depressant Myth*. New York: Basic Books.
Kramer, P.D. (2005) *Against Depression*. New York: Viking.
Lehmann, P. (ed.) (2004) *Coming Off Psychiatric Drugs*. Berlin: Peter Lehmann.
Lerman, H. (1996) *Pigeonholing Women's Misery: A History and Critical Analysis of the Psychodiagnosis of Women in the Twentieth Century*. New York: Basic Books.
Martin, E. (2000) 'The rationality of mania', in R. Reid and S. Traweek (eds.) *Doing Science and Culture*. London: Routledge, 177–197.
Moncrief, J. (2009) *The Myth of the Chemical Cure: A Critique of Psychiatric Drug Cure*. London: Palgrave Macmillan.
Murphy, M. (1997) 'Relationship-centeredness, the essential nature of human health care', *Human Health Care*, 13, 142–143.
Peterson, M. (2009) *Our Daily Meds: How the Pharmaceutical Companies Transformed Themselves into Slick Marketing Machines and Hooked the Nation on Prescription*. New York: Picador.
Sadler, J.Z. (ed.) (2002) *Descriptions and Prescriptions, Values, Mental Disorder, and the DSMs*. Baltimore: Johns Hopkins University Press.
Seikkula, J. and Arnkil, T. (2006) *Dialogic Meetings in Social Networks*. London: Karnac.

Sinaikin, P. (2004) 'Coping with the medical model in clinical practice or "How I learned to stop worrying and love DSM"', *Journal of Critical Psychology, Counselling and Psychotherapy*, 4, 36–48.

Timimi, S. (2014) *Pathological Child Psychiatry and the Medicalisation of Childhood*. London: Routledge.

Whitaker, R. (2011) *The Anatomy of an Epidemic: Magic Bullets, Psychiatric Drugs and the Astonishing Rise of Mental Illness in America*. New York: Broadway.

Part III
Users' Perspectives

5
Personal versus Medical Meanings in Breakdown, Treatment and Recovery from 'Schizophrenia'

Tom Cotton and Del Loewenthal

[G:51:1] it was [*seen as*] this arbitrary symptom of mental illness... a piece of biological bad luck to be endured, rather than a complex, or significant, or meaningful experience to be explored. [G:52:1] it was the beginning of this horrendous, demoralising, vicious cycle of exhaustion and hopelessness and loss of self respect that just drains you into this shadow of yourself. [G:42:4] I think I went in [*to hospital*] a sort of distressed, unhappy teenager, and I came out a schizophrenic.

(Participant (G) in Cotton 2015)[1]

In this chapter we explore the gap between what we call 'personal' and 'medical' meanings of 'schizophrenia',[2] and how this gap may have important implications for the treatment that is offered to those with this diagnosis. In his heuristic (Moustakas 1990) doctoral research, which explored the psychotherapeutic experiences of those with a 'schizophrenia' diagnosis (Cotton 2015), one of the authors found that personal meaning – both its loss and its restoration – was central to the participants' understanding of their 'schizophrenic' breakdown and their subsequent recovery. However, it was also found that a crisis of personal meaning in breakdown was unwittingly compounded by medical meaning treatment, which was argued to be grounded in modernist 'objective' models of knowledge, whose 'mass of quasi-theoretical speculation' has become estranged from the subjective knowledge that is 'fundamental' (Bateson 2000: xxvii) to human experience.

Meaning, breakdown and recovery

Eight people, Participants (A)–(G), with a 'Schizophrenia'[3] diagnosis (APA 2005: 298–317) took part in the study mentioned above, which asked: 'What are your psychotherapeutic experiences?' The personal meaning that participants attributed to their experiences was presented as a composite chronology, which is briefly summarised here in the sections below entitled 'Life experience and breakdown', 'Inpatient and residential treatment', 'Where psychotherapy was unhelpful', 'Where psychotherapy was helpful' and 'Recovery'.[4]

For most participants, psychotherapy was used in conjunction with peer-support organisations, such as the Hearing Voices Network (HVN) in the UK, to promote a process of recovery through exploring the meaningfulness of their 'symptoms'. This process seemed to aid recovery because it moved the expression of painful experiences from an attenuated, metaphorical 'psychotic' domain of voices and images into a 'non-psychotic' dimension, where, as Lauveng (2012) summarises from her own experiences of 'schizophrenia', they could be recognised as 'just emotions – recognizable human feelings. That was all' (p. 36). Recovery from 'schizophrenia', therefore, could be said to involve the recovery (as in retrieval) of meaningfulness, which Bracken (2002) argues may be withdrawn in response to trauma (p. 1). A growing body of empirical research (Read and Bentall 2012) supports this argument.

Participants' recovery processes also provided startling insights into the often unwitting currents of meaning which underlie treatment. These findings lead to the argument made towards the end of this chapter – that facilitating another's recovery through this kind of meaning-making is similar to Heidegger's (2008) concept of *Vorspringende Fursorge* (p. 158) or 'anticipating care' (Boss 1963: 73). By contrast, treatment that was felt to be an obstacle to this meaning-making process seemed to be unhelpful, and this is likened to Heidegger's (2008) concept of *Einspringende Fursorge* (p. 158) or 'intervening care' (Boss 1963: 73). Boss and Binswanger, who both transposed Heidegger's work into a psychotherapeutic framework (Burston 2000), noted the significance of this reading of care when applied to the psychotherapeutic relationship. For Craig (2007), who summarises both approaches, 'intervening care' subjects Being (in Heidegger's sense) to a preconceived notion of health and may use 'control' to instil this preconception, while 'anticipating care' might facilitate possibility, authentic meaning and therefore freedom (p. 10). Before looking at how the findings of Cotton (2015) suggest the implications of personal and medical meaning and the above models of care in treatment, we will briefly describe what is meant here by these meanings.

Medical and personal meanings

Heidegger's phenomenological description of 'fundamental ontology' (Gelven 1989: 16) presented in *Being and Time* ([1926] 2008) distinguishes a 'present-at-hand' world of objects from a 'ready-at-hand' world where meaning is derived from the way in which we use those objects. In this sense, 'the way in which I make use of the world is meaningful. Meaning, then, is a mode of Being here in the world' (Gelven 1989: 98). By contrast, an 'objective meaning' (which here, we argue, underpins medical meaning) becomes 'misleading, if not downright inaccurate' in its attempt to exclude any subjective or existential influences (p. 101).

Heidegger insists that to look meaningfully at human experience, the entire *Dasein* ('There-Being') of the individual must be taken into account because '[t]he structure of the world's worldhood is such that Others are not proximally present-at-hand as free-floating subjects along with other Things, but show themselves in the world in their special environmental Being' (Heidegger 2008: 160). Summarising Heidegger's (2008) position, Gelven notes that human consciousness when viewed through this lens poses the following vital questions in relation to meaning.

> What does it mean to be one's self? to be afraid? to be such that one understands? In this way, 'world,' 'self,' 'fear,' and 'understanding' are not objective entities divorced from the type of subjective concern about them, nor are they 'definitions' in any abstract or verbal sense. Each is, instead, a *way* in which one exists...
> (Gelven 1989: 14)

Writing from a critical psychiatry perspective that draws on this Heideggarian view, Bracken (2002) notes that it is this uniquely human capacity for 'self-interpreting' (p. 98) that places the search for meaning at the core of human experience. From this perspective, personal meaning might be seen as intrinsically bound up in one's unique position in the world and how one uses both this position and the world itself. To adapt Gelven's (1989) example, the latch to one person's front door may be the lock to another person's prison. In this sense, the voices that one person hears may mean something entirely different to another. As Romme et al.'s *Living with Voices: 50 Stories of Recovery* (2009) illustrates, those who have recovered from 'schizophrenia' tend to conceptualise voices on a continuum with thought. In this sense, to suggest that either the voices that one hears or the thoughts that one has have a universal, non-personal meaning would be problematic.

However, it is precisely this assumption of universalised meaning that DSM,[5] the definition of medical meaning that we use here, starts with. This is because the 'medicine of the tissues' epistemology (Bracken et al. 2012: 430) that underpins DSM assumes that voices and other 'symptoms' of 'schizophrenia' are the meaningless expression of a 'disease process'. This 'objective' meaning leads one 'further away' from the 'proper' ontological meaning (Gelven 1989: 95) of the experiencing person because the context of their use of their world has been excised. This leaves 'the medical story' (McCarthy-Jones 2012: 316) with a fundamental dilemma in attempting to 'know' something about problems that it attempts to treat.

These personal and medical meanings run like train tracks that shadow each other but rarely meet. Jacqui Dillon, chair of HVN England, offers a vivid illustration when she describes being hospitalised after experiencing traumatic visions and persecutory voices. When she told her psychiatrist that she felt that these experiences were connected to the sexual abuse that she suffered as a child, he patiently explained to her that she was describing the 'symptoms' of 'schizophrenia', and that he had encountered many other patients who had experienced similar 'delusions'.

> What I was experiencing was never considered to be a natural and human response to things that had happened in my life. The fact that I listened to my voices was evidence of my illness, and wanting to keep them in order to understand more about myself was seen as me being resistant to treatment.
> (Dillon in Romme et al. 2009: 190)

This often unbridgeable gap between meanings leads McLaughlin (2000), who draws on the empirical research of Romme and Escher (1993) as well as his own experience of facilitating an HVN group, to argue that 'the dominance of psychiatric and psychological discourse is not legitimate' in the area of 'schizophrenia' (McLaughlin 2000: 11). Laing's (1965, 1967) 'existential-analytic' approach (Loewenthal 2011: 4), which is grounded in Heidegger's philosophy, explores these issues in relation to 'schizophrenia' and so offers one way of thinking about what is at play in this meaning gap.

Laing (1965) features a deconstruction of influential psychiatrist Emil Kraepelin's analysis of Hans, a young man deemed to suffer catatonic excitement (a diagnostic forebear of 'schizophrenia'). Kraepelin comments on Hans' seemingly incomprehensible mumblings when 'presented' to an audience of student psychiatrists. Laing notes that Kraepelin explains Hans' behaviour from an 'objective' perspective as ' "signs" of a "disease" ' (p. 31) with pre-existing 'categories of thought' (p. 33). However, if one sees Hans' behaviour as 'expressive of his existence' (p. 31), and the meaning that he attributes to the world as being expressive of his way of being in it (p. 32), then one is led to a radically different understanding of his situation. Moreover, Hans' disturbance may be a manifestation of '*our* inability or unwillingness to understand *him*' (Burston 2000: 69). To explain someone's actions with medical meaning and to attempt to understand their personal meaning, then, are 'to see and to hear in radically different ways' (Laing 1965: 33), both of which may then impact on the 'behaviour' that is 'seen and heard'. Heidegger's conception of intervening and anticipating care offer one way of thinking about how these issues play out in treatment.

For Heidegger (2008), to understand another person is to see the meaningfulness of their world as a range of possibilities beyond an enslaving 'actual' (p. 239). In the context of the extract from Laing (1965) above, and this chapter as a whole, the 'actual' might be both the distress that a person finds themselves in and the theoretical categories of thought that might be used to explain that situation and how it should be treated. To keep open this kind of possibility for oneself and another, and anticipating the personal meaning that might emerge from it, is an essential act of care because it offers freedom from such enslaving actuality. Meanwhile, to close down, or dominate the possibility of understanding another's personal meaning with a medical meaning that is used to explain their experiences might be seen as an uncaring violation. The experiences presented below illustrate the implications of these divergent meanings in treatment, or care given to another (*Fursorge*, Heidegger 2008: 157), and how they have impacted on the recovery of the participants featured. We should acknowledge first, however, that while we have tried to do justice to the participants' personal meanings here, our representation of them may be no less an uncaring violation.

Life experience and breakdown

Most participants experienced traumatic relationships (or sometimes a lack of relationships) within the family. Parental inability to express love was a common theme; overcontrol was another, as well as parental psychological distress. Participant (D), who experienced a range of physical and psychological abuse as a child, described how he learned to manage his distress from his mother:

> [D:116:4] she kind of like bottled in everything... which led to her having this kind of, this very deep relationship with a voice. Which I gather, from the way she was talking to them, they came from God. And that was my earliest experiences. And I did the same thing, I bottled everything up.

Most participants seemed to be psychologically fragile by the time they experienced a first trauma in childhood. This included neglect, bullying, and physical and sexual abuse, and it seemed to reinforce existing feelings of insecurity and self-loathing. Not being able to speak about these experiences led to increasing internalisation and withdrawal:

> [G:6:1] I think I was somebody who literally buried my past, but I buried it alive. And so throughout all of my adolescence and early adulthood, and to some extent even now, it was almost like screaming to get out.

Most participants then experienced a second trauma during their entry into adulthood. This included being raped, relationship breakdown, being bullied, drug use, violence and attempting suicide.

> [H:37:13] I wasn't equipped to enter the world at all and I think that's one reason I broke down, because I couldn't face entering life.

This second trauma seemed to shatter a wall that had been constructed to suppress past trauma, which now seemed to come flooding back in the form of voices and 'hallucinations'. The significance that participants placed on these experiences in the development of 'psychosis' echoes the findings of Read and Bentall (2012), mentioned above.

Inpatient and residential treatment

At first, medical meaning diagnosis and treatment was reassuring for most participants. It was a relief to feel that someone 'knew' what the problem was. For some, hospital was a secure refuge during this terrifying time of crisis, and medication dampened down troubling 'symptoms', such as voices. However, a feeling began to develop for many that the 'medical story' presented a way of not thinking about complex underlying issues.

> [A:136:1] Social workers, CPNs, doctors, my family. My family were *really* into the genetic thing as an explanation. Because the thing about genetics is it's a chance thing that you carry with you, you know. Nobody's to blame... [A:135:1] I understood myself, as there's something wrong with me...

This 'there's something wrong with me' narrative seemed to be the iceberg tip of a deeper problem that unfolded from intervening care, which unwittingly exacerbated 'symptoms' – a process that Participant (G) summed up at the start of this chapter. We can see this process now in more detail.

First, the narrative mirrored a self-loathing image associated with earlier traumatic experiences, and so deepened associated despairing feelings. Second, only the parts of participants' experiences that stayed within the hermeneutic of 'the medical story' could be talked about in the clinical encounter; the rest was either unnoticed or considered irrelevant.

Third, treatment was focused on the suppression of 'symptoms'. Not only was this often ineffective but also it seemed to encourage an alienation from Self because to believe that suppressing a 'symptom' is helpful one has to mistrust one's personal meaning associated with it. Intervening care then tended to replace this meaning with a nonpersonal medical meaning 'disease' concept, which left participants helpless and cut adrift from their own meaningfulness, as Participant (F) illustrated:

> [F:89:1] After experiencing [*voices*] through the medical model for 20 years... they were just sort of noise in my head and [*I thought*] I was psychologically flawed.

This process seems to illustrate how intervening care 'takes over for the Other that which he is to concern himself', and in so doing, '[t]he Other is... thrown out of his own position' (Heidegger 2008: 158) as the driving force behind caring for himself. This may then have the disastrous consequence that the 'Other can become one who is dominated and dependent, even if this domination is a tacit one and remains hidden from him' (*ibid.*). For participants, this domination was felt to unwittingly reflect earlier experiences, in this instance, of being controlled, abused or made to question one's own 'reality', which, like the first three points mentioned above, was felt to compound feelings of 'depersonalisation', 'derealisation' and 'dissociation' – the 'associated features' of 'schizophrenic symptoms' noted by DSM (APA 2005: 304).

Participant (G) described how the unwitting consequence of this treatment was that she took 'an aggressive stance' against her own mind (G:44:8). This led to 'a sort of psychic civil war' (G:44:7) in which the initial voice that she heard – and was not troubled by – multiplied into 12 voices that 'became stronger and more aggressive...' (G:46:3). Ironically, the consequence of this was that 'my behaviour and emotions just began to deteriorate so rapidly (*in hospital*) that by the end they couldn't have let me go...' (G:42:4).

Where psychotherapy was unhelpful

Where psychotherapy was offered by statutory mental health services, it was often short-term cognitive behavioural therapy (CBT) with a community psychiatric nurse (CPN), which was geared towards 'symptom' management. The perpetuation of treatment focus on this medical meaning conception of 'symptoms', and the meaning dynamics underlying it, were a prominent feature of therapy that was found unhelpful. To a lesser extent, the rigid application of psychoanalytic theory constructs was also found unhelpful for similar reasons. Psychotherapy – whatever the theoretical orientation - that *explained* with theory before attempting to *understand* what was experienced seemed to share 'modern descriptive psychiatry's' tendency to ignore 'important data' (Roe and Lysaker 2012), and its 'naïve realist stance' (Cromby and Harper 2009) towards experiences whose context cannot be explicitly (Polanyi 2009) explained within its 'objective' framework. Binswanger, who transposed Heidegger's work into a psychotherapy setting, notes that this 'perfect tense of theoretical investigation' in the therapy relationship involves replacing a 'reciprocal, "personal" communication within a we-relationship' with a 'one-sided, i.e. irreversible, relationship between doctor and patient' (Binswanger in Friedman 1991: 414). This relational aspect was important because feeling unable to develop a human connection, in feeling that the therapist was not interested in their experiences, was an obstacle to building a trusting relationship, as Participant (F) seemed to suggest in his work with a psychoanalyst:

> [F:154:1] I didn't feel like he treated me like a human being. He didn't value my pain, you know. And I've been turned into a thing by people before...

(A) meanwhile, found that CBT made inflexible 'perfect tense' judgements about what was 'normal' thought, and what was not:

(A:160:3-6) [I]t relies on the idea that certain thought patterns are pathological, it's kind of telling you that you're thinking wrong, whereas I think that the way I think is perfectly normal considering my experiences...

(C) thought this kind of inflexibility closed down the possibility of exploring meaning:

(C:88:14) [T]here was no talking around it or kind of exploring what it meant to me – [CBT] was a conveyor belt, it just felt really prescribed.

This closing down of personal meaning not only felt oppressive, it also led (C) to make up experiences that better fitted her therapists' framework, in order to please her (C:92:1).

The study was not structured in a way where empirical comparisons between modalities was useful: there were not enough participants, and modality comparison was not an aim. However, it is interesting to note that both CBT and psychoanalysis were mentioned most often in relation to these unhelpful qualities. This may be because they were the most ubiquitous modalities encountered. Equally, their ubiquity tends to hinge on their ability to work with the mainstream medical model – CBT because it 'supports the positivist psychiatric project of codifying human suffering into disease-like categories' (Rapley et al. 2011: 1), and while currently out of favour with NICE, the latter 'often functions as a compliment to the mainstream medical model' (Parker et al. 1995: 23). In this sense both may, at times, replicate the totalising, intervening care impulse of medical meaning.

Where psychotherapy was helpful

Helpful therapy was not modality specific but spanned art therapy, family therapy, counselling, psychoanalytic and psychodynamic therapy, personal construct therapy, dissociative identity disorder therapy and CBT. However, a unifying theme was that it was almost always found outside statutory mental health services, and with a psychotherapist of participants' choosing. For roughly half of the participants, this meant having to access it privately.

An important starting point for what was considered to be helpful was removing the 'symptom' as the all-encompassing focus. A second key aspect was forming a human connection with the therapist, which encouraged participants to explore difficult underlying issues. Participant (G) illustrated how these elements came together for her:

> [G:108:4] in therapy we spent relatively little time talking about the voices but a *lot* of time talking about me and the way I sort of feel about myself. [G:95:6] Actually, part of that was just going through my relationship with my mum and dad. Because in a way I'd sort of never really acknowledged, or understood how much that had hurt me. And... and then the year after that – and this is still very much work in progress – is stuff around the abuse.

Having the freedom to explore life experiences without being shut down by technique, or being told what these experiences meant by the therapist, helped participants to develop their own meanings. This was particularly important given that they had experienced considerable confusion in childhood in relation to others' meanings, whether implied, directly imposed or disguised. Participant (D) illustrates this process of meaning unfolding through the exploration of experiences:

> [D:134:1] I started talking a bit about... how I felt towards my victim, 'cos I thought he was Ronnie Kray, who was a well known homosexual man. [D:133:1] I told him that... the reasons why I killed my victim was because I didn't want to turn gay. I suppose I was very confused at the time. I didn't know who I was, so I was confused about a lot of things, especially about my sexuality... [D:82:19] So I realised that I wasn't mad. I was *traumatised*, but I wasn't mad. [D:135:7] And that's when I realised that basically I'm not a raving lunatic after all, and I can have control over myself.

However, connecting with past trauma was painful at first, and this acted as a powerful disincentive. Similar to the accounts of recovery in Lauveng (2012) and O'Brien (1960), most participants saw 'psychosis' as a refuge from traumatic feelings, and experiencing these in therapy was difficult, as Participant (C) illustrates:

> [C:28:1] Therapy for me is like having your insides ripped out... looking at your stuff as having meaning hurts, it's a lot easier to talk about it in terms of alien conspiracies and kind

of – one time I went saying I'd kind of started to believe that I was, Bladerunner... [C:28:7]. Which basically meant that I didn't have a history and that I was basically made and all... the bits my voices were remembering weren't real and I was just given those memories and that I'm not human...

Being able to explore issues of power and powerlessness within the therapy relationship was also helpful because it worked through aspects of past experience that found expression in the present of the therapeutic relationship. Reconnecting with alienated emotions, although painful, lessened their power and led to a decrease in the threatening quality of 'symptoms'. This relationship is shown in more detail in the next section.

Recovery

When combined with external peer-support networks,[6] which encouraged taking responsibility for recovery, psychotherapy was an important process through which personal meaning could be recovered. Participant (G)'s journey vividly illustrates the impact that restoring personal meaning had on 'symptoms' for many participants. As described above, an intervening care approach to suppressing her 'symptoms' had led to the initial voice she heard multiplying into 12. One voice dominated the others:

[G:47:2] There was this figure of just immense fear and terror... a man, sort of immensely tall, swathed in black, black hat, black cloak and was very shadowy and nebulous and the only thing about him that was clear was instead of a right hand, he had a hook, sort of like a butcher's hook and this figure would sort of appear and sort of like almost slither around the ward... [G:47:10] when it did speak it was hugely articulate and fluent, and I'd been sort of studying Paradise Lost at the time and it would sound almost a bit like Satan...

However, when Participant (G) began to listen to this voice, and to explore what he represented, a radical transformation came about:

[G:48:1] [H]ow I ultimately came to understand him was that he was a hugely amplified version of that original voice that reflected my own emotion. I think he represented the aspects of me that identified with the people who'd harmed me. So the part of me that felt, 'You deserved it, you asked for it, you're bad, you're dirty, you're flawed, you're destined to suffer, your whole life is going to be cursed.' But ultimately he also represented the part of me that had been harmed the most and in that respect, he needed the most care and compassion. But obviously I responded to him with the most fear and resistance, and you know, worked to the point of exhaustion to try and blot him out and not acknowledge him.

Through developing her own meaning of what the voice represented, it changed dramatically:

[G:60:4] over the years... [he] visually disappeared completely and I haven't actually seen him or any image for many years now. But every time he came back he was more benevolent. And he became calmer and calmer and kinder. [G:60:10] It's almost like he became more integrated into me... [G:61:1] he was the voice that definitely caused me by far the most problems. But he was also the voice that held the real key to the healing in him as well...

This seems a startling illustration of how anticipating care might give 'back to him authentically as such for the first time... it helps the Other to become transparent to himself *in* his care and to become *free for* it' (Heidegger 2008: 158–159). This is because in being open to possibilities beyond the enslaving states of 'actual' that we are caught up in, we may find a meaning that is more authentically our own (Gelven 1989: 70). Bollas (2013) makes a similar argument from a psychoanalytic perspective. For him it is in the state of 'breakdown' that the psyche attempts to throw up its contents into consciousness to be worked with, and for meaning to be addressed (p. 18). The experiences represented above suggest that an approach to care that anticipates this meaning might help another to live meaningfully and with possibility. By contrast, an approach to care that intervenes and dominates might close down this possibility. Bollas (2013) argues that in missing the opportunity to work with the contents of breakdown, the Self risks closing up again with its contents in disarray. As this disarray has to become incorporated in order for the psyche to function, the Self may become a longer-term 'broken self' (p. 13) that medical-meaning treatment (and medication in particular) seals over and so 'unwittingly ensure(s) its permanence' (p. 18). In, at times, unwittingly deepening 'schizophrenic symptoms', might intervening care therefore facilitate the passage from breakdown (or a 'prodromal' phase of 'schizophrenia'; APA 2005: 302) to 'broken self' (or 'acute' phase of 'schizophrenia'; p. 307), rather than help to facilitate recovered Selves (in all senses)?

Conclusion

The experiences referred to here are a startling illustration of how the supposedly fixed mechanisms of 'disease' seem to be, in fact, intrinsically linked to emotional states, and are delicately responsive to a process of psychical evolution in which personal meaning seems to occupy a central role. While psychotherapy that facilitated the recovery of personal meaning was helpful in this process, peer-support organisations, such as Hearing Voices Network, were seen as instrumental, not least because they provided an alternative to the 'medical story' (McCarthy-Jones 2012) that most had felt 'colonised' by. Friends, family, work, social workers and drop-in facilities were also felt to be important sources of support and hope, when they did not close down personal meaning.

Geekie (2012) notes that '[c]linical approaches to psychosis are dominated by efforts to control positive symptoms' (p. 93). This control may be one reason why, in almost all cases, these resources for facilitating personal meaning were found outside statutory mental health services, which was likened to 'an abusive parent' (G:40:5), and a 'dumping ground' (C:158:1). Rather than an anomaly, this seems to be a depressingly common experience among those with the diagnosis. This is not to say that there are not many dedicated, gifted and passionate people who work with, what can be at times, overwhelmingly distressed and distressing individuals. Both of us have worked in the mental health system and appreciate the immense pressures involved. However, while control might be useful at times, it seems to have a disastrous impact on recovery when used as a template for care. As Bracken (2002) notes, when such modernist urges to intervene and control are applied to psychotherapy, 'new forms of oppression and suffering' can be expected (p. 202).

Rapley et al. (2011) note that the reversal of this status quo is a 'massive and multifaceted task' (p. 5). Where to start? Opening up 'psychiatrized and psychologized' theory (*ibid.*) to 'what emerges in practice' (Loewenthal 2011: 4) seems to be a critical starting point. As Parker (1999) notes from a critical psychology perspective, because we are 'always embedded in a particular set of perspectives' (or the 'actual' for Heidegger and 'categories of thought' for Laing), to be critical 'does not mean finding the correct standpoint, but it means understanding how we come to stand where we are' (p. 4). Understanding this might help us to appreciate how caught up we might be in the theories we use to 'uncaringly' explain (in a Heideggerian sense) a person's experiences before we are able to understand their personal meaning. Similarly, post-existential thought (Loewenthal 2008, 2011), which draws on both Laing and Heidegger, might be a helpful way of keeping something open, and resisting the urge to retreat into the totalising theories that systems and the psychotherapies used within them are embedded. The task that Rapley et al. (2011) envisage seems pre-Copernican in scale, and the arguments raised here may be, to some, just as heretical. If mainstream psychotherapy cannot enable personal meaning, then the least we can do is reserve the name 'critical' psychotherapy for such purposes.

Notes

1. Interview codings used in Cotton (2015) have been retained throughout this chapter.
2. The use of inverted commas around 'schizophrenia' acknowledges that the scientific validity of the term is widely held in contention.
3. The capitalised form of 'Schizophrenia' refers to the DSM diagnosis, rather than the wider concept of 'schizophrenia', the medical definition of which may vary.
4. There is not the space here to provide a balanced representation of the experiences of all eight participants. This reduced chronology focuses on Participant (G), whose text opened this chapter, and is contextualised in places with other participants' experiences.
5. *Diagnostic and Statistical Manual of Mental Disorders: DSM-IV-TR* (APA 2005) is referenced in this chapter.
6. Six of the eight participants had varying degrees of involvement with the Hearing Voices Network.

References

American Psychiatric Association (APA) (2005) *Diagnostic and Statistical Manual of Mental Disorders: DSM-IV-TR* 4th ed. New Delhi: Jaypee.
Bateson, G. (2000) *Steps to an Ecology of Mind.* Chicago and London: Chicago University Press.
Bollas, C. (2013) *Catch Them before They Fall: The Psychoanalysis of Breakdown.* London: Routledge.
Bracken, P. (2002) *Trauma: Culture, Meaning and Philosophy.* London: Whurr Publishers Ltd.
Bracken, P., Thomas, P., Timimi, S., Asen, E., Behr, G., Beuster, C., Bhunnoo, S., Browne, I., China, N., Double, D., Downer, S., Evans, C., Fernando, S., Garland, M.R., Hopkins, W., Huws, R., Johnson, B., Martindale, B., Middleton, H., Moldavsky, D., Moncrieff, J., Mullins, S., Nelki, J., Pizzo, M., Rodger, J.,

Smyth, M., Summerfield, D. and Wallace, J. (2012) 'Psychiatry beyond the current paradigm', *British Journal of Psychiatry*, 201, 430–434.
Burston, D. (2000) *The Crucible of Experience*. London: Harvard University Press
Cotton, T. (2015) ' "Schizophrenia" and the crisis of meaning: A heuristic exploration of the psychotherapeutic experiences of those who have a "Schizophrenia", diagnosis', Research Centre for Therapeutic Education, Roehampton University. Unpublished doctoral thesis.
Craig, E. (2007) 'From daseinsanalysis to taopsychotherapy', *International Federation for Psychotherapy Newsletter*, December 2007, 5–17.
Cromby, J. and Harper, D.J. (2009) 'Paranoia: A social account', *Theory & Psychology 2009*, 19, 335–361.
Friedman, M. (ed.) (1991) *Worlds of Existentialism*. New Jersey: Humanities Press.
Geekie, J. (2012) 'The uncertainty of being: Existential aspects of the experience of psychosis', in J. Geekie, P. Randal, D. Lampshire and J. Read (eds.) *Experiencing Psychosis*. London: Routledge, 87–95.
Gelven, M. (1989) *A Commentary on Heidegger's Being and Time* revised ed. London: Northern Illinois University Press.
Heidegger, M. (2008) *Being and Time* trans. Macquarrie, J. and Robinson, E. London: Harper Perennial Modern Classics.
Laing, R.D. (1965) *The Divided Self*. London: Penguin Books Ltd.
Laing, R.D. (1967) *The Politics of Experience and the Bird of Paradise*. Middlesex: Penguin Books Ltd.
Lauveng, A. (2012) *A Road Back from Schizophrenia*. New York: Skyhorse Publishing, Inc.
Loewenthal, D. (2008) 'Introducing post-existential practice: An approach to wellbeing in the 21st century', *Philosophical Practice*, October 2008, 3:3, 316–321.
Loewenthal, D. (ed.) (2011) *Post-Existentialism and the Psychological Therapies: Towards a Therapy without Foundations*. London: Karnac.
McCarthy-Jones, S. (2012) *Hearing Voices: The Histories, Causes and Meanings of Auditory Verbal Hallucinations*. Cambridge: Cambridge University Press.
McLaughlin, T. (2000) 'Psychology and mental health politics: A critical history of the hearing voices movement', Unpublished PhD thesis.
Moustakas, C. (1990) *Heuristic Research: Design, Methodology, and Applications*. Newbury Park, CA: Sage.
O'Brien, B. (1960) *Operators and Things*. London: Elek Books.
Parker, I., Georgaca, E., Harper, D., Mclaughlin, T. and Stowell-Smith, M. (1995) *Deconstructing Psychopathology*. London: Sage.
Parker, I. (1999) Deconstruction and psychotherapy. In Parker, I. (ed.) *Deconstructing Psychotherapy*. London: Sage.
Polanyi, M. (2009) *The Tacit Dimension*. Chicago and London: University of Chicago Press.
Rapley, M., Montcrieff, J. and Dillon, J. (2011) 'Carving nature at its joints? DSM and the medicalization of everyday life', in M. Rapley, J. Montcrieff and J. Dillon (eds.) *De-Medicalizing Misery: Psychiatry, Psychology and the Human Condition*. London: Palgrave Macmillan, 10–26.
Read, J. and Bentall, R. (2012) 'Negative childhood experiences and mental health', *British Journal of Psychiatry*, 200, 89–91.

Roe, D. and Lysaker, P. (2012) 'The importance of personal narratives in recovery from psychosis', in J. Geekie, P. Randal, J. Read and D. Lampshire (eds.) (2012) *Experiencing Psychosis*. East Sussex: Routledge, 5–14.

Romme, M. and Escher, A. (1993) *Accepting Voices*. London: MIND.

Romme, M., Escher, S., Dillon, J., Corstens, D. and Morris, M. (2009) *Living with Voices*. Ross-on-Wye: PCCS Books.

Part IV

Critiques Coming More from Outside

6
Critical Theory and Psychotherapy

Anastasios Gaitanidis

In the face of the monumental events that took place during the first half of the twentieth century (for example the First and Second World Wars, the Holocaust and Hiroshima), a group of theorists which came to be collectively known as the Frankfurt School (established in 1923 as the Institute of Social Research in affiliation with the University of Frankfurt) developed a specific type of interdisciplinary approach to the examination of social, psychological and cultural phenomena called critical theory. In this chapter, I intend to present the work of two of the most important figures of the Frankfurt School – Walter Benjamin and Theodor Adorno – by focusing on their analyses of the catastrophic nature of history, their emphasis on the importance of remembrance and redemption, and their portrayal of our post-Holocaust social reality. I will then attempt to explore how their insights could be employed for the development of a radical psychotherapeutic practice.

History as a permanent catastrophe

The Frankfurt School (critical) theorists begin with what West (2009) calls 'the catastrophic' as it manifests itself in the course of world history. This idea is clearly formulated in Benjamin's description of the 'angel of history', based on a painting by Paul Klee. Benjamin writes:

> A Klee painting named 'Angelus Novus' shows an angel looking as though he is about to move away from something he is fixedly contemplating. His eyes are staring, his mouth is open, his wings are spread. This is how one pictures the angel of history. His face is turned toward the past. Where we perceive a chain of events, he sees one single catastrophe which keeps piling wreckage upon wreckage and

hurls it in front of his feet. The angel would like to stay, awaken the dead, and make whole what has been smashed. But a storm is blowing from Paradise; it has got caught in his wings with such violence that the angel can no longer close them. This storm irresistibly propels him into the future to which his back is turned, while the pile of debris before him grows skyward. This storm is what we call progress.

(1992: 249)

This depiction of history as one single, permanent catastrophe is in direct conflict with the Enlightenment notion of human history as a teleological progression towards greater autonomy and freedom. This idea is based on a history that is written from the standpoint of the victors (after all, 'to the victors belong the spoils' of history), whereas Benjamin wants to view history from the standpoint of the vanquished. From this perspective the historical advancement of civilisation is nothing more than the constant repetition of acts of monstrous, destructive barbarity. As Benjamin (1992) puts it, 'There is no document of civilisation which is not at the same time a document of barbarism' (p. 248). This view corresponds with Freud's (1930) thesis in his *Civilisation and Its Discontents* that the development of civilisation entails the progressive hold of superegoic violence (i.e. internalised social violence) over the individual's libidinal kernel (with its concomitant increase in individual unhappiness), and Nietzsche's (1887) proposal in his *On the Genealogy of Morals* that our present, precious moral codes are based on a long-forgotten history of past immorality and violence.

According to this perspective, the idea of a 'plan for a better world that manifests itself in history and unites it' (Adorno 1973: 320) is completely erroneous. The only notion of a unified, continuous universal history that can be legitimately construed is a negative one – history is continuous in its catastrophic discontinuity. As Adorno states,

Not to be denied for that reason, however, is the unity that cements the discontinuous, chaotically splintered moments and phases of history – the unity of the control of nature, progressing to rule over men, and finally to that over men's inner nature. No universal history leads from savagery to humanitarianism, but there is one leading from the slingshot to the megaton bomb.

(1973: 320)

Even the development of technology which is usually employed as evidence for the existence of positive historical progress should be viewed as contributing to the continuous expansion of the destructive structures of domination. Instead, true progress would mean

> escaping from the magic spell, including the spell of progress that is itself nature. This happens when human beings become conscious of their own naturalness and call a halt to their own domination of nature, a domination by means of which nature's own domination is perpetuated. In this sense, we might say that progress occurs where it comes to an end.
>
> (Adorno 2006: 152)

In other words, true progress has not yet begun, because the domination of nature (implying here both the human domination of nature and nature's domination) has not ceased. All history is fundamentally prehistory (reflecting Marx's view that proper human history – that is, history without the presence of violent social antagonisms – has not yet commenced) as it compulsively repeats its prehistoric, catastrophic relation to nature. Beginning with the first human beings' destruction of other animals and each other, human history has always involved violence and destruction. In the form of advanced civilisation, the increase in technological power signifies an increase in violent destructiveness.

It is not an accident, therefore, that in a century in which the advanced development of technology and means of production could have allowed for global peace, fair distribution of wealth and the end of starvation and deprivation, the greatest 'break' in the history of civilisation took place – the Holocaust. In the midst of one of the most technologically and culturally advanced countries in the world (twentieth-century Germany), a barbaric ideology of racist superiority created an apocalyptic system of selection and extinction that led to the industrially organised mass killings of millions of human beings.

Yet it is neither that the potential for totalitarian practices, racist killings and genocides has actually diminished nor that the global powers have really given up their means of total annihilation – their arsenal of weapons of mass destruction. Everyday acts of 'micro-genocide' are also 'conducted in the normative social spaces of public schools, clinics, emergency rooms, hospital wards, nursing homes, court rooms, prisons, detention centres and public morgues' (Scheper-Hughes 2002: 369), which reduce 'Others' to non-persons, illegal aliens and terrorising monsters who 'contaminate' our public spaces and thus need to be violently excluded or subtly and silently exterminated.

It seems that this destructive historical path has never been abandoned. There is something obsessive in the ways in which we continue to pursue our own and Others' destruction in our very attempts to secure our self-preservation, especially if we think of our ruthless appropriation of the world's resources. And the fact that we can discuss and address this obsessive tendency, on the one hand, seems to indicate that there is enlightened criticism and awareness, but, on the other, this seems to have no effect at all – despite (or, perhaps, because of the abstract character of) our awareness of our situation, we are still unable to arrest the catastrophic course of world history.

It feels as if we are trapped within a historical nightmare from which we cannot awake (to paraphrase Joyce's famous line from *Ulysses*). Although we temporarily seek to escape from this nightmare by repressing the memories of past traumas, we are still haunted by the ghosts of the dead who constantly seek justice for all of the cruelty and mindless suffering that they had to endure. To quote Marx (1852), 'the tradition of all the dead generations weighs like a nightmare on the brains of the living' (p. 5). However, we cannot simply awake from this nightmare by deciding, like Marx (1852), to 'let the dead bury their dead' (p. 6). If we do not listen to their persistent wailing and interminable lamentation, if we decide to either ignore or forget them, then we are bound to repeat the traumas of the past and condemn ourselves (and the dead) to the never-ending confinement, the purgatory of catastrophic history.

Remembrance and impossible redemption

If we have indeed been haunted by the ghosts of the dead and their wailing voices, what can we do in order to redeem their tormented souls and create for us a space to live? According to Benjamin (1992), we can only redeem the dead by exhibiting our anamnestic solidarity with them, by keeping alive the memory of all of those who suffered at the slaughter-bench of history. Like preceding generations, we have been endowed with a 'weak messianic power' which enables us to restore and mend what has been historically broken. Ours is a 'weak' messianic power because this restoration will not come about via an external divine agency but only through our sustained efforts to remember the dead.

Crucially significant for this 'messianic restoration' (the Hebrew *tikkun*) is Freud's notion of *Nachträglichkeit* (Freud 1918; Freud and Breuer 1895), or 'afterwardness'. This is a form of causality that works both forwards and backwards in time. For this reason, although our present situation is shaped by the traumatic experiences of past generations, it is not reducible to these experiences. Every original trauma must find a present experience for its continued expression. At the same time, repetition is never merely 'repetition'. There is always something new in the present experience which, if it is supported by our acts of remembrance and persistent recollection of the sufferings and injustices inflicted on past victims, could lead to the potential healing of their original traumas and the recovery of *tempe perdu* (lost time). As Benjamin (1992) states, 'nothing that has ever happened should be regarded as lost for history. To be sure, only a redeemed mankind receives the fullness of its past – which is to say, only for a redeemed mankind has its past become citable in all its moments' (1992: 246).

However, the fullness of the past cannot be recovered by our attempts to integrate it into a seamless and consistent historical narrative. The creation of this coherent narrative can only function as a defence against the possibility of genuinely remembering the traumatic experiences of the past – in the same way that transforming the fragmented segments of a dream into a coherent narrative only helps to further disguise and repress its latent traumatic content. Rather, redemption becomes possible when the historical continuum is arrested by blasting 'an image of the past' out of 'the magic circle' of homogenous history. The reawakening of the dead takes place through a 'shock' that happens when the horrors of the past are fully witnessed in an instant. It is as if, in a moment of present and deadly danger, all of the past catastrophes (and the traumatic lives of history's victims) 'flash' before our eyes (see Benjamin 1992: 247).

For this reason, Benjamin's concept of anamnestic solidarity with the dead does not seek empathy or identification with past generations. He requires us to initiate a 'messianic cessation of happening' that lends a voice to past suffering and allows it, through our mediation, to speak its own truth. This prohibits us from fully appropriating the memory of our suffering ancestors for our own purposes. As Cornell (1992) puts it, 'We run into the limit of our narcissism, however, as we realize that, will what we might, we cannot rewrite the other back into life, remaking history so that she is still with us. She is gone. In her very absence we feel the pull of otherness' (1992: 30).

We confront the traumatic materiality of actual history not so much through the confrontation with our own death (as Heidegger (1927) claims), which seems to result in the enhancement of our subjective self-governance, but instead through the recognition of our inability to fully recuperate the 'Otherness' of the dead. As Freud (1915) explained in his *Thoughts for the Times on War and Death*, the fear of death is the fear of losing the loved Other; it is the fear of being helpless before our own grief and of feeling powerless to bring the lost Other back into life.

Yet it is precisely because we cannot know the dead except in their absence, and as our loss, that we are always in danger of doing violence to their Otherness by imposing our own meaning to this loss. This is also the danger with certain simplistic interpretations of Freud's concept of *Nachträglichkeit*, which seem to involve the recuperation of the catastrophic past through our successful internalisation and narrativisation of the traumatic experiences of the dead. However, this process is bound to fail, precisely because the absence of the dead cannot be repealed. The precedence of the dead whose memory trace continues to be felt in their absence brings to a halt our attempt to fully internalise them or narrativise their experiences. Paradoxically, it is only through this impossibility to fully internalise the dead that it is possible to restore them as Other to us (see Cornell 1992).

This is also reflected in the much quoted last paragraph of Adorno's (2005) *Minima Moralia*, where he proposes that it is both necessary 'to contemplate all things as they would present themselves from the standpoint of redemption' (2005: 247) and also impossible to assume this standpoint. However, he goes on to say: 'Even its own impossibility it must at last comprehend for the sake of the possible. But beside the demand thus placed on thought, the question of the reality or unreality of redemption itself hardly matters' (Adorno 2005: 247).

Despite the impossibility of contemplating things from the standpoint of redemption, what is essential for Adorno is the demand placed on thought to imagine itself capable of occupying this standpoint. This is why the reality or unreality of redemption hardly matters. What is important is the messianic demand itself and not whether this demand is going to ultimately lead us to some kind of redemption. This is why the impossibility of the redemptive standpoint must be comprehended 'for the sake of the possible'. In its very impossibility, the demand leaves open the prospect of the possible that is understood as something that is yet to come from the future (a meaning contained in the French word for future: *avenir* – to come).

For Adorno, the promise of the future inherent in the messianic demand is only 'there' as the trace of the Other that marks the impossibility of fully recovering, and thus redeeming, the Other. Even when Adorno (In Adorno and Horkheimer 1979) argues that 'all reification is a forgetting' (p. 230), he does not mean that its overcoming would follow from the anamnestic recovery of an original meaning, our reunification with the Other. Unlike Hegel's (1817) defence of *Erinnerung* as the reinternalisation of our externalised Other, Adorno agrees with Benjamin in stressing the redemptive power of *Gedächtnis*, the reverential recollection of the Other always prior to the remembering subject.

The reversal of forgetting that Adorno recommends is thus not the same as the 're-membering' of the dismembered Other, the recovery of a perfect wholeness or original plenitude. It means rather the restoration of the Other's difference and non-identity which will no longer be subsumed under the subject's identity but will coexist with it as part of a non-hierarchical and non-coercive constellation. The future is revealed in our remembrance of the non-identity of the suffering Other, which acknowledges the limits of our capacity to internalise the Other, the very finitude of our memory that makes any vision of 'true' redemption of the Other impossible, and yet absolutely necessary.

Life and/or death after Auschwitz

Adorno's insistence on the necessity of the remembrance of the Other's non-identity requires a subject which is mindful of its own limitations as a result of its intersubjective and historical embeddedness. The idea of a 'pure, autonomous subjectivity' is a distorted notion that denies the reality of the subject's inseparability from the world. Therefore any idea of autonomy must be conceived of as a relation between the subject and Others and the subject and the collective.

It is useful here to employ Benjamin's (1977) distinction between *Erfahrung*, the understanding of present events within the context of collective and personal traditions, and *Erlebnis*, the isolation of events from any such meaningful context, communal or individual. For Benjamin, *Erfahrung* has been steadily replaced by the meaningless, atomistic *Erlebnis* in the culturally bankrupt world of late capitalism. Therefore it is crucial that, in order to rescue *Erfahrung* from the current individualistic assault of *Erlebnis*, 'the attempt must be made anew to wrest tradition away from a conformism that is about to overpower it' (Benjamin 1992: 247).

Adorno shares Benjamin's animosity to *Erlebnis*, a term which has been extensively used by the existentialists because it is supposed to privilege a kind of experiential pseudoimmediacy and existential isolation which unwittingly replicates the irrationality and uprootedness of modern social experience. However, he also realises that in a deeper cultural and psychological sense, our inability to feel truly at home anywhere in the world means that we are all uprooted, alienated, effaced – that is to say, we have lost our faces, we are no longer πρόσωπα (personae or personalities). Like Kafka's key characters, we are the anonymous, rootless persons always in search of a community but unable to find it because we are trapped by a form of rationalised, lucid madness – the world of modern administration (Adorno 2003a). Even worse is that the hope for a 'promised land' has evaporated. This goal is unattainable because it is the suffering physical world we are dealing with rather than a transcendent realm. Thus despair arises because existence in the modern world is as an exile; there is no true 'home' anymore; there is no secure place where we could avoid the anxiety of modern life apart from the confines of the 'totally administered' world – that is to say, a world in which every aspect of our lives is 'managed' by state apparatuses, the culture and entertainment industry, and practices of social and individual 'normalisation' and control (including psychotherapy). To the extent that Adorno's vision is true – that is, to the degree that the administrative mode is totalised – we are like Gregor Samsa in Kafka's *Metamorphosis* (1961 [1933]), who wakes up from an uneasy dream only to realise that he has been transformed into a gigantic insect caught in the web of an 'administrative' spider to whose power he cannot help but aspire (Adorno 2003a).

Perhaps the only remedy for this negative, totally administered life – a 'life that does not live' (Adorno 2005: 19) – is to embrace the positivity of death, a solution that echoes Heidegger's (1927) proposal to fully come to terms with the supreme ontological 'truth' that we are 'beings-towards-death'. For Adorno, however, there is a problem with this solution: we cannot choose to die, or even accept it as our ultimate existential possibility, because we are not aware of the fact that, under the current social conditions, we are no longer really alive. As he puts it,

> the very people who burst with proofs of exuberant vitality could easily be taken for prepared corpses, from whom the news of their not-quite-successful decease has been withheld for reasons of population policy. Underlying the prevalent health is death. All the movements of health resemble the reflex-movements of beings whose hearts have stopped beating.
>
> (Adorno 2005: 59)

Moreover, we cannot embrace death as 'our' possibility because we can no longer properly die. Our death does not belong to us since it is now controlled by the totally administered world: 'So the experience of death is turned into that of the exchange of functionaries, and anything in the natural relationship to death that is not wholly absorbed into the social one is turned over to hygiene' (Adorno 2005: 232).

It comes as no surprise, therefore, that we are currently extremely fascinated by the figure of the 'zombie' – the 'un-dead dead'. We are condemned to roam the earth without being able to either really live or properly die. This is echoed in Adorno's (2003b) reading of Beckett in which he argues that Beckett's major plays (especially *Waiting for Godot* and *Endgame*) do not deal with the inevitability of death, as in a classical tragedy, but with the fact that even after all is over, after the destruction of all our cherished cultural values and beliefs in historical progress (i.e. after Auschwitz), one has to go on. We are stranded in this abysmal region 'between life and death' that the Nazi death camps have enacted with a vengeance. Beckett's characters run, leap, tumble, grow restless, feel awkward, brawl; crave a glance, a handshake, a caress, but are left so unsatisfied by fate, by love, even by pity. Although they contemplate the possibility of taking their own life, they can never actually do it. And this is not because they are afraid of death; they are totally consumed by the fear that 'death could miscarry' (Adorno 2003b: 289). They call forth pity and fear, and pass through pity and fear so as to achieve catharsis, only to realise that catharsis is impossible and their life is nothing but an animated wasteland. For Adorno, Beckett's parody of tragedy is a most candid mirror held up to our post-Holocaust individual and social reality. As Adorno (1973) puts it, 'Beckett has given the only appropriate reaction to the situation of the concentration camp, that he never names, as if it lay under an image ban (*Bildervebot*). What is, is like a concentration camp' (p. 380).

It is for this reason that Adorno believes that Heidegger's attempt to rescue Being from the merely existent is at best futile and at worst deeply cynical and ideological because it ignores our post-Holocaust reality. As Beckett states in his 1961 interview with Tom Driver,

> One cannot speak anymore of Being, one must speak only of the mess. When Heidegger and Sartre speak of a contrast between being and existence, they may be right, I don't know, but their language is too philosophical for me. I am not a philosopher. One can only speak of what is in front of him, and that now is simply the mess.
>
> (quoted by Driver 1961: 23)

And 'the mess' for Beckett is so overwhelming that it overflows into his form. This is why he breaks with Joyce, who is still trying to find a form that he can impose upon the catastrophic chaos of history. Beckett believes that this catastrophic mess is so overpowering that the only solution is to enact an 'aesthetics of failure'. But his aesthetics of failure, as Adorno (1973) correctly points out, does not only aspire to 'fail' – that is, it is not simply 'nihilistic'; it is 'a legacy of action' that 'silently screams that things should be otherwise. Such nihilism implies the opposite of an identification with the Nothing' (p. 381). It is a 'nihilism' which is redemptive in the specific sense presented above – namely, that in our post-Holocaust era, we need to view things from the standpoint of redemption, which is impossible, and yet this impossibility must be comprehended for the sake of the possible.

To offer (as Heidegger (1927) does) a picture of our positive reconciliation with the Being of the world in this point in history through our anticipatory resoluteness (i.e. through the way in which our possibilities are shown as our own through our being-towards-death) would be to suggest that the only way out of our current historical (zombie-like) predicament is to transform ourselves into 'vampires' – that is to say, creatures who derive their power from knowing that they are already dead and survive by sucking the life out of human (and other sentient) beings. This would conspire with the very forces that resulted in the concentration camps. This is why Adorno (1973) insists that the real nihilists are not writers such as Beckett, but are those active nihilists (for example Heidegger) 'who oppose nihilism with their more and more faded positivities, and through this conspire with all extant meanness and finally with the destructive principle' (p. 381).

The role of psychotherapy

After exploring Benjamin's and Adorno's views about history as a permanent catastrophe, their belief in the importance of remembrance and 'impossible' redemption, and their position regarding our current individual and social reality 'after Auschwitz', I will now attempt to draw three conclusions regarding the role of psychotherapy in contemporary society.

First, it is absolutely crucial that we, as therapists, become aware of the historical and social contexts which 'frame' our relationship with our patients. We have to abandon notions of therapeutic 'success' which amount to the normalisation of our patients, their adaptation to the catastrophic functioning of society and the reinforcement of the illusion of their separateness from the world. The crucial achievement of critical theorists such as Benjamin and Adorno is precisely their explanation of how individual mental distress results from the very structure of the existing social order which 'alienates' people from each other and from themselves. As Rozmarin (2011) explains in his article 'To be is to betray', 'The potential for freedom lies in the difference between a subject who is conscious of his embeddedness in society and his consequent dependence and responsibility and a subject intent on defying his embeddedness, destined to existence in self-estrangement in a foreign world that is hostile to his pleas' (p. 328).

For this reason, we need to transform the therapeutic encounter with our patients so that the question they ask is not only 'What's wrong with me?' 'For there to be freedom we must also ask and allow the subject to ask "What's wrong with the world?"' (Rozmarin 2011: 329).

Second, we need to develop a practice which promotes our patients' potential for examining the consequences of 'living' their lives in the face of the countless traumas, losses and sufferings of past and present Others. We have to be mindful of the conflict that exists between our patients' tendency to forget and repress the traumas of past and present Others in order to be able to carry on with their lives, and the guilt that this forgetting generates. It is also essential to realise that there is no satisfactory solution to this conflict: if they decide to deny the past and present injustices in order to allow themselves to live, then they inevitably betray the past and present victims and become complicit with the very forces that perpetuate these injustices. And if they decide to remember and recognise these injustices, then they must do this without believing that they can appropriate them for their own purposes and without any guarantees of immediate or imminent salvation. This appears to be an unbearable position; and yet it is only by staying with the unbearable feelings that this position generates that they can become fully aware of their current entrapment between 'a life that does not live' and the impossibility of viewing things from the standpoint of redemption. However, as mentioned above, this impossibility must be contemplated for the sake of the possible. As Rozmarin (2011) puts it,

> we all live in a spellbound society, in denial of unbearable injustice and violence – each individual who steps into our offices is the bearer of much more trouble than he or she can handle... We must choose whether to resign to living and practicing under the spell, to asking our patients to renounce their concern for others as mere fantasy replaceable with healthy self-servitude, or to embark on a journey of remembrance and recognition, and of critique of things as they are, towards unknown consequences. (p. 344)

Finally, we must employ Benjamin's and Adorno's insights in such a way as to both criticise existing forms of conformist psychotherapeutic practices which function as instruments of individual adjustment and resignation, and promote a form of radical psychotherapy which can provide the means by which patients can retrieve some of their ability to realise the extent of their alienation and fragmentation, recognise a small part of themselves in the fractured mirror of the social world and try to find a way to build on it. In other words, we need to facilitate our patients' development of an elegant self-togetherness that is able to withstand the monstrous and calamitous effects of past and present history without violating the 'Otherness' of the suffering Other. However, in order for this to be effective, the therapeutic relationship should remain independent of the control of the 'totally administered world', which constantly attempts to regulate the psychotherapeutic field and 'manage' its practices. It is only in this way that psychotherapy can act as a 'privileged kind of laboratory, a place where something new appears: that which transpires through the examined living *together* of the thought, ideology and history in which each singular subjectivity, each intersubjective relation and each collectivity are constituted' (Rozmarin 2011: 323).

References

Adorno, T.W. (1973) *Negative Dialectics* trans. Ashton, E.B. New York: Continuum.
Adorno, T.W. (2003a) 'Notes on Kafka', in Rolf Tiedermann (ed.) *Can One Live after Auschwitz? A Philosophical Reader*. Palo Alto: Stanford University Press, pp. 211–239.
Adorno, T.W. (2003b) 'Trying to understand *Endgame*', in Rolf Tiedermann (ed.) *Can One Live after Auschwitz? A Philosophical Reader*. Palo Alto: Stanford University Press, pp. 259–294.
Adorno, T.W. (2005) *Minima Moralia – Reflections on a Damaged Life* trans. Jephcott, E.F.N. London: Verso.
Adorno, T.W. (2006) *History and Freedom: Lectures 1964–1965*, R. Tiedemann (ed.) trans. Livingstone, R. Malden: Polity Press.
Adorno, T.W. and Horkheimer, M. (1979) *Dialectic of Enlightenment* trans. Cumming, J. London: Verso.
Beckett, S. (1961) Quoted by Tom F. Driver, 'Beckett by the Madeleine', *Columbia University Forum*, 4, pp. 21–25.
Benjamin, W. (1977) *The Origin of German Tragic Drama*. London: NLB.
Benjamin, W. (1992) 'Theses on the philosophy of history', in Hannah Arendt (ed.) *Illuminations* trans. Zohn, H. London: Fontana Press, pp. 245–255.
Cornell, D. (1992) *The Philosophy of the Limit*. London: Routledge.
Freud, S. (1915) 'Thoughts for the times on war and death', in J. Strachey (ed. and trans.) *The Standard Edition of the Complete Psychological Works of Sigmund Freud (SE), Vol. 14*. London: Hogarth Press, pp. 273–300.
Freud, S. (1918) 'The history of an infantile neurosis', *SE, Vol. 17*, pp. 7–122.
Freud, S. (1930) 'Civilisation and its discontents', *SE, Vol. 21*, pp. 57–146.

Freud, S. and Breuer, J. (1895) *Studies on Hysteria, SE, Vol. 2*. London: Hogarth Press.
Hegel, G.W.F. (1817) *Science of Logic* trans. Miller, A.V. Atlantic Highlands: Humanities Press, 1969.
Heidegger, M. (1927) *Being and Time* trans. Stambaugh, J. New York: State University of New York Press, 1996.
Kafka, F. (1961) *Metamorphosis and Other Stories* trans. Muir, W. and Muir, E. Middlesex: Penguin Books, 1933.
Marx, K. (1852) *The Eighteenth Brumaire of Louis Bonaparte* trans. Padover, S.K. Marx/Engels Internet Archive (www.marxists.org/archive/marx/works/download/pdf/18th-Brumaire.pdf), 1999.
Nietzsche, F. (1887). *On the Genealogy of Morals* trans. Smith, D. Oxford: Oxford University Press, 1996.
Rozmarin, E. (2011) 'To be is to betray: On the place of collective history and freedom in psychoanalysis', *Psychoanalytic Dialogues*, 21:3, pp. 320–345.
Scheper-Hughes, N. (2002) 'Coming to our senses: Anthropology and genocide', in A. Hinton (ed.) *Annihilating Difference: The Anthropology of Genocide*. Oakland: University of California Press, pp. 348–381.
West, C. (2009) 'Cornell West: Truth – an interview with Astra Taylor', in A. Taylor (ed.) *Examined Life: Excursions with Contemporary Thinkers*. New York: The New Press, pp. 1–24.

7
When Love Is Not All We Want: Queers, Singles and the Therapeutic Cult of Relationality

Mari Ruti and Adrian Cocking

Psychoanalysts and psychotherapists understand that relationships – particularly intimate ones – can be difficult to navigate: they know that their patients are likely to complain about their relationship troubles; they expect to hear about the failures of love, about loss, betrayal, suffering and disappointment; and they seek to use transference in subtle ways to guide their patients to more successful modes of relating. But what they may be less attuned to is the extent to which their assumptions about what constitutes 'success' in the context of relationships are determined by normative social narratives of what the so-called 'good life' is supposed to look like. Do they define 'healthy' relationships as monogamous, permanent and stable? Do they expect their patients to be willing to work through their relationship dilemmas with a degree of patience and diligence? If so, psychoanalysis and psychotherapy find themselves at odds with many of the central arguments of contemporary queer theory. And they also find themselves out of joint with the growing body of work on how singles – whether queer or straight – are discriminated against in our society. Indeed, what the queer and the single have in common is that both refuse to adhere to our society's heteronormative expectations regarding the proper organisation of sexuality. This has prompted the queer critic Michael Cobb (2012) to state that he has started to attach the letter 'S' to the LGBTQ acronym in order to affiliate those who are single 'with the ever-elongating list of nonmajority sexualities that deserve more sustained attention, political interventions, and cultural investigations' (p. 5).

The aim of this chapter is to urge psychoanalysts and psychotherapists to become more critical of their foundational assumptions regarding relationality. Essentially, we are asking the reader to consider the possibility that psychic wellbeing might not always demand thriving relationships, or at least not the kinds of relationships that are conventionally recognised as thriving. By this we do not mean to downplay the importance of relationality in any global sense, let alone to imply that caring relationships – whether romantic, familial or friendship-based – are not worth striving for. We merely wish to call attention to cultural and ideological factors that all too easily produce the impression that, without enduring relationships, particularly romantic ones, an individual's life is somehow intrinsically incomplete. Perhaps even more radically, we wish to reassess the idea that 'love', conventionally understood, is what all of us want (or should want).

Consider the following clinical vignette. During the initial assessment session for psychoanalytic treatment, the following exchange occurs:

Patient (one of the authors of this chapter): I'm not currently in a relationship.
Analyst: But you have been previously?
Patient: Yes, I've had quite a few relationships.
Analyst: Well, in that case, we have nothing to worry about.

This is a seemingly innocent exchange – one in which the analyst reassures the patient that he is not pathologising her for being single. Yet the analyst's comforting response contains a number of loaded assumptions: that the patient possesses the potential for a productive analysis because she has already proved herself capable of relationships; that if she is not currently in a relationship, it is because her previous attempts have 'failed' (rather than been voluntarily relinquished); and that – most fundamentally – she is seeking analysis because she wants to be in a relationship and hopes that analysis will enable her to fulfil this wish. At this moment the analyst does not realise that his patient is thinking:

> If I tell him that I have no interest in being in a long-term relationship – if I mention that I find permanent relationships stifling – he'll think that I'm crazier than I actually am; he'll think that I'm putting up defences, that I'm fleeing from the pain of past relationship failures, that I have fortified myself with the impenetrable walls of a false self in order to protect the vulnerable core of my true self, and so on.

So the patient says nothing, thereby shutting down a number of potentially interesting therapeutic avenues. As Laura Kipnis (2003) observes, saying no to love, in our society, seems virtually impossible: according to the dominant cultural ethos, rejecting love 'isn't just heresy, it's tragedy... the failure to achieve what is most essentially human. And not just tragic, but abnormal' (p. 26).

The approach we take in this chapter is heavily indebted to queer theory, not because queer theory is the first to outline the coercive aspects of the ideology of love – the theme was already prevalent in feminist criticism of the 1960s and 1970s – but because queer theory has done so with noticeable energy during the last decade, thereby renewing general critical interest in the topic. Moreover, the capaciousness of the term 'queer' – which implies a more fluid notion of both identity and sexuality than, say, 'gay', 'lesbian' or 'straight' – makes it possible for us to stress that the overvalorisation of relationality in our society impacts individuals of various sexual orientations. (This will become evident in our discussion of singles in the second half of this chapter.) In a way, queer theory has made visible a predicament that many straight people have also experienced but have not necessarily been able to name.

In this context it is important to specify that we are by no means arguing that psychoanalysis and psychotherapy should, generally speaking, abandon their emphasis on relationality. Obviously, relationships form an essential part of many (perhaps most) human lives. And, equally obviously, many patients seek analysis or therapy because they would like to improve the quality of their relationships; we are well aware of the enormous psychic toll that intimate relationships often take on people. As a result, we are not calling for a reorientation of the entire analytic-therapeutic undertaking. We are merely asking for a greater degree of sensitivity to the plight of those who do not, for various political or personal reasons, wish to follow what the feminist philosopher Sara Ahmed (2010) calls the dominant 'happiness scripts' (p. 90) of Western society.

The promise of happiness

Ahmed explains that because virtually no one in Western society contests the notion that happiness should be the goal of human existence, the way in which we are taught to conceptualise its parameters has a tremendous impact on our lives; dominant cultural imaginaries of happiness can, quite literally, dictate which life directions we choose to pursue and which to avoid. And, predictably enough, our society tells us that one of the most reliable indicators of happiness is the capacity to sustain enduring relationships, especially married monogamy. Marriage, according to Ahmed, is defined as

> 'the best of all possible worlds' as it maximizes happiness. The argument is simple: if you are married, then we can predict that you are more likely to be happier than if you are not married. The finding is also a recommendation: get married and you will be happier! (p. 6)

Ahmed notes that in every society the promise of happiness clings to particular goals – goals that are deemed necessary for the attainment of the good life – so that those who are perceived as falling short of such goals are also perceived as falling short of happiness. In our society, heterosexual marriage, and increasingly homosexual marriage, is foremost among such privileged goals, which is why it can be hard to avoid the sense that if one opts out of marriage, one opts out of happiness.

'The public investment in happiness', Ahmed specifies, 'is an investment in a very particular and narrow model of the good' (p. 70). This investment, she continues, 'blocks other possible worlds', rendering 'possibles impossible, such that possibles are lost before they can be lived, experienced, or imagined' (p. 165). That is, a large array of life paths are deemed either undesirable or untenable before they even become possibilities, before we even get a chance to imagine what it would be like to pursue them. Furthermore, our commitment to dominant happiness scripts can be so strong that when a given script does not deliver what it promises, when it makes us unhappy rather than happy, we do not think of questioning the script (say, the marriage script) but instead assume that somehow we have failed to live out the script correctly. Simply put, when we have been invested in the notion that a certain kind of life is the happy life, it can be very difficult for us to admit that this life has not actually made us happy; it can be hard to admit that our faith in a specific happiness script has led us astray. Instead, we cling to the hope that if we keep at it, if we try hard enough, this script will eventually usher us to the threshold of happiness.

Lauren Berlant (2011) characterises this predicament as one of 'cruel optimism': the stubborn, irrational belief that social arrangements and ways of life that hurt us will eventually pay off and make us happy. She specifies that 'a relation of cruel optimism' exists when something that we desire is in reality an obstacle to our flourishing (p. 1). That is, cruel optimism entails the fantasy that our relentless efforts will bring us the love, intimacy, success, security, harmony or financial reward that we crave even when they are extremely unlikely to do so. Berlant explains, for instance, that the economically disadvantaged may at times form optimistic attachments to the very power structures that oppress them, so that a poor person might support a conservative political agenda even when it is clear that it will never help them to overcome poverty. Or the daughter of working-class parents who has watched her parents toil without reward for two decades might still place a great deal of faith in the ideals of hard work and social mobility, hoping against hope that the American dream will one day rescue her even if it did not rescue her parents. As Judith Butler (1997) has also suggested, such an optimistic attachment to potentially wounding modalities of life tends to arise from the desire to feel normal: we want to feel like we are a part of something familiar, like we belong to – and are recognised by – the world in which we live, with the result that we go along with the expectations that render this world comprehensible to us. In Berlant's terms, our investment in the notion of 'a dependable life', 'a life that does not have to keep being reinvented' (p. 170), can be so persistent that we remain attached to specific fantasies of satisfaction even after they have repeatedly disappointed us. In short, we endorse forms of life that are not in the least bit good for us, coming, as it were, 'to misrecognize the bad life as a good one' (p. 174).

Misery, marriage and capitalism

Arguably, the happiness script of marriage is uniquely designed to induce us to misrecognise a bad life – a life filled with domestic squabbles, hurt feelings, the tedium of routines and lacklustre sex lives – as a good one. This is not to say that there are no happy marriages – obviously these exist. Yet there is no doubt that, for many, the alliance that was supposed to guide them to the heart of the good life is causing a great deal of misery. Indeed, one of the paradoxes of our society is that we are taught to expect from marriage an almost miraculous power to right all of the wrongs of our lives, heal the wounds of our past and grant us enduring satisfaction, yet the reality of married life is often quite removed from this fantasy. Many married people experience their marriages as deadening, suffocating, frustrating and sometimes even frightening. Sniping, bickering, resentment, the silent treatment and other forms of psychological warfare seem to be among the standard devices of modern marriage. Speaking of the high levels of everyday irritation that often accompany married lives, Kipnis notes that relatively trivial things – such as who forgot to run an errand, take out the recycling, return the scissors to their designated spot or leave the toilet seat the way it is supposed to be – serve as emotional trigger points that govern the tone of a couple's daily interactions. 'Considering the amount of psychological space such issues come to occupy,' Kipnis states, 'irritation would seem to be domestic coupledom's default setting' (p. 79).

We want to stress that we have nothing against happy marriages. We believe that all social institutions – including marriage – can be revitalised, so that it is conceivable to be married without buying in to the repressive ideologies that have traditionally accompanied marriage. At the same time, it is impossible to deny that the social glorification of marriage serves to hide the fact that, as Kipnis puts it, 'toxic levels of everyday dissatisfaction, boredom, unhappiness, and not-enoughness are the functional norms in millions of lives and marriages' (p. 190). When they are not bickering or screaming at each other, married couples often spend countless hours negotiating, adjusting and resolving their 'issues', frequently even paying analysts or therapists to play umpire to their domestic dramas. Sometimes the mere tone of a mate's voice demands countless therapy sessions to work through, for even a hint of disapproval can open the floodgates of a long history of bruised egos, callous rejections, painful letdowns and stinging disenchantments. And, strangely enough, our society considers this 'normal', so that if we start to question the value of this way of channelling our energies, we are told to grow up, become more realistic and ask less from our marriages. As Kipnis points out, marriage researchers, relationship experts, religious authorities and couples counsellors are all telling us that the secret to a good marriage is to lower our expectations (pp. 173–175). That this 'Ask Less from Life plan' (p. 175) directly contradicts the cultural hype about marriage being the cure for all of our problems – social and personal alike – seems to go unnoticed, as does the fact that lowering our expectations hardly represents the solution that it professes to be.

If the rewards of marriage are frequently so meagre, why does our society work so hard to sell us this particular ideal of the good life? According to social theorists, the reason is primarily economic. Critics from Antonio Gramsci (1930) to Herbert Marcuse (1955) and Michel Foucault (1978–1979) have proposed that the idealisation of marriage constitutes the linchpin of Western capitalist society, facilitating the smooth functioning of its economy. Gramsci noted that Henry Ford was among the first to recognise the socioeconomic benefits of marriage. When Ford updated the technology of his car factories in the 1920s – shifting to an assembly line process that increased his workers' productivity hugely – he capitalised on the link between marriage and (presumed) productivity by demanding proof of marital status as a precondition of higher wages. He even had a cadre of investigators who conducted spot-checks at workers' homes to verify that their domestic arrangements were what they had reported. This is because he understood that stable domestic arrangements tended to produce more stable, and therefore more efficient, workers. As Gramsci states,

> The new industrialism wants monogamy: it wants the man as worker not to squander his nervous energies in the disorderly and stimulating pursuit of occasional sexual satisfaction. The employee who goes to work after a night of 'excess' is no good for his work. The exaltation of passion cannot be reconciled with the timed movements of productive motions connected with the most perfected automatism.
> (pp. 304–305)

In other words, from the perspective of capitalism, it is better that you are married, no matter how miserably, than that you cruise sex clubs until 3.00 am, ending up at the conveyor belt (or desk) at 8.00 am, hungover and bleary-eyed.

Marcuse in turn argued that Western societies are governed by what he called 'the performance principle': an ideal of productivity that asks us to sacrifice a large portion of our pleasure for the sake of the economic machine. And he observed that restricting sexuality to the confines of the marital bed is an effective way to exact this sacrifice. This is how, in Marcuse's words, man's 'erotic performance is brought in line with his societal performance' (p. 46). Along related lines, Foucault proposed that marriage is one of the biopolitical tools of producing compliant subjects – the kinds of subjects who are relatively reliable, relatively responsible and relatively likely to do what the social order would like them to do. Every society has a stake in producing the kinds of personality types that suit its socioeconomic purposes, and marriage has always been a means of moulding such characters, of creating psychological structures that reflect the normative codes of our culture. More generally speaking, Foucault argued that societies invent institutions such as factories, schools, prisons and asylums to guarantee that people can be disciplined into predictable routines, which is why such institutions tend to regulate both mobility and timetables, essentially forcing individuals to conform to confined spaces and the ticking of the clock. Faithful to Foucault's vision, Kipnis asks: 'What current social institution is more enclosed than modern domesticity? What offers greater regulation of movement and time, or more precise surveillance of body and thought to a greater number of individuals?' (p. 93). The answer to this rhetorical question, of course, is that there is no modern institution that tames people more effectively than marriage.

Gay rights vs. queer rebellion

It is against this theoretical backdrop that we can understand a phenomenon that may at first glance seem counterintuitive – namely, that the most prominent queer critics of the last 15 years (for example Michael Warner (1999), Judith Butler (2004), Lee Edelman (2004), Jasbir Puar (2007), Heather Love (2007), Jack Halberstam (2011) and David Eng (2010)) have all, without exception, condemned the mainstream gay and lesbian movement's attempts to secure marriage rights in the USA. Though many of these critics understand that there may be situations where marriage rights are desirable, as, for instance, when one's access to social benefits or one's partner's hospital bed depends on these rights, they see gay marriage as a narrow political agenda that merely reproduces the core values of neoliberal capitalism, including its privileging of one relational modality (marriage) over all others. Social benefits should be granted to everyone regardless of their relationship status, such critics argue. Additionally, they accuse the mainstream LGBTQ movement of pandering to the desires of the most domesticated – and usually the most privileged – members of the gay, lesbian and queer community. From their perspective, what is happening right now is that some well-healed, mostly white gays and lesbians are using marriage as a way to purchase their way into 'normality' at the expense of those who cannot be so easily assimilated: poor queers, racialised queers, gender-variant queers, immigrant queers and so on. In other words, from the queer theoretical viewpoint, gay and lesbian mainstreaming merely intensifies the problem of social marginalisation, so that while some gays and lesbians now 'make it' to dominant culture, others are all the more irrevocably excluded and exploited.

Perhaps most fundamentally, queer theorists question the desire to 'make it' in dominant culture in the first place. That is why they have supplemented their critiques of heteronormativity with fierce critiques of homonormativity, accusing the mainstream gay and lesbian movement of buying into an inherently oppressive system. Among other things, queer theorists problematise the ideals of success, achievement, individualism and self-actualisation that neoliberal capitalism promotes as the route to happiness. They point out that such ideals blind us to structural inequalities such as poverty, racism, sexism and homophobia, which make it impossible for some people to succeed no matter how hard they try. Essentially, if the neoliberal creed tells people that their individual efforts can surmount any and all obstacles, queer critics of neoliberalism emphasise that this creed is just a convenient way to gloss over the fact that some people will never attain the American dream. More specifically, from a queer theoretical perspective, gays and lesbians who agitate for marriage rights are caught up in the tentacles of cruel optimism, deluded in their hope that the patriarchal, state-controlled institution of marriage will make up for the legacies of gay and lesbian abjection.

In many ways we are dealing with a rift that has always complicated progressive politics – namely, the battle between those who want to improve the existing system by making it more inclusive and those who want to blow this system into smithereens and replace it with something completely different. That is, we are dealing with a division between rights-based political approaches on the one hand and more revolutionary approaches on the other: the supporters of gay marriage want equal rights within the system whereas queer critics of gay marriage see marriage as the corrupt foundation of a thoroughly corrupt system. Indeed, queer critics recognise that the LGBTQ movement's attempts to gain entry to a marriage-based system – a system that automatically vilifies those who reject monogamy – threaten to wipe out queer subcultures that have historically been organised around promiscuous, anonymous and fleeting sexual encounters. For many queer critics, the disappearance of such subcultures equals the death of queer culture as such. There are, of course, enclaves of resistance that persist, such as the barebacking communities that Tim Dean (2009) explores in *Unlimited Intimacy*. As he explains, barebackers see risky, promiscuous sex as a way of subverting the normative expectation that we all want to lead long, healthy and reasonable lives – lives bathed in the soft glow of enduring love. Yet the mainstream LGBTQ movement's effectiveness in highjacking the queer agenda is making it increasingly difficult for such resistant communities to survive. Ironically, it is because the LGBTQ movement has managed to make gays and lesbians sound 'just like' straight people, eager to endorse the family values of married monogamy, that it has made such tremendous political strides. Essentially, the gay and lesbian subject has been stripped of their disturbing 'Otherness' in order to make them more palatable to straight society. For many queer critics, this is a short-sighted victory that drastically undermines more radical efforts to gain social justice.

The cult of relationality

What are the implications of this for psychoanalytic and psychotherapeutic contexts? The obvious answer is that to the degree that such contexts valorise monogamy, and to the degree that they perpetuate the idea that enduring relationships are the hallmark of psychic health, they are explicitly supporting a heteronormative and homonormative vision of the good life, thereby damaging the clinical experience of patients who either cannot or do not wish to uphold this vision. Somewhat paradoxically, this problem may be easier to discern in the treatment of singles (queer or straight) than in the treatment of coupled-up gays, lesbians and queers for the simple reason that analysts and therapists, these days, are unlikely to condemn their patients for being queer, whereas the therapeutic cult of relationality can lead them, however subtly, to disparage their single patients for having failed to attain the prize that everyone is assumed to covet: a loving relationship. In this sense, negative attitudes toward singles allow social normativity to persist in seemingly LGBTQ-friendly analytic and therapeutic settings. In saying this, we do not wish to equate the struggles of queers and straight singles, for obviously queer subjects – whether single or not – experience a greater degree of stigmatisation within mainstream society. We are merely calling attention to the fact that in analytic and therapeutic contexts, pro-couple sentiments are one way in which heteronormative notions slip under the radar. And the fact that these notions constitute the crux of homonormativity as well makes it all the more difficult to see them as a continuation of homophobia. Given that many homonormative gays and lesbians use the same rhetoric about the value of loving relationships as therapeutic professionals (queer or straight), it can be hard to recall that this rhetoric does not represent the desires of all queer subjects.

Negative pronouncements about singles are all the more insidious in often being couched as attempts to help people to avert various misfortunes. Some clinicians, for instance, equate singleness with pathological loneliness and social isolation. Consider the following statement by Yalom and Leszcz (2005):

> Contemporary research...documents the pain and the adverse consequences of loneliness. There is, for example, persuasive evidence that the rate for virtually every major cause of death is significantly higher for the lonely, the single, the divorced, and the widowed.

Social isolation is as much a risk factor for early mortality as obvious physical risk factors such as smoking and obesity. (p. 20)

In this stark assessment, 'the lonely' and 'the single' are treated as virtually synonymous. Sue Johnson (2008) in turn writes in *Hold Me Tight* (a primer for couples therapy):

> Historians long ago observed that in the death camps of World War II, the unit of survival was the pair, not the solitary individual. It's long been known, too, that married men and women generally live longer than do their single peers... Loneliness raises blood pressure to the point where the risk of heart attack and stroke is doubled... Emotional isolation is a more dangerous health risk than smoking or high blood pressure. (p. 24)

Here again we witness a facile sliding from the single to the lonely (and emotionally isolated), not to mention the taken-for-granted assumption that coupled people fare better under stress than single people. Finally, Clarke et al. (2010) report in their collection on queer psychology that 'the very limited research in this area tends not to view being single as especially positive, with reports of lesbian and gay male couples having fewer sexual problems and greater well-being than single lesbians and gay men' (pp. 185–186). Such striking statements surely do not go unnoticed by readers – ordinary citizens and therapeutic professionals alike. In Cobb's words, they 'make you want to run to the nearest available partner and pop the question' because they leave readers with the impression 'that social connection is absolutely necessary [and] that a menacing, debilitating feeling of loneliness lurks everywhere' (pp. 15–16).

On the whole, singles in our society, while sometimes envied for their freedom, tend to symbolise the disgrace of undesirability and unhappiness. At worst, singleness is a reviled state of being; at best, it is, as Cobb observes, 'a conundrum to be solved by coupling off, and as soon as possible' (p. 4). Ultimately, Cobb continues, 'no one is *really* supposed to be single': 'there are no *real* single people out there – they're all just waiting for the chance to find that special someone, sometime soon' (p. 5). That is, our culture is so strongly oriented towards enduring intimate relationships that being single is seen as a transitory state, something to be overcome rather than something to be enjoyed for its own distinctive rewards. In addition, as Bella DePaulo (2006), who has written extensively about the ways in which singles are shunned in our society, remarks, now that increasing numbers of people no longer see marriage as an essential component of their lives, our culture is engaged in a frantic effort to 'instill in an entire populace the unshakeable belief that marriage is exactly what it is not: utterly and uniquely transformational' (p. 13). According to this mythology, DePaulo asserts, marriage

> transforms the immature single person into a mature spouse. It creates a sense of commitment, sacrifice, and selflessness where there was none before. It is the one true place where intimacy and loyalty can be nurtured and sustained. It transforms a serious sexual partnership from a tryout to the real thing. (p. 13)

Along similar lines, Cobb maintains that, in our cultural imagination, marriage is supposed to end 'our tragic twists and turns, nullifying all the bad feelings of misunderstanding and misconnection that preceded it' (p. 13).

The idealisation of marriage as a 'cure' for the pathology of singleness can infiltrate clinical discussions with frightening ease. For example, Johnson (2008) writes in the introduction to *Hold Me Tight*:

> My response to my parents' pain was to vow never to get married. Romantic love was, I decided, an illusion and a trap. I was better off on my own, free and unfettered. But then, of course, I fell in love and married. Love pulled me in even as I pushed it away. (p. 3)

We are used to seeing such storylines in romantic comedies, but when they are articulated by clinical 'experts' they contribute to the naturalisation of marriage as the only genuinely valid way to go about our love lives. Johnson in fact explicitly relies on naturalised evolutionary accounts of love, arguing that the 'drive to emotionally attach...is as basic to life, health, and happiness as the drives for food, shelter, or sex. We need emotional attachments with a few irreplaceable others to be physically and mentally healthy – to survive' (p. 15). Against overwhelming evidence regarding the socially constructed character of our romantic ideals, she here insists on portraying long-term coupling as a quasibiological human need. No wonder, then, that she claims that therapy is for those 'seeking a lifetime of love' (p. 8). More specifically, therapy – for the patient – involves admitting 'that you are emotionally attached to and dependent on your partner in much the same way that a child is on a parent for nurturing, soothing, and protection' (p. 7).

In this manner, Johnson fans the common conception that – as DePaulo and Morris (2005) mockingly put it – 'people without a stable sexual relationship are wandering adrift with open wounds and shivering in their sleep' (p. 75). Indeed, one has to wonder about the ideological forces that figure into Johnson's efforts to make singles bear the burden of being labelled as lonely outcasts when it is obvious to anyone with a degree of critical discernment that many married people are terribly, heartbreakingly lonely.

Working for love

To the extent that we continue to view love as an 'essential nutrient' that our cells yearn for – as Barbara Fredrickson (2013: 4) describes it – we will find it difficult to envision alternative versions of the good life, alternative happiness scripts. This naturalisation of love may, moreover, explain the wide acceptance of the social mantra which dictates that good relationships require a great deal of work. Precisely because so many people believe that enduring relationships are the only 'natural' way to go about their love lives, many are willing to work at their ailing relationships to an almost irrational degree – and this is the case even though a moment of reflection would reveal that whatever is 'natural' should not require so much manipulation. Those who dare to complain about the state of their marriages are often met with a wall of rhetoric along the lines of 'everyone has problems', 'no one said it would be easy', 'it could be worse – count your blessings' or 'marriage takes hard work'. This last notion – that marriage takes hard work – has become so prevalent that it is these days almost impossible to talk about marriage without conjuring up the language of mines, factories and sweatshops. 'Yes, we all know that Good Marriages Take Work', Kipnis quips: 'we've been well tutored in the catechism of labor-intensive intimacy. Work, work, work: given all the heavy lifting required, what's the difference between work and "after work" again? Work/home, office/bedroom: are you ever *not* on the clock?' (p. 18).

We 'work at' intimacy, at getting along, at not getting on each other's nerves, at doing what we are supposed to do, at not doing what we are not supposed to do and so on. Indeed, as Kipnis observes, one of the incredible feats of our social order is to make 'working for love' (p. 20) sound admirable – as the thing we should all want to do. Many of us take it for granted that 'grown-up' love is going to be a labour-intensive enterprise. We even elevate this type of love, a 'love' that feels like an endless boot camp, over less permanent but more vitalising affairs. Yet who is to say that an enduring marriage that offers security but no passion is better than a dozen short-lived but ardent affairs? Who is to say that a deep emotional connection to a life partner is healthier than a string of anonymous sexual encounters at various queer venues? Might there be something more troubling about the desperate quest for constant connection that characterises some married people than there is about the attempts of singles (queer or straight) to avoid lethal forms of relationality? Why is the single person who contently dwells within solitude deemed to be more distressed than the married person who cannot tolerate their spouse's bouts of unavailability? And, for heaven's sake, why do so many of us accept the idea that there is something laudatory, even noble, about the endless effort that we put into relationships that are clearly past their expiration date?

Clinical settings may be particularly prone to accepting the Protestant work ethic as their default approach to relationships. After all, if the patient is not working to improve their relationship – or at least working through the psychic knots that are keeping them from having a rewarding relationship – what is there left to do? Starting to imagine a viable answer may require sacrificing the cult of relationality; it may require that analysts and therapists not only recognise a variety of legitimate relational modes but also entertain the possibility that, for some patients, non-relational ways of living may be equally or even more important.

There is also something to be said for acknowledging that people in our society tend to be overly invested in love to begin with. Many are so centred on relationships that they neglect other aspects of life, with the result that a clinical focus on relationality may merely further impoverish them. Nor is it always to the benefit of patients to celebrate the healing potential of love – as Johnson, for instance, does – for doing so drastically underestimates the destructive frequencies of Eros; it contributes to the deluge of sugar-coated images of love that our society throws at us in an attempt to convince us that love is more benign than it actually is (see Ruti 2011). Against this backdrop, it might be productive to remind everyone – clinicians and patients alike – that the ever-so-seductive notion of a 'soul mate' may merely be a means of obscuring the utter naïvety of handing over the key to one's wellbeing to another person. We are not saying that people should not fall in love – they will undoubtedly continue to do so. But it seems to us that those who have a realistic sense of love's intrinsically unreliable nature – and those who see relationships as merely one element of the rich tapestry of their lives – are better protected than those who have been lulled into false complacency about the power of love to grant everlasting happiness. Working for love may sometimes make sense, but only if it is accompanied by the willingness to work for other things as well. And sometimes it is nothing but a dreadful waste of emotional resources that could be better spent elsewhere – an instance of cruel optimism and therefore an obstacle to flourishing.

Conclusion

Rachel Hare-Mustin (1997) reminds us that clinical encounters often take place in a figurative 'mirrored room' that upholds dominant discourses 'through discursive practices that reflect and reenact the traditions, power relations, and institutions of the society' (p. 558). In this chapter we have attempted to illustrate that insofar as clinicians – consciously or unconsciously – endorse our society's hegemonic happiness scripts, they can pathologise queer and single patients, thereby denying such patients a constructive therapeutic experience. As Lyndsey Moon (2008) observes, 'therapy, it has to be said, has not been queered, despite there being much to query!' (p. 1). Yet Moon correctly perceives that queer theory holds a great deal of potential for unsettling conventional analytic and therapeutic practices because it demands a serious rethinking of relationality. We would like to add that queer theory also offers clinicians the perhaps even more fundamental insight that socially defiant subjects – which is what non-heteronormative and non-homonormative subjects often deliberately are – may not, generally speaking, be interested in our society's success narratives. Judith (Jack) Halberstam's *The Queer Art of Failure* (2011), for instance, counters the neoliberal capitalist emphasis on success narratives with narratives of utter failure, including stories of ignorance, forgetfulness and losing one's way. If neoliberal capitalism asks us not only to work hard at our jobs but to tirelessly, and narcissistically, work on ourselves, Halberstam proposes that our various failures can be read as a form of rebellion, of opting out of the rat race. As Halberstam states,

> We might read *failure*, for example, as a refusal of mastery, a critique of the intuitive connections within capitalism between success and profit... Let's leave success and its achievements to the Republicans, to the corporate managers of the world, to the winners of reality TV shows, to married couples, to SUV drivers (pp. 11–12, 120).

We wonder, in closing, what it would mean for analysts and therapists to take seriously this queer plea to embrace failure. What would it mean, for example, to stop trying to fix the lapses of love?

References

Ahmed, S. (2010) *The Promise of Happiness*. Durham, NC: Duke University Press.
Berlant, L. (2011) *Cruel Optimism*. Durham, NC: Duke University Press.
Butler, J. (1997) *The Psychic Life of Power: Theories in Subjection*. Stanford: Stanford University Press.
Butler, J. (2004) *Undoing Gender*. New York: Routledge.
Clarke, V., Ellis, S., Peel, E. and Riggs, D. (2010) *Lesbian, Gay, Bisexual, Trans, and Queer Psychology: An Introduction*. New York: Cambridge University Press.
Cobb, M. (2012) *Single: Arguments for the Uncoupled*. New York: New York University Press.
Dean, T. (2009) *Unlimited Intimacy: Reflections on the Subculture of Barebacking*. Chicago: University of Chicago Press.
DePaulo, B. (2006) *Singled Out: How Singles Are Stereotyped, Stigmatized, and Ignored, and Still Live Happily Ever After*. New York: St. Martin's Press.
DePaulo, B. and Morris, W. (2005) 'Singles in Society and in Science', *Psychological Inquiry*, 16:2/3, 57–83.
Edelman, L. (2004) *No Future: Queer Theory and the Death Drive*. Durham, NC: Duke University Press.
Eng, D. (2010) *The Feeling of Kinship: Queer Liberalism and the Racialization of Intimacy*. Durham, NC: Duke University Press.
Foucault, M. (1978–1979) *The Birth of Biopolitics: Lectures at the Collège de France, 1978–1979*. New York: Picador, 2010.
Fredrickson, B. (2013) *Love 2.0: How Our Supreme Emotion Affects Everything We Feel, Think, Do, and Become*. New York: Penguin Books.
Gramsci, A. (1930) *Selections from the Prison Notebooks*, edited by Q. Hoare and G. Nowell Smith. New York: International Publishers, 2010.
Halberstam, J. (2011) *The Queer Art of Failure*. Durham, NC: Duke University Press.
Hare-Mustin, R. (1997) 'Discourse in the mirrored room: A postmodern analysis of therapy', in M. Gergen and S. Davis (eds.) *Toward a New Psychology of Gender*. New York: Routledge, pp. 553–574.
Johnson, S. (2008) *Hold Me Tight: Seven Conversations for a Lifetime of Love*. New York: Little, Brown, and Company.
Kipnis, L. (2003) *Against Love: A Polemic*. New York: Vintage.
Love, H. (2007) *Feeling Backward: Loss and the Politics of Queer History*. Cambridge: Harvard University Press.
Marcuse, H. (1955) *Eros and Civilization: A Philosophical Inquiry into Freud*. Boston: Beacon Press.
Moon, L. (ed.) (2008) 'Introduction: Queer(y)ing a psychosocial approach to sex, sexuality and gender in therapeutic settings', in *Feeling Queer or Queer Feelings? Radical Approaches to Counselling Sex, Sexualities, and Genders*. New York: Routledge, 1–6.

Puar, J. (2007) *Terrorist Assemblages: Homonationalism in Queer Times*. Durham, NC: Duke University Press.
Ruti, M. (2011) *The Summons of Love*. New York: Columbia University Press.
Warner, M. (1999) *The Trouble with Normal: Sex, Politics, and the Ethics of a Queer Life*. New York: Free Press.
Yalom, I. and Leszcz, M. (2005) *The Theory and Practice of Group Psychotherapy*. New York: Basic Books.

8
Relating to People as Revolutionaries

Lois Holzman

What do you do in your moments of despair upon hearing or seeing the latest horror that human beings have inflicted upon each other – in your own neighbourhood or thousands of miles away from it? Sometimes, what happens with me is that a certain phrase or two will 'pop into my head' and ground me, by which I mean allow me to locate the horrific events in the contradictory totality of human history and its dialectic with human society, in the human capacity to continuously overthrow (recreate) that which we have created. One of these phrases is a quote from the Soviet psychologist Lev Vygotsky: 'A revolution solves only those tasks raised by history' (Vygotsky, quoted in frontispiece, Levitin 1982). Another is from French cultural theorist Sylvère Lotringer: 'One does not cure neurosis, one changes a society which cannot do without it' (1977). And a third was spoken by Dr Martin Luther King Jr: 'The salvation of our world lies in the hands of the maladjusted' (King 1956). Each of these propositions speaks to me in the performative: 'Don't mourn, organize!' They convey not a critical but a practical-critical approach to the therapy professions.

In 2003, Fred Newman and I wrote an article entitled 'All power to the developing', which appeared in *Annual Review of Critical Psychology*. There we presented a picture of our practical-critical psychotherapy by foregrounding its debt to Marx's radical humanism – by which we meant his insistence on the sociality of human beings and, in particular, his conception of revolutionary activity. In our discussion of social therapy, which was created by Newman in the 1970s, we focused on its activity of relating to all people as revolutionaries:

> Relating to patients as revolutionaries entails relating to them as world historic in everyday, mundane matters, that is, as social

beings engaged in the life/history-making process of always *becoming* (assimilating 'all the wealth of previous development'). For what is history/making history if it is not the dialectic what is/what is becoming?

(Newman and Holzman 2003: 11)

This feature of social therapy was first articulated in a 1986 speech by Newman to the Congress of the Interamerican Society of Psychology, held in the Karl Marx Theater in Havana, Cuba. The following quote says more of what we mean by relating as revolutionaries:

> We speak of social therapy as revolution for non-revolutionaries. This radical Marxist conception – that the fundamental or essential human characteristic is being capable of carrying out revolutionary activity (what Marx calls practical-critical activity) – that's the foundation of anything which can be called or should be called a Marxist psychology. Ours is a radical insistence that we not accommodate reactionary society by relating to people – *any* people – as anything but revolutionaries.
>
> (Newman 1991: 15; Newman and Holzman 2003: 11–12)

It is now 2014, nearly 30 years since the Havana speech and more than a decade since our aforementioned article appeared. Over these years, Newman and I continued to work together until he passed away in 2011 – organising, writing and expanding social therapy practices as well as other environments and activities that relate to people as revolutionaries. The methodology of social therapy (social therapeutics) has broadened to education, healthcare, youth work and organisational development. In the past decade the chasm that existed between theoretical critical psychology and alternative practices in psychology and psychotherapy has begun to blur. New critical practices have developed and, to some extent, this has advanced the overall substance and quality of the intellectual conversation. The debate continues, but critique and practice are now closer together. At the same time, the bureaucracy and institutionalisation of the helping professions of psychology, counselling, social work, psychiatry and psychotherapy have become more oppressive, and harder and harder to get around. The medical and natural science models of understanding and relating to human beings are so dominant that non-mainstream approaches are rarely taught in universities or professional schools and the options available to those seeking help are becoming more and more limited. The work continues.

This article is an invitation to go beyond the critical to create practical-critical psychotherapy and counselling approaches.

Origins of social therapy

Social therapy originated in the 1970s as part of the social-cultural change movements of the time, which tied the 'personal' to the political. It was developed by a community of activists who began by working in the poorest communities of New York City and who have since gone on to organise middle-class and wealthy people to support poor people to develop and provide leadership to the process of positive social change, free of government, corporate or university dependence. In this organising process, new kinds of relationship are created between rich and poor, and all develop emotionally, socially and culturally. This organising has led to international training in the social therapeutic methodology, the development of out-of-school youth programmes, a free-of-charge developmental learning centre for inner-city youth and adults, a political theatre, a research and training centre, an emergent international movement of performance activists, independent electoral campaigns, and partnerships with organisations on a national and an international stage. With this significant quantitative and qualitative expansion over the decades, the inseparability of human development from community development has become more and more obvious.

Central to all of the activities, organisations and projects of this activist community is an understanding of the necessity of affording opportunities for all people to engage in the practical-critical activity of creating their own development – in other words, of relating to people as revolutionaries. The mode of relating is performatory, grounded in the discovery that performing (as the 'always becoming' activity) is what allows human beings to develop beyond instinctual and socially patterned behaviour.

Similar to other new psychologies that were springing up at the time, social therapy was ideology-based – in the belief that living under capitalism makes people emotionally sick and in the hope that therapy could be a tool in the service of progressive politics. Like the radical therapies of the 1970s, social therapy engaged the authoritarianism, sexism, racism, classism and homophobia of traditional psychotherapy. But social therapy's unique feature, even in its earliest years, was its engagement with the philosophical underpinnings of psychology and psychotherapy. It rejected explanation, interpretation, the notion of an inner Self that therapists and clients need to delve into, and other dualistic and problematic foundations of traditional psychology. These are characteristics of what are now known as postmodern psychologies (for example Gergen 1991; Gergen and Gergen 2012; Holzman and Morss 2000; Kvale 1992). As an emerging practical-critical epistemological and ontological critique, social therapy was influenced by Newman's study of Marxian dialectics and the philosophy of science and language (Wittgenstein's work in particular), and my study of human development, psycholinguistics and Vygotsky, and work as a qualitative researcher. Their methodological innovations helped us to see the potential for ordinary people to effect radical social change and to better understand the subjective constraints that need to be engaged so as to actualise this potential (for example Holzman 2006; Newman and Holzman 2006/1996, 2003). In particular, we read Marx and Vygotsky as valuable contributors to dissolving the dualist gap between Self and world, between thought and language, between who we are and who we are becoming, and between theory and practice, in such a way that it becomes possible to approach human beings as activists and activity-ists, not as knowers and perceivers.

Unpacking Marx

In actualising Marx's dialectic understanding of history/making history in the service of supporting people to perform as revolutionaries, we had to 'postmodernise Marx'. Ironically, we find the seeds for such postmodernisation in Marx's own work (his earliest, most philosophical writings rather than his later work on political economy). He was no psychologist and didn't particularly address psychological issues, but he was nevertheless a fine critical psychologist. In the *Economic and Philosophical Manuscripts* and *The German Ideology*, for example, he speaks clearly about the social nature – that is the ontology – of human activity and of human development:

> *as* society itself produces *man* as *man*, so it is *produced* by him. Activity and mind are social in their content as well as in their *origin*; they are *social activity* and *social* mind.
> (Marx 1967: 129)

This is as clear a rejection of the dualisms of the mental and the physical, thought and action, and the individual and the social upon which psychology is based as I have ever read.

We have further shown that private property can be abolished only on condition of an all-round development of individuals, because the existing character of intercourse and productive forces is an all-round one, and only individuals that are developing in an all-round fashion can appropriate them, i.e., can turn them into free manifestations of their lives.

(Marx and Engels 1974: 117)

Here we have a rejection of the psychological understanding of human development and the field of psychology's claim to investigate and come to understand it. Development does not happen to us, unfolding in a predetermined progression of stages towards some end. For Marx, development is 'all-round'. All-round development is revolutionary, a practical-critical activity. This social, communal and reconstructive activity of human beings exercising their power to transform the current state of things is what makes individual and species development possible (Holzman 2009; Newman and Holzman 2014/1993, 2003).

These passages from Marx presage contemporary postmodern concerns with psychological and psychotherapeutic methods that are premised on individuals – that is, entities which exist in social surrounds but are not themselves social; and development as a characteristic of such entities, specifically, of particular aspects or parts of such entities.

Social therapy is an actualisation of the above critique. First, its focus, meaning the work of the therapist and the group, no matter the size – that is, a group of 2 (therapist and client) or a group of 30 – is the activity of the social unit developing. By engaging in this new kind of activity of creating their group, people are simultaneously creating who they are and who they are becoming, emotionally speaking. Such a focus on development is rare in the psychotherapy world, which focuses on 'curing' the individual, relieving their symptoms, or some other form of correction of something presumed to be internally faulty and causing problematic outward manifestations.

Second, emotions in social therapy are not understood as products or possessions of individuals or as something internal that is made manifest in outward behaviour, but rather as social, relational activity ('social activity and social mind'). In social therapy, the group is working to exercise its power to overthrow – to the extent that is possible under current political, economic and sociocultural conditions – the alienation and commodification necessary for everyday life, including the professional and everyday psychological understanding of what emotions are and where they 'reside'.

Social therapy is most often conducted in groups, and it is not the individual members of the group but the group itself that is the therapeutic unit. This is different from most group therapies, in which the group serves as a context for the therapist to help individuals with their emotional problems. Clients who come together to form a social therapy group are given the task of creating their group as an environment in which they can get help. This group activity is a collective, practical challenge to the assumption that the way in which people get therapeutic help is to relate to themselves and be related to by others as individuals, complete with problems and with inner selves.

In the US-based centres for social therapy, groups range in size from 8 to 30 people, a mix of women and men of varying ages, ethnicities, sexual orientations, class backgrounds and economic status, professions and 'presenting problems'. This heterogeneity is designed to challenge people's notion of a fixed identity (for example based on gender, ethnicity, diagnostic label, or 'That's the kind of person I am'), and to maximise the diversity of 'material' that the group has to create with. Group sessions are typically 90 minutes long and meetings are weekly on an ongoing basis. Some group members remain for years, others months; people leave and new members join. The therapeutic environment and its potential 'building material' are thus in continuous flux.

In a sense, each social therapy group is working to relocate itself in history while remaining in society. For we all live in that dialectic. But we don't experience it. Most people do not experience their world historicalness; they experience only their societal location (temporal, spatial, cultural, etc.). Our social identities are versions of the many ways there are to be alienated, commodified, separated and objectified. Our historical identity is as revolutionaries, as social, cultural, historical creators of something new out of what exists.

The many hundreds of practitioners trained in social therapy who work in institutionalised settings modify their practices accordingly. Additionally, in other countries, social therapy is practised in a structure and manner that is coherent with the specifics of the given cultural environment.

Vygotsky's contribution

Vygotsky has been invaluable to our understanding of the contemporary relevance of Marx's radical historical humanism just discussed, and to the continued development of our practical-critical psychotherapy (Holzman 2009, 2013; Newman and Holzman 2014/1993). During the revolutionary times of the early twentieth century when both the first communist state and the new discipline of psychology were beginning, Vygotsky saw his task as that of having to create a new kind of method (method as dialectical activity) in order to study psychological activity and create a new psychology that would be coherent with and support the development of a new kind of society: 'The search for method becomes one of the most important problems of the entire enterprise of understanding the uniquely human forms of psychological activity. In this case, the method is simultaneously prerequisite and product, the tool and the result of the study' (Vygotsky 1978: 65).

Here Vygotsky is suggesting a radical break with the accepted scientific paradigm in which method is a tool that is applied and yields results. There, the relation between tool and result is linear, instrumental and dualistic (coined 'tool for result methodology' in Newman and Holzman 2014/1993). Vygotsky's 'search' is a qualitatively different conception of method – not a tool to be applied but an activity that generates both tool and result at the same time and as a continuous process. Tool and result are not dualistically separated; neither are they the same or one thing. Rather, they are elements of a dialectical unity/totality/whole. Method to be practiced, not applied, is what Vygotsky was advocating. To capture the dialectical relationship of this new conception, Newman and I called this 'tool-and-result methodology' (Newman and Holzman 2014/1993). Importantly, this new conception of method is neither objective nor subjective but something outside that dualistic box.

In addition to proposing a qualitatively new way to study human life, Vygotsky is pointing to the dialectical nature of human development and how to reinitiate it if it has been stopped. For human beings are not only tool-users but also tool-makers. We do not merely respond to stimuli, acquire societally determined and useful skills, and adapt to the determining environment. The uniqueness of human social life is that we ourselves transform the determining circumstances. Human development is not an individual accomplishment but a sociocultural activity.

Understanding Vygotsky's conception of method as dialectical tool-and-result provided a new way of seeing social therapy – namely, as the group's activity of creating itself as the tool-and-result of their (becoming) emotional development. We identified Vygotsky as a forerunner to 'a new psychology of becoming', in which people experience the social nature of their existence and the power of collective creative activity in the process of making new tools(-and-results) for growth (Holzman 2009). Relating to people as revolutionaries is akin, we came to believe, to relating to them as tool-and-result-makers/methodologists/practical-critical dialecticians.

Further Vygotskian insights followed from this methodological one. For example, his understanding of the role of play in early childhood remains today unique and uniquely dialectical: 'In play a child always behaves beyond his average age, above his daily behavior; in play it is as though he were a head taller than himself' (Vygotsky 1978: 102). We took this as a metaphor for the being/becoming dialectic of human development and expanded it to adolescence and adulthood. Recognising that performers on stage are also simultaneously who they are and the characters that they are playing, we came to understand performance as a Vygotskian kind of play, and to understand that human beings perform our development. This became not only the topic of our subsequent investigations and writings but simultaneously the direction that our practices and those of our colleagues took in therapy as well as in educational, organisational and cultural settings (Friedman 2011; Holzman 1997, 2009; Holzman and Newman 2012; Lobman and O'Neill 2011; Martinez 2011; Newman and Holzman 1997, 2006/1996).

In order for social therapy participants to create their therapy group and simultaneously create new emotional activity, they must perform therapy. Such an ensemble performance is the difficult work/play of engaging in the activity of speaking and creating conversation as transformative of 'saying what's on your mind'. Here, Vygotsky's challenge to the received wisdom that language expresses thought was essential: 'Speech does not merely serve as the expression of developed thought. Thought is restructured as it is transformed into speech. Thought is not expressed but completed in the word' (Vygotsky 1987: 251). We synthesised this instance of Vygotsky's dialectical understanding of human activity with that of Wittgenstein, taking Vygotsky's 'speaking completing thinking' as a Wittgensteinian 'form of life' (Wittgenstein 1958: 11, para. 23). We expanded the concept of 'completion' to other people; others could 'complete' for you. Very young children become speakers of a language with and through others, and we posited that caregivers 'complete' babbling babies, and that the babies creatively imitate their completers.

We drew out the implications of this Vygotskian insight throughout the lifespan and concluded that the human ability to create with language – to complete, and be completed by, others – can be, for adults as well as for very young children, a continuous process of creating who we are becoming. In terms of therapy, it suggests that speaking about 'what's going on for you' is therapeutic because and to the extent that it is a socially completive activity and not a transmittal of so-called private states of mind. Thus the social therapist's task is to support the group in practising method so as to relate to emotional talk relationally and activistically rather than individualistically and representationally. In this process people experience that they can create, and that developing comes from participating in the process of building the groups in which one functions (Holzman 2009; Holzman and Newman 2012).

The focus of therapy is no longer the individuated Self who discovers deeper insights into their consciousness. The focus has become the collective that is engaged in the continuous activity of creating a new social unit. The typical therapeutic question – 'How is each individual doing?' – becomes 'How well is the group performing its activity?' This shift from the individual to the group reorganises what is traditionally related to as a dualistic and antagonistic relationship between individual and group into a dialectical one. Mainstream psychology has tended to negate the group or reduce the group to the individual. Mainstream Marxism has tended to negate the individual or reduce the individual to the group. However, recognising the 'groupness' of human life does not inevitably negate individuals. The social therapy group is producing something collectively and, as with many life activities, individual members contribute in different ways and to differing degrees. Focusing on how the group is performing its activity does not preclude seeing individuals: one can see and relate to both simultaneously.

In terms of Vygotsky's understanding of play, social therapy can be understood as a playful activity in the 'head taller' sense. The adult clients are being supported by the therapists to do what is beyond them – to create new ways of speaking and listening to each other, and new ways to understand and relate to talk and to emotionality. By their language play, they are creating new performances of themselves as a way out of the rigidified roles, patterns and identities that cause so much emotional pain.

Areas to explore (practical-)critically

As a practical-critical process ontology, social therapeutic group activity raises some questions that those working to develop critical psychotherapy might wish to explore, as described below.

Individual therapy

What is the purpose of individual therapy? If the unit of study is the group creating itself, and the group activity is the tool-and-result practice of reconstructing Marx's species identity/history-making, then perhaps the entity experiencing distress (an individual client) need not be the focus of the therapy. Perhaps individuals need to be organised as social units in order to carry out the task of developing. This is, after all, the case for countless other human endeavours in which people become organised as social units to get a specific job done. (Manufacturing, most team sports, theatrical and other performance activities – not to mention the military – come immediately to mind as examples.)

Alienation

A second area for exploration is alienation. The alienation that Marx (1974) describes – relating to the products of production severed from their producers and from the process of their production (i.e. as commodities) – is not limited to smartphones, cars and Big Macs, not even for Marx: 'Production does not only produce man as a *commodity*, the *human commodity*, man in the form of a *commodity*; in conformity with this situation it produces him as a *mentally* and *physically dehumanized* being' (Marx 1967: 111). It has become the normal way of seeing and relating to everything in contemporary Western (and, increasingly, global) culture. People relate to their lives, their relationships, their feelings, their culture and so on as things, torn away from the process of their creation and from their creators. Such 'thingification' is a major factor in people's emotional problems, but rarely spoken about by psychotherapists as something that is engaged in their practices.

However, if, following Marx, we are commodified and alienated individuals, then any transformative social change necessitates decommodifying and de-alienating such human 'products' through a positive and constructive process of producing sociality and regaining humanity. Vygotsky's psychology of being/becoming can be employed (as it has in social therapy) to decommodify and de-alienate, through a reconstruction-deconstruction of the ontology of modernist psychology in which human beings are understood to be only who we are (hardly world historic, in Marx's sense). In social therapy's process ontology, human beings are both who we are and who we are becoming. And who we are becoming is creators of tools(-and-results) that can continuously transform mundane specific life practices (including those that produce alienation) into new forms of life. Creating these new kinds of tool is the becoming activity of creating/giving expression to our sociality and historicity as revolutionaries.

Power

Finally, we would do well to rethink how we understand and speak of power. Critical psychologists (and educators, economists and...) speak of 'power' as a pejorative, something bad or even evil, the property of those who rule. Instances of this abound: this book's editors, as one example, speak of 'the exercise of power' in the negative. When and how did 'power' lose its revolutionary meaning? What happened to 'power to the people'? What does it mean to 'empower people' if the 'exercise of power' is to be avoided? But these are merely different uses of 'power' in different contexts, you might be thinking. Yes, they are. And more. To relate to people as revolutionaries (engaged in 'all-round development') these multiple meanings need to be deconstructed.

A starting point is to see power in its sociopolitical sense as distinguished from authority – power being created from the bottom and authority being imposed from the top. From this vantage point, being 'in power' and 'exercising power' are as different as can be. Newman and I drew out the implications of the power/authority dialectic as it is manifest psychologically as we argued that the activity of power is a practical-critical, revolutionary activity:

> But being 'in power' (somewhat ironically) does not at all involve the activity of power. It is, rather, the commodification of power (labor power) into authority. And while commodities can be sold, they do not develop; they are consumed. Authority stifles growth. It is not a necessary evil. It is an unnecessary evil. What is necessary for development is the activity of power, the exercise of power, the development of power by the many – collectively, democratically and creatively. It is the work of the laborer, Marx teaches us, that creates value (Marx 1967). It is the authoritarian commodification of this process that yields a *realization* of this value which, in turn, maintains the authority of the owners of the means of production.
>
> But authority (vs. power) goes well beyond the economic sphere. It is constantly present, under capitalism, in the psychological sphere. The human capacity to authoritarianly commodify oneself is in constant psychological struggle with the human desire and capacity to exercise power *without commodification*, i.e., freely.
>
> (Holzman and Newman 2004: 75)

'Authoritarian commodification' aptly describes professional, institutionalized psychotherapy, counselling and social work in the USA and, increasingly, elsewhere. It is epitomised by the nearly universal necessity of a DSM or *International Classification of Diseases* diagnosis in order to help or be helped. In the face of such dehumanising by authority, the practical-critical practice of social therapy is one method of supporting people to exercise power without commodification. It is this psychological struggle that I urge critical psychotherapy and counselling to support in their work with clients.

References

Friedman, D. (2011) 'Good-bye ideology, hello performance', *Topoi: An International Review of Philosophy*, 30:2, 125–35.
Gergen, K. (1991) *The Saturated Self: Dilemmas of Identity in Contemporary Life*. New York: Basic Books.
Gergen, M.M. and Gergen, K.J. (2012) *Playing with Purpose: Adventures in Performative Social Science*. Walnut Creek, CA: Left Coast Press.
Holzman, L. (1997). *Schools for Growth: Radical Alternatives to Current Educational Models*. Mahwah, NJ: Lawrence Erlbaum.
Holzman, L. (2006) 'Activating postmodernism', *Theory & Psychology*, 16(1): 109, 123.
Holzman, L. (2009) *Vygotsky at Work and Play*. London and New York: Routledge.
Holzman, L. (2013) 'Critical psychology, philosophy and social therapy', *Human Studies*, 36(4): 471–489. [Chinese translation, 2013, in Bo Wang (ed.) *Special Issue of Register of Critical Theory of Society: Critical Psychology*. Nanjing: Jiangsu People's Publishing House.]
Holzman L. and Morss, J.R. (eds.) (2000) *Postmodern Psychologies, Societal Practice, and Political Life*. New York: Psychology Press.
Holzman, L. and Newman, F. with Strong, T. (2004) 'Power, authority and pointless activity: The developmental discourse of social therapy', in T. Strong and D. Paré (eds.) *Furthering Talk: Advances in Discursive Therapies*. New York: Kluwer Academic, 73–86.
Holzman, L. and Newman, F. (2012) 'Activity and performance (and their discourses) in social therapeutic practice', in A. Lock and T. Strong (eds.) *Discursive Perspectives in Therapeutic Practice*. Oxford: Oxford University Press, 184–195.
King, Dr. M.L. Jr. (1956) 27 June 1956 address to the Annual Convention of the NAACP in San Francisco. http://www.mindfreedom.org/kb/mental-healthglobal/iaacm/MLK-on-IAACM. Accessed 24 July 2014.
Kvale, S. (1992) *Psychology and Postmodernism*. Thousand Oaks, CA: Sage.
Levitin, K. (1982) *One Is Not Born a Personality: Profiles of Soviet Education Psychologists*. Moscow: Progress Publishers.
Lobman, C. and O'Neill, B. (eds.) (2011) *Play and Performance, Vol. 11, Play & Culture Studies*. New York: University Press of America.
Lotringer, S. (1977) 'Libido unbound: The politics of schizophrenia', *Semiotexte*, II:3, 7.
Martinez, J.E. (2011) *A Performatory Approach to Teaching, Learning and Technology*. Rotterdam, The Netherlands: Sense Publishers.

Marx, K. (1967) 'Economic and philosophical manuscripts', in E. Fromm (ed.) *Marx's Concept of Man*. New York: Frederick Ungar Publishing Co, 90–196.

Marx, K. (1974) 'Theses on Feuerbach', in K. Marx and F. Engels (eds.) *The German Ideology*. New York: International Publishers, 121–123.

Marx, K. and Engels, F. (1974) *The German Ideology*. New York: International Publishers.

Newman, F. (1991) 'The patient as revolutionary' in F. Newman (ed.) *The Myth of Psychology*. New York: Castillo International, 3–15.

Newman, F. and Holzman, L. (1997) *The End of Knowing: A New Developmental Way of Learning*. London: Routledge.

Newman, F. and Holzman, L. (2003) 'All power to the developing!', *Annual Review of Critical Psychology*, 3: 8–23.

Newman, F. and Holzman, L. (2006/1996) *Unscientific Psychology: A Cultural Performatory Approach to Understanding Human Life*. Lincoln, NE: iUniverse Inc. (originally published Westport, CT: Praeger).

Newman, F. and Holzman, L. (2014/1993) *Lev Vygotsky: Revolutionary Scientist*. London: Routledge.

Vygotsky, L.S. (1978) *Mind in Society*. Cambridge: Harvard University Press.

Vygotsky, L.S. (1987) *The Collected Works of L.S. Vygotsky, Vol. 1*. New York: Plenum.

Wittgenstein L. (1958) *Philosophical Investigations*. New York: Palgrave Macmillan.

9
Work in Contemporary Capitalism
Michael Rustin

Historical introduction

It might be as well to begin with a historical sketch, to situate the topic of work in a larger context than that of immediate preoccupations.

In the ancient world (including that of Greece and Rome, which has had most influence on modernity), work was undertaken largely by slaves, and was therefore accorded little moral value. Ancient societies were not economically or technologically dynamic, for the most part, so the idea that work might be an essential means of social improvement or human transformation was scarcely considered. Questions raised by the great ancient philosophers, such as Plato and Aristotle, on the nature of the good life and the good society for the most part paid little attention to labour as such. The cultivation of the mind and body, the activities of political life and (in some societies, such as Sparta and imperial Rome) the capabilities necessary for war were far more important as sources of value. Physical labour was what cultivated men (women did not come into the equation) avoided wherever possible as a mark of their superior social status.

Hannah Arendt (1959) in her classic book *The Human Condition* on the whole follows ancient writers in assigning primary value to the political life (*vita active*), and to a lesser extent the contemplative life (*vita contempliva*), over both menial forms of labour oriented to subsistence (*homo laborans*) and those forms of labour through which objects of worth are designed and made (*homo faber*).

In rural medieval society, labour was also assigned little value. The soil was tilled by serfs, while the high places in the social hierarchy were occupied by warriors (knights), monks or priests. Castles, churches and monasteries were the high-value sites in these societies. The development of cities brought changes, as skilled artisanal production grew in its importance, with exchange taking place through trade routes, markets and fairs, sometimes of international scope. It is obvious that high qualities of work, involving great artisanal skills, were achieved in medieval craftsmanship, as we see in the fields of architecture, textiles, statuary and illustration, even machines. Such labour and exchange were organised through guilds, organisations of producers set up to establish standards of production, and to support the material and social wellbeing of their members, no doubt in large measure by the exclusion of competitors. The aesthetic and social values embodied in the guild system became a positive point of reference for critics of the degradation of human labour through the organisation of capitalist machinofacture, such as John Ruskin (1853) and William Morris (1884), in the latter years of the nineteenth and the early twentieth centuries. It was, however, capitalism which brought full recognition to labour as the principal source of economic value. For the classical economists and their philosopher associates – Locke, Adam Smith, Ricardo, John Stuart Mill – it was through the application of labour to land and other raw materials that value was created. Whereas in pre-capitalist society what mattered socially were entitlements to wealth materially produced by others – in other words, entitlements to rents and tithes – in capitalism a new form of entitlement rose to prominence: profits from material production and the market exchange of its products. Rents and profits were obtained through the application of labour to the two other major factors of production: land and 'capital' (the 'dead labour' accumulated as tools, buildings or machines). Value was increased by improving methods of production (whether by agricultural improvement or manufacture), and this required the efficient use of labour. A new theory of entitlements emerged which could legitimately derive from the ownership of land, the ownership of capital or the sale of one's labour.

The most pro-labour version of the theory of the conjoining of factors of production (that of Marx) argued that all value ultimately derived from labour power, since without this neither capital (tools, machines, means of transport) nor land produce any value at all. John Locke argued that man's entitlement to land should be related to the amount of land that an individual could himself cultivate, not that this theoretical principle seemed to have much influence on the actual distribution of land in John Locke's England.

In other words, I want to propose that it is under capitalism that 'work' acquired the salience that it still has as a central and valued form of life for both individuals and society.

Instrumental and expressive conceptions of work

One can identify an extrinsic or instrumental and an intrinsic or expressive view of work and labour in the discourse of modernity. The instrumental view, associated with Adam Smith, saw labour primarily as a means for the production of goods. It should be deployed in the most efficient manner, this being determined by the processes of exchange in the market. Enhancements of efficient production (for example through a division of labour) were desirable, since they would increase available wealth, even if their consequence might be to diminish individual skills in work and the satisfactions that are derived from undertaking it. Thus there was the paradox of Adam Smith's famous pin factory (Smith 1776) in which specialisation in various elements of the production process could vastly increase the number of pins produced with a given input of resources, even if the skills of the craftsmen, formerly responsible for the entire process (and thus their satisfaction in their work), might be greatly diminished. The benefits were largely seen in quantitative rather than qualitative terms, as competitive efficiency brought higher levels of both output and profits. The quality of the experience of the labourer was accorded no intrinsic value in this model. Production was for an end (profit being the means by which its benefits were spread), and the activities which made it possible were merely means. 'Economic growth' (the growth of aggregate money income and wealth) is the modern version of this goal.

The increases in output and productivity, and of money income, which this instrumental or extrinsic conception of labour has helped to bring about, have obviously been in many respects beneficial. The argument that whatever needs to be done in the field of work to ensure such increases ought to be done, almost regardless of its consequences for the intrinsic satisfactions of labour, has therefore usually carried great weight. The process of economic modernisation has involved the ceaseless displacement of one form of labour by another, and it is often held to be reactionary, selfish or Luddite to defend less 'efficient' forms of labour against 'improvements' on the grounds of the loss of their intrinsic satisfactions.[1] Such arguments usually dominate economic decision-making. In an epoch of neoliberal hegemony such as has prevailed for the past three decades, it is difficult to gain much support for a different view. The more that existing income levels and 'living standards' (not quite the same thing) are threatened, and expectations of their future growth diminished, the greater the insistence there is likely to be on maintaining a tough instrumental approach to the economy and to the deployment of labour within it. The conventional wisdom has come to be that only what brings the highest material returns (whether it be to capital, land or labour) can be permitted.

Contrary to this is the 'expressive' or intrinsic view of the labour process. Here, labour is seen as a form of self-realisation, as the creative vision and power of the worker was joined with its material object. Objects acquired value in so far as they had been transformed by human vision and skill. Human lives acquired value through the quality of the artefacts which their labour produced. The most eloquent and influential exponent of this was Karl Marx in his *Economic and Philosophical Manuscripts* of 1844, a work which became very influential in socialist circles in the 1960s and 1970s. Marx here wrote about 'alienated labour', labour as it should not be:

> In what does this alienation of labour consist? First, that the work is external to the worker, that it is not part of his nature, that consequently he does not fulfil himself in his work but denies himself, has a feeling of misery, not of well-being, does not develop freely a physical and mental energy, but is physically exhausted and mentally debased. The worker therefore feels himself at home only during his leisure, whereas at work he feels homeless. His work is not voluntary but imposed, *forced* labour. It is not the satisfaction of a need, but only a *means* for satisfying other needs.
>
> (Marx 1844)

He contrasted his view of labour with that of Adam Smith, whom he quotes:

> In his normal state of health, strength and activity, and with the common degree of skill and facility which he may possess, he must always give up the identical portion of his tranquillity, his freedom and his happiness. Whatever may be the quantity or composition of the commodities he obtains in reward of his work, the price he pays is always the same. Of course, this price may sometimes buy a lesser, sometimes a greater quantity of these commodities, but only because their value changes, not the value of the labour which buys them. Labour alone, therefore never changes its own value.

Marx goes on: ' "In the sweat of thy brow shalt thou labour!" Was Jehovah's curse.' And this is labour, for Smith, a curse. 'Tranquillity' appears as the adequate state, as identical with 'freedom' and 'happiness'. It seems quite far from Smith's mind that the individual 'in his normal site of health, strength, activity, skill, facility' also needs a normal portion of work and the suspension of tranquillity. These ideas are echoed later in the writings of John Ruskin and William Morris. Here, for example, is Morris:

> But a man at work, making something which he feels will exist, because he is working at it and wills it, is exercising the energies of his mind and soul as well as of his body. Memory and imagination help him as he works. Not only his own thoughts, but the thoughts of men of past ages guide his hands: and, as part of the man race, he creates. If we work thus we shall be men. And our days will be happy and eventful. Thus worthy work carries with it the hope of pleasure in rest, the hope of our pleasure in our using what it makes, and the hope of pleasure in our daily creative skill. All other work but this is worthless: it is mere slaves' work – mere toiling to live that we may live to toil.
>
> (1884–1885)[2]

One can see that different forms of work correspond to these intrinsic and extrinsic perspectives. The work of a sculptor or skilled furniture-maker corresponds best to the intrinsic view; work on a mass-production assembly line, or at the supermarket checkout, to the extrinsic or instrumental view.[3] Workers of the former kind have particular skills, related to one another in particular ways. There are limits to their interchangeability. Production processes which depend on particular skills and the knowledge of particular contexts confer bargaining leverage on employees, since replacing these capabilities has a distinct cost to employers. Workers of the latter kind need only limited skills and are more replaceable, one for another. This gives them little bargaining power. In production processes, technicians who are responsible for maintenance enjoy powers (and rewards) that are denied to routine production workers, since their skills, 'local knowledge' and ability to cope with contingencies make them more valuable to employers than workers whose tasks have been fully routinised.

In practice, of course, even the most 'instrumental' forms of work have some intrinsically beneficial aspects, and 'expressive' forms of work usually produce outputs with measurable value. Different forms of work possess these attributes in different balances.[4]

Different conceptions of the individual within modernity

Capitalist societies generated two different versions of the relationship between the individual and society. The instrumental version saw individuals as motivated by rational self-interest, rooted in the desire for pleasure and the aversion to pain. A system which maximised the total sum of 'utilities' (fulfilled wants of whatever kind) would be the optimal system, hence the utilitarian doctrine of the greatest happiness of the greatest number. The romantic or expressive view, by contrast, saw individuals as having a creative potential or essence, which became realised through the development of their capabilities, by giving an expressive form to entities outside the Self, through work with material objects, or within human relationships.

This difference can be theorised as the difference between a utilitarian and an Aristotelian worldview. The former is a conception of the good equated with the aggregate sum of individual human satisfactions or pleasures, regardless of what these may be. The latter involves a conception of human 'flourishing' – the development of recognised capabilities within an ordered society based on shared values. Aristotle's ancient world vision of what those capabilities and that social order should be is different from ours. But many contemporary writers, such as Alasdair MacIntyre (1981), Amartya Sen (1999) and Martha Nussbaum (Nussbaum and Sen 1993), find the idea that good societies involve different kinds of 'flourishing' (capabilities developed within a system of recognised roles and responsibilities) to be compelling. They contrast this with a model of individual self-interest in which the satisfaction of wants of whatever kind is held to be the only good.[5]

'Aristotle versus Bentham' is one version of this debate, but John Stuart Mill brought this argument into the centre of utilitarianism itself when he argued that 'pleasure' and 'happiness' were not unproblematic ends in themselves. What counted as pleasure or happiness was itself a matter for choice and reflection, and good societies were those which allowed space for this reflection to take place.[6] Hence the priority which Mill accorded to individual freedom, and to the cultivation of self and society through education. Mill thought that Bentham's assertion that 'pushpin was as good as poetry' (i.e. anything that gave pleasure was as good as anything else) was wrong.

We can see that these contrasting conceptions of individual and society have long remained active and in contest with one another, finding their strongest adherents within different social fractions and their subcultures. There are occupations and forms of life which are more oriented to 'values', and those which are more oriented to 'interests', and these differences have persisted over a long period of time. The vocational spheres of 'culture', education and religion have a tendency to be more 'value-oriented', and those of industry, business, trade and finance to be more 'interest oriented'.[7] Raymond Williams' early masterwork, *Culture and Society* (1958), described a cultural critique of British capitalism which had been developed in largely aesthetic and moral terms, with such figures as Wordsworth and Coleridge, nineteenth-century realist novelists such as Dickens and Hardy, and writers and artists such as William Morris and George Orwell, featuring prominently. On the whole, we expect those who choose to work in finance houses to have a more mercenary or 'interest' orientation than those who choose to work as actors or teachers.

Generally the distinction between 'extrinsic' and 'intrinsic' conceptions of labour is reflected in preferences for quantitative and qualitative measures of output and performance. 'Quantities' of their nature require the homogenisation and standardisation of units of value, whereas 'qualities' identify and value differences between them.[8]

All of this is perhaps merely a sketch of a familiar philosophical landscape. But what may be less obvious is how different views of the meaning of labour are part of this larger argument between instrumental and expressive views of the individual. The 'extrinsic' view of the meaning and value of labour corresponds to the interest-based theory of the individual and individualism. The 'intrinsic' view corresponds to the expressive, romantic or Aristotelian view of the person and their essentially social nature. Arguments about how work should be valued and configured in society are thus also inherently arguments about the nature of the individual and society themselves.[9]

Labour's ascendancy in the 1970s: Instrumental and expressive dimensions

There was a period in the 1970s when labour, as a 'factor of production' distinct from land and capital, and as a class asserting its collective interest, acquired more power and influence than it had perhaps ever previously had. (This was, however, experienced in conservative social circles as a situation of near social breakdown.) This followed a period of full employment, economic growth and enhanced social protection, which brought about a heightened bargaining power for organised labour. This was the time when Harold Wilson memorably demanded that Jack Jones and Hugh Scanlon, leaders of the two largest trade unions, 'take your tanks off my lawn'. This moment of crisis was short-lived. In 1979, Margaret Thatcher was elected to power with the intention of putting the trade unions, and the anti-capitalist mentalities which she believed had acquired too much influence in society at large, back in their place, an ambition which she and her successors have achieved.

Labour's relative ascendancy in this period found its expression in both 'extrinsic' or instrumental, and 'intrinsic' or value-based terms. These two interpretations of working-class interests were in tension with one another. The 'extrinsic' expression of labour's claim to power took the form of 'money wage militancy' – the use of bargaining powers (arising from the scarcity of labour, and the effective organisation of its recruitment and deployment) to force up wages, and also to exert control over the work-effort bargain. Its 'intrinsic' form was seen in concerns – in Sweden, for example – about the 'quality of working life', and by Japanese manufacturers in the idea that workers' own knowledge of the production process could be mobilised (through 'quality circles' and the like) in both their interests and those of their employees.

The movement for workers' control in the UK, which reached the point of influence of a major official report (the Bullock Report) in the 1970s, was another instance of this 'intrinsic' focus, since the aim of increased industrial democracy was not simply to advance workers' economic interests but to enhance their participation and sense of ownership of the productive process – to add a kind of 'economic citizenship' to the idea of political citizenship.[10] However, most trade unions, predominantly committed to an 'extrinsic' and 'economistic' view of their function, were ambivalent about the campaign for workers' control, fearing that if workers became involved in taking joint responsibility for their enterprises, the cutting edge of 'collective bargaining' would be blunted, and the trade unions' usefulness for their members would diminish. The absence of trade union interest in this development was one reason why it made no progress, although the major defeat suffered by social democracy and consensus politics more generally in 1979 and after pushed these issues right off the agenda in any case.[11]

We can see the development of the Tavistock Institute and associated conceptions of the human relations approach to industrial management, and its theories of sociotechnical systems, as also located in this 'intrinsic' view of work and the labour process. Indeed, the implication of studies such as Trist and Bamforth's investigation of the coal industry (Trist and Bamforth 1951; Trist et al. 1963/1987) was that the mobilisation of workers' knowledge and capabilities, assigning them more responsibility for the organisation of their work at the coal face, would both improve the quality of working life and enhance production, and therefore bring economic returns for all. This was in contrast with systems of work organisation which treated workers in a wholly instrumental way, and which were hierarchical if not authoritarian in their assignment of responsibility. The 'sociotechnical systems' approach to these questions thus seemed to offer a resolution of the contradictions between 'extrinsic' and 'intrinsic' approaches to work (since it offered gains on both dimensions), and between the interests of capital and labour, employers and employees, since both sides were expected to benefit. The very idea of a 'sociotechnical' system involves a conceptual shift in the direction of the intrinsic, qualitative or value-oriented conception of work insofar as it insists that there is scope for social choice in determining how technologies are deployed. This model thus made it possible to pay attention to the 'total work experience' in the organisation of a system of production, without prejudging what was or was not feasible in a given case.

The concept of 'democratic leadership', developed at the Tavistock Institute and elsewhere during this period, to which David Armstrong and I have recently drawn fresh attention (Armstrong and Rustin 2012), is another expression of these same concerns. Democratic leadership was conceived as a means both of enhancing the quality of working life, through the enhanced respect, scope for self-expression and responsibility which it assigned to workers, and of making production processes more efficient and effective. It also sought to reconcile antagonistic conceptions and interests, arguing that attention to 'expressive' values could also enhance 'instrumental' outputs, and that democratic methods could benefit the interests of both capital (whether this was in public or private ownership) and labour.

Reconciling the instrumental and expressive elements of work

These two conceptions – and the utilitarian and romantic worldviews to which they correspond – have remained in continuing argument and competition with one another throughout the capitalist era. This is because each corresponds to an essential aspect of the economic and social environment, and to how men and women understand their situation in it.

According to the instrumental or extrinsic view, work is understood as a sacrifice of time and energy, made voluntarily (within capitalism, unlike slavery, labour is contracted freely from the point of view of law if not material necessity) in return for wages. In other words, labour, invested in production, is undertaken for the benefit of the consumption that it ultimately makes possible. Its intrinsic qualities are deemed to be irrelevant to the measure of its economic value. Insofar as its intrinsic quality (or its attractions for the worker) has relevance, it is in affecting the price that has to be paid for it. That is to say, people are liable to work for smaller material rewards where their work gives them intrinsic satisfaction but to demand more if it does not. Capitalist economies have increased their output of goods and services immeasurably by creating settings for labour which have provided few satisfactions other than the pay packet received at the end of the week. Sometimes such increases in efficiency and output have had as their by-product an actual reduction in the satisfactions found in work.[12]

Satisfactions include those that are derived from the exercise of skills, from relationships with work colleagues, clients or customers, from the exercise of autonomy and control, or from the aesthetic properties of a product or process. There is a long history of lament at such losses. We can think of the protests at the destruction of hand-loom weaving faced with the onslaught of the 'dark satanic mills' in the early nineteenth century, or at the replacement by supermarkets today of specialist shops, such as the baker, butcher or fishmonger; or of those hardware stores where one could once buy screws, nuts and bolts in brown-paper bags, sold by knowledgeable assistants wearing remarkably similarly coloured dustcoats.

This was the occupation immortalised by Ronnie Corbett and Ronnie Barker's 'Fork Handles' sketch. I recently encountered an assistant in a building supplies warehouse in Bury St Edmunds who, standing behind his counter, looked and sounded very similar to Ronnie Barker (although, in the sketch, Barker was the customer). I told him of this resemblance and, to my delight, he told me that the 'Fork Handles' sketch was a favourite of his too. Perhaps he too saw it as a celebration of his trade (www.youtube.com/watch?v=Cz2-ukrd2VQ).

This standard 'market model', positing an exchange of the disutility of labour for the utility of money, has always found it difficult to take account of the fact that paid (or unpaid) work is rarely regarded by those who do it as wholly extrinsic or instrumental. Most work is experienced as having some value for those who do it apart from the money that it earns.[13] We know that the loss of work, through redundancy or even normal retirement, on average produces a measurable and significant reduction in wellbeing, health and even life expectancy for reasons which are not the consequence of material impoverishment (although that may also occur). The explanation is essentially to do with the non-material benefits of inclusion, recognition, finding meaning and structure in a life, and putting capabilities to use, which paid work normally provides to some degree.[14]

The neoclassical economic view of work, which is that it is a sacrifice of one assumed good (time and effort) in exchange for another 'fungible' benefit (money and the powers that it brings), fails to account in its metrics for these non-monetised benefits of labour. This is because its underlying model of human nature, as self-oriented and pleasure-maximising, does not intrinsically value dispositions which are not self-oriented, or those satisfactions which derive primarily from relationships, whether with other persons, or with material or natural objects.

In practice, different compromises are struck all the time between 'intrinsic' and 'extrinsic' conceptions of work, both by employers and employees. People will say, 'I would prefer to work in a more interesting field, but I can't afford to', trading intrinsic satisfactions for extrinsic ones. Or employers will make some economic sacrifice to provide more satisfying conditions of work, even beyond its possible economic benefits to them arising from their workers' greater commitment.[15]

Because it is no one's responsibility to assess levels of work satisfaction in the aggregate (unlike wage and salary levels, which are continually measured), it is difficult to know what such average levels of satisfaction are and how they have changed over time. There might be reason to suppose that in times of relative prosperity, employees are more prepared to trade economic rewards for greater work satisfaction, and employers might therefore find themselves pressed to provide greater satisfaction, even at some economic cost, in order to retain workers. A concept of 'post-material goods' emerged in the 1970s,[16] proposing that there was a secular tendency for non-material (or intrinsic) goods to become valued more highly over merely material rewards. This was perhaps a sociological and psychological version of the radical political critique of 'alienation' in that period, all of these reflecting in their different idioms expressive rather than instrumental conceptions of human activity.

Back to the instrumental

In the last few years it has become more difficult to argue for the enhancement of the meaning of work, either for the benefit of workers or for organisations, than it was at the high point of post-war economic and social aspirations, in the 1960s and 1970s. One explanation for this lies in the effects of globalisation, in exposing firms to low-cost competition. Insulated by the barriers of strong nation states, and what seemed like secure competitive advantages, 'surpluses' existed which could safely be spent on 'non-material' benefits of various kinds, both within an enterprise and in the larger society, in the form of 'welfare'. But as capital became more mobile, and firms chose or felt obliged to move their operations to lower-wage economies, these apparent 'surpluses' disappeared.

One view of how to deal with such competition, which had strong support in the New Labour governments from 1997 to 2010, was that 'advanced' economies should try to maintain their competitive advantage in the global marketplace by moving from low-value to high-value forms of production, making the most of their supposedly superior resources of knowledge, education and skill. A focus on the knowledge and creative industries, and also in fact on the financial and business services sectors, was a reflection of this. Tony Blair's reiterated priority – 'education, education, education' – made this strategy into a soundbite, but the economic crisis of 2007–2008 undermined confidence in this possible economic future.

Instead, governments in the UK and elsewhere have taken the view that only reducing the costs of production in their economies can solve their competitive disadvantage. Their hope seems to be that rising wage levels in emerging economies such as China's will at some halfway point meet falling wage levels in the West. The aim of 'austerity programmes' in Europe is essentially to bring down the local costs of production, to restore the competitiveness both of weaker and stronger European economies (southern versus northern Europe) and of Europe with its rivals on other continents. (Thus diminishing welfare protections and increasing unemployment have the effect of driving down wages, and lower corporation taxes of increasing company profitability and attracting inward investment.) Whether this will be a successful strategy for restoring competitiveness remains to be seen.

However, for many people in this context, finding and keeping a job, any job, becomes an overriding concern. Finding the lowest-cost method of producing goods or services takes precedence, for both private and public providers, over whatever higher-level aspirations they might once have had. It may be less agreeable to make a purchase from a machine rather than a shop assistant, but, because it pays them to do so, companies like Sainsbury's or WH Smith switch to checkout machines where they can. The disciplines of routinisation and standardisation, described in the 1970s by Harry Braverman (1974) as the essence of the profit-seeking methods of capitalist employers, are being extended beyond manufacturing to many other spheres, including schools, universities and even mental health services. Targeted and measured 'outputs' (for example literacy and numeracy in schools) take precedence over more complex objectives. Why give a disturbed child psychotherapy for a year or more with a highly skilled practitioner if a short-term manualised treatment delivered by someone with less training and lower pay will do? But, of course, the question in such a case is how much will it do, and with what quality? How damaging is the substitution of measurable but one-dimensional 'quantities' of output for less measurable but more multidimensional 'qualities' of output?

The larger economic situation as far as the UK and Europe are concerned is one of significant relative decline in comparison with the huge emerging economies of Asia and Latin America, and perhaps soon of Africa too. Their competitive advantages in terms of low wages, where these become combined with higher technical and organisational capacities, seem irresistible. This relative decline – it is an experience of collective downward mobility, usually psychologically damaging for both individuals and groups[17] – is more serious than the immediate financial and budgetary crises which are probably its mere symptoms.[18]

The contemporary paradox – instrumental pressures versus expressive needs

Thus there are increasing economic pressures to displace concerns with the intrinsic values of work, in favour of instrumental concerns to ensure that there is at least some work available, through which livelihoods can be maintained. The enormous levels of youth unemployment in the European Union are evidence of a huge problem.

How can one think about enhancing the quality of life and work when people feel they are sliding down a slope on which there seem to be few footholds? These are hard times to be arguing for a rebalancing of the nature of work in a more 'intrinsic', expressive and 'qualitative' direction, and away from its extrinsic, instrumental and quantity-maximising functions.

Yet in one way it still does make sense to argue that human labour both can and should now be made more fulfilling and satisfying. This is because of the ever-increasing role of machines – mechanical and electronic – in the production of goods and services. The reduction in the labour required to process, for example, annual tax returns or road tax licences, when these functions are computerised, of course brings a loss of employment. But there are potentially more fulfilling things for people to do than to process the mountains of paperwork that such systems used to require. We are long familiar with the automation of manufacturing processes, and the automation of routine bureaucratic functions is just as significant a form of sociotechnical revolution.

A humane and rational society, concerned with flourishing and its population's wellbeing, would ask: What work can be done which enhances people's capacities and contributes to the wellbeing of others? When the former roles of serfs and slaves come to be taken by machines and computers, it ought to become possible for the majority to devote themselves to the callings – democratic deliberation; social interaction; the development and care of persons; the achievement of physical, intellectual and expressive excellence; relations with the natural world – which were once accessible only to the privileged minority. In a biographical study of the socially excluded that I once was part of, 13 years ago (well before the financial crisis and in a relatively prosperous period), we found that the difficulty of the unemployed graduates whom we interviewed across Europe was not in finding work as such, but in finding work which was interesting and satisfying to them in the light of their educational experience and aspirations.

We now know also that increases in material standards of living have little or no relationship to measures of subjective wellbeing, for populations taken as a whole, once a level of subsistence much lower than present-day Western living standards has been reached.[19] There are inescapable natural resource constraints on the feasible pursuit of further 'economic growth', which are defined in terms of material outputs and consumption. That growth which is feasible in any case needs to be directed towards achieving a reasonable standard of life (which one can objectively measure by the indices of life expectancy and education) for the billions of the world's poor.

Thus, less economic growth, more equally distributed and directed towards less material goals is the adaptation of society to present conditions which is actually needed. It is said that we live in a time of economic greed, and of course there is evidence of this. But is this not also a time of suppressed economic panic, only partially disavowed? The spectre conjured up in 2009–2010 that the UK might suffer the economic fate of Greece was an example of this, far-fetched and exploited politically as it was. And might not the guarded mansions, offshore bank accounts and luxury yachts of the super-rich have some of the attributes of refuges, essentially cutting them off from meaningful transactions with most of humanity, compared with the location of great houses in former times within the communities and neighbourhoods on which they depended.

But in this atmosphere, it is difficult to find space for discussion of the alternative futures which utopian thinkers have previously imagined could exist once material scarcity has been overcome. This would be a world of intrinsic rather than extrinsic goods, of the pursuit of ends rather than means. Work would in such a world be a means of self-expression, and engagement with 'objects' (as the object-relations psychoanalysts call them – whether they be persons, natural entities or ideas) valued as goods in themselves. Work would cease to be a merely instrumental activity.

In some respects, this seems to be precisely the time when such a debate should be taking place, about how to turn the necessity of material constraint into human benefit. Even the goals of economic survival might be served by such a change in emphasis, since the goods and services which a society committed to enhanced wellbeing could produce might find their own competitive niches.[20] Yet, for the moment, such a debate has been completely displaced. We now live in the grip of a degraded version of economic competition as a struggle for the survival of the fittest, and one which is already grossly distorted by the prior possession of its assets and by the widespread substitution of actual production by predation and rent-seeking.

If one wishes to see due attention given to the nature and quality of work in our society, it seems that nothing less is needed than a cultural and social revolution, comparable to that which has taken place under the flag of neoliberalism[21] during the past 30 years.

Notes

An earlier version of this paper was given at the Annual Conference of ISPSO (the International Society for the Psychoanalytic Study of Organisations) at St Catherine's College Oxford, July 12–13, 2013.

1. Very large sources of employment – for example, in agricultural labour, domestic service and horse-drawn transport – have been largely or completely displaced, while the total numbers engaged in paid work have nevertheless grown vastly.
2. Alasdair Clayre's anthology *Nature and Industrialisation*, written for the Open University in 1977, has valuable material from these debates. Its date of publication is significant.

3. Marx was keenly aware of this difference. He wrote that 'even the semi-artistic worker of the Middle Ages' did not fit into Smith's definition. Marx thought work should be like that of artists or writers. 'When labour becomes attractive work, the individual's self-realisation in no way means that it becomes mere fun, mere amusement... Really free working, for example composing, is at the same time precisely the most damned seriousness, the most intense exertion' (from *Outline of the Critique of Political Economy – the Grundrisse* 1859).
4. Psychoanalytic psychotherapy belongs at the 'intrinsic' end of this spectrum, being experienced as inherently satisfying by its practitioners, and even by its human subjects. It is not a field which people mostly enter in the expectation of becoming rich.
5. Some (Chau 2003; Murphy 1993) have argued that Marx's early view of labour as a form of self-fulfilment was Aristotelian in inspiration. His later views became more instrumentalised – the class struggle is about the pursuit of collective interests, and self-fulfilment is postponed until after it has been won. The instrumental idea that human fulfilment and its prerequisites should be deferred until the final victory of the working class over its enemies has been achieved had a disastrous heritage in Soviet communism.
6. Richard Wollheim (1993) offers a fine account of Mill's argument.
7. Psychoanalysis as a field belongs on the 'expressive' or values-oriented side of this divide, being committed to a diffuse conception of human development. Some other forms of psychology are more instrumental in their perspective.
8. It has recently been argued (McGilchrist 2009) that differences of this kind reflect the ascendancy of the right or left hemispheres of the brain.
9. Murphy (1993) has argued for an Aristotelian concept of work. 'Work has dignity when the worker executes what he has first conceived in thought, and work is degraded when one worker merely executes what is conceived by another.' Chau has examined these ideas in her 2003 Stanford Master's thesis. http://economics.stanford.edu/files/Theses/Theses_2003/Chau.pdf.
10. The Institute for Workers' Control, founded in 1964 by Ken Coates, was its most active advocate.
11. The high point of this movement was the Occupation of the Upper Clyde Shipyards in 1973 under the leadership of Jimmy Reid, in protest against their closure. This had both 'extrinsic' and 'intrinsic' dimensions since it aimed both to protect employment as such and to demonstrate that workers themselves had the capacity to manage an enterprise.
12. That this is happening is now a common complaint of employees in public health and education services, for example.
13. I once had to make a purchase in the haberdashery department of John Lewis (I was looking for replacement buttons of some uncommon kind) and was struck by the pleasure that the assistants took in their knowledge of the materials, their capacity to please their customer (me), and their feeling that working in John Lewis was a privilege relative to other retail employment. John Lewis enjoys notably strong public trust.
14. Hegel (1807) famously argued, in his parable of the relations between master and slave, that the slave gained a sense of wellbeing, relative to the master, because of his relation to material production, through which he could experience the effect of his creative power. The master, by contrast, depended

for his sense of worth on recognition by a category of person to whom he assigned no worth.
15. A cousin of mine had inherited and developed a family business. He took pride in allowing his (mainly Asian) employees to continue to work sometimes into old age, holding parties for them and making presentations to celebrate special anniversaries. It was plain that his pleasure in this was far from 'economic'. Indeed, when he died, one of his close relations told me ruefully that the firm had become his family.
16. Inglehart (1977) developed a sociological version of this thesis, which was founded on Maslow's (1954) psychological theory of a hierarchy of needs.
17. Its harmful concomitants include persecutory anxiety, irrational dependence on leaders, scapegoating and projection of unworthiness into others. It is the main recruiter of the radical right.
18. The misplaced speculative financial investments which preceded the crash of 2007-2008 took place in the absence of more solid investment opportunities, just as the 'subprime' mortgage market filled a dearth of solvent mortgageholders.
19. For the debate about the disconnect between income and happiness, see Offer (2006) and Layard (2005), and for a summary account, see Rustin (2007).
20. If the UK's defunct economic planning system could now even map the different kinds of 'production' that actually take place, and their relative growth and decline, it might well be evident that this is where most of its competitive advantage already lies.
21. *After Neoliberalism? The Kilburn Manifesto* (edited by Hall, Massey and Rustin) is developing a case for such changes over the next 12 months. http://www.lwbooks.co.uk/journals/soundings/manifesto.html.

References

Arendt, H. (1959) *The Human Condition*. New York: Anchor Books.
Armstrong, D. and Rustin M.J. (2012) 'What happened to democratic leadership?', *Soundings*, 50, 59-71.
Braverman, H. (1974) *Labour and Monopoly Capitalism: The Degradation of Work in the Twentieth Century*. New York: Monthly Review Press.
Chau, A. (2003) *On Aristotle and Marx: A Critique of Aristotelian Themes in Marxist Labor Theory*. Stanford University master's Thesis. http://economics.stanford.edu/files/Theses/Theses_2003/Chau.pdf.
Clayre, A. (ed.) (1977) *Nature and Industrialisation*. Oxford: Oxford University Press.
Hall, S.M., Massey D. and Rustin M.J. (eds.) (2014-2015) *After Neoliberalism? The Kilburn Manifesto*. http://www.lwbooks.co.uk/journals/soundings/manifesto.html.
Hegel, G.W.F. (1807/1977) *The Phenomenology of Spirit* trans. Miller, A.V. with analysis of the text and foreword by Findlay, J.N. Oxford: Clarendon Press, 1977, para. 179, 111.
Inglehart, R. (1977) *The Silent Revolution: Changing Values and Political Styles Among Western Publics*. Princeton: Princeton University Press.

Layard, R. (2005) *Happiness: Lessons from a New Science*. London: Penguin Books.
MacIntyre, A. (1981) *After Virtue*. London: Duckworth.
Marx (1844) *Economic and Philosophical Manuscripts*. London: Lawrence and Wishart (1959).
Maslow, A.H. 1987 (1954) *Motivation and Personality* 3rd ed. New York: Harper and Row.
McGilchrist, I. (2009) *The Master and His Emissary: The Divided Brain and the Making of the Western World*. New Haven, CT: Yale University Press.
Morris, W. (1884) 'Useful Work versus Useless Toil', reprinted in *William Morris, Selected Writings*. London: Nonesuch Press (1948), 603–623.
Murphy, J.B. (1993) *The Moral Economy of Labor: Aristotelian Themes in Economic Theory*. New Haven, CT: Yale University Press.
Nussbaum, N. and Sen, A. (eds.) (1993) *The Quality of Life*. Oxford: Oxford University Press.
Offer, A. (2006) *The Challenge of Affluence: Self-Control and Well-Being in the United States and Britain since 1950*. Oxford: Oxford University Press.
Ruskin, J. (1853) 'The Nature of Gothic', from *The Stones of Venice, Part 2*. Reprinted in *John Ruskin: Selected Writings*, ed. D. Birch. Oxford: Oxford University Press (2009), 32–63.
Rustin, M.J. (2007) 'What's wrong with happiness?', *Soundings*, 36, 67–84.
Sen, A. (1999) *Development as Freedom*. Oxford: Oxford University Press.
Smith, A. (1776) *The Wealth of Nations*. Harmondsworth: Penguin (1970).
Trist, E.L. and Bamforth, K.W. (1951) 'Some social and psychological consequences of the longwall method of coal-getting', *Human Relations*, 4, 3–38.
Trist, E.L., Higgin G.W., Murray H., Pollock A.B. (1963/1987) *Organisational Choice: Capabilities of Groups at the Coal Face under Changing Technologies*. London: Tavistock Publications.
Williams, R. (1958) *Culture and Society*. London: Chatto and Windus.
Wollheim, R. (1993) *The Mind and Its Depths*. Cambridge, MA: Harvard University Press.

Part V
Critiques Coming More from Inside

10
Everything You Always Wanted to Know about Therapy (But Were Afraid to Ask): Fragments of a Critical Psychotherapy

Andrew Samuels

To be critical without reference to the critic would be fatuous. This chapter attempts to share some of what I have learned in the past 40 or so years about the challenges and crises facing psychotherapy and counselling (see Samuels 1989, 1993, 2006). Prominent experiences have been the founding and successful operation of the Alliance for Counselling and Psychotherapy, which led the campaign to thwart the government's plans for state regulation of counselling and psychotherapy in the UK. The minister responsible for the regulation of health professionals was kind enough to say to the Alliance that we had 'won the argument'. It was not all due to a change of government. Indeed, it is fascinating to observe, as with whites in apartheid South Africa, that for a period of time it was hard to find anyone who supported the absurd and overblown regulatory plans of the then Health Professions Council. Nevertheless, at the time of writing (August 2014) there has been a private members' bill with the aim of bringing counselling and psychotherapy into statutory regulation under the newly named Health and Care Professions Council. It could be that the whole divisive battle will be fought all over again.

Created in 2006, the Alliance brought together progressive thinkers from all of the modalities and traditions of psychotherapy. We had Lacanian analysts working alongside libertarian humanistic people who rejected the very term 'psychotherapist'. Putting aside considerable distrust of legal process, the Alliance strongly supported the successful application for judicial review that a group of psychoanalysts mounted.

Although this was by no means my first exposure to working harmoniously via difference in the professional field – a similar pluralism characterised the earlier formation (by Judy Ryde and me) in 1994 of Psychotherapists and Counsellors for Social Responsibility (PCSR) – it was a memorable experience.

PCSR also tangled with the government by drawing the attention of the then health ministers to discrimination against members of sexual minorities with regard to training at a number of psychoanalytic institutes and also in some important NHS centres of excellence in psychotherapy. The campaign was greatly helped by what some have called the idiocy of the most prominent theoretician (Charles Socarides) who had been invited to give an important NHS lecture and to get an award. The dressing-up of his out-of-date prejudices as psychoanalytic theory was so obvious that even a Conservative politician was incredulous. It has been gratifying to see how the institutes that I referred to above nowadays stroke themselves with pride at having scrapped their discriminatory practices. But what is actually taught on those trainings regarding sexuality may be another matter entirely.

A second relevant experience was my unexpected (though decisive) election as chair of the UK Council for Psychotherapy (UKCP) in 2009. In my three years in office I was made forcefully aware of the destructive threats facing psychotherapy, especially but not exclusively in the public sector – and also of the significant extent to which psychotherapy had contributed to its own crisis: by incorrigible infighting, pathological deference to authority, adoption of a falsely 'deep' perspective on issues that inhibited action, and, generally, living in a series of interconnected bubbles. There was a failure to engage with new thinking about therapy provision, such as national low-cost schemes, community-based endeavours and ideas about there being a psychological 'commons' (Postle 2013, 2014). Sometimes it was clear to me that, despite the overall goodness of the project to defend and extend psychotherapy in the NHS, some of what existed prior to the cuts was difficult to justify. For example, certain modalities had 'captured' certain localities, and people with different training backgrounds could not get jobs. People reading this may be interested to note that, where UKCP and its sister organisations were successful in campaigning against cuts, the support of the local community and its elected councillors was decisive.

On a more personal level, finding myself established in the profession, in recent years I have been more able to reconnect to the earlier passions of my life: to political activism, to an ongoing love affair with the theatre, and to humanistic psychology. My first work as anything resembling a therapist was in the context of theatre work with massively deprived young people. Then followed a time as an encounter group leader, leading, as a result of an epiphany, to training as a Jungian analyst. Subsequent extra periods in body psychotherapy, marital therapy and systemic therapy on an individual basis have helped to give me a sense of proportion with regard to many of the issues that upset colleagues.

For years I quoted the French writer on religious themes, Charles Peguy, who claimed: 'Everything starts in mysticism and ends in politics.' Perhaps now, as I enter my mid-60s, the poles of that aphorism are starting to reverse. Hence these fragments of a critical psychotherapy are intended to be compassionate as well, and to look to the future as well as bemoaning and slashing the present.

I write as an insider so, if there is a bubble in place, enveloping the world of counselling and psychotherapy, I am definitely in it. Hence, what I and many others in the bubble see as radical will, to someone who believes themselves to be outside the bubble, seem rather conservative. While this may be so, I doubt that anyone is so free of their context as to be 100% outside the bubble. One way of reconciling this is to say that the bubble will benefit if ideas developed externally penetrate it.

In this chapter, I discuss three assertions about psychotherapy that, as far as I can tell, would find substantial if not universal support. (You never will find unanimity in the therapy field.) Then, as stated, I will discuss each of them critically, compassionately and with an eye to the future. They are as follows:

- Counselling and psychotherapy can be free and independent professions provided that, acting together, we fight for them to be that way. (See 'Freedom' below.)
- Counselling and psychotherapy are private and personal activities, operating in the realms of feelings and emotions – the psyche, the unconscious, affects rooted in the body. Above all other factors, the single most important thing is the therapy relationship between two people. (See 'Relationship'.)
- Counselling and psychotherapy are vocations, not jobs. Therapists are not only motivated by money. (See 'Vocation'.)

Freedom

Much of what follows derives from reflection after the successful campaigns to remove discrimination against sexual minorities in terms of psychoanalytic training, and to stop the project of state regulation. While I am pleased that all of it happened, I have come to see that a notion has developed that, provided that we are organised and energetic enough, we can 'save' psychotherapy and can recuperate its independence and its awkward nature (awkward from the point of view of the powerful, that is). Now, painfully, I am not sure.

These are never going to be free and independent professions (and nor are any of the other professions in our society). Some would say that psychotherapy isn't really a profession at all. But the point is that the state is omnipresent, and this is true even if its mode of regulation is said to be 'voluntary'. The legal system, including legislation about 'equality', sets parameters for clinical work. Therapy takes place within what sometimes seems like an immutable economic system with its concomitant values of an anti-humanistic nature. We are all subject to ethics codes, sometimes called 'fitness to practise'. Supervision, and even peer supervision, tempers any illusion of freedom. There is no free association, in all senses.

The 'supervisor on your shoulder' is a phrase with which every therapist is familiar. I have often wondered if the old-fashioned term 'control analysis' doesn't describe the supervisory process more precisely. There is a politics of supervision to do with power generally but also with clashes of values and experiences. Also, your supervisor has desire too. I do not refer here to the erotics of supervision, a powerful phenomenon that has yet to be written about very much. I am referring to the manifold ways in which supervisors seek mirroring that they are good and even brilliant supervisors. It would then mean that they are good and even brilliant therapists. This requires, *au fond*, agreement, and it remains true even when the official line is that robust differences of opinion are welcomed. One learns pretty quickly, if one's supervisor is psychoanalytically oriented, that you must not see your work as educative, you must not reassure or promise the client that things will be okay, and you really need to think extremely carefully, reflect deeply and discuss with the supervisor before you disclose any personal information. If you make a mistake then saying sorry is not the default position.

I turn now to what could be called 'the profession in the mind of the therapist' – a serious inhibitor of freedom. The various experiences described in the Introduction have made me sensitive to the internalised professional hierarchies that exist in the therapy world. Though things are changing, one can still discern, by interpreting the intensity of cries of protest that it is not so, that psychoanalysis remains at the top of the therapy pile, something that belies its general cultural decline. It is clear that when therapists undertake second therapies wherein they can choose the modality of their therapist, they go to psychoanalysts. Jungians can tell you a lot about the hierarchy. Many years ago, aping Avis in its battle with behemoth Hertz, I said: 'We're number two – we try harder.'

Humanistic and integrative psychotherapists have tended to welcome government projects to map the skills of therapy practice, and even to welcome regulation, because it would 'level the playing field'. All state-regulated therapists would be equal. I have always said that, in this particular regard, such humanistic and integrative supporters of regulation have got a point. But the fact that some people are complaining that the playing field is not level means, surely, that they are admitting that the playing field is not level, which is the point I am developing here.

Finally, therapists do not strike me as wanting to be free. I have already noted a deference to authority and, given unconscious dynamics, this deference may also be present in some shadowy form when therapists seem rabidly against authority of any kind. We are, for the most part, a conventional and conformist group of people. Generally, the highest clinical value is attached to settled long-term relationships that produce children, to 'normal' families and not to lone-parent families or families headed by two parents of the same sex. The profession is not as reprehensibly homophobic as it used to be but the plumb-line for the majority remains heteronormative.

We know now how much the composition of the therapy pair or group matters, and that it profoundly affects the therapy process – as does everything in society, such as violence, war, ecological disaster, unemployment and poverty, and major state-sponsored surveillance intrusions into privacy. Therapy is not hygienically insulated from the infection of such phenomena, and, if we continue in critical vein, we find that it means that therapy is not really free to define itself in any way. Differing cultural and ethical specifics may make an approach based on the therapy relationship or the therapeutic alliance inappropriate or damaging in some instances. In a sense, the client may have to resist the way in which the therapist predefines their joint activity.

Let me pose a few relevant questions at this juncture. The matter of therapists from minorities working with clients who are not from those minorities (i.e. so-called 'majority' clients) is important. How white clients feel when confronted with Black therapists, or straight clients with a therapist from a sexual minority (yes, such things can sometimes be visible or are acknowledged/disclosed) are not talked or written about very much. Yet in conversation with Black and ethnic-minority therapists there is a considerable fear that therapists will be sequestered into working only with clients who resemble them.

We know, too, that the history of relations between the groups that the two participants come from is important. There are ancestral as well as here-and-now dynamics when a Black person and a white person work therapeutically together, or when a German and a Jew find themselves in the same therapy room.

In addition, economic inequality, and its concomitant envy and sense of failure or success, skew the transference – countertransference. Sometimes the client has more wealth, sometimes the therapist. Money is always a hot issue (see Samuels 2014b). Much the same can be said about the physical health and disability characteristics of both participants.

What about similars working together as therapist and client? Of course, it is a truism that apparent cultural and identity similarities mask deeper differences in culture and background so there is always cultural difference in the room. But to focus on it avoids the sharp point that I wish to make here: palpable difference and inequality inevitably impact on the level of professional freedom that can exist.

Relationship

'It's the relationship, stupid!' Taking off from ex-US President Bill Clinton's famous 'it's the economy, stupid!', this slogan was seriously considered for use in an advertising and public relations campaign in support of psychotherapy and counselling. This was possible because it was the therapy relationship that was considered to be the unique selling point of psychotherapy and counselling. This is stated to be what the clients want, and it is what the therapists want to offer. It has become a marker of difference between psychotherapy and CBT, which may be one rhetorical reason why CBT practitioners these days emphasise that there, too, the client will find a relationship. We're all relational now (see Loewenthal and Samuels 2014a).

Hence in a recent paper (Samuels 2014a) I have asked whether relationality in therapy was still cutting edge or had become conformist. I said it could well be both. But I also argued that the emphasis on the relationship, with notions of safety, containment, holding and diminution of risk, tended in the conformist direction. Without going so far as to say that making therapy safe is all done in the interests of the therapist, I think we have to consider what our professional expectation – that safety is what clients need – has done to the way in which we work. Does it not reinforce the idea of the client as needy, dependent, infantile and caught between flight and fight? Such clients exist. Perhaps every client is like this at some time. But, pushed just a little bit further, this apparently profoundly psychotherapeutic set of assumptions about clients comes perilously close to imitating what the government's state therapy scheme (Improving Access to Psychological Therapies (IAPT)) wants to see in its clients. The clients of state therapy are to be compliant and grateful, do what the therapist wants them to do and, above all, get off state benefits and back to work. The therapist is situated as an expert, working from an evidence base, something like a surgeon whose recommendations one would be very misguided to disobey. When psychotherapists and counsellors say to clients 'You must relate to me', they are as mistrustful of the client's autonomy as anyone working as a state therapist would be.

What we are seeing in the literature, and hence we may assume is taking place in practice, is the emergence of a wholly different conception of the client, a perspective that sees them as the motor of therapy (summarised in Norcross 2011). This client is a heroic client, a client who knows what they need, a client who can manage their own distress. As Postle (personal communication 2013) has pointed out there is also a client who engages less in a process of healing or cure and more in a process of ongoing enquiry. This multifaceted new client is potentially a healer of others, especially the therapist, and, in a sense, of the world. Client as healer.

Summarising a mass of research findings, Norcross (2011) has forced us to consider whether it truly is the therapy relationship that is the decisive factor. Is the private and highly personal therapy relationship the main thing that makes therapy work? Not really. Unexplained and extratherapeutic factors amount to some 40% of efficacy variance, the client accounts for 30%, the therapy relationship 12%, the actual therapist 8%, and the school or tradition or modality of the therapist 7%. Of course, Norcross would be the first to admit that therapy is a melange of all of these, and I would add that the findings do no more than force us to consider our ideas about our clients. These figures are far from veridical. But let us take them as heuristic, stimulants to critical thinking about clients. Who they are, what do they want and what point in their life journey have they reached? What stage have they reached in what Norcross calls their 'trajectory of change'?

There are some clients from whom one learns great lessons. My first training 'case' had a dream early on in the analysis. She dreamt: 'I visit a doctor who is ill in bed. He begs me to stay.' Her associations to 'bed' were of illness, not of sexuality. How else could we understand this dream? Was the doctor in fact me? Or was this an assumption, intended to justify what has been called a 'you mean me' interpretation (also known as a here-and-now transference interpretation)? Was there denial here, in that she is the ill one and I am truly the doctor? Or is she in the grip of an inflation, of herself as the one who brings life and succour, more than a human mother? Or was this dream, perhaps, an accurate perception? I did need something from her, and not just that she would stick with me so that I could get through the training. Crucially there would be a further accurate perception in the dream: that she could in fact help/heal this doctor. This was in 1974 and at that time it would have been difficult to think of the client as a healer. Has much changed? (I write at length about working with this client, 'D', in Samuels 1985.)

Thinking of the client as a healer, we see that recent thinking about the client has moved in that general direction. From the person-centred approach we find Bohart and Tallman (1999) referring to the 'active client'. Rogers (1951), in the era when the discourse was about 'client-centred' therapy, makes it clear that the client knows for themselves what is needed and where they want to go. Jung (1946) writes of entropy in the client, an innate process of self-regulation. From relational psychoanalysis, we read that Hoffman (2006) regards the client as having responsibilities to the analyst and the analysis, more than just for the co-creation of the therapy relationship.

So the therapist is, in a way, adjunct to the therapy process. But she is also a contingent figure, a product of a particular social circumstance. Franks (1961) suggested that what makes the therapist is not only training, techniques and wounds but also being socially sanctioned as a therapist, a sort of overarching placebo effect. The therapist is being socially sanctioned, granted permission to be a therapist – by society and by the client. This is a new version of the client who does not want the analyst to be the one who knows, or even one who is supposed to know.

Let us see what happens if we re-vision the therapy relationship with all of these thoughts about the client in mind. I am putting it like this because it has gradually dawned on me that clients sometimes do not dare to deploy their tacit knowledge and emotional literacy. We therapists are cool with this because it leaves us free to do our work. But that could, and from a critical perspective perhaps should, change.

Almost no one argues for discarding the idea of the therapy relationship completely, which is a rare phenomenon in our field. As already mentioned, even CBT therapists are now aware of it and work it these days. But the therapy relationship is a limited lens through which to view therapy. It is also far too monolithic. Based on Jung's alchemical metaphor for transference – countertransference – I suggested (in Samuels 1985) that the question that we should ask is: 'One therapy relationship or many?' Similarly, in 1986, Clarkson acutely delineated five levels of the therapy relationship. So what gets called 'the therapy relationship' is in fact only one aspect or level of the relationship. Sticking my neck out, and aware that I am generalising, could it be that we have conflated all of the others into what is accurately termed the therapeutic alliance or working alliance? If there is co-creation, it stems from the alliance. If there is an intersubjective process, it is sustained by the therapeutic alliance. But there are problems with the idea of the therapeutic alliance, and these are not much discussed.

Focus on the therapeutic alliance can also be a very one-sided perspective on therapy. For it is as if the therapist is the one who is ready, willing and able to enter the alliance, whereas the client has to struggle to enter it. 'Well done, client, for getting to where I, your therapist, have already got!' Now, I expect some people who are therapists to object to this and say that they do sometimes struggle to enter the alliance. But be honest about it: don't you usually regard your struggle to enter the alliance as more to do with the client or type of client you are with? The client is a sort of obstacle to your entering the therapeutic alliance. How can borderline, traumatised or regressed clients do what their therapists have done – reach the level of therapeutic alliance readiness?

If what I am saying is at all reasonable then the very attempt to have a kind of ethical equality in therapy – the stress on the therapeutic alliance – can lead to a radical inequality. Herein the therapist is the one who is 'sorted' about the project of therapy, and the client is having to 'commit' to it. Not fair. I don't think that much of what is regarded as the therapy relationship can achieve what Jung (1946: 219) meant when he wrote: 'The meeting of two personalities is like the contact of two chemical substances: if there is any reaction, both are transformed.'

A number of specific critiques of the proposition that it is 'the relationship' that is central to the therapy process will now be outlined.

Social critiques

Therapy is an induced relationship, not a natural one. The therapy relationship is imbued with the history, power dynamics and authority structures of therapy itself.

Systemic critiques

Focus on the therapy relationship misses out the presence and impact of the wider human systems in which client and therapist are embedded: families, friends, other people at work and so on. Just to give a simple example, it has been illuminating to listen to the answers when I ask a potential new client what their partner or family thinks about their having therapy. Paradoxically, nothing is more potent in this regard than to be told that the client hasn't told anyone.

Reality critiques

This is a critique of those, mainly but not only in psychoanalysis, who see hints and references to the therapist in the discourse of the client. Sometimes, as I mentioned earlier, these are called 'you mean me' interpretations, so the inefficient car mechanic is the inadequate therapist in disguised form. Or there is simply a symbolic interpretation made. Margaret Thatcher is your mum, David Cameron (or Saddam Hussein) your shadow. But sometimes the car mechanic (or the boss at work) is just the mechanic or the boss, Margaret Thatcher is Margaret Thatcher, and David Cameron plays himself. (And sometimes clients are late because there really has been a dead body on the train line.)

Ecological and political critiques

Emphasis on the therapy relationship makes it even more difficult for the client to express the impact on themselves of planetary/environmental crisis or any other collective field of emotional distress. When I first began to advocate the therapist picking up on political aspects of the client's material, I was told that I might be depriving the client of the opportunity to talk about their mother if I kept her references to Margaret Thatcher on the level of Margaret Thatcher. I replied that I was worried about the opposite: that a client who needed to talk about Margaret Thatcher would be definitely, if indirectly, discouraged from so doing because talking about one's mother is what one does in therapy. In principle, any political theme can be taken under the umbrella of the therapy relationship, and it is an important development in our field that people are doing that to an ever-increasing extent. But whether the focus moves off the two humans in the room is another question, and one that deserves a fuller discussion at some point.

Ethical and epistemological critiques

Without intending it, proponents of the centrality of the therapy relationship are buying in to a particular view of human relationships. In this view, people are regarded as atomised, isolated beings who have to struggle into a relationship and, when they achieve a relationship with a therapist, the two people in the relationship 'own' it. But this is not the only narrative of relationality. What about those in which people are always already in connection and relationship? They do not meet each other via the hurling of projections (from the Latin *proicere* – to throw a spear) across empty space. For there does not exist any empty space between people, even though it may look that way. What if we conceive of a rhizome, or nutrient tube to be, buried out of sight, which throws up separate stalks that are, nevertheless, already connected? What if we understand the two people as linked by their citizenship, their membership of the polis, no matter how different that experience might be for them? Or, as Totton has suggested (personal communication 2013), perhaps we should understand the members of the therapy pair as linked via their experiencing and perhaps exploring the manifold bodily, physical phenomena present in the therapy room?

It would be ironic as well as tragic if, just as we discover the importance of the created therapy relationship, we omit to recognise (and experience) the relationship that is always there. One need hardly add that the autonomous, separate, 'individuated' person is exactly the person whom capitalism and free market theorising assumes exists. So relationality in therapy is not a politically neutral notion.

The Activist Client

This observation on the politics of the idea of the therapy relationship leads me to suggest that the new model client, the client as the motor of therapy, is increasingly a politically active and aware client. One possible goal of therapy might be that, during the work, the client develops their capacity for alterity, meaning, among other things, an empathic concern for the Other. Yes, this does mean other people, but there is a more-than-personal version of alterity to consider. For example, in a multicultural world, meeting one's inner diversity could lead to support for outer (cultural) diversity and hence to support for those who were hitherto subject to social inclusion. To the idea that a client is also a healer, we can now add that clients have the potential to be citizen-therapists for the wider world, with its environmental problems, economic injustice and ubiquitous violence. The therapy client, re-visioned as a healer, may now be understood to be a socially responsible agent of *Tikkun Olam*, the drive to repair and restore the world.

My research (2006) shows that, in many countries, clients bring political, social and cultural material to therapy much more than they did (and, I would add, they will bring even more when they know that it is permitted to do so). Therapy becomes a place where, in political dialogue, client and therapist work out their political attitudes and engagements. This can be as transformative as a more personal alchemy, and can be done even when one of them finds the political positions of the Other to be horrid or reprehensible.

As so often, when one thinks one is gathering in some new ideas in the therapy field, one finds that there is a back story. In 1957, Racker stressed that analysis is not something done by a sane person to a neurotic one. In 1975, Searles wrote his paper 'The patient as therapist of his analyst'. If part of 'mental health' is to want and be able to help and heal others, then isn't this something to work on in analysis? If so, then isn't the obvious relationship within which the client can develop skills as a healer the one with the analyst?

A few years earlier, in *Power in the Helping Professions*, the Jungian analyst Guggenbuhl-Craig (1971) pointed out that the sharp split in Western culture between health and woundedness impacts on psychotherapy: therapists get assigned health and clients are left with their woundedness. But in the inner worlds of each resides the opposite. We know about wounded therapists but even Guggenbuhl-Craig does not write much about clients as healers.

The word 'healing' is much used, and I suppose there is intended a contradistinction to curing and cure. This was developed in some detail by Gordon (1978) in her book *Dying and Creating: A Search for Meaning*. But, with healing in mind, perhaps one doesn't have to do very much. Meier (1967) showed this in his account of classical Greek healing practices in *Ancient Incubation and Modern Healing*. If you are ill, enter the *temenos* – the sacred temple precinct – lie down, sleep and take your dreams to the priests.

Vocation

This section is written with students and recently qualified therapists in mind, though the concerns raised apply to all of us. Therapy is not only a vocation, it is a job. This brings up the usual range of trades union issues: money, job security, status. Conventionally, money is the shadow of vocation but, as Stone suggests (personal communication 2013), there is a complicated relationship between vocation and money.

New entrants into the profession find themselves in what I have called a 'battle for the soul'. This is the context in which today's therapy is being practised. In the USA and the UK, with resonances in other Western countries, a full-scale war has broken out regarding emotional distress (and 'illness'): how we talk about it, whether we try to measure it or not and, crucially, what we do about it. Behind this battle for ownership of the soul lies contemporary culture's profound ambivalence regarding psychotherapy and counselling. Many countries have now opted for what they believe to be a quick and effective form of therapy – CBT – which, proponents maintain, has been scientifically measured to have proven effects in relation to those who are suffering from anxiety and depression.

But if you read the previous sentence again, you will see just below its surface the main grounds upon which the war is being fought. Are there really separate illnesses or diseases called 'anxiety' and 'depression'? No one in the field seriously believes that, hence the coinage 'co-morbidity'. And whether or not one can measure either the illness or the cure is such a hot topic that it will be keeping university philosophy of science departments busy for years. Is there such a thing as an 'effective' therapy? Don't people keep coming back?

Recently, a further front opened up in connection with the fifth version of the DSM. Many established professional bodies are concerned that 'the psychiatrists' bible' adopts an over-easy pathologisation of what are really ordinary – if difficult and painful – human experiences, such as grief. Others have protested that DSM-5 is not scientific enough, failing to consider genetic determinants of mental illness. At the time of writing it seems that the DSM psychiatrists have seen off the opposition. What is your problem, they say, with taking a systematic approach to mental illness? How can that fail to help? The media agreed.

But will they actually win? The stock-in-trade of psychiatry remains drug treatments and, recently, a series of books and scholarly papers have appeared (notably Irwin Kirsch's *The Emperor's New Drugs: Exploding the Antidepressant Myth* 2010) that cast doubt on the reliability of the research that seems to support such treatments. Kirsch's point, made by many others as well, is that the methodology that underpins such research – RCTs – is liable to many kinds of distortion. For example, if a patient is given a placebo with a mild irritant in it, they will assume that they have been given the actual drug being trialled (everyone knows that drugs have side-effects, you see), and, hey presto, they get better.

In the UK there is great interest now in discussing the pros and cons of RCTs because they are used to ration therapy on the NHS. Well-established approaches, such as humanistic, integrative, family systemic and psychodynamic are vanishing from the NHS. Either CBT, or a watered down version of it that I call 'state therapy', secures the funding. This has led some to say that we should do RCTs of our own.

I understand the tactic of 'If you can't beat them join them', but what if it doesn't work?

Others point to the fact that there is a huge amount of non-RCT evidence for the efficacy of psychotherapy and counselling. But the government agency that draws up guidelines for treatments on the NHS does not recognise the methodologies that underpin this research. At times, NICE does seem to have been captured by the proponents of RCTs and – due to the way in which it has been researched via RCTs – CBT. The Department of Health claims that NICE is beyond its control, which has left many observers speechless.

This is the world that a new therapist is going to encounter. But there is worse to consider. We also need to ask what it means to train to be a therapist in the age of austerity. Where are the jobs going to come from? If courses in counselling and psychotherapy are not transparent and honest, is there not a risk of a scandal of mis-selling?

Ending: The future, failure and the trickster therapist

I said I would be compassionate and look to the future.

Here are a few intuitive suggestions for the themes of the future: deconstructing the idea of trauma, deepening our understanding of how one variant of masculinity has shaped our world, debating whether or not the past really does shape the present, how we apprehend relations between individual and collective – can individuals make a contribution to social and political change? Above all, it would be constructive to engage with these themes as a cohesive profession, putting aside preciously held in-house ideas and assumptions. If we are going to arrest the decline of psychotherapy in our society, we had better do it from as united a base as possible.

In terms of compassion, I think it is very important not to be too hard on ourselves. However, we will fail to be self-compassionate. Yet failure is at the centre of what we do and what we deal with. Consider:

- 'every attempt is a wholly new start, and a different kind of failure' (Eliot);
- 'fail better' (Beckett);
- 'there's no such thing as failure and failure's no success at all' (Dylan);
- 'failure is the key to the kingdom' (Rumi).

But it is hard to let a thousand flowers bloom if we are frightened that the garden is going to get untidy and overgrown. I am not sure that there is a solution to many of the problems I have been writing 'critically' about in this chapter. Hence, even a critical project has the most severe limitations and is subject to critique.

I wish that therapists were more spontaneous, trusting more in the revelatory aspects of their own minds. Perhaps we should be less frightened of embracing contradictory positions. And perhaps we should show more respect for people's pet ideas, the bees in their bonnets, the *idées fixe*, today's bright ideas. Do not be afraid to be foolish, do not seek to avoid shame, let it all hang out, for no one in our profession is all wise, all deep, all spiritual, always reflective or always related.

This lacklustre characterisation of today's therapist brings me to some thoughts about the legendary figure of the Trickster in general, and to Hermes in particular. These personifications are intended to jazz things up a bit in our field. What attracts me to the Trickster-therapist is their very lack of a coherent psychological project. In fact, they lack ambition to do good. If they do good it is often by accident. This is how I have come to think of healing and cure in psychotherapy. There can be little or no cleaning up of our Trickster-therapist. Primitivity and amorality make Tricksters what they are.The Greek Trickster god was Hermes, who was responsible for trade and commerce, maintenance and penetration of boundaries, and carrying the messages of the gods, as well as carrying out practical jokes and mockery of the powerful. Can this coarsely energetic figure be refashioned so as to speak to therapists? This is perhaps the deeper project of the chapter.

On this note, let me end by providing a brief summary of the overall thrust of this essay in critical psychotherapy. I wanted to show how many of the core ideals, values and practices of psychotherapy are not what they seem, not as valuable as they seem, and even capable of doing harm to whatever therapeutic project might exist. It was not a comfortable chapter to write because there is so much self-criticism in it, but that's my punishment at the Trickster's hands, I should think.

Acknowledgements: I had great feedback on drafts from Moira Duckworth, Richard House, Denis Postle, Sissy Lykou, Martin Stone and Nick Totton. Thank you.

Note

This chapter was originally published as 'Everything you always wanted to know about therapy (but were afraid to ask): Social, political, economic and clinical fragments of a critical psychotherapy' (Andrew Samuels (2014), *European Journal of Psychotherapy & Counselling*, 16(4): 315–330) and it is reprinted here by permission of the publisher, Taylor & Francis Ltd.

References

Bohart, A. and Tallman, K. (1999) 'Empathy and the active client: An integrative, cognitive-experiential approach', in A. Bohart and L. Greenberg (eds.) *Empathy Reconsidered: New Directions in Psychotherapy*. Washington DC: American Psychological Association, pp. 73–101.
Clarkson, P. (1986) *The Therapy Relationship*. London: Whurr.
Frank, J. (1961) *Persuasion and Healing*. New York: Basic Books.
Gordon, R. (1978) *Dying and Creating: A Search for Meaning*. London: Society of Analytical Psychology.
Guggenbuhl-Craig, A. (1971) *Power in the Helping Professions*. New York: Spring Publications.
Jung, C.G. (1946) The Psychology of The Transference, Vol. 16. *Collected Works of C.G. Jung*. London: Routledge and Kegan Paul; Princeton: Princeton University Press.
Kirsch, I. (2010) *The Emperor's New Drugs: Exploding the Antidepressant Myth*. New York: Basic Books.
Meier, C.A. (1949) *Ancient Incubation and Modern Psychotherapy*. Evanston, IL: Northwestern University Press, 1967.
Norcross, J. (2011) *Psychotherapy Relationships That Work*. Oxford: Oxford University Press.
Postle, D. (2013) The psyCommons – Ordinary wisdom and shared power, http://youtu.be/5lipKokm5-A.
Postle, D. (2014) The psyCommons and its enclosures – professionalized wisdom and the abuse of power, http://youtu.be/pxuFnUuLqyc.
Rogers, C. (1951) *Client-Centered Therapy*. Cambridge: Riverside.
Samuels, A. (1985) *Jung and the Post-Jungians*. London: Routledge and Kegan Paul.
Samuels, A. (1989) *The Plural Psyche*. London: Routledge.
Samuels, A. (1993) *The Political Psyche*. London: Routledge.
Samuels, A. (2006) 'Working directly with political, social and cultural material in the therapy session', in L. Layton, N. Hollander, and S. Gutwill (eds.) *Psychoanalysis, Class and Politics: Encounters in the Clinical Setting*. London: Routledge, pp. 11–28.
Samuels, A. (2014a) 'Shadows of the therapy relationship', in D. Loewenthal and A. Samuels (eds.) *Relational Psychotherapy, Psychoanalysis and Counselling*. London: Routledge, pp. 184–192.
Samuels, A. (2014b) 'Economics, psychotherapy and politics', *International Review of Sociology*, 24(1), pp. 77–90.
Searles, H. (1975) 'The patient as therapist to his analyst', in *Countertransference and Related Subjects: Selected Papers*. New York: International Universities Press, 1979, pp. 256–279.

11
Critical Priorities for the Psychotherapy and Counselling Community

Colin Feltham

I have promoted the idea of thinking critically about the psychological therapies (and more broadly about human distress and the human condition) for many years, initially in Dryden and Feltham (1992). Feltham (1999) attempted to categorise critiques, and most recently my *Critical Thinking in Counselling and Psychotherapy* (2010) and *Counselling and Counselling Psychology: A Critical Examination* (2013) have continued this critical trajectory. Since the origins of the British Association for Counselling & Psychotherapy (BACP) in 1970 we have seen many enthusiasms in the form of new schools of therapy; a great deal of professionalising in the form of ethics documents, training and supervision norms, accreditation procedures and statutory regulation; and a push for research activity and its dissemination in conferences and journals. But the field still suffers, in my view, from wholly insufficient critical thinking. In this chapter, I want to explore (1) the place of thinking and theorising in counselling; (2) the neglect of and suspicions about such thinking; (3) areas in which critical thinking might suggest some priorities for our profession and beyond; and (4) some reflective afterthoughts on the sources and limits of my own thinking.

Thinking and theorising

We could begin by asking questions about thinking per se, but that would take us into philosophical areas that some readers might believe to be irrelevant and that I lack the expertise to explicate rigorously. Heidegger, for example, wrote about this matter (Heidegger 2011), arguing that thinking seriously must be explicitly learned, but most trainees do not have the necessary background to read him, nor is there space in most training courses to accommodate such study. *Sapere aude* (dare to think) was Kant's recommendation and Heidegger commended *aletheia* (truth as unconcealment), yet we make the assumption that such original and critical thinking can be left to philosophers and is not the business of psychotherapists, or perhaps belongs to critical psychologists and not to counsellors and psychotherapists. We could, it is true, lose ourselves in philosophical enquiries about the meaning and place of polemics, contrarianism, deconstruction, discourse analysis, scepticism and nihilism, and these may be better left to philosophers of epistemology, mind and mental health.

Pragmatically, I begin instead by asking how tutors come to subscribe to and recommend certain theories of psychological therapy and how trainees are (or are not) taught to evaluate such texts that are prescribed in course reading lists. It seems doubtful that many tutors of whatever academic or professional background, however evidence-espousing, devote years to sifting earnestly through therapy-related texts on theory and research before concluding: 'Yes, this one ticks all the boxes and can be recommended.' Much more likely is that the process that Kahneman (2011) refers to as the 'affect heuristic' is responsible. In other words, those leading the promotion and training of therapy like, or are strongly emotionally influenced by, certain texts and related therapy experiences, and they fall under their sway, becoming relatively uncritical about them. This phenomenon has been referred to as belief-dependent realism, but I think the term 'personality-dependent realism' is more comprehensive and accurate (Feltham 2015). The choice of and adherence to a therapeutic approach seems part of the powerful emotional faith that most counsellors invest in the therapeutic enterprise.

Now, it is also true that intraprofessional promoters, tutors and researchers may commit themselves to developing their chosen approach on the basis of what may look like critical thinking, by adding certain concepts and references to research. But how often do we hear anyone pronouncing: 'I have rigorously evaluated these claims and, since I find them wanting or defective, I have decided to abandon this approach'? Very rarely indeed, unless we include all of those who were originally wedded to psychoanalytic practice principles but defected or created their own approaches (for example Jung, Perls, Reich, Berne, Assagioli, Ellis, Beck, Frankl, Janov) based on disaffection with psychoanalysis. But why should early emotional investments in various therapies so rarely change significantly? Well, perhaps we have here not only an emotional path dependency but the financial one of sunk costs: unless people are paid to be objective regardless of where their thinking takes them, most cannot afford to abandon livelihood-related theoretical beliefs.

Most training now takes place in, or is validated by, academic institutions, where in principle it has always been an expectation that students will learn to think, discuss and write analytically and critically. Indeed, given the rise of doctoral demands in counselling, counselling psychology and psychotherapy training, we ostensibly expect high levels of rigorous critical thinking. We should probably ask what differences exist between undergraduate level (for example foundation degree) and doctoral level (for example PhD, D.Couns., D.Couns.Psych, Prof.Doc) training standards and how these impact on practice competency, but we don't. I am frequently surprised to read doctoral theses that, apart from obligatory discussions of the merits of qualitative methodologies and some Foucauldian or similar jargon, demonstrate somewhat superficial levels of critical thinking. Doctoral candidates mostly remain wedded to their beliefs, make microanalyses of selected practice issues and go through the motions of discovery but uncover little, if anything, genuinely new (Brooks 2013). It is conceivable that all of this work makes for significant incremental advancement of knowledge in the field, but I doubt it. Incidentally, for brevity's sake I am not here raising the critical question posed by some about the possible negative effects of basing psychotherapy training within academia instead of the arguably less cerebral and more down-to-earth, freethinking independent sector.

Once qualified and in practice, what kind of thinking do we expect from practitioners? Requirements for supervision, accreditation and continuing professional development entail a certain amount of clinical and ethical reflection, theory-into-practice case studies and engagement in self-chosen workshops, conferences and additional training. But there are no real markers of the level or originality of thinking expected, only the amount of activity and sometimes a justification of rationale. This may be due to BACP's well-intentioned, historical refusal to align training standards with higher academic levels, but, even if all this were to be particularised and mandated, it would be no guarantee of rigorous, authentic, independent critical thinking; rather, it would probably lead simply to more artful hoop-jumping.

Typical training texts summarise some historical and professional issues before going on to extol uncritically the merits of particular theoretical/clinical approaches. Almost all of these are based on what has happened in one's life and head (and perhaps one's body) – that is, they assume intrapsychic aetiologies. Critical psychology usually adds an anti-capitalist dimension but avoids having any truck with evolutionary psychology, for example. All theorists have prejudices and a limited range of reference. Very few include any examination of human history and evolution, or biology generally. All assume an anti-determinist position, and most avoid discussing biological truths of disease, deterioration and death. Most avoid the idea that life contains a large element of suffering, tragedy, absurdity and (probably) meaninglessness. Not only trainees struggle to think and theorise at the macrolevel but founders and interpreters of theoretical models too lack breadth and depth.

Neglect of critical thinking

It is natural to wonder if the enthusiastic faith-oriented, often emotion-loaded ethos of counselling is at odds with critical thinking. It has been argued that trainees need first to be immersed in therapeutic dogma before being encouraged to apply stringent and even radical analytical thinking to it. Intellectualisation portrayed as a psychoanalytic defence mechanism may colour our views about the value and importance of thinking over emotional investment. Suspicions may be engendered by the Critical Parent of Transactional Analysis. The emphasis given in training to relational factors, personal awareness and emotional openness may discourage too much play being given to critical thinking. The well-known phrases 'He's so much in his head' or 'I asked you what you feel, not what you think' (more often heard in humanistic contexts than in others) may militate against thinking. Even presumably more thinking-oriented CBT courses are likely to severely limit the free rein that could be given to fulsome critical thinking which sceptically challenges the very foundations of all therapeutic theory and outcome claims. And let's note too that passion and critical thinking are not necessarily mutually exclusive.

Those opposed to statutory regulation who were vocal in their arguments often discovered that the pro-regulation lobby simply refused to engage in the core arguments, as if an attitude of 'Of course we must have regulation' was self-evidently true. Try to engender a debate about whether or not supervision, or personal therapy in training, is necessary and you meet the same, or worse, kind of indignation and an unwillingness to discuss the issue logically. This kind of non-engagement has been called 'ignoring [one's opponents] to death'. Jeffrey Masson, who dared to rock the psychoanalytic establishment in the 1980s and 1990s, was not ignored so much as vilified by many therapists, and his accusations that most therapists are abusive were often derided or ignored (Dryden and Feltham 1992). As a published 'critical friend' of counselling and psychotherapy since 1992, I am quite used to book reviews that offer bland pseudoappreciation or identify minor faults (a dubiously placed semicolon here, an inconsistency there, etc.) rather than engaging seriously in the core issues raised. The irresistible picture that emerges is that critical thinking isn't wanted here, any more than Richard Dawkins is welcome in church. 'We know therapy works and our traditions are sacred' may be backed up with predictably confirmatory research, but that's usually the end of the discussion.

For some unknown reason, empirical research has been elevated as the premier mode of analysis of theoretical and practice issues. I glibly write 'unknown' but we must suspect that the reason is linked to an aping of other social science bids for scientific status, or if not scientific then 'reflective practitioner' status (which is code for a modified kind of humanistic science that is broad enough to include subjectivity). Hundreds of postgraduate dissertations and theses now routinely investigate nuances of counselling phenomena, and researchers confidently proclaim that the effectiveness debate stemming from the 1950s is over, the battle is won, 'we know therapy works'. But critics are far from satisfied that the research can ever get at the complex variable experiences of thousands of actual clients. Meanwhile, much research tries to establish the most effective therapeutic ingredients and relational qualia, as if new, key practice variables are waiting to be discovered that will significantly improve therapeutic delivery. But who really believes that typical therapy practice will improve a great deal, indefinitely, or indeed that it has improved hugely across the last few decades? Can we even entertain an idea like 'the cure for depression' to compare with medical research into a cure for cancer?

Priorities for critical thinking

My hunch is that views such as this are regarded by the majority of practitioners as a minor nuisance at best or waved aside with a dismissively humouring 'there he goes again' response. I meet relatively few in our field who believe that we face serious problems of credibility, particularly since counselling and CBT have been established within the NHS. Academics with psychoanalytic affiliations and private practices are those who are most likely to oppose 'state therapy' in often floridly obtuse language. There is understandably not too much appetite for inconvenient critical thinking among most hard-pressed practitioners, nor among those with public relations responsibilities for therapy. Therapy's harshest critics remain a mixture of sociologists, journalists, philosophers, scientists, ex-clients and others who have variable motives and a not always accurate grasp of the field. Internal debates about, and schisms around, regulation, research, inter-approach wrangling and pluralism continue. But the pressures from critics don't go away, recent additions including Moloney (2013) and Madsen (2014), and paradoxically amounting to what we could call a parasitical industry of critique. What are some of the main objections to therapeutic theories and practice, either perennial or topical, and what might be learned from them if taken seriously?

Aetiologies of distress

The field of psychological therapies is somewhat detached from the question of, and research into, the deeply intertwined causes of widespread human distress. Psychotherapy is something like a 100-year-old set of touted theories and practices (albeit modified over the decades) at odds with each other, yet all claiming to identify the key, intrapsychic and interpersonal, causes of distress and claiming to bring significant and lasting relief via disciplined listening and talking. Is it too much to ask for an attempt to produce an interdisciplinary and coherent picture of the probable causes of mental distress, to include genetic, neurological, socioeconomic, individual-developmental and other inputs? Are we so partisan in our thinking that we must espouse sociopolitical aetiologies of distress, say, and deny evolutionary accounts, or vice versa?

Competing models

Is it credible and inevitable that we have hundreds of different and competing therapeutic theories? On top of that we have eclecticism, integrationism, pluralism and unification – that is, different but indeterminate bids to link, blend or rationalise diverse therapies. By some estimates we now have around 500 differently named models. We could produce a theory of the underlying causes of such multiplicity, we could investigate the problems caused by this fragmentation, we could also philosophically analyse the possible merits of this proliferation. But we don't. Instead, new approaches are constantly invented unchecked.

Why? What prevents greater cooperation rather than such sprawling creation? Can we really defend the idea that pluralism is good and anything looking monolithic is bad? And how can we prioritise such intraprofessional matters when we know that meanwhile many distressed people are simply not getting the help that they need, if any help at all?

The outcome question

It suits us to see research conducted into outcomes, usually by insiders of the psychological professions, that always happens to confirm the effectiveness of therapy, seemingly regardless of the therapeutic approach or the psychological condition being investigated. Yet much anecdote, the reservations of some psychologists and sociologists, client publications and ex-client websites (for example www.disequilibrium1.wordpress.com, www.therapyabuse.org, www.trytherapyfree.wordpress.com, www.debunkingprimaltherapy.org) suggest that significant levels of dissatisfaction persist. Is it ethical to rest on the laurels of still-questionable research? Anecdotally, I heard of one ex-client, who volunteered to take part in a research programme to investigate the views of dissatisfied consumers, who was simply ignored when he declared that he had very grave reservations about therapy. Some of us suspect that it isn't only the 20% who are acknowledged as not benefiting from therapy, but a concealed greater figure who have appeased researchers, who officially appear as successes however ambivalent they are, or whose benefits dissolve in time. This is not mere cynicism but knowledge gathered in informal networks.

Professional issues

If we accept, or put aside, some of the above 'messiness' of the field, we are still confronted with a reality of unknown numbers of clients with a variety of personal problems being seen by thousands of practitioners in different institutional settings, each of whom have trained in various, often incompatible theories and associated skills, and who bear different professional titles. Many therapeutic outcomes may be modest or indeterminate rather than wholly successful. We do not ask who make the best therapists (practitioners are self-selecting) but we know that the majority of counsellors and therapists are women. Are there no significant questions for us to disentangle here? Neither within research nor in new theory do we seriously pose any of these questions. This may well be due to an unconscious recognition that our professional mess is beyond reform and that none of us is capable of addressing such major matters.

The training and employment question

Related closely to the above question is the problem of training courses turning out annually far greater numbers of qualified practitioners than employment openings, and probably many more than can find enough clients to provide a living in private practice. Many therapists continue to practise into late life (I have heard of active practitioners in their 80s and even 90s), which also reduces the work available for younger qualified practitioners. This problem has economic and ethical dimensions (the overselling of training), which have been raised over the years but received almost no critical attention or action. I have even heard it said that this is not a topic for serious critical thinking, compared with supposedly more intellectually worthy questions. There is arguably a kind of snobbery at work among well-remunerated academics in the field who are more interested in, for example, refining Lacanian theory than in helping sad 'hard-to-help' clients. Who will take these questions on?

Disciplinary stances

Our field has neglected inputs and criticisms from evolutionary, genetic, philosophical and political analysts of the human condition. This is probably due to a combination of sincere opposition to those proffered aetiologies and the urgent, practical orientation of most therapists, whose business is primarily interpersonal and clinical rather than intellectual in nature. Critical psychologists are usually well informed politically and invariably oppose pharmacological and other psychiatric treatments, but they are often critical of low levels of political engagement among counsellors. A small cadre of critical psychiatrists question psychodiagnosis and medication from within psychiatry; formerly we would have spoken of anti-psychiatrists and we should pause to wonder at the impotent recirculation of old ideas and titles. Many therapists have humanistic affiliations and spiritual inclinations, and they oppose medical interventions with people suffering from psychological distress. Is some sort of unarticulated pro-science vs. pro-spiritual vs. pro-political dynamic at work here? Contrary to person-centred claims to a 'quiet revolution', might not most therapy constitute a rather conservative, indeed collusive, anti-revolutionary quietism (Epstein 2006)?

Scope and limits of the field

Somewhat in contrast with the above point, we see an emergence of climate change-engendered models of ecotherapy. This development seems to show that at least some therapists are seriously engaged with the threat of climate change and the need for a radical psychological change to meet its challenges. But here we have disagreement, many also arguing that the business of therapy must only reflect what the individual client brings, that we are practitioners involved in deep therapeutic relationship work, not social activists. Can there be any consensus on these matters? Are the more conservative practitioners correct to point out the limits of psychotherapeutic reach and the folly of political grandeur? Feltham (2009) and Isack and Hook (1995) offer quite different perspectives on such questions.

We could easily add more critiques. One conclusion we might come to is that the complexity and messiness of the therapy world simply reflects the human condition. No one can know everything or cover all angles, no one is an enlightened saint or fully functioning person, we're all just doing our limited best in our own circumstances. Marie Adams' (2014) book *The Myth of the Untroubled Therapist*, based on her own doctoral research, shows that therapists are probably no more free of depression, anxiety, relationship problems, accidents, illness and physical pain than anyone else, though they presumably retain sufficient skill and discipline to attend meaningfully to others' distress. But would we equally accept that the entire 'profession' of therapy can be described in terms of 'the myth of professing to understand and address all psychological distress successfully'?

James Joyce referred to us as 'unhappitants of the earth', and Samuel Beckett declared: 'You're on earth, there's no cure for that.' A growing band of depressive realists argue that life is fairly grim, a struggle that ends in death, and that this view should not be pathologised as merely a projective cognitive distortion of depressed individuals. This is the tragic view about common unhappiness that Freud shared, while humanistic therapists tend to hold a romantic view of inevitable progress, and CBT folk hold fast to an ever-upward problem-solving optimism. Could we even see a humanistic-CBT truce soon, as former antagonists agree on a pro-positive psychology agenda? It's quite possible that counselling and psychotherapy (the enduring dichotomy of these and allied professional titles reveals a central problem) will never achieve a consensus of views, language and practice. Not only do we suffer periodically or incessantly as human beings, but also we generate endless social and professional absurdities and impasses, and seem unable to resolve these. Indeed, we even seem to have little appetite even to discuss them.

Critical afterword

I have often wondered why I share neither the optimism nor the taste for abstruse critical theory and some strands of continental philosophy that some of my colleagues appear to. The answer in fact is probably very clear. I now describe myself as a depressive realist because I am tired of apologising for being (perceived as) cynical and negative (Feltham 2015), although I might feel honoured to be associated with the cynic Diogenes. Although I have been involved in the psychotherapy and human growth world for almost 40 years, little of what I have experienced or witnessed has lived up to the early dreams and promises. I know many trainees and mature practitioners (actually far fewer of the latter) who are full of optimism about personal and social change. I have to accept that I am different, more inclined to see the negatives or limits. I am a downbeat minority in the world of therapeutic optimism. Depressive realists are stigmatised, I have come to believe, in a way that is similar to homophobia, say: one has always been this way, it is in the bones, or genes, it cannot be cured and it should be regarded as unethical to even suggest a cure for it. A difference exists between modifiable clinical depression and constitutional depressive realism. Some academics using the term 'affect studies' are now challenging the privatisation or individualisation of depression (Cvetkovich 2012).

Coming from a working-class family but now a middle-class man in my mid-60s, I have never shaken off the working-class concern for utility, concreteness and disdain for snobbery, pretence and grandeur. Although I am not quite in the blunt-speaking spade-is-a-spade category, I often feel like H.C. Andersen's little boy watching the vain emperor parading nakedly and calling him out. I have earned my living for many years now partly by producing books that relatively few read. I am a 'working-class hero' in having left the working class and become a professor, but I have never become truly and comfortably middle class, nor do I even now have much money. Yet had I lived in Mao's China I might have been made to return to work on the land. I cannot always distinguish between envy and a sense of injustice at income inequality. I could never vote right wing but neither can I identify with today's version of politically correct left wing. I find some sympathy with the critique of Torrey (1992), who chides not only Freud but also many anthropologists such as Boas, Mead and Benedict, who, he claims, distorted their findings to fit a liberal, left-wing view of noble human nature. Perhaps to some extent it is hard to appreciate others' pain or fully trust others when a core of one's own pain remains inside. The current Israeli-Palestinian conflict shows how deeply and chronically such dynamics can run at the collective level.

Most of us have long abandoned any myth of pure objectivity, and yet we somehow make the unfounded assumption that human subjectivities will naturally coincide in their own best interests. They do not. A realistic view of diversity will acknowledge that a pro-multiculturalist, Lacan-loving, anti-positivist and progressivist agenda is certainly not endorsed by all. It represents only a very small part of the possible range of views in academia and society. Ultimately we each remain in our phenomenological silos, seeing the world through the highly specialised lens of our own biology, sociology and psychology. We tend to bleed for ourselves and those we identify with, not for inimical perceptions and causes. We use the language that we are comfortable with, not an alien conceptual language. So, like everyone else, I am limited by what has determined me, any changes I make are modest and my continuing errors are inevitable: empathy can be developed for the clinical situation but it still has limits. Other romantic myths that we must confront are those of infinite neuroplasticity and endless stoicism. The heart of therapy involves a willingness and ability to hear others' experiences (empathy) but congruence demands that one be oneself. 'Work on oneself' sounds like an admirable lifelong quest but it also has its limitations, which it would be folly to deny.

Meanwhile, we must wonder if the profession has any real interest in serious reforms, and also whether it has the capability to change seriously. What was a countercultural psychoanalysis or humanistic movement long ago became a professional juggernaut, small rebellious factions notwithstanding. Well-intentioned but surface earnestness and token change are always possible. The Quality Assurance Agency's (QAA's) subject benchmarks for counselling and psychotherapy now require 'criticality' at levels 6 and 7, and this is supported by the BACP. But who can really believe that the QAA, BACP or any other establishment institution understands and values radical criticality in action? Critiques like those above are met mostly with silence from the establishment, and also with more or less silence from those who regard themselves as the real representatives of intellectual and political criticality – that is, in the main, the heavyweight critical psychologists.

In the meantime, yet more qualified counsellors join the unemployment queue or go back to their day jobs; more depressed people cast around for suitable (and, if necessary, affordable) help, in some cases trying again after previous therapeutic disappointments; sober professional and ethics committees meet regularly to examine complaints and produce worthy documents; the research bandwagon rolls on (with research academics queuing at airport security gates for their flights to exotic international conferences); and psychotherapeutic models continue to proliferate like new, competing consumer brands. Do these accusations emanate from an unworthy depressive cynicism or are they accurate perceptions and fair comment? Is it empty iconoclasm or justifiably angry critique? Should, and will, anything here change? If so, who will change it?

There are many varieties of critique in our field, at various levels, conducted with varying degrees of energy and with different motivations. Most of the critical literature is produced by academics, sometimes in conjunction with dissatisfied colleagues in the health professions. On the negative side of this matter, it is (1) not only part of an academic's job description to think critically and to produce new research but academics are also under pressure to produce publications, many of which appear in high-ranking but little-read journals. But we should add to this point three easily ignored further points: (2) that academics in the arts, humanities and social sciences have a very strong left-leaning tendency which, however 'natural' and laudable, probably distorts the flavour of debate and production of knowledge; (3) academics are middle-class intellectuals whose preoccupations and vocabulary tend to reflect their own lives, interests and ambitions; and (4) significant shifts in conceptual understanding usually take a considerable time to make their impact on social change. When you add these four points together, the result may show why the so-called critical literature actually relates poorly to the everyday world in which the majority of the population are left untouched and unhelped by such debates.

It is true that, in recent times, academics have been squeezed by the New Public Management so that stridently critical, independent thinking is minimised. Many complaints have been made about the disappearance of the public intellectual, for example, and the dumbing down of academic discourse. Academics themselves usually complain that the wickedness and short-sightedness of government is to blame for this state of affairs but it cannot be truly separated from the problem that we live in a time of capitalist realism: however angrily critical social science academics are, few if any have any actual revolutionary zeal when a salary and pension have to be protected. Anecdotally, I know of a few retired clinical psychologists with holiday homes in France or Italy – hardly a testament to a radical socialist lifestyle.

Some of the greatest intellectuals of the past have had no academic affiliation, or only peripheral and difficult academic links, such as Schopenhauer, Kierkegaard, Nietzsche, Darwin, Marx, Freud, Sartre, Cioran, Wittgenstein and many artists and novelists. A private income, rich friends or a willingness to live very frugally (remember Diogenes) often underpin original and authentic work. Some of the most interesting critical literature comes from superannuated academics or thoughtful outsiders, such as journalists. In the meantime, I am afraid that most of us are merely talking rarefied jargon to ourselves in our critical coteries and narcissistically expecting to be taken seriously.

An original, much shorter, version of this chapter first appeared as Feltham, C. (2014) 'Whatever happened to critical thinking?', *Therapy Today*, 25(3): 14–18.

References

Adams, M. (2014) *The Myth of the Untroubled Therapist*. London: Routledge.
Brooks, O. (2013) 'Methodolatry, irony, apricot cocktails', *Self and Society*, 41(1): 48–53.
Cvetkovich, A. (2012) *Depression: A Public Feeling*. Durham, NC: Duke University Press.
Dryden, W. and Feltham, C. (eds.) (1992) *Psychotherapy and Its Discontents*. Buckingham: Open University Press.
Epstein, W. (2006) *Psychotherapy as Religion: The Civil Divine in America*. Las Vegas, NV: University of Nevada Press.
Feltham, C. (forthcoming) *Depressive Realism: Interdisciplinary Perspectives*. London: Routledge.
Feltham, C. (1999) 'Facing, addressing, and learning from critiques of counselling and psychotherapy', *British Journal of Guidance and Counselling*, 27:3, 301–311.
Feltham, C. (2009) 'Revolutionary claims and visions in psychotherapy: An anthropathological perspective', *Journal of Contemporary Psychotherapy*, 39:1, 41–54.
Feltham, C. (2010) *Critical Thinking for Counselling and Psychotherapy*. London: Sage.
Feltham, C. (2013) *Counselling and Counselling Psychology: A Critical Examination*. Ross-on-Wye: PCCS Books.
Feltham, C. (2015) *Keeping Ourselves in the Dark*. Charleston, WV: Nine-Banded Books.

Heidegger, M. (2011) *Basic Writings*. London: Routledge.
Isack, S. and Hook, D. (1995) 'The psychological imperialism of psychotherapy', Paper presented to the *First Annual Qualitative Methods Conference*, 22 October, University of Witwatersrand, South Africa, http://www.criticalmethods.org/hook.htm.
Kahneman, D. (2011) *Thinking, Fast and Slow*. London: Penguin Books.
Madsen, O.J. (2014) *The Therapeutic Turn: How Psychology Altered Western Culture*. London: Routledge.
Moloney, P. (2013) *The Therapy Industry: The Irresistible Rise of the Talking Cure, and Why It Doesn't Work*. London: Pluto.
Torrey, E.F. (1992) *Freudian Fraud: The Malignant Effect of Freud's Theory on American Thought and Culture*. New York: Harper Perennial.

12
The Deleuzian Project
Chris Oakley

The publication in 1972 of the book *Anti-Oedipus: Capitalism and Schizophrenia* by Gilles Deleuze and his co-conspirator Felix Guattari was in part an endeavour to distance themselves from the overarching reach of the teachings of Jacques Lacan, which was particularly virulent in France at that time. And Lacan, faithful to his paranoia, knew something of this. The story goes that for a number of years Guattari, nicknamed 'Lacan' by some of his contemporaries owing to the compulsive mimesis of his master, was seen as one of the most prominent of the young Turks, along with Jacques-Alain Miller, converging on Lacan's infamous seminar at rue d'Ulm. Undoubtedly canny, long in the game, aware of the impending publication, Lacan of the gravel whisper, summoned Guattari to an evening of fine dining on the banks of the Seine. Whereupon, promptly dispensing with superfluous social energy, the good doctor proceeded to interrogate, to tap up Guattari as to what exactly was due to appear. Apparently murmuring approval, Lacan at one point made some suggestion that all might be enhanced if 'an analyst were involved', conveniently glossing over the fact that at the time Guattari was indeed a practising analyst. At a later point, rumour has it that Lacan set about smearing Guattari's analytic reputation. Step outside the circumference of fawning idealisation and all fellowship was rescinded. Terminal rustication. The evening came to a close with Lacan, with a faint limp, heading for the door, which closed with a resounding bang – and he and Guattari were never to meet again. Sadly there is no record of who picked up the tab.

Welcome to the Deleuzian project, which hopefully does not attempt to airbrush Guattari out of the narrative. And in their fashion I should like to begin with a reversal: rather than ask what questions might be put to them we shall examine certain questions that they pose for psychoanalysis. But, and I believe this to be faithful to their initiatives, in lieu of a more linear, goal-orientated purposefulness, may we allow a more nomadic, meandering ramble, potentially receptive to surprise, all with the possible rendezvous with a denunciation of the conspiracy that envelops us all, all marinated in their reconceptualisation of our being as a flow of multiple connecting and disconnecting intensive forces.

But as we head across the border into this curious territory, there can be no attempt to summarise, to break down the complexities, but rather to offer a small sampling, suggestive of the lurking delights within. Prior to any other considerations, a few words about Deleuze and his ideas with regard to reading. Not for him the prescription of a syllabus. Rather, he proposes allowing a book, a text, a film (after all, Deleuze had a serious cinema habit) to 'come to you'. Only then will there be a genuine readiness to engage. All of this is suffused with his maxim 'to be on the lookout'. And one might think that it is curious, to say the least, that in part there is this invitation to return to *Anti-Oedipus*, which initially appeared to such acclaim, in France at least, over 40 years ago. At that time I was beginning my involvement with R.D. Laing and the Philadelphia Association, where, hardly surprisingly, there was awareness of the book, although Laing himself was a little muted in his enthusiasm to the point of being faintly dismissive, irretrievably detached. This was despite Guattari, through his involvement with the hugely unorthodox psychiatric clinic at La Borde in the Loire Valley, having established a position within the international anti-psychiatry movement. Put most simply, I was not ready for their book; nor, until more recently, for Deleuze, despite the claim from Foucault that 'perhaps one day this century [twentieth] will be known as Deleuzian' (Foucault 1970: 885).

But early this year it 'came to me'. It began by my picking up, having been seduced by the cover with its photograph of the two of them, the hefty biographical study by Francois Dosse (2011) entitled *Intersecting Lives*. This was followed by a good friend, Adam Phillips, whom I regularly meet up with to engage in a reading of various psychoanalytic texts, suggesting that we look at *Anti-Oedipus*. Then, almost immediately, another friend, Eric Harper, proposed that we set up a small group to watch together the film *From A to Z*, in which Deleuze is interviewed by Claire Parnet, or more accurately encouraged to speak on a variety of topics, prompted by a letter of the alphabet: A for animals, B for boire, boisson... drinking, drink (at some point in his life, Deleuze was something of an alcoholic)... and so forth. And now I can't get enough of it. Why? Not because they are entirely anti-psychoanalytic, while denouncing elements of it, but more pertinently because of the questions that they raise. And, perhaps crucially, the introduction to the book by the aforementioned Foucault and his manifesto for an anti-fascist life provokes a particular thinking. Here we are called upon not to read fascistic as the historical fascism of Hitler and Mussolini but that which we all can engage in, in our everyday dealings with others, our desire to strut like cardinals, our lust for power, 'to desire the very thing that dominates and exploits us' (Foucault 2004: xv).

How, to use Foucault's words, might we 'ferret out the fascism that is ingrained in our behaviour'? The proposal is to focus on one principle from the multiplicity of suggestions or principles in this anti-fascistic polemic. I quote: 'Withdraw allegiance from the old categories of the Negative (law, limit, castration, lack, lacuna)... so long held sacred as a form of power and an access to reality' (Foucault 2004: xv).

In Lacan's (1977) theorising, desire is irretrievably linked to lack ('No lack, no desire', and some of you may recall the report of Foucault standing up in one of Lacan's seminars to insist: 'Dr Lacan, I do not lack!'). We might pause for a moment to reflect on Andre Green's criticism at the time of the book's emergence: Is there a confusion between the experience of satisfaction, for in that moment we are free from lack, but note that Green at least allows for that as a possibility, and with desire itself, which will always be linked to lack by making an absent satisfaction return? Right here, Deleuze and Guattari would in all probability seek to unhandcuff desire with any linear objective, installing something more nomadic, meandering, open to possibility.

It would seem that psychoanalysis sees lack as inherently negative rather than as a constitutive element within a whole. Examples of the latter would be silences that punctuate a conversation or pauses in a piece of music. Let us note that Deleuze is with the stoics at this critical threshold: he sees philosophy and ideology as heading off in the wrong direction, as fundamentally going astray, in the moment that truth is upheld, elevated – in other words, outside Plato's cave, in the heavens purified of all earthly illusions, where truth involves an ascent, a loftiness or indeed a transcendence we lose our way. However, if we head off in the opposite direction, where truth is now hidden, buried in the depths, Deleuze sees this as philosophy with a hammer, mistakenly attempting to crack open the truth that is insistently veiled. In fairness to Lacan, he opened his *Ecrits* (1977) with his reading of Edgar Allen Poe's *The Purloined Letter*, and showed that so often in our psychoanalytic attentiveness we miss the large letters written across the map to designate the name of the country. Meanwhile, the stoics looked laterally to the East where the sun emerges. In other words, the answer lies at the surface. What is valorised is a philosophy of immanence, and Lacan was indelibly concerned with the transcendent. Via his use of mathemes and topology, he sought to break down the (in his view) overly descriptive nature of psychoanalytic enquiry, what he dubbed 'Linguistery', to arrive at an entirely formal procedure. Deleuze and Guattari saw this as his being ensnared by the fantasy, the fiction of a pure signifier, whereby the unconscious, whether structured as a language or not, becomes static, congealed, is reduced to an empty form, where all desire and affects have been evacuated. They wanted there to be far greater emphasis on the 'I feel'. For them, unconsciousness is linked to the production of flows, lines of flight. For them it is a machine of production, crucially it produces. Thus blurring the specificity of the political, the economy and the psychic, we have not a theatre within which the Oedipal drama is played out but none other than a factory. Thus the foundation of desire would never be lack but the will to produce. How often are we faced in our work by the question: Do I need to come for analysis? Therapy, call it what you will. Their need is so redolent of the suggestion that there is some form of lack, only for the message to be returned to the sender: 'The question is one of desire.' In other words, do you want to go on producing?

Fundamentally, their claim is that desire does not lack anything, has no concern to aim for what it does not have, or was originally lost or gone missing. Nor does it inherently create a fantasy world to fend off the horror of the reality of absence. Crucially, desire is a productive force. What precisely does it produce? The answer is the real world in all of its multiplicities. It is only a secondary issue to acknowledge as a potential effect of social organisation that we can all be led astray into the simulated world of gratification, of imaginary compensation. If psychoanalysis continues to subscribe to the insistence on lack (Foucault described Lacan as a 'poor technician of desire' through his persistent and pernicious subjugation of the 'multiplicity of desire to the twofold law of structure and lack'; 2004: xiv) then it merely becomes a reactive, 'slave' psychology. And, to paraphrase Nietzsche, 'under the cloak of the psychoanalyst we smell a priest'.

Certain consequences stem from such an insistence. One is that there would be the idea of a foundational split between the subject of enunciation and the subject of the statement, thus inaugurating an ongoing, continuous agonising frustration at not being at one with oneself, not being self same. In lieu of this we substitute the alienating, representational passions of identity with the attendant concern with hierarchy.

A second consequence is that a concern with sexual pleasure, erotic fulfilment, will always already be subordinated to this issue of lack. While paying tribute to Freud for having liberated sexuality from reproduction, psychoanalysis is indicted for reducing orgasmic intensity to mere discharge, both temporary and excessive, the little death of release, all in pursuit of a futile search to be reunited with the maternal body, always leaving something to be desired.

Leaving aside that in all probability this is an entirely male version of things, let us for a moment examine the issue of pleasure, erotic pleasure, and its place in the field of desire. Intriguingly, pleasure appears to give rise to numerous difficulties for our intrepid two, and we might note that something similar can crop up in psychoanalysis. There is a tilt in the direction of it being cultured out through an emphasis on the suffering, the bravery of the one submitting to the experience. All is to be upheld as work on the trail of a particular outcome. So often it feels as if there is considerable anxiety about the possibility of the two protagonists enjoying themselves too much.

Can we allow that sexual delight is both entirely relevant on an individual and personal level while simultaneously being entangled with the political, cultural and conceptual or philosophical level as well. Some mere illustrations of this would be the issue of the entitlement to certain sexual identities and practices, the concerns regarding sexual abuse and the issue of reproductive rights. But Deleuze is deeply sceptical regarding the productive potential of sexual pleasure. Rather, he sees it as actively inhibiting a fuller fruition of his notion of desire. Not for him the persuasive wail of the band Bikini Kill pulsating in the Moscow club, the Knitting Factory, with the chorus line 'I believe in the radical possibilities of pleasure... I do, I do, I do' (Bikini Kill 1998). The orgasm is now read as being on the side of capture, as merely this, and this is – his word – deplorable, temporary release. Of course his emphasis is on the plateau, an infinity of plateaus, unquestionably on the side of immanence. But this seems to be at the expense of the peak, a devaluation of the heights of sexual ecstasy. For a moment there appears to be something of Tantric sexual wisdom here. In contrast with the objective of orgasm we have the potential for a quivering pitch of intensity which is not inherently finalised by climax. In other words, the form that the pleasure might take, to follow a Deleuzian trope, would be a multiplicity of intense states through which any number of connections and disconnections might unfurl. All well and good, one might think. Nevertheless, there appears to be a fundamental conflict between the plateau and the orgasmic, in whatever form it might emerge, for

Deleuze, while they might have been sustained as both having a place within the productions of the desiring machine.

If desire as a mode of production is much more on the side of an openness to the multiplicities of life – back to Deleuze's idea of being 'on the look out' – then perhaps we can begin to glimpse why he appears to be so dubious about pleasure, so persistently seeking to disentangle it from desire. As mentioned previously, orgasm for him is linked to capture. The body appears spoken for, claimed, chained to pro-ordained insistencies of – their word – territoriality (an example of this would be the erotogenic zones), thus preventing rather than permitting an expressivity of the body in the widest possible sense: an emergence of multiple intensities. Thus desire, rather than pleasure production, is upheld as a far more productive force.

Post-Foucault, sexuality may be acknowledged as a convention of cultural and historical construction, saturated by political subjectification. It can be seen as becoming sedimented via a stratification of our desire, with the emphasis on orgasm now associated with a closing-down rather than an opening-up of possibilities within our embodiment. Politically there is an organised seizure of our bodies, all coerced into historically specific forms of subjectivity. Here, Guattari, who used to organise vigilante groups that would take it upon themselves to disrupt any potential monogamous couplings on the verge of taking place at La Borde, emerges as the more militant. In his work *Three Billion Perverts on the Stand* (1996), he vigorously endorses what he sees as new and direct expressions of desire, all on the side of a proposed creativity through eluding the prevailing discursive and dominant order, what he enthusiastically saw as libidinal disruptions aligned with multiplicity and fluidity. Simultaneously he is only too aware of the potential enclosure, converging on a fixity, of the dialectic, the back and forth between liberation and repression.

Nevertheless, something of this continues to haunt the scene: an unceasing oscillation regarding capture and emancipation, en route to a freeing-up of desire production. And all of this is framed by the concerns particularly in *Anti-Oedipus* with the unquenchable link between capitalism and the Oedipal. Both are seen as modes of enslavement. To cover a bit of ground very quickly – in other words, risking a simplification, the capitalist project is seen as unwaveringly involved in capture and codification. And the claim is that psychoanalysis is engaged in precisely an identical operation. At the microlevel we can bear witness to exactly that – the pathetic concerns at an organisational level with regard to registration and the codification of identity. Will we ever learn that as far as Joe Public is concerned we are all shrinks. But Deleuze and Guattari have much larger fish to fry.

The capitalist system turns territory into land, facilitating the aggregation of stock, pushes activity into labour, and exchange into the accumulation of capital. A recoding emerges whereby market calculations replace more primordial values and belief systems. Money becomes the prevailing signifier of worth, of value. Simultaneously the movement and behaviour of bodies become subordinated to the system via abstraction and commodification. While a degree of deference is acknowledged to Freud for his configuration of desire as libido – we all have sex lives even if we are not all having sex – he is accused of his involvement in a disastrous recoding of desire by delimiting it to the confines of the family, all underwritten by normative Oedipal considerations. He closes down 'the wide open spaces glimpsed for a moment', replacing them with the 'dirty little secret' with the claim that all we ever truly want is to either kill or fuck the other, just as we are captured, captivated by the capitalist concerns with money so that our libidinous lives are confined, made docile, manageable through submission to the Oedipal recoding. The boss, the governor, is money. We all want the boss, thus Oedipal desire, even though it regulates and defiles us, reconfigured as a despotic image, is what we seemingly willingly sign up for. The form that the capture takes is via the representations and repression of sex into an Oedipal economy, all subject to a recoding into the genital, reproductive and familial. As Slavoj Zizek (2006) claims, the superegoic imperative is that we 'enjoy', but the danger is that pleasure of an erotic kind, coerced into these Oedipal cul-de-sacs, propped up by the economy of lack, merely serves the capitalist order. We are led to believe that we are always frustrated, always wanting more, propelling us into a frenzy of continuous consumption – a capitalist imperative writ large. Yet by placing our trust in their anti-Oedipal conceptualisation of desire, we align ourselves with the intoxicating invitation to free desire from the interweave of capitalist and Oedipal recoding. By so doing we extrude 'the dirty little secret', which is not to say that there is no truth to it, but we recognise its potential to stand in the way of those glorious wide open spaces. And an initial step in that project would be to acknowledge – and they suggest this through the utilisation of the notion of 'the desiring machine' – the juxtaposition of the libidinal and the industrial, economies that are more usually kept apart, thereby sustaining a mystification as to the trouble that we are in.

Perhaps it is not too difficult to allow how capitalism exploits sexual pleasure. Lyotard (2007) for one links the postponement of orgasm in order to enhance, to increase pleasure, to certain types of commercial purposefulness. Indeed, one potential effect is the insistent blurring of whatever we might mean by 'real' pleasure and pleasure that is merely an effect of commodity consumption. But can we genuinely dispense with the pleasure principle so easily? Of course, we can say with Lacan that what lies beyond the pleasure principle is enjoyment, aka *jouissance* – never to be conflated with joy. Deleuze seemingly writes it off as too contaminated in its formation through Oedipal insistencies. Instead he wishes to underline the virtues of a desire that is now potentially released from the codes and images of psychoanalytic and capitalist concerns.

Inevitably in our contemporary world the issue of pornography looms large. In the USA approximately 400 films are made for the cinema and television each year, while the porn industry makes somewhere in the region of 10,000–11,000 per annum. So it is not difficult to argue that our sexuality is continually organised through representation and commodification. This perhaps most explicitly and simultaneously in all of its banality is exemplified by the 'money shot' – a man coming on a woman's face. Now in part, and this is obvious, this is a reference to its intrinsic value to the film – no come shot, no porn movie.

The orgasm now has a particular quality of visuality. Here we might recall one reading of the claim that it's a man's world: that there is a cultural insistence on the erection of the visible, the representable, the specular, the specularisable. And this can be seen as emblematic of capitalist coding: waving your wad, shooting your load, loads of money, loads of surplus value. Linda Williams (1999) in her book *Hard Core: Power, Pleasure and the 'Frenzy of the Visible'* claims that the money shot is the perfect testimony to the illusory one-dimensional society of the spectacle of advanced capitalism. Ultimately we are as concerned with consuming images as much as we seek to consume things. In the money shot the inflated 'spending penis' exemplifies the late capitalist pleasure-orientated world – pleasure now not the acquisition of a seriality of fetishised objects but all converging on the surplus value of spending, of coming, of spunking up your wad. This is what Deleuze and Guattari might designate as machinic enslavement, or at other moments describe as paranoiac capture – paranoia as understood as a system of absolute belief where all meaning is fixed, sedimented and defined by an absolute authority. Hereby the money shot is a violent manifestation of the capitalist production of a paranoid sexuality, and representation is always in the foreground when we seek, are on the lookout for, indications of capture.

But immediately, after all it is staring us in the face, this model of sex that generates such an understanding is an inherently masculine version, heading off in the direction of a misleading conflation of erotic pleasure and paranoid functionality. It is as if in their very act of endeavouring to unloosen the ties of such paranoid, fascistic modalities, Deleuze and Guattari are caught in that which folds back on itself, returning us to more of the same.

Let us now turn to the issue of another trajectory: that of schizoanalysis. Deleuze always claimed that one amid the multiple tasks of philosophy was to generate new concepts. Fair enough, but as to whether this is an entirely felicitous one I have my doubts. They, to do justice to their project, attempt to head off such criticisms at the pass, claiming – in advance – that any such reading would be a 'bad reading' if all that one saw amid their initiatives was an identification of the revolutionary with 'the schizo'. Even at that moment there is something of the colloquialism that evokes a wince every bit as much as when anybody refers to a woman as a 'bird', 'chick' or 'babe'. Now a principle point of differentiation of schizoanalysis is to 'overturn the theatre of representation into the order of desiring- production' (Deleuze and Guattari 2004: 294). Or, to put it another way, the project is to disperse notions of private identity without a blurring of our singularity. Identity is the concern of being this rather than that – those questions of 'Am I man or am I a woman?', of 'Am I alive or am I dead?' dislodged by an embrace of ourselves as 'collective agents of enunciation that for their part refer to machinic arrangements' (Deleuze and Guattari 2004: 294). It is instructive to recall the authors' prolonged resistance to all and any attempts to establish which parts of the book belonged to whom.

An initial hesitation stems from their recruiting of the 'schizo', the schizophrenic, potentially compounded by the rallying call 'A schizophrenic out for a walk is a better model than a neurotic lying on an analyst's couch' (Deleuze and Guattari 2004: 2). This is partly because this appears to be antithetical to the Foucauldian anti-fascistic manifesto where he proposes 'develop[ing] action, thought, and desires by proliferation, juxtaposition, and disjunction, and not by subdivision and pyramidal hierarchization' (Foucault 2004: xv), and partly because it raises the question: 'better model' for what? Once we step onto the terrain of psychosis, so wedded to the issue of only ever being driven mad by those who in their turn were driven mad themselves, via the insistent trigger of thought appropriation, we come up against the issue of thinking. Now clearly, and after all why not? Deleuze and Guattari propose a thinking differently with regard to the crucial issue of desire, but a thinking nevertheless. And the hallmark of psychosis is precisely that there is an impairment of the capacity to think. The psychotic lives in a world of ideas, but ask them to have an idea about those ideas – and that's what thinking is – we will inevitably draw a blank. It is not resistance but rather that this appropriation has provoked a foreclosure of just such possibilities. So why uphold this state of affairs as a model for anything? What revolutionary potentialities lurk within? Ultimately it is difficult to resist putting the question to them: Would you really prefer your child to be that schizophrenic out for a walk? That's not because they would be less than, or that there would be something wrong with them, but because something would have gone wrong – seriously wrong.

In all probability that would be to understand the term too concretely. Rather, it is utilised as a strategy to gesture towards a particular mode of functioning that is both facilitated, encouraged by 'a schizophrenic accumulation of energy or charge' (Deleuze and Guattari 2004: 37), and simultaneously suppressed by the capitalist economy. Schizophrenia is now to be understood as a process, linked to paths of excess, free from concerns with normative structures of human interaction. But when our capitalist world is unable to countenance this, when the so-called 'disturbed' become too disturbing, the result is 'madness'. The process submits to a repression, a suppression usually of a pharmaceutical nature, that inexorably culminates in the installation of schizophrenia as an entity. In other words, we are amid the terrain of operators and things, which is acknowledged as a locus of intense suffering.

So what might be meant by schizophrenia as a process? One of the more prominent Deleuze and Guattari commentators, Eugene Holland (1999) from Ohio State University, has come up with two intriguing and potentially rehabilitating possibilities: jazz and football. Let us jettison any associations, although this takes some doing, with anything associated with so-called mental illness. Instead, let us set up a continuum of possibility with improvisational jazz at one end and a symphony orchestra at the other; or football, as we know it here in Europe and beyond, and American football. In both the latter and with the orchestra we may note fairly rigid specialisation, with order imposed from above by either the coach or the conductor. Now contrast this with football and jazz, where both would appear to allow for something more free-flowing. In football the best referees are those who allow the game to flow, one of the more treasured terms within the Deleuzian trajectory, in a breaking-free from those Oedipal confines where what is to be privileged is the chance, the random, the spontaneous, the nomadic, the meandering. This is curiously somewhat akin to psychoanalysis at its best. Indeed, let us give the last word to R.D. Laing, who inevitably had considerable affinity with these concerns. When asked what he was trying to achieve in his psychoanalytic work, he said that it was to the best of his ability to enable the other 'to be as alive as they could possibly be'. What else could anyone possibly desire?

References

Bikini Kill (1998) 'I like fucking', in *The Singles* CD, Olympia, WA and Portland, OR: Kill Rock Stars, KRS298, Track 8.
Deleuze, G. and Guattari, F. (2004) *Anti-Oedipus: Capitalism and Schizophrenia*. London and New York: Continuum Books.
Foucault, M. (1970) 'Theatrum philosophicum', *Critique*, 282, November 1970, pp. 885–908.
Foucault, M. (2004) 'Preface', in G. Deleuze and F. Guattari (eds.) *Anti-Oedipus: Capitalism and Schizophrenia*. London and New York: Continuum Books, pp. xiii–xvi.
Francois, D. (2011) *Gilles Deleuze & Felix Guattari Intersecting Lives*. Colombia University Press.
Guattari, F. (1996) 'Three billion perverts on the stand', in G. Genesko (ed.) *The Guattari Reader*. Cambridge: Blackwell, pp. 185–192.
Holland, E. (1999) *Deleuze and Guattari's Anti-Oedipus: An Introduction to Schizoanalysis*. London and New York: Routledge.
Lacan, J. (1977) *Ecrits: A Selection*. New York: Norton.
Lyotard, J.-F. (2007) *Libidinal Economy*. London: Continuum Books.
Williams, L. (1999) *Hard Core: Power, Pleasure and the 'Frenzy of the Visible': Expanded Edition*. Berkeley: University of California Press.
Zizek, S. (2006) *How to Read Lacan*. London: Granta Publications.

13
Psychoanalysis and the Event of Resistance

Steven Groarke

Does psychoanalysis matter politically? Further to Freud's own involvement in the institutional politics of the psychoanalytic movement, the relationship between psychoanalysis and politics has been addressed on any number of occasions. In this chapter, I shall focus particularly on the Freudian interpretation of resistance as a critical and political resource. For Freud, the 'whole theory of psycho-analysis is...in fact built up on the perception of the resistance offered to us by the patient when we attempt to make his unconscious conscious to him' (1933: 68). But does the treatment of the patient's internal resistances (*innere Widerstände*) exhaust the critical reach of the Freudian concept of resistance? I don't think this is necessarily the case. I will argue in fact that the political significance of psychoanalysis rests on the historical as well as the personal meaning of resistance.

How to link the therapeutic practice of psychoanalysis (the apolitical nature of treatment in its clinical specificity) to practical politics is not something that can be decided theoretically. The relationship between the analysing situation and the unfolding of events isn't subject to prediction outside a particular institutional and historical context, and I certainly have no intention of making any general pronouncements along these lines. I shall limit myself to the more modest aim of outlining a strategic conception of the Freudian interpretation. It seems to me that we can assess the political significance of psychoanalysis most effectively by approaching Freud as a strategist. In adopting this approach, I shall argue that the concept of resistance has a wider critical range when it is worked through rather than pitted against psychoanalysis.

I shall present this argument through a selective reading of the three lectures, dating from the early 1990s, collected in Derrida's *Résistances de la psychanalyse* (1996). The chapter isn't intended as a comprehensive evaluation anymore than a summary overview of Derrida's arguments.

Instead, I shall elaborate on some of the questions that are raised in the lectures, which Derrida (1996: 48) himself preferred to think of as 'discussions' with posthumous interlocutors. A few preliminary comments may help to clarify what I aim to achieve here.

First, the distinction that Derrida makes between 'resistance-*to*-psychoanalysis' and 'resistances-*of*-psychoanalysis' provides the basic framework for this chapter. Opposition to psychoanalysis has been abundantly clear from the beginning, and the verdict delivered by Gustav Aschaffenburg, in 1906, at a congress of neurologists and psychiatrists in Baden-Baden is representative of the widespread rejection of Freud at the time across Europe and the USA (Gay 1988: 194). A professor of neurology and psychiatry at Heidelberg, Aschaffenburg's dismissal of the psychoanalytical method as wrong, objectionable and unnecessary turns out to have been an accurate forecast of the current state of play. I take up these objections in the third and final part of the chapter as part of the increasingly scathing attacks on psychoanalysis in contemporary culture. It is important to note, however, that Derrida doesn't prioritise this aspect of resistance in his lectures. He is primarily concerned with the resistances of psychoanalysis, which I attempt to elaborate as a philosophy of defiance under the headings of plurality, helplessness, and the archive. Taking the three lectures as a point of departure, I also draw on Caygill's (2013) indispensable rereading of Clausewitz in order to draw out the critical potential of psychoanalysis. My basic argument is that the courage and conviction that go with speaking out against the consensus are integral to the analytic experience and, as such, form part of the historical event of resistance.

Second, although it isn't my intention here to recount the history of anti-psychiatry, nonetheless I think it is important to note that the questions that Derrida raised in his lectures may be seen more broadly in this context. Certainly, the political implications of Derrida's questions are, in many respects, consistent with the alternative movement of resistant psychiatry in a range of interventions: most notably the work of Tosquelles and Fanon at the hospital of Saint-Alban; the work of Jean Oury and Félix Guattari at the Clinique de La Borde; and the treatment of schizophrenia by David Cooper and R.D. Laing in Villa 21 at Shenley Hospital, and later at Kingsley Hall. The alternative movement of psychiatry along these lines intersects, albeit in complex and divergent ways, with the history of psychoanalysis understood as a series of controversial discussions.

Third, as for the shadows that fall across the lectures, I think it is possible to extrapolate a philosophy of defiance from Derrida's ghostly schema, a philosophy that 'can only *maintain itself* with some ghost, can only *talk with or about* some ghost [s'entretenir *de quelque fantôme*]' (1993: xviii). No one since Freud has given as much thought as Derrida has to ghosts; he belongs in the wake of the Shakespearean precedent with Joyce, Beckett and Sebald among the great ghost-writers of modern European literature. It would, I fear, take us too far afield to include the arguments from *Spectres de Marx*, suffice it to note here that Derrida's critique of psychoanalysis is theoretically and politically consistent with his critique of Marxism. I am not suggesting that Derrida attempted a combined reading of Marx and Freud, for instance, in the critical tradition of Marcuse, Habermas and Axel Honneth. Nevertheless, he did open up further possibilities along these lines, particularly with respect to the spectral logic of the Marxian theory of ideology. An extensive work of exegesis would be required to link the themes of justice and the gift, on the one hand, to the problems of legacy and the archive, on the other. What should we stress in the meantime? For Derrida, Marxism and Freudianism denote pluralities that cannot be intercepted or captured by the proper names 'Marx' and 'Freud'. The general point is that the dead cannot be outwitted by the living. Rather, as the lectures under discussion demonstrate time and again, speaking out in the name of truth results in a haunted dialogue that takes in the living along with the dead. We have before us Kent's warning not to vex the King's ghost. And yet, Derrida appears to take it upon himself, so to speak, to disturb the Heideggerian *Geist* on the contentious grounds that it is only at the border or limit between life and death that the courage of truth and of truth-telling becomes an event.

With the aim of describing the historical event of resistance as synonymous with the invention of psychoanalysis, I shall elaborate in turn on three basic propositions. First, the work of the negative exceeds the dialectic through the resistances of psychoanalysis in the plural. Second, the retreat before death articulates the destructive drive as an occasion of resistance. Third, the politics of psychoanalysis is essentially a politics of memory, inheritance and the transmission of unconscious forces across generations. In short, my argument covers a strategic field ranging from psychoanalysis in the plural through the predicament of distress to the paradoxes of the archive.

Plurality

That psychoanalysis is the occasion rather than the object of discussion in Derrida's lectures is a salutary reminder that there is still time today for distinctions that matter. The philosophical imperative of working through the Freudian interpretation is driven by the distinction between 'objects of knowledge' and 'occasions of thinking'. Events occur through the occasions of thinking and, as Derrida never allows us to forget, no event would take place without the making and remaking of thoughts. As such, Freudianism may be seen as one of the events of our time and, in his concluding remarks on Foucault's *Histoire de la folie*, Derrida points out that the historical-critical project itself cannot but give voice to the Freudian controversies that it continues to stir up. For Derrida it is always a case of working through (*Durcharbeitung*) psychoanalysis, even where it is assumed that the analysis is wrong, objectionable and unnecessary. Working through thus allows for the resistance of resistance-to-analysis; hence a counter-resistance which resists the totalising thought of resistance per se.

We can posit an initial hypothesis on the strength of Derrida's claim concerning the unavoidable encounter with the Freudian interpretation – namely: resistance resists being totalised to the extent that working through psychoanalysis renders resistances in the plural. The controversial discussions that constitute the history of psychoanalysis may be seen in terms of the contested passage to the plural. It is important to emphasise that the latter denotes 'more than one' rather than a particular doctrine or political philosophy. In other words, I am not suggesting that the political significance of psychoanalysis may be inferred from notions of the so-called pluralist society. Rather, the point is that there is always 'more than one' resistance in the occasions of thinking that comprise the psychoanalytic movement. I take it that this is what Derrida (1996: 19) means when he says: 'there is no unity of the concept of analysis... from philosophy to psychoanalysis'.

While tradition no doubt presides over individual talent, the archaeological determination of analysis is nonetheless subject to dissolution or dismantlement, insofar as we are driven to undo what we believe we have done. The conservative hypothesis, which appears from a certain vantage point as the very meaning of tragedy, is at once undeniable and impeachable. Derrida posits the historical situation of psychoanalysis in these terms (whether or not we insist on the tragic dimension of our modernity) with respect to the infinite play of enmity and affinity. Psychoanalysis does not have a unified concept of resistance, as Derrida points out, precisely because it is determined, so to speak, 'in relation to what resists it' (1996: 20). The same argument applies to the institution of psychoanalysis itself: there is no unified concept of psychoanalysis either as a system of thought or as a national or international organisation. Once again, it is important not to confuse the idea of psychoanalysis in the plural with the relatively trivial formulation of plurality – namely, 'the many voices of psychoanalysis'. The strong version of the 'plural' (*pluriel*) means that there isn't something called 'psychoanalysis' (*la psychanalyse*), something to which 'many voices' could be attributed. Put simply, there is 'more than one' from the beginning – that is, insofar as the passage to the plural constitutes the very possibility of psychoanalysis.

Starting, then, from the concrete occasions of clinical and critical thinking, the possibility of psychoanalysis in the plural comes into play in various ways, above all in terms of the 'resistance of others [as] the condition of our own development [*progrès*]' (Certeau 1969: 217). The same holds for Foucault as for Derrida when it comes to the irreducibility of resistance as an historical event: 'resistance comes first, and resistance remains superior to the forces of the process; power relations are obliged to change with the resistance' (1984: 167). In this respect the concept of the plural provides a way of theorising the political subject of psychoanalysis that is consistent with the critique of the historical *a priori* in Foucault. At the same time, the idea of psychoanalysis in the plural is clearly at odds with the growing consensus that psychoanalysis is wrong, objectionable and unnecessary.

Of course, by assuming the objectifying logic of right or wrong, it is possible to condemn psychoanalysis in advance. It is the invariability of the verdict delivered along these lines, the juridical presupposition that psychoanalysis cannot and never will be right, that comes sharply into focus in Derrida's discussion of Foucault's *Histoire de la folie*. Where 'history' and 'madness' are rendered as objects of science, resistance to psychoanalysis on so-called 'critical' grounds may turn out to be another kind of obedience. Notwithstanding the critical reach of his thought, Foucault's history of madness may actually play into a politico-juridical framework in which Freud stands accused in advance. That the facts are determined by trials of one kind or another is always a matter of urgency in the controversies that constitute the history of psychoanalysis. The critical import of the Foucauldian project, therefore, which Derrida certainly doesn't reject out of hand, is nonetheless put in jeopardy so long as madness as such – the 'lightning flashes and cries... in Nerval or Artaud, Nietzsche or Roussel' (Foucault 1954: 87–88) – remains an object of historical inquiry.

Contrary to the objectification of Freud and psychoanalysis, the resistance of the resistance-to-analysis keeps both defiance and a resistant subjectivity permanently in play as an historical event. It is the game of defiant resistance, understood as an invention of psychoanalysis, which determines the political import of the Freudian interpretation. This, at least, is my main argument: the analysing situation is continuous with the actualisation of potentials of life in the political field. Together, psychoanalysis and politics provide specific occasions for human social contact, where resistance retains the upper hand and remains the critical driving force. I am not suggesting (assuming it were possible) that one should aim to avoid resistance to analysis altogether. The idea of avoiding resistance to analysis, clinically speaking, makes about as much sense as wanting to protect psychoanalysis from the latest attacks in the public sphere. Neither of these manoeuvres is viable so long as we admit the strategic conception of psychoanalysis in the plural. Resistances of presuppose resistance to.

The potential space of psychoanalysis, therefore, must be defended permanently as a matter of course. Philosophically, this places the articulation of resistances in the plural under the Kantian modal category of 'actuality' rather than the modal categories of 'possibility' or 'necessity'. The Kantian distinctions in fact are no less important for the strategic argument than the distinction between 'occasions' and 'objects'. It will be evident here, as I have already indicated, that my application of the strategic argument is informed by Caygill's (2013) radical reappraisal of resistance and its place in contemporary politics. Based on a re-evaluation of Clausewitz's *On War* (1832/1982), Caygill allows us to identify the politics of psychoanalysis with the actualisation of a capacity to sustain courage; to demand political justice; and to exercise prudence. In particular, the relationship of a resistant subject to appearances may be seen as essentially 'defiant, governed by chance and enmity and dedicated to the actualization of a capacity to resist in the face of this predicament' (Caygill 2013: 97). As such, the problematic of defiance offers a viable critical alternative to the classical Freudian ideal of freedom through autonomy. Although not set out explicitly until the late works, Freud acknowledged from the beginning that the predicament of helplessness becomes an occasion of resistance. It would be fair to say that my argument is essentially a gloss on this fundamental insight.

The idea that resistance marks out the contemporary Freudian subject in its actuality as well as its plurality, indeed as a political and historical subject, undercuts the homogeneity of the analytic situation but also the general ideology of consensual times. The realisation of resistances in the plural necessarily involves the kind of contrapuntal listening that Jonathan Sklar (2011: xiv) applies to the analytic situation. Politically speaking, resistance and counter-resistance constitute a dynamic framework of permanent defiance, manifest as an interminable doubling of sense and non-sense, a ceaseless work of exclusion/inclusion, or, as Derrida emphasises repeatedly, an inexhaustible *fort/da* acted out historically as well as personally. As such, resistance of the resistance-to-analysis presupposes 'the other side of psychoanalysis' (Foucault 1954: 31) within the analytic situation. Resistance understood as a capacity common to all institutes a contingent suspension of the rules of analysis within the very institution of psychoanalysis. Potential is more important here than the 'freedom to relate', insofar as the latter fails to account for the desiring subject in its connection to the pure immanence of life along the energetic trajectory of affects and drives.

To give an example of what I mean by a progressively democratic arrangement of analysis, it seems to me that Jonathan Sklar's reflections on the potential for 'a new European analytic dialogue' (2011: 169) may be seen as an occasion of resistance. There is no guarantee how things will turn out, but the emphasis on new forms of analytic subjectivity within the context of the European Psychoanalytic Federation keys in with the political and philosophical stakes that are identified in Caygill's reappraisal of Clausewitz. Thus, based on Caygill's philosophical critique of resistance, we can extend the new forms of collective institutional activity envisaged by Sklar – indeed, 'in the spirit of Freud's legacy' (2011: 169) – to a framework of non-dialectical reciprocity of forces. The clinical focus of the Freudian interpretation, in this case, is linked to an affirmative and inventive type of resistance through the question that continues to animate the resistant subject – namely, how to construct a transformative history under traumatic or catastrophic conditions.

The question of how to appropriate the potentiality of the negative as history, how to experience the unthinkable in the past tense, is fundamental for the event of resistance. And as Sklar's clinical examples demonstrate, it isn't simply a question of breaking down the resistances on the classical Freudian model of repression and interpretation. Further to the model of repression-recollection, the philosophy of defiance, according to Caygill's rereading of Clausewitz, eschews the idea of history as *telos* in favour of the actualisation of the capacity to resist. Thus, rather than a reconciliation of destruction modelled on the philosophical eschatology of Hegel's fulfilment, the presupposition of counter-resistance involves a strategic model of psychoanalytic thinking. The latter presupposes the identification of potentiality and the negative, as opposed to the logic of the dialectic. In characteristic fashion, Lacan (1986: 310) clarifies matters for us from the structural point of view of desire, pointing out that Oedipus, having journeyed with his faithful daughter to the hamlet of Colonus, remains unyielding to the end and absolutely unreconciled.

Helplessness

I am not proposing a clear-cut distinction between critical theory and *Geist der Utopie* (the spirit of utopia). Nor do I think Derrida's critique of psychoanalysis operates with any such distinction in mind. The strategic conception of the Freudian interpretation, on my understanding at least, is essentially redemptive rather than reconciliatory; it involves a redemptive promise of reclamation together with a defiant and permanent capacity to resist. To demonstrate the politico-theological framework of analytic thinking, I shall consider the utopian appropriation of psychoanalysis in Winnicott and Marcuse. We can take Derrida's interminable reading of Lacan as our model: reading for the Other in the name of love ('for the love of...') involves not only a sense of responsibility suffused by history, but also a gesture of helpless compassion as the ground-tone for the critical occasion. By 'helpless' I mean the fact that, according to the appearance of the face which speaks even in its nakedness and destitution ('Thou shalt not kill'), one or other party is always left in the solitude of questioning rather than the enjoyment of peace in non-violence. This is what I call the predicament of distress, in which resistance seems to me to be a fundamental resource.

At the heart of every discussion or critical occasion, lending life to the controversy that it continues to generate in its wake, there is an emptied voice shaken by the feeling that it is too late; someone is inevitably left alone to imagine the other person's response. The predicament of distress issues inevitably from what Levinas (1998) calls 'the mortality of the face'. In this case, remaining (*restance*) involves a way of listening to listening (Faimberg 2005), or listening out, listening in (Parsons 2014) without guarantees of any kind. Most importantly, what repeats itself between remaining and resistance doesn't go into memory. Repetition isn't a form of honouring the dead, anymore than concern for the other's death translates into public testimony. Where remaining doesn't lend itself to 'dialectical sublation' but remains 'unanalyzable' (Derrida 1996: 30), the activity of listening itself exceeds *in memoriam*. What Derrida describes as 'the remaining of the rest [*la restance du reste*]' (1996:

26) is played out not as remembrance or the reminiscence of being but, rather, as contact with reality beyond the reality principle, or as memory without recollection (Botella and Botella 2005).

Remembering (*Er-innerung*) the forgotten doesn't account for the possibility of survival, at least not when it comes to the demands of psychic negativism and its traumatic implications. One is helpless precisely in the sense of not being able to answer for the other person, even as one is obliged to find the resources in oneself to respond without reserve. Such is the incomparable weight and paradox of the archive as the potential space of the real. While Levinas parts company with Heidegger on these grounds, similarly, Derrida articulates the predicament of distress as a political and an ethical predicament. We should also include the religious framework, which comes into play, for instance, in Derrida's address for Foucault. In this case, Derrida acknowledges that we must reckon with ghosts in doing justice to them – that is, not in the attitude of being-towards-death (*Sein zum Tode*) but in living on (*sur-vie*). In a reckoning that is anything but final, we must do justice to the dead in the sense of 'a survival whose possibility in advance comes to disjoin or dis-adjust the identity to itself of the living present as well as of any effectivity' (1993: xx).

The predicament of distress, therefore, is confirmed by one's responsibility for the death that all along would not fail to arrive; it is as if it had always been so, even before the beginning. The commitment to justice ('we must do justice to...') will have carried life beyond a life, reaching a tragic level, as Lacan (1986: 300) points out, in Antigone's *Atē*. That we do justice to the dead only by accepting something that issues before us in previous generations is exemplified to the point of tragedy in *Antigone*. This, then, is the arch-use of the French future perfect (*futur antérieur*), the future anterior in the conditional, that underpins the strategic conception of psychoanalysis in the plural. It isn't simply the inevitability of death as such, the *factum brutum* that one dies (*Man stirbt*), or that I am dying (*sum moribundus*) from the first, which animates the deep resistances of psychoanalysis. Death means something more than the perishable – indeed, something that doesn't fall under the jurisdiction of the hermeneutics of reason.

What does it mean to say that the meaning of life is that it ends? To what extent is it a question of meaning at all? Does something other than sense insist beyond the perishable? Or does life itself resist meaning because it ends? In the history of psychoanalysis, questions regarding the sense of an ending, or the failure to come to any understanding in these terms, are synonymous with the occasions of resistance and controversy. Not surprisingly, then, the hypothesis of the death drive (*Todestriebe*) is among the most contentious issues in psychoanalysis. And in his lecture on Lacan, Derrida addresses what seems to me the most profound difficulty in the resistances of psychoanalysis, a difficulty that turns on the question of 'primordiality' (*Ursprünglichkeit*) and the other person. How is it that, even where one may be subject to death at the hands of an enemy, the death of the Other is nonetheless primordial? What does it mean to say that 'to die for...' is prior to authentic death?

Let me rephrase what I think is a pivotal question for psychoanalysis but also for critical theory in general. How does turning away from death, the retreat before death, bear the weight of accepting responsibility for something that one hasn't done? Levinas is an indispensable reference here. We rely on him (1998: 216) for the ethics of sacrifice as 'the primordial inflection of the affective as such'. And yet within the domain of clinical thinking itself it seems to me that Winnicott provides a complementary argument. Through his central preoccupation with mothers and babies, he (1945: 152) effectively retrieved the utopian dimension of life by positing that 'the mother and child *live an experience together*'. Living together is not primarily a matter of one's own being or being in its own right. Rather, living an experience together consists of being alive towards concern. Maternal devotion brings life into a state of concernment from the beginning as a manifestation of concerned living.

What is crucial here, of course, is that psyche cannot come about without love. Thus concern for being, the achievement of going on being, comes about in and through love or devotion to the Other. The further point I wish to make is that death confirms what is at stake here. I think that the retreat before death shows that the excessiveness of sacrifice ('to die for...') and the pure immanence of life are coextensive, insofar as the presentiment of death is manifest as love, be it ruthless love to begin with. Let me propose a second hypothesis at this point: the matrix that constitutes being alive is put under stress from the beginning by the possibility of death. And by 'stress' I don't mean a concern for one's own skin so much as an anxiety over 'the nakedness of the face and its mortality' (Levinas 1998: 217). The baby clings to the experience of his mother's face before establishing the contours of his own body. The clinging suggests that life comes under stress to begin with as a concern for the Other's death. More primordial than an anxiety arising in anticipation of one's own death, one is stressed or worried over the death of the Other.

When my child is able to say what has been harassing him all along, when he finds words for the worry, he asks if I am going to die. How will he keep me from dying? His question is the groundwork of concern over the Other's dying, and I want to suggest that the hesitation to which it gives rise amounts to 'a surpassing of the *conatus essendi* of life' (Levinas 1998: 215). Once again, it is incumbent on me to account for the coexistence of life and concern, or to say how I think life affects itself in conjunction with the innate morality of concern. I believe that this requires a redistribution of the sensible from object-relating to object-usage. My argument is especially indebted to Winnicott at this point, although I don't necessarily share his developmental model.

In a remarkable late paper on the use of an object that has yet to be read in the direction of its overwhelming vitality, Winnicott describes a situation where the subject destroys the object and the object survives destruction by the subject. Summaries of the paper are readily available in the secondary literature, but the essential point needs to be made. In proposing that use alone gives the object its value, Winnicott reveals himself in the Anglican tradition of Thomas Traherne on the formal causes of God's kingdom. The arch-use of object-usage isn't simply a developmental proposition; it isn't the case, in my view, that concern develops out of some more primordial state of life. Nor does ontology account for a situation in which the continuity of being presupposes devotion to the other's longing for life and happiness. The predicament that is presented in Winnicott (1968: 222–223) as a paradox entails an 'acceptance of the ongoing destruction in unconscious fantasy relative to object-relating'. To put it more simply, 'While I am loving you I am all the time destroying you in (unconscious) *fantasy*.' The Winnicottian life, at its most radical, allows for the inextricable link between ruthlessness and devotion, as distinct from the fusion of the drives.

It is perhaps only 'the becoming real because destroyed' that provides a viable context for Derrida's unequivocal claim that 'we loved each other very much, Lacan and I' (1996: 42). No doubt this is a fantasy, although it may also be the only personal-historical reality in which life goes on being life. In any case, the claim presupposes an occasion in which the resistances of psychoanalysis are emphatically on the side of defiance rather than compliance. In positing the situation in which becoming real is possible, Winnicott had in mind a mother who enjoys her baby's appetite for life, with greedy desire and passion on both sides. However, as well as being an object of satisfaction, this is a mother who also remembers the baby who will have forgotten her. Love's legend feeds the family romance, even as life manifests itself in memory and forgetting. Again, the *futur antérieur* in the conditional demarcates a forgetfulness that goes with living and, therefore, has nothing to do with denial or repudiation. The overlap between memory and forgetting demarcates what will and will not have come about towards a living-on rather than a being towards death. As such, the destructive gesture of forgetfulness comes about spontaneously following the baby's devouring of the breast, but also in the wake of the yet more primitive tie of foetus–placenta. In unconscious fantasy, the question of being alive precedes the question of where babies come from; life is a going concern before it exists within the world (*innerhalb der Welt*), or belongs somewhere in the world.

I want to make something of a leap now with the aim of placing the Winnicottian formulation 'becoming real because destroyed' in an explicitly political context. While this takes us beyond anything Winnicott actually said about destruction and survival, nonetheless the leap approximates to his utopian use of hope. It is the sense of utopia, what has also been called in its various millenarian interpretations the 'new Jerusalem', that I wish to emphasise here. Indeed, Freud was exercised by a similar obligation in *Civilization and Its Discontents*, although, unlike Winnicott, his conclusions cannot be gathered under the heading of 'Utopia'. Rendering the tragic fate of modern culture consistent with the sociological arguments in Simmel, Weber and others, Freud (1930: 140) defined a situation in which 'the urge towards happiness' seems to be fundamentally at odds with 'the urge towards union with others'. Lacan, who shared Freud's political conservatism, came to the same conclusion. However, in light of the inherent conflict that Freud identified between Eros and *socius*, we are prompted to ask whether the promise of joy at the object's survival is the best hope we have against the nihilistic response to the problem of nihilism. The question of hope arises in Winnicott on the grounds of a pre-lapsarian plenitude. For Derrida, on the other hand, the question of survival, insofar as it arrives at all, 'questions with regard to what will come in the future-to-come [*l'à-venir*]' (1993: xix). The different emphases notwithstanding, the radical gesture is aimed at working through the 'here and now'. In effect, Derrida and Winnicott alike draw out the temporal complexity of the political redress in the historic formulation 'now is the time'. But whereas Winnicott posits hope through the treatment of the unlived life, Derrida (2002) addresses the question of survival in terms of 'the sense to come'.

In psychoanalysis and elsewhere, critical occasions repeatedly turn on the conjunction of survival and utopia. Let us take another example. Further to my comments about Winnicott, the problematic of survival also underpins the utopian thought of Herbert Marcuse. It is instructive to note the alternative uses that they make of the Freudian interpretation. Winnicott posits contact with the real by means of illusion – that is, prior to the reality principle. By contrast, Marcuse (1955) renders Freudianism in social-historical terms, mobilising the resistances of psychoanalysis against Freud by identifying a future beyond the reality principle. Basically, Marcuse elaborates on the utopian interpretation on two counts, both of which seem to me to be essential for the relationship between psychoanalysis and politics.

On the one hand, elaborating on the Freudian notion of libidinal ties and the idea that 'love alone acts as the civilizing factor in the sense that it brings a change from egoism to altruism' (Freud 1921: 103), Marcuse subsumes the dialectic of history under the pleasure principle. On the other hand, he envisaged us learning to live finally the *gaya sciencia*, while at the same time identifying the reification of the reality principle as an expression of the fate of the destructive drive. Drawing on the Marxian concept of false consciousness, the false needs that Marcuse identifies may be compared to the darkness of the lived moment in the explicitly utopian thought of Ernst Bloch, or to Sartre's *mauvaise foi*. I take it that nihilism is the degenerate form of distress, in which case it would appear that Marcuse initially underestimated the political task (cf. the Political Preface, 1966), where the value of nil in the form of compliance remains the overwhelming predicament of our times. Nevertheless, in his attempts to extend the Freudian interpretation to Marxism and critical theory, I think Marcuse made an invaluable contribution under the heading of 'Profane utopia'. In particular, we are indebted to him for our understanding of the utopian drive, distinct from Freud's final dual instinct theory.

To conclude this part of the chapter, I shall attempt to bring the psychoanalytical and the political uses of utopian thought into closer dialogue through some additional clinical references. More vociferous in his analysis of 'the work of the negative' than any of his contemporaries, André Green (1999) consistently draws our attention to Winnicott's preoccupation with the negative side of relationships. Moreover, the same holds for Green as for Lacan: one resists in the face of a crisis of the symbolic. On this reading, the resistances of psychoanalysis are invariably manifestations of the longing for happiness in the face of the unlived life, tragic as it may be. And yet, whereas Green (1999: 197) took his bearings from 'a deletion at the heart of representation', for his part, Lacan testified to the inevitable violence of death together with the illusory nature of happiness. He paid homage to Derrida, for instance, with the words: 'as it may please him [Derrida]' (quoted in Derrida 1996: 51). We can take this entreaty to mean that the dead return on the authority of the living, which remains fundamentally at odds with Derrida's idea that the dead cannot be outwitted by the living. But once again, in addition to emphasising the contested word of the (dead) father, the general point I wish to make here is that the predicament in which one can no longer speak but only listen is inextricably tied to resistance as a retreat before death. To be clear, by 'retreat' I don't mean denial or disavowal anymore than a withdrawal into interiority. On the contrary, while questioning invariably actualises itself as self-questioning in terms of the destructive activities that will have come from the heart, at the same time a kind of mute resistance outplays the pathos of resolute decision as a break with the totality of resistance. The baby who forgets their mother, and who goes on forgetting her as they destroy her over and over again in unconscious fantasy, thereby enters a life with all its hopes and utopian dreams, a life that feels real and is better than death because of its hopes.

The fact that one experiences a life that is made stressful from the beginning by love, rather than feelings of envy and hatred, presupposes the *limbus* of memory without recollection. Psychoanalysis thus retraces the infant's predicament in terms of 'the initial helplessness [*Hilfösigkeit*] of human beings' (Freud (1950 [1895]: 318). From Freud onwards, analysis repeatedly stakes its claim for the greatest freedom of interpretation, including above all the interpretation of resistance, on deciphering the insignificant details of mute speech (Rancière 2001). And yet Derrida reminds us that hermeneutic deciphering isn't primarily what psychoanalysis is engaged in doing. Certainly, it isn't the case that meaning is simply waiting to be revealed; the Freudian interpretation, at its most radical, doubles the retreat before death through reclamation of the unlived life. Winnicott called this reliving, which he saw as distinct from the lifting of repression. Death is in the detail at any moment, at every instant, not only as the nothing of beings or the abyss of not-being, but also as the occasion for the forestalment of not-yet. We hear the latter voiced without end in the Freudian interpretation as the primal source of ethics. This isn't simply a matter of speaking truly of oneself; it also involves the promise of what Marcuse (1955: 19) called 'the beginning of the reversal' understood as the groundwork of the political. Accordingly, the political or critical occasion is inscribed in the retreat before death along the related axes of Eros and utopia – a force of counter-resistance modelled on libidinal necessity and, at the same time, a sense of concern for the other's death in a moment of hesitation. In the language of philosophical theology we speak of God revealing Himself in and through a world that is made heavenly insofar as we are given to live the life of Heaven therein. Thus one awaits in moments of concerned hesitation the life not-yet-conceived, even amid the pure immanence of life.

To resist in a profound sense is to hinder by way of hesitation. Freud said as much with the notion of the *fort/da*, which, to push our critical reading to an extreme, may be seen as the basis of Freudian ethics. Resistance maintains the critical occasion, not least of all as so many moments of hesitation in an eternal engagement. Listening and forestalling, whatever else they may do, decide nothing that together we might receive the life to come. To offer a third hypothesis: we retreat before death as life affects itself according to its innate potential. Far from a denial of death, the retreatant subject draws back from death through an affirmation of the pure immanence of life. Again, more than a turning towards life, resistance is actually a manifestation of life; we can think of withdrawal itself, in all its errant wanderings and inner retreats, as a non-objectifying experience of feeling oneself in the sensation of aliveness. After all, the eternal recurrence of the same (*die ewige Wiederkehr des Gleichen*) doesn't identify the love of life with the afterlife; resistant subjectivity is alive and defiant to the extent that one retreats before death as one might withdraw before an enemy – that is to say, without any withdrawal of affect.

Understood as a 'vital phenomenon' (Genet 2004: 171), resistance presupposes the affective interplay of enmity and affinity, destruction and survival, disaster and hope. In what amounts to a life protest rather than a withdrawal into a pathological organisation, Genet differentiates the brutal gesture that has nothing to do with the life process on the one hand, from the inherent aggression and germinal force of the spontaneous gesture on the other. The resistances of psychoanalysis, at best, are violent in the sense that life draws its very vitality from violent resistance and ruthless love. As a 'law of life' (in Gottfried Benn's Nietzschean phrase), violent resistance resists the gratuitous violence of brutality, self-destructiveness, nihilism and the deadening of life. Paradoxically, looked at in terms of Freud's compulsion to repeat, we could say that retreating keeps one alive beyond the pleasure principle. Of course, this is the very paradox of the death drive seen from a certain vantage point, the fact that it extends beyond 'the problematic of the principle' (Derrida 1996: 117) altogether, beyond pleasure but also beyond principality as such, in ensuring (if one could speak here of a guarantee) that life itself, what is most alive in life, remains available. To state the critical argument at its most far-reaching, the retreat before death is continuous with the 'violence of a bud breaking forth' (Genet 2004: 172) and, as such, stands opposed to the lure of death in all of its grotesque mastery.

The Archive

Let us now add some final thoughts regarding the resistance to psychoanalysis. Although hardly a new development, the century-long history of repudiation, modelled on the analytic concept of resistance to interpretation, seems to have taken a more vociferous turn in a triumphant free-market society driven by acquisitiveness and short-term gains. I don't know that psychoanalysis, in Europe or elsewhere, has ever been admitted willingly, or given much in the way of a reception by the host culture. But it certainly isn't a welcome customer today, not when intellectual life itself is under attack on any number of fronts. Derrida alerts us to the question of 'today', to the analysis of what 'today' means, especially when it comes to doing justice to Freud. It is therefore a certain state of analysis – the situation of psychoanalysis at the moment – that should and does concern us here.

Generally speaking, the progressive possibilities of Freudianism, which I have suggested are at large in the future of utopia and synonymous with psychoanalysis in the plural, have narrowed considerably in line with the new forms of economy and society in late capitalism. The limits placed on the intellectual and spiritual affinity between Freud and Nietzsche, for instance, may be seen as symptomatic of the cultural-political consensus *contra* psychoanalysis. Mindful of these limits, and starting with the idea that Freud 'restored the possibility of a dialogue with unreason to medical thought' (Foucault 1972: 339), let us elaborate on the political and critical implications of Derrida's reading of Foucault.

The ambivalence of unreason in the Freudian interpretation extends to the critical occasion itself, particularly to our own divided sense of belonging today, where, alongside *la folie du jour* or 'madness in its present form' (Foucault 1966: 375), Freud is found wanting in advance by a heterogeneous alliance of administrators, policy-makers, managers, educators, social workers and psychological therapists of one kind or another. Where the anarchy of madness continues to speak out against the conservatism and mediocrity of consensual times, by the same token the Freudian dialogue with madness may be seen as a driving force in the historical archive of resistances. The very idea of a definable 'age of Freud' is called into question here. Thus what is getting archived is not a question for Derrida but an exclamation. While it remains difficult to know exactly what is being archived, not least of all on account of the developments in technology and electronic media, the historical archive of resistances is actually part of this very difficulty. We don't know what is getting archived, precisely, because it isn't a question of knowledge. Resistances thus resist the order of knowledge in what amounts to a constitutive paradox of the archive itself. To repeat the fundamental point that we noted with regard to Lacan and André Green: one resists in the face of a crisis of the symbolic.

Two questions present themselves: What does psychoanalysis have to say about its own historical paradox? And what can the treatment of psychoanalysis tell us about the paradox of the archive? The question of resistance, which is also a way of speaking out in the name of the archival gesture, turns not only towards the 'blanks' in the archive but also, more important, to 'the radical destruction of the archive' (Derrida 1996: 44) beyond the theme of repression. In his discussion of Foucault's resolutely philological, if in all other respects ambivalent, encounter with Freud and psychoanalysis, Derrida foregrounds the contested principle of reason. The judicious attempts to prove someone wrong (*donner tort*) or to prove them right (*donner raison*) demonstrate what is at stake in the relationship between psychoanalysis, history and the archive. As Foucault's own efforts to 'do justice to Freud' (1972: 339) testify, the resistance of psychoanalysis is inextricably linked to the controversies that continue to turn on the juridical question of what it means to be right or wrong – what it means to do justice to someone, or to do them harm. The resistance to psychoanalysis comes into play, accordingly, in the form of a trial and a verdict, where analysis is indicted and Freud stands accused on any number of counts.

To be clear, I don't believe that psychoanalysis inevitably or consistently demonstrates a capacity to resist. On the contrary, we can see that under certain historical and political conditions, if anything, Freudianism and its various institutional applications render social order functional. Ego psychology, updated versions of attachment theory, and the rapprochement with neuroscience are only the most obvious examples of a general trend in which post-Freudian thinking facilitates social regulation and the supervised life. The classical Freudian interpretation itself, operating in conjunction with the general regulation of markets in advanced liberal societies, has undoubtedly demonstrated its expediency as a technique of self-management (Groaikc 2014). Its usefulness to governmental institutions, as Donzelot (1977: 233) has pointed out in an indispensable critique of psychoanalytic reason, is evident not in its capacity to resist but, rather, in its concerted efforts 'to justify and renovate the two major frames of reference of a social order that functioned on the basis of a maximum avoidance of political issues: *the social norm as a reality principle* and *the family*, its effacement and its privileges, *as a value principle'*.

The Freudian interpretation has clearly played an important role in presenting the entrenched inequalities of class society as consistent with modern democratic values. It has played its part, in other words, in the reduction of politics to a form of social administration and technocratic management. However, to delve into the politics of the reality principle, not to mention a culture of value predicated on the dishonourable secrets of the modern liberal family, would require a much larger canvas than I have at my disposal here. Nevertheless, the fact that psychoanalysis has been deployed as a subtle and flexible mechanism of adjustment of social order and inner security is not in question. If, as I suggest, we start with a strategic model of force relations, then it is perfectly clear that psychoanalysis continues in a society of managers to fulfil a longstanding historic function as a displacement of politics. As it turns out, the function of displacement remains entirely consistent with the freedom of the marketplace over a period of considerable and significant historical change. New forms of finance capitalism under global conditions demonstrate exactly what the 'freedom to relate' can achieve – indeed, with little or no concern for the principles of democratic politics – through a strategic alliance between the reality principle and the social norms of free-market meritocracy.

The initial claim on psychoanalysis as an alternative to politics was made in the social sector. The destructive potential within society, in this case, is identified through a strategic combination of the working-class family and the antisocial tendency. The strategies of 'applied analysis', however, turn increasingly towards the domain of culture and its management in the latter part of the twentieth century, marking an important shift in the institutional application of psychoanalytic thinking from social welfare to a preoccupation with new technologies, the media, identity politics, emotional capital and lifestyle. Essentially, discredited as a type of treatment in the public health sector, and found wanting therein as a combined mechanism of security and freedom, psychoanalysis sets up shop instead (or in tandem) as a form of 'cultural studies' under the auspices of the university. While I think it is important to attend to the specificity of its applications, nonetheless the Freudian interpretation clearly responds to similar demands from the welfare state and the market meritocracy of managed society. The well-managed life is the common objective from economy and society to culture.

However, as with political utopianism, technocratic management is an option in which the Freudian interpretation may or may not be invested; regulation and the requirements of control culture certainly don't exhaust the theoretical or institutional capacity of psychoanalysis. The general point here, as Foucault and others have argued, is that new demands for control give rise to new capacities for resistance, and this applies to the history of Freudianism as much as it does to anything else. A regulatory mechanism, as Deleuze (1977: 121) reminds us with an appropriately spectral metaphor, 'is haunted by what overflows it and makes it burst from the inside'. Indeed, it is the divisibility of the so-called 'inside', promising as well as excessive, which comes through repeatedly in Derrida's reading of the resistance of psychoanalysis as a resistance to itself. The implication is that the analytic institution is deconstructed from the 'inside'; something comes through by coming back, precisely, according to the haunting backdrop that lets it appear. In this respect at least, resistance is seen as something which helps or comes to the aid of psychoanalysis despite itself.

But what does it mean to say that 'resistance of psychoanalysis – to psychoanalysis' (Derrida 1996: 24) returns as one of the cards dealt to our time? What are we to make of this so-called deconstruction from the 'inside', or the inclusive exclusion of the Freudian interpretation, as an historical claim? To put it another way, is there an 'outside' the archive? The question of resistance is before us in Derrida's lectures not only in the name of Freud and the (possible) effacement of the name but also in the provocation of Lacan with the philosophers, and, again, in the irreducible ambivalence of Foucault's relation to Freud and psychoanalysis. There is, I think, a strong argument to be made that the latter is indicative of the ambivalence of reason itself under the conditions of modernity. In any case, taken together the three lectures collected in *Résistances de la psychanalyse* lend weight to the oppositional stance of Freudian thought.

In conclusion, the lectures may be seen as prolegomena to a time when it will be possible, once again, to believe in the historical dimension of life without the burden of historical judgement. I am thinking of a time when belief itself carries beyond the historic imagination of time in the form of a defiant gesture. Derrida was careful to remind us that Foucault's history of sexuality was not a historian's history and, taking him at his word, Derrida himself takes his chances – in order to be able not to arrive – between analysis (the general concept of analysis) and psychoanalysis. He certainly doesn't avoid the word 'resistance' any more than the idea of an archive that exists beyond the alternatives of presence and absence. Throughout the lectures, Derrida (1996: 2) contemplates 'an idiomatic interest...in the word "resistance"' *contra* the repudiation of political memory. The question itself, the question of what remains to be thought through, takes a turn when it comes to resistance, understood as 'the most beautiful word in the politics and history of [France]' (1996: 2). In not shying away from 'history' on this occasion but 'recalling' *la Résistance française* as a series of resistance movements, albeit unified in due course under the political logic of the Conseil nationale de la Résistance ahead of the Normandy and Provence landings, Derrida avoids neither the word 'resistance' nor the interminable working through of its actuality in civil and political society.

That resistance turns out to be a matter of living well in the face of the Other's death is the main conclusion that I draw from the lectures. The paradox of the archive amounts to more than an *agon* with nothingness, more than the authenticity of courage. For Lear, who would grasp the mystery of things in his daughter's company only at the moment of her death, the ranting itself remains exemplary. In the meantime, Derrida takes the work of resistance upon himself, so to speak, as a problem of destruction and survival. Lear is destroyed in a final hankering after the telling of old tales. Alienated in becoming what old age has made of him, Lear's identification with the will to knowledge amid the mortality of the face ('a chance which does redeem all sorrows') may be seen as the problem of the archive itself. The worst that comes of the endless wrangling and controversial discussions of sects and sectarian parties, the worst that will have been done as if it had always been so, is condensed in the exclamation that echoes throughout the entire archive of resistances: she lives! The sad times to which we are obligated, today and henceforward, require an archive that the obligation of sadness itself might be accommodated, which is another way of saying that the entire politics of the archive are at stake in what does and does not remain.

References

Botella, C. and Botella, S. (2005) *The Work of Psychic Figurability: Mental States without Representation*. Hove and New York: Routledge.
Caygill, H. (2013) *On Resistance: A Philosophy of Defiance*. London: Bloomsbury.
Certeau, M. (1969) *L'étranger; ou, L'union dans la différence*. Paris: Desclée de Brouwer.

Clausewitz, C. (1832/1982) *On War*. Harmondsworth: Penguin Books.
Deleuze, G. (1977) 'The rise of the social', in G. Deleuze (ed.) *Two Regimes of Madness: Texts and Interviews 1975–1995*. New York: Semiotext(e), 2006, pp. 113–121.
Derrida, J. (1993) *Spectres de Marx* trans. Kamuf, P. (1994) *Specters of Marx* New York and London: Routledge.
Derrida, J. (1996) *Résistances de la psychanalyse* trans. Kamuf, P., Brault, P.-A. and Naas, M. (1998) *Resistance of Psychoanalysis*. Stanford: Stanford University Press.
Derrida, J. (2002) 'Responsibility – of the sense to come', in J. Derrida (ed.) *For Strasbourg: Conversations of Friendship and Philosophy*. New York: Fordham University Press, 2014, pp. 56–86.
Donzelot, J. (1977) *La police des familles* trans. Hurley, R. (1980) *The Policing of Families: Welfare versus the State*. London: Hutchinson University Library.
Faimberg, H. (2005) *The Telescoping of Generations: Listening to the Narcissistic Links between Generations*. London and New York: Routledge.
Foucault, M. (1954) *Maladie mentale et psychologie* trans. Sheridan, A. (1976) *Mental Illness and Psychology*. New York: Harper and Row.
Foucault, M. (1966) *Le mots et les choses* trans. Sheridan, A. (1976) *The Birth of the Clinic*. London: Tavistock Publications.
Foucault, M. (1972) *Histoire de la Folie à l'âge classique* trans. Murphy, J. and Khalfa, J. (2006) *History of Madness*. London and New York: Routledge.
Foucault, M. (1984) 'Sex, power and the politics of identity', in P. Rabinow (ed.) *Ethics: Subjectivity and Truth, Volume 1, The Essential Works of Michel Foucault 1954–1984*. London: Allen Lane, 1994, pp. 161–173.
Freud, S. (1921) 'Group psychology and the analysis of the ego', in J. Strachey (ed. and trans.) *The Standard Edition of the Complete Psychological Works of Sigmund Freud (SE), Vol. 18*. London: Hogarth Press, pp. 65–143.
Freud, S. (1930 [1929]) 'Civilization and its discontents', *SE, Vol. 21*, pp. 57–145.
Freud, S. (1950 [1985]) 'Project for a scientific psychology', *SE, Vol. 1*, pp. 281–397.
Gay, P. (1988) *Freud: A Life for Our Time*. London: Dent.
Genet, J. (2004) 'Violence and brutality', in J. Genet (ed.) *The Declared Enemy: Texts and Interviews*. Stanford: Stanford University Press, pp. 171–177.
Green, A. (1999) *The Work of the Negative*. London: Free Association Books.
Groarke, S. (2013) *Managed Lives: Psychoanalysis, Inner Security and the Social Order*. London and New York: Routledge.
Lacan, J. (1986) *Le seminaire, Livre VII, L'ethique de la psychanalyse, 1959–1960* trans. Miller, J.-A. (1992) *The Ethics of Psychoanalysis*. London: Routledge.
Levinas, E. (1998) 'Dying for...', in E. Levinas (ed.) *Entre Nous: On Thinking-of-the-Other*. London: Athlone Press, pp. 207–217.
Marcuse, H. (1955) *Eros and Civilization*, with a new Political Preface in 1966. London: Abacus, 1972.
Parsons, M. (2014) *Living Psychoanalysis: From Theory to Experience*. London and New York: Routledge.
Rancière, J. (2001) *L'inconscient esthétique* trans. Keates, D. and Swenson, J. (2009) *The Aesthetic Unconscious*. Cambridge: Polity Press.
Sklar, J. (2011) *Landscapes of the Dark: History, Trauma, Psychoanalysis*. London: Karnac.

Winnicott, D.W. (1945) 'Primitive emotional development', in D.W. Winnicott (ed.) *Through Paediatrics to Psychoanalysis*. London: Hogarth Press, 1978, pp. 145–156.

Winnicott, D.W. (1968) 'The use of an object and relating through identification', in C. Winnicott, R. Shepherd and M. Davis (eds.) *Psycho-Analytic Explorations*. London: Karnac, 1989, pp. 218–227.

14
Psychology, Psychotherapy – Coming to Our Senses?

Paul Moloney

Despite its centrality in our lives – or perhaps even because of it – the science and practice of the psychology industry is largely bogus. After more than 100 years of psychological therapy, there are few signs that people are any happier or less disturbed – quite the opposite, in fact.[1]

Back in the eighteenth century, Anton Mesmer was among the first to use the mantle of modern science in the pursuit of mental healing. His chief mistake was the ease with which his techniques could be put to the test with the mere substitution of dummy magnets (Szasz 1978). The same cannot be said of Sigmund Freud, who set the pattern for what was to come when he depicted a hitherto concealed mental landscape, visible only to the expert practitioner who alone could guide the patient to a healthier mind. His theories were successful largely because they arrived at the right time: when belief in religious truth and humanist progress were being shaken by Darwinism and by world war, with faith in medical expertise at its height (Webster 1995). But there may be a further side to this familiar tale. Freud's fanciful ideas and the success of his teachings in the absence of independently confirmed discoveries or cures may have owed something to the 15 years of cocaine addiction that marked the peak of his inventiveness and messianic conviction (Crews 2011).

Freud's spiritual descendents are seldom fuelled by the use of recreational drugs, but they share his abiding faith. Like most other fashions, the taste for psychological therapy has spread from the rich right across society, even to the poor. New therapies have emerged steadily, branching and intermingling to spawn more descendents, the vast majority following a familiar pattern: high levels of enthusiasm and success to begin with, followed by a slow descent into middling results or worse, as each new variant enters day-to-day practice and its limitations become harder to deny (Cushman 1995; Fancher 1996; Feltham 2013).[2]

Scientists are taught to think rationally. This can make them surprisingly naïve, and never more so when studying other human beings who are equally busy trying to understand or outwit them. It has never been conjurors but always scientists (including psychologists) who have been the most deceived by spiritualism and the paranormal (Couttie 1988). Something similar seems to have happened with the world of psychological therapy, where poor-quality research has met with wishful acceptance on the part of researchers, clinicians, clients and the wider public – to yield unwarranted faith in the potency of the talking cure (Midlands Psychology Group 2009).

If the arguments made by a handful of sceptics down the years have been largely ignored, then this is not for want of substance, depth or sharpness on the part of these critics. Careful scrutiny shows that the research literature within the talking therapy field has long been biased towards the selective reporting and publication of those studies that show only the desired positive results (Boyle 2002; Epstein 1993), and that much of this literature has depended upon inadequate control groups, comprising people who have remained, untreated, on a waiting list, or who have received a less plausible form of pseudotherapy, delivered with half-hearted commitment by the researchers (Holmes 2002; Mair 1992). There has been too much reliance upon carefully chosen research populations, such as university students or people with less severe, complicated or longstanding problems than are found among those who seek treatment in the public health services where many counsellors and therapists work. Too many investigations have been built upon shaky foundations comprising small client samples, and failure to prevent or allow for client drop-out rates that are either unacceptably high or biased in favour of the treatment wing of the clinical trial (Dineen 1999; Eisner 2000; Feltham 2013; Kline 1988). Average outcome scores which appear favourable in aggregate have disguised large numbers of people for whom psychotherapy has been unhelpful, and perhaps even harmful (Epstein 2006, 1995). Unanswered questions remain about the validity of widely used clinical measurement scales and diagnostic inventories, including the Beck Depression Inventory, for example (Epstein 2006; Stein 2012). Most of these scales fail to do any justice to the full personal or clinical significance of distress (see Newnes 2014; Parker 2007; Tolman 1994).

Moreover, the claims of the field are supported largely by appeal to meta-analytic studies, which entail the pooling and examination of the data from large numbers of different clinical trials. In the context of psychological therapy, this approach has always been dubious, given the disparate nature of the studies that customarily get lumped together (often likened to an ill-judged attempt to treat apples and oranges as the same kind of thing), and given that those who carry out the meta-analysis rarely have a good practical knowledge of the realities of clinical research. Without the benefit of such experience, it is impossible to judge the adequacy of the data chosen for any given review (Charlton 2000; Feltham 2013; and see Polanyi 1955). These (and many other) flaws go beyond the academic literature, to afflict the cited research which forms the basis of the guidelines for psychological therapy that are issued by national organisations, such as NICE in the UK and the National Institute for Mental Health (NIMH) in the USA.

As far as any attempt to assess the validity and value of psychological treatments is concerned, the issues discussed so far (serious as they might be) are not the end of the matter. Aside from (decidedly) modest indications of the greater potency of behavioural therapies with regard to phobias, the comparative research literature lends small support to the view that any one approach is more helpful than another (Assay and Lambert 1999; Little 2010; Smith et al. 1980). It is not easy to reconcile this observation with the confident claims about the power and precision of psychological treatments that are aimed at specific disorders, as broadcast by the marketers and supporters of the mainstream therapies (see Hansen et al. 2003). Yet within the field there has always been 'tremendous resistance to accepting this finding as a legitimate one' (Bergin and Garfield 1994: 822).

Current evidence implies that, rather than specified techniques, a host of so- called 'non-specific' factors may explain most of the reported beneficial effects of psychological treatment. Among these features, the quality of the therapeutic relationship and the client's 'motivation to change' (which, arguably, reflects the influence of the individual's environment rather than of any internal psychological faculty of willpower) seem to be the most central (Bergin and Garfield 1994; Bohart and Tallman 2010; Little 2010; Mahrer 1998).

Comparisons of qualified practitioners with amateurs, unschooled in therapeutic methods and theories, suggest that there are few tangible differences between them in effectiveness, regardless of how this is judged. This is a surprisingly durable finding which has persisted across more than two-dozen research projects conducted over a period of two decades (Dawes 1996; McLenan 1998; Moloney 2013a; Stivers 1999).

A reliable trend within the psychotherapy outcome literature is that the closer the study comes to real-life clinical settings and the more carefully it has been carried out, the less significant the outcomes (Dineen 1999). For instance, the American multicentre research trial known as the Fort Bragg Demonstration Project involved the analysis of the treatment of several thousand clients (largely children) over a span of five years. Despite widely reported parental satisfaction with the psychological therapy, there was no sign that it improved the wellbeing of these recipients, many of whom were struggling with significant social disadvantage. As the clinical psychologist Tana Dineen observes, 'these results should raise serious doubts about some current clinical beliefs about the effectiveness of psychological services... there is scant evidence of its effectiveness in real life settings' (Dineen 1999: 128).

Recent attempts to ground the validity and effectiveness of talking therapy in brain imaging research, which allegedly shows that certain forms of counselling can 'transform the central nervous system' (for example Cozolino 2010), do not fare any better, upon closer examination. So far the very small-scale psychotherapy studies upon which the neurological scanning research is based seem to have replicated (or even amplified) the methodological shortcomings that are found within the general talking therapy research field described above. Predicated upon the assumption that 'therapy works', many of these studies appear to be lacking in proper control groups and in the longer-term follow-up of their recipients that would be needed to show that the claimed 'neurological rewiring' has proved to be stable (Moloney 2013). The products of this imaging research are heavily dependent upon the assumptions of the programmers and researchers, and the technology has not yet reached full maturity as a reliable investigative tool for psychologists (Noe 2009; Uttall 2014). At best, these scanning procedures might demonstrate a (not very surprising) correlation between undergoing an experience such as talking therapy on the one hand, and subtle changes in cerebral activity on the other. This is not the same as saying that the observed changes have been caused by the therapeutic techniques, or that they have particular implications for how the treated individual will fare in the world outside the brain scanning suite – the world in which their distress is incubated and given meaning (Choudhury and Slaby 2012; Kagan 2013; Moloney 2013).

Finally, we should recall that what people say about their experience of talking therapy has to be treated with unusual caution, owing to the powerful social and cultural expectations that saturate this healing ritual, and that make it difficult for its initiates to think about it in a detached or measured way (Frank and Frank 1991). If most psychotherapy clients are already vulnerable to persuasion – by virtue of their having revealed hitherto private worries or traumas – then their would-be healers have at their fingertips yet further tools of influence. Humanist counsellors, for instance, seek to nurture a therapeutic relationship that surpasses most ordinary professional–layperson encounters in emotional depth and strength (Gendlin 1981; Mearns 1994); psychodynamic therapists make much of their claimed ability to read and manage the intricacies of the transference relationship (for example Casement 1995); and cognitive behavioural practitioners solemnly assert the authority of 'cognitive science' behind all that they do (for example Clark and Layard 2014; Greenberger and Padesky 1995; Hawton et al. 1989). If the practice of psychological therapy has never moved far from its roots in the religious confessional, then all involved are likely to share strong and culturally sanctioned beliefs, which equate failure to benefit with a wilful rescinding of the inner moral strength that is needed to overcome adversity (Epstein 2006; Smail 2005; Throop 2009). And it may be hardest of all for the client to admit – even to themselves – that their therapy has not been as helpful as they had hoped (Kelly 2000).

Rather than trying to grapple with these complex issues, investigators have instead fallen back – almost exclusively – upon simple tick-box measures collected from clients, clinicians and other employees of the agencies and institutions that support the therapeutic work and research, but without any independent attempt to follow each treated person's subsequent progress in the wider world beyond the consulting room (Eisner 2000; Epstein 2006, 2013). More recent analyses of the literature on community-based therapeutic 'empowerment' initiatives, and of the long-term effects of psychological treatments, have done nothing to improve this picture (Epstein 2013; Moloney 2013).

The main issue, of course, is to what extent each client's assessment of their own treatment might be distorted by this mixture of wishful thinking and self-censorship. Here it is instructive to compare these evaluations of the claimed curative power of psychotherapy with estimates of the strength of what are known as 'demand characteristics'. These are the subtle cues that behavioural scientists have been shown to emit – unawares – to the participants in laboratory-based psychological experiments that are designed, for instance, to understand how people recall different sorts of information, or how different presentational styles can influence the extent to which people are swayed by a given argument. Without thorough efforts to control such unconscious cues, the results of any psychological study can be significantly skewed in the direction favoured by the researcher (Cialdini 2007; Sutherland 1990). Even the behaviour of laboratory animals can be shaped by these signals, which operate in situations that are relatively dull, impersonal and brief when contrasted with most psychotherapeutic interventions, in which everyone involved should have a far higher stake in the outcome (for a full discussion, see Rosenthal and Rubin 1978). It is telling that these estimates of researcher influence equal (and often surpass) the average gains reported for psychotherapy, even for the minority of better-controlled studies. This situation has led many critics, in particular the American social scientist William Epstein, to conclude that the talking therapies are little more than placebos. There has 'never been a scientifically credible study that attests to the effectiveness of any form of psychotherapy for any mental or emotional problem under any condition of treatment' (Epstein 2006: 220).

If the sheer difficulty of personal transformation is hard for consumers and professionals to countenance, then there is no mystery as to why. Belief in the power of prayer, self-affirmation and now therapy to change lives is deeply embedded within Western culture, and increasingly in many others (Howard 2005; Thomas 2009). Too many of us feel ashamed that we cannot solve our personal problems or steer the happier and more productive course through life that must surely be within our grasp. Where previous generations wanted to suppress or modify undesirable conduct, we have become obsessed with examining our motives – partly out of a fear that our control might be slipping, and partly out of an urgent desire to maximise our 'enjoyment'. Either way, we remain insecure (Illouz 2008; Moloney 2013).

An international banking crisis, the inevitable cost of unfettered free-market capitalism, has presented a convenient excuse for an unprecedented attack upon the wages, living conditions and democratic rights of ordinary people (Clark and Heath 2014; Dorling 2013; Midlands Psychology Group 2014). In place of common cause and protest, too many of us gratefully seek our daily doses of counselling and happiness psychology. A widespread belief in the value of talking treatments has nurtured the fantasy that there are simple, bargain-basement answers to enduring and complicated social and political problems.

Even if it hasn't got us very far as a society, perhaps this abiding faith at least reflects a growing humanitarian impulse and sensitivity toward one another? In the USA, the spiritual and economic home of psychological therapy and techniques as a commercial industry (see

Hansen et al. 2003; Moloney 2013; Newnes 2014), public opinion surveys routinely show generous, humanitarian impulses towards fellow citizens in the grip of poverty. Food and cash assistance to the disabled and the underprivileged elderly are regularly endorsed, and the needs of deprived children aren't far behind (Epstein 2010). However, these expressions of goodwill may amount to little more than insincere public rhetoric, not unlike the civic-minded but disingenuous explanations that are given by middle-class Americans in support of their liking for petrol swilling, and dangerous sport utility vehicles, and guns. The proof is in the pudding. The real views and intentions of the American public are glimpsed in the longstanding inadequacy of social programmes that are ostensibly designed to help the disadvantaged, and in the indolence of both national and state legislatures when it comes to helping such families and children in public care. Since the Reaganite era, most of these public-spirited citizens – too often including the destitute themselves – have voted for tight-fisted and punitive social welfare policies that speak of a 'characteristic indifference, even spitefulness toward fellow citizens and a persistent deceptiveness, perhaps hypocrisy, in reporting beliefs' (Epstein 2002: 117).

The UK is not the USA. Even so, it is hard to deny that something similar has been going on in a country that has not been so socially divided since the 1930s, but in which those who cannot work through illness or disability have lately begun to face regular vilification and hatred from the media, and too often from their fellow citizens, and to a degree that would have been unthinkable just a few years earlier. Public attitude surveys in the UK are, if anything, less disingenuous than their American counterparts and indicate a growing antipathy, if not contempt, towards the jobless and the poor (Harkness et al. 2012).

Meanwhile, central government, financial organisations and employers increasingly tell citizens that more and more they need to stand on their own two feet and look after their own welfare. All notions of social class disadvantage, let alone fairness and justice, have been quietly sidestepped to fashion a new minority – 'the socially excluded'. This is a term that hides the financial and material nature of inequality, and casts its objects as failures in responsible self-control and motivation who are unwilling to abandon their bad habits of gluttony, drinking, smoking and lazy parenting, and especially their pauperism (Jones 2012; Moloney 2013; Throop 2009).

Where the Victorians saw impoverishment and fecklessness as proof of inferior breeding, the enlightened managerial classes of the early twenty-first century see them as a willfully sustained mental outlook.

Any hint that the disadvantaged might be suffering from malign circumstances, exploitation by wealthier citizens or just ill luck gets short shrift. They are viewed simply as the rusty detritus of an era of industrial class conflict, now long gone. If such attitudes and policies are not entirely the creation of the therapy industry then they owe a large debt to that industry's fondness for victim-blaming, and for prescribing a better world through better mental hygiene.

By any standard, all of this is pretty damning. Does it mean therefore that every therapist should pack up their bags and choose another vocation? Not necessarily. There will always be distressed and confused people, and any humane society should strive to offer them some form of comfort, advice and care. Even if all of the therapists were to disappear tomorrow, a new caste of professional listeners would emerge, if only because the unhappiest people are often so because they have no one else to whom they can turn in their confusion or hopelessness (Cushman 1995; Smail 1996).

Some practitioners appear to be better than others at providing the kind of help that people appreciate in times of trouble, and this may account for differential client satisfaction rather than verifiable cure. This topic has received surprisingly little attention from researchers, but it is likely to reflect personal qualities such as intelligence, self-belief, warmth, charisma and even wisdom (Gordon 1998). Perhaps there is a place for counselling or therapy as a very modest affair, where the therapist might listen and then point people towards possible sources of practical, material and financial help, and, if they are lucky, of friendship or escape.

If we ignore the pscyhobabble and exaggerated claims, then the so-called systemic therapies approach this template, to the extent that such practitioners often work with groups that are explicitly acknowledged to lack power: the elderly, people with learning and other disabilities, and children. Here the professionals often find themselves negotiating on their clients' behalf to try to help them to change their position in the world (Newnes and Radcliffe 2005). The problem, of course, is that for many such clients, these windows of opportunity are few and, in the arid economic climate, growing fewer, while nobody can be trained to be genuine, charismatic or wise. There is no good evidence either that these systemic methods yield better outcomes than traditional individual therapy. Families and care homes can be remarkably resistant to change, especially after the psychologists have departed the scene and things have settled down into their familiar, well-worn grooves. On the other hand, perturbations in the outside world can upset the most carefully piled apple cart. Still, in their willingness to see mutual entanglement between person and situation, these therapies are ahead of the rest. It is only in the last 15 years or so that the field of adult mental health treatment, for example, has begun to catch up.

At the very least we need more and better science, starting with improved research. Like most of us, psychologists have to earn their living and are not always the best critics of their field. This is not to suggest any willful distortion or impropriety, but to observe that few of us can quite escape our commitment to the institutions in which we work, or to the colleagues whom we might prefer not to offend. One way of getting round this problem might be to invite, for example, a rigorous critic, such as the American academic William Epstein, to design a large-scale research trial that seeks to definitively answer all of the fatal methodological flaws that he has identified in the clinical RCT literature. This is unlikely to happen because of the prevailing view, now congealed into dogma, that psychological therapy 'works', because of the huge expense and effort that would be involved, and because too many people would stand to lose.

The mythology of the therapy industry needs to be replaced by a genuine human science, but what form this might take is not immediately obvious. After more than a century, the discipline of psychology still lacks a unified theory or standpoint of the sort that we find in an established natural science, such as biochemistry or geology. Each day we all have the experience of going to sleep and of awaking to consciousness. Nothing could be more obvious. Yet there is no widely accepted view of what consciousness is, of what it does or even of its relationship to the physical brain (Blackmore 2005). It is easy to lose sight of this basic fact, of our fundamental ignorance, when therapists, trainers and television experts confidently pronounce the 'scientific basis' for what they do. Moreover, human experience has a bewildering complexity and variety, and a propensity to change over time and from place to place, making a complete and monolithic science of humanity an unlikely goal (Howard 2005; Throop 2009). The failure of psychological therapy itself underlines this point, and perhaps it is one for which we should be thankful. As the late David Smail astutely argued, if human beings really could be reprogrammed into healthier and happier versions of themselves via some set of individual psychological techniques, then these would long ago have been refined and then deployed for a more sinister purpose; we would already be the outright slaves of governments and corporations (Smail 1987).

Nevertheless, by drawing upon the work of a number of critics and thinkers, it is possible to sketch some of the likely elements of a more accurate and truthful account of human experience. What might be called a social-materialist version of psychology seems to point in the right direction: where thoughts, feelings and wishes are seen, not as the messengers of an autonomous realm but as a kind of music, arising from the interweaving of worlds, bodies and social and material power (Midlands Psychology Group 2012; Smail 2005). This kind of psychology can comfortably accommodate the mounting evidence of the environmental causation of distress (Clark and Heath 2014; Wilkinson and Pickett 2010) on the one hand, and for the relative impotency of talking therapy on the other. It does not deny that humans have agency, astonishing creativity (when the circumstances are right) and fascinating vistas of elusive subjective experience – far from it. But the human faculty of self-awareness is scaled down to its proper size – from inner galaxy to a realm of fragile gossamer – befitting the lives of creatures that must always 'walk warily among their kind' (Eisely 1969: 188).

As Wittgenstein observed, 'The sickness of a time is cured by an alteration in the mode of life of human beings, and...the sickness of philosophical problems...only through a changed mode of thought and life' (Wittgenstein 1956). Because psychology is so much a part of our culture, the very place in which we dwell, it is unlikely that any large-scale change can be engineered from within the discipline, unless it was ushered in by developments in wider society. In the foreseeable future, this is unlikely to happen, and in any case it would not be healthy to replace one set of sweeping dogmas with another. The best outcome might be to ensure that there is room for a wider range of views than is currently the case, to warrant that the culture of psychology avoids the dead end that now confronts it.

It is possible that recurring economic and ecological crises will force us to develop a different view of ourselves. To some extent, this is already happening, as the international banking collapse of the early twenty-first century has led many people to question the pretensions of the economists and other prophets of globalisation (Chang 2011). If recent warnings about planetary climate change are accurate, then as a matter of survival we may be heading towards a society in which even the pretence of democracy is dispensed with (Oreskes and Conway 2013). A more optimistic view suggests that a gentler way of communitarian life might instead become the norm, celebrating the duality of human beings as both social and solitary creatures, with a need for belonging as much as for privacy, and so undercutting the hyperindividualistic brand of psychology that we have now.

The gap between the confident writings of the therapy trainers and the far more tentative and thoughtful things that at least some practitioners say about their own experience of providing therapy might give an indication of where we need to be heading.

Indeed, any kind of psychology that ignores the views of people who are suffering emotional and mental torment (whether in relation to their experience of anguish or of the treatments that they are given for it) would be woefully inadequate. In many ways, this is what we already have in the shape of biomedical psychiatry and of the more simplistic, but widespread, forms of CBT and other quick-repair talking therapies (Willoughby 2013). However, it is equally remiss to take the things that people say about themselves and their problems entirely at face value, without any recognition of the many uncertainties, lacunae, oversights and unconscious distortions to which such accounts are prone (Schwitzgebel 2011) – not least because many of us place so much faith in the talking cure, and because of the larger social and political realities that shape and limit what we can say, sometimes as much to ourselves, as to anyone else. If an adequate psychology must occupy the troubled zone between these conflicting requirements, then it is clear that the discipline will always be a contested one, and that a range of scientific methods will need to be brought to bear upon its subject matter, which should also include the beliefs and actions of its practitioners (Parker 2007).

Above all, we need to shed spurious certainty and to regain a spirit of open enquiry, guided by what the world teaches us and supported by a renewed commitment to the idea of truth. At its best, science is not a set of doctrines. In the words of the humanist and scientist Jacob Bronowski, it is

> a very human form of knowledge, we are always at the brink of the known, we always feel forward for what is to be hoped. Every judgment in science stands on the edge of error and is personal. Science is a tribute to what we can know although we are fallible.
> (Bronowski 1973: 374)

Science advances through dedication to solving the unknowns, but first they have to be recognised. Selective ignorance is endemic within the field,[3] and practitioners should be encouraged to think a lot harder about where these gaps occur and whose interests they serve. This kind of outlook can only flourish where public institutions allow, and their creation and maintenance is a matter for politics far more than for the profession of psychology.

We already know enough about what ails us to at least make a start towards putting things right. One of the best historical examples is probably the actions of the post-Second World War British Labour government and its creation of a robust welfare state on the back of massive electoral victory. These housing, health and educational programmes, though paternalistic and flawed in their execution, nevertheless represented primary prevention on a grand scale. A unique set of circumstances helped to make them possible. Mass conscription meant that many working-class men (and some women) were by now trained combatants, and members of a militant and economically powerful labour movement, demanding more than dole and charity as the reward for two world wars and 20 years of starvation. There was also the presence of nominally socialist states in other parts of the globe – enough to scare the elites into believing that the threat of revolution was real – and a political leadership with at least some ideals. These were among the key contributions to the post-war settlement (Hobsbawm 1994; Todd 2014). Unfortunately, few to none of these conditions obtain today. In both the UK and the USA, growing social inequalities and corporate financial abuse exist side by side and can be sustained, in part, because many middle-class people remain keen to distinguish themselves from those clinging to the rungs beneath them. Rather than challenge the main source of their own (and almost everyone else's) economic and social troubles, they have embraced a politics of envy (Jones 2012; Kampfner 2009).

In their summary of the scientific literature on the prevention of mental suffering written nearly 40 years ago, the American psychologists Marc Kessler and the late George Albee observed that no medical cure had ever been enough to eradicate or even control disease. In every case, from the Broad Street pump onwards, prevention led the way, and the same applies to mental distress: 'Everywhere we looked, every social research study we examined, suggested that major sources of human stress and distress generally involve some form of excessive power' (Albee and Joffe 1977: 379). These conclusions are still valid. Before the discovery of the malarial parasite and of its transmission by mosquito, people used to drain malarial swamps as a defence against their 'bad airs', long believed to be the root of the sickness. This theory was, of course, wrong in detail but close enough to the wider truth to work. The same insight applies to the origins of personal distress and to the attempt to ease it. We don't have to know every pathway that fosters misery in every person. If despair and madness are wrought by material things happening to material bodies – outright abuse on the one hand, and soul-deadening labour, squalid impoverishment, the boredom of joblessness, the moralising sermons of the privileged (to name but a few of the officially approved torments) on the other – then it seems sensible not to try to talk people out of their unhappiness but to change the world from which it descends.

Acknowledgements: With grateful thanks to Dave Crook and William Epstein, who commented upon earlier drafts of this chapter.

Dedicated to the memory of David Smail.

Notes

1. See, Hillman, J. and Ventura, M. (1989) *We've Had a Hundred Years of Psychotherapy: And the World's Getting Worse*. Townsend: Copper Canyon Press. This is surely one of the best book titles ever.
2. This progression, a historical pattern that is well known within the talking therapy world, was described by one speaker at a national conference as being 'rather like when you are still in the first blush of romantic love with your new partner, and then you hear them fart, for the first time'. He went on to say, with questionable accuracy, that 'we haven't heard CBT fart as yet'. See, Midlands Psychology Group (2010).
3. Recently a new branch of sociology has emerged which is dedicated to studying how certain forms of knowledge (and even fundamental questions) become neglected or forgotten, not because they are illegitimate or irrational but because they are inconvenient. See, Proctor, R.N. and Schiebinger, L. (2008).

References

Albee, G.W. and Joffe, J.M. (eds.) (1977) *The Issues: An Overview of Primary Prevention*. Hanover, NH: University Press of New England, p. 379.

Assay, T.P. and Lambert, S.J. (1999) 'The Empirical case for common factors in therapy: Quantitative findings', in M.A. Hubble, B. Duncan and S.D. Miller (eds.) *The Heart and Soul of Change: What Works in Therapy*. Washington, DC: American Psychological Association.

Bergin, A. and Garfield, S. (1994). 'Overview, future trends and issues', in A. Bergin, and S. Garfield (eds) *Handbook of Psychotherapy and Behaviour Change* 4th ed. New York: John Wiley, pp. 821–830.

Blackmore, S. (2005) *Conversations on Consciousness*. Oxford: Oxford University Press.

Bohart, C. and Tallman, K. (2010) 'Clients: The neglected factor in psychotherapy', in M.A. Hubble, B.L. Duncan, S.D. Miller and B.E. Wampold (eds.) *The Heart and Soul of Change: Delivering What Works in Therapy*. Washington, DC: American Psychological Association.

Boyle, M. (2002) *Schizophrenia: A Scientific Delusion?* London: Routledge.

Bronowski, J. (1973) *The Ascent of Man*. London: BBC Books.
Casement, P. (1995) *Further Learning from the Patient: The Analytic Space and Process*. London: Tavistock Publications.
Charlton, B.G. (2000) 'The new management of scientific knowledge: A change in direction with profound implications', in M. Hampton and B. Hurwitz (eds.) *NICE, GHI and the NHS Reforms: Enabling Excellence or Imposing Control?* London: Aesculapius Medical Press, pp. 13–32.
Chang, H. (2011) *23 Things They Don't Tell You about Capitalism*. London: Allen Lane.
Cialdini, R.B. (2007) *Influence: The Psychology of Persuasion*. London and New York: Harper Business.
Choudhury, S. and Slaby, J. (eds.) (2012) *Critical Neuroscience: A Handbook of the Social and Cultural Context of Neuroscience*. New York: Wiley-Blackwell.
Clark, D. and Layard, R. (2014) *Thrive: The Power of Evidence Based Psychological Therapies*. Harmondsworth: Penguin Books.
Clark, T. and Heath, A. (2014) *Hard Times. The Divisive Toll of the Economic Slump*. New Haven, CT and London: Yale University Press.
Cozolino, L. (2010) *The Neuroscience of Psychotherapy: Healing the Social Brain* (Norton Series on Interpersonal Neurobiology) 2nd revised ed. New York: W.W. Norton & Company.
Couttie, B. (1988) *Forbidden Knowledge: The Paranormal Paradox*. Bury St Edmunds, Suffolk: Edmonsbury Press Ltd.
Crews, F. (2011) *Physician Heal Thy Self: Part I*. The New York Review of Books. 29 September 2011. http://www.nybooks.com/articles/archives/2011/sep/29/physician-heal-thyself-part-i/?pagination=false&printpage=true. Accessed 2 May 2013.
Cushman, P. (1995) *Constructing the Self, Constructing America: A Cultural History of Psychotherapy*. Cambridge, MA: Perseus Publishing.
Dawes, R. (1996) *House of Cards: Psychology and Psychotherapy Built on Myth*. New York: Palgrave Macmillan.
Dineen, T. (1999) *Manufacturing Victims: What the Psychology Industry Is Doing to People*. London: Constable.
Dorling, D. (2013) *Unequal Health: The Scandal of Our Times*. London: Polity Press.
Eisely, L. (1969) *The Unexpected Universe*. San Diego: Harvest Brace and Company. Chapter 8. The Inner Galaxy, p. 188.
Epstein, W. (1993) *The Dilemma of American Social Welfare*. New Brunswick: Transaction Publishers.
Epstein, W. (1995) *The Illusion of Psychotherapy*. New Brunswick: Transaction.
Epstein, W. (2002) *American Policy Making: Welfare as Ritual*. Lanham, MD: Rowan and Littlefield, p. 117.
Epstein, W. (2006) *The Civil Divine: Psychotherapy as Religion in America*. Reno: University of Nevada Press.
Epstein, W. (2010) *Democracy without Decency: Good Citizenship and the War on Poverty*. University Park, PA: Pennsylvania University Press.
Epstein, W. (2013) *Empowerment as Ceremony*. Piscataway, NJ: Transaction Publishers.
Eisner, D. (2000) *The Death of Psychotherapy: From Freud to Alien Abductions*. New York: Preager.

Fancher, R.E. (1996) *Cultures of Healing. Correcting the Myth of the American Mental Health Professions*. San Francisco: W.H. Freeman.

Feltham, C. (2013) *Counselling and Counselling Psychology: A Critical Examination*. Ross-on-Wye: PCCS Books Ltd.

Frank, J.D. and Frank, J.B. (1991) *Persuasion and Healing: A Comparative Study of Psychotherapy*. Baltimore: Johns Hopkins University Press.

Gendlin, E. (1981) *Focusing*. New York: Bantam.

Gordon, P. (1998) *Face to Face: Therapy as Ethics*. London: Constable.

Greenberger, F. and Padesky, C. (1995) *Mind over Mood: Change How You Feel by Changing the Way You Think*. New York: Guildford Press.

Hansen, S., McHoul, A. and Rapley, M. (2003) *Beyond Help: A Consumer's Guide to Psychology*. Ross-on-Wye: PCCS Books, p. 12.

Harkness, S., Greg, P. and MacMillan, L. (2012) *Poverty: The Role of Institutions, Behaviours and Culture*. Joseph Rowntree Foundation.

Hawton, K., Salkovskis, P., Kirk, J. and Clarke, D. (1989) *Cognitive Behaviour Therapy for Psychiatric Problems: A Practical Guide*. Oxford University Press.

Hobsbawm, E. (1994) *Age of Extremes: The Short Twentieth Century 1914–1991*. London: Michael Joseph.

Holmes, J. (2002) 'All you need is cognitive behaviour therapy?', *British Medical Journal*, 324, pp. 288–291.

Howard, A. (2005) *Identity and Counselling*. London: Palgrave Macmillan.

Hubble, M.A., Duncan, B.L., Miller, S.D. and Wampold, B.E. (2010) 'Introduction', in M.A. Hubble, B.L. Duncan, S.D. Miller and B.E. Wampold (eds.) *The Heart and Soul of Change: Delivering What Works in Therapy*. Washington, DC: American Psychological Association.

Illouz, E. (2008) *Saving the Modern Soul: Therapy, Emotions and the Culture of Self-Help*. Berkley and London: University of California Press.

Jones, O. (2012) 'Introduction', in *Chavs: The Demonization of the Working Class* 2nd ed. London: Verso.

Kagan, J. (2013) *The Human Spark: The Science of Human Development*. New York: Basic Books.

Kampfner, J. (2009) *Freedom for Sale: How We Made Money and Lost Our Liberty*. London: Simon and Schuster.

Kelly, A.E. (2000) 'A self-presentational view of psychotherapy', *Psychological Bulletin*, 126(4), pp. 475–494.

Kline, P. (1988) *Psychology Exposed: Or The Emperor's New Clothes*. London: Routledge.

Little, J.H. (2010) 'Evidence based practice: Evidence or orthodoxy?', in M.A. Hubble, B.L. Duncan, S.D. Miller and B.E. Wampold (eds.) *The Heart and Soul of Change: Delivering What Works in Therapy*. Washington, DC: American Psychological Association.

Mahrer, A. (1999) 'Embarrassing problems for the field of psychotherapy', *BPS Psychotherapy Section Newsletter*, 23.3, pp. 3–25.

Mair, K. (1992) 'The myth of therapist expertise', in W. Dryden and C. Feltham (eds.) *Psychotherapy and It's Discontents*. Buckinghamshire: Open University.

McLenan, J. (1998) 'Becoming an effective counsellor: Are training and supervision necessary?', in C. Feltham (ed.) *Controversies in Counselling and Psychotherapy*. London: Sage.

Mearns, D. (1994) *Developing Person Centred Counselling*. London: Sage.
Midlands Psychology Group (2009) 'Post qualification training in selective ignorance: A report from two recent national conferences', *Clinical Psychology Forum*, 212, pp. 46–51.
Midlands Psychology Group (2010) 'Welcome to NICE world', *Clinical Psychology Forum*, 212, pp. 52–56.
Midlands Psychology Group (2012) 'Draft manifesto for a social materialist psychology of distress', *Journal of Critical Psychology, Counselling and Psychotherapy*, 12(2), pp. 93–107.
Midlands Psychology Group (2014) 'Charting "the mind and body economic"', *The Psychologist*, 27(4), pp. 46–51.
Moloney, P. (2013a) *The Therapy Industry: The Irresistible Rise of the Talking Cure and Why It Doesn't Work*. London: Pluto Press.
Moloney, P. (2013b) 'What can brain scans really tell us about the effectiveness of psychological therapy?', *Journal of Critical Psychology, Psychotherapy and Counselling*, 4, pp. 252–264.
Newnes, C. (2014) *Clinical Psychology: A Critical Examination*. Ross-on-Wye: PCCS Books Ltd.
Newnes, C. and Radcliffe, N. (eds.) (2005) *Making and Breaking Children's Lives*. Ross-on-Wye: PCCS Books Ltd.
Noe, A. (2009) *Out of Our Heads: Why You Are Not Your Brain, and Other Lessons from the Biology of Consciousness*. New York: Hill and Wang.
Oreskes, N. and Conway, E.M. (2013) *The Collapse of Western Civilization: A View from the Future*. Daedalus.
Parker, I. (2007) *Revolution in Psychology*. London: Pluto.
Polanyi, M. (1955) *Personal Knowledge: Towards a Post-Critical Philosophy*. London: Routledge.
Proctor, R.N. and Schiebinger, L. (2008) *Agnatology: The Making and Unmaking of Ignorance*. Stanford: Stanford University Press.
Rosenthal, R. and Rubin, D.B. (1978) 'Interpersonal expectancy effects: The first 345 studies', *Behavioural and Brain Sciences*, 3, pp. 377–415.
Schwitzgebel, E. (2011) *Perplexities of Consciousness*. Cambridge: MIT Press.
Smail, D. (1987) *Taking Care: An Alternative to Therapy*. London: Dent.
Smail, D. (1996) *How to Survive without Psychotherapy*. London: Dent.
Smail, D. (2005) *Power, Interest and Psychology. Elements of a Social-Materialist Understanding of Distress*. Ross-on-Wye: PCCS Books Ltd.
Smith, M.L. and Glass, G.V and Miller, T.I. (1980) *The Benefits of Psychotherapy*. Baltimore: Johns Hopkins University Press.
Stivers, R. (1999) *Technology as Magic: The Triumph of the Irrational*. New York: Continuum.
Stein, D. (2012) *The Psychology Industry under the Microscope*. New York: University Press of America.
Sutherland, S. (1990) *Irrationality: The Enemy Within*. London: Constable.
Szasz, T.S. (1978) *The Myth of Psychotherapy: Mental Healing as Myth, Rhetoric and Repression*. Syracuse, NY: Syracuse University Press.
Thomas, K. (2009) *The Ends of Life: Roads to Fulfillment in Early Modern England*. Oxford: Oxford University Press.
Throop, E. (2009) *Psychotherapy, American Culture, and Social Policy: Immoral Individualism*. New York: Palgrave Macmillan.

Todd, S. (2014) *The People. The Rise and Fall of the Working Class 1910–2010.* London: John Murray.

Tolman, C. (1994) *Psychology, Society, Subjectivity: An Introduction to German Critical Psychology.* London: Routledge.

Uttall, W. (2014) *Neural Theories of Mind: Why the Mind-Brain Problem May Never Be Solved.* New York: The Psychology Press.

Webster, R. (1995) *Why Freud Was Wrong: Sin, Science and Psychoanalysis.* London: HarperCollins.

Wilkinson, R. and Pickett, K. (2010) *The Spirit Level: Why Equality Is Better for Everyone* 2nd ed. London: Penguin Books.

Willoughby, C.J. (2013) 'Tied to the mast on a ship of fools: The delusions of "Big Psy"', *Journal of Critical Psychology, Counselling and Psychotherapy,* 13(4), pp. 236–251.

Wittgenstein, L. (1956) *Remarks on the Foundations of Mathematics,* edited by G.H. von Wright, R. Rhees and G.E.M. Anscombe. Oxford: Blackwell.

Part VI
Critiques of Training and Learning

15
Contesting the Curriculum: Counsellor Education in a Postmodern and Medicalising Era

Tom Strong, Karen H. Ross, Konstantinos Chondros and Monica Sesma-Vazquez

What is required to become a good counsellor these days? Most answers start with mention of ethical and responsive relational and conversational skills. However, beyond this initial answer, consensus would be hard to find. Look beyond graduate programmes in counsellor education, to what counsellors are expected to do in their everyday practice, and different notions of good counselling become evident. Counsellors are increasingly regulated as health practitioners whose services are funded by healthcare finances (Grohol 2013; Hansen 2007). With such medically oriented changes in funding and regulation have come professional identity challenges (Eriksen and Kress 2006). Counselling's professional organisations have been renaming themselves as counselling and psychotherapy associations to position their members to receive health system funding (for example from the Canadian Counselling Association to the Canadian Counselling and Psychotherapy Association; De Cicco 2007). Such changes, beyond but still relevant to the universities, may be factors that are changing counsellor education.

The recent publication of the *Diagnostic and Statistical Manual of Mental Disorders* – Fifth Edition (American Psychiatric Association, 2013, hereafter APA, 2013), despite controversies over its development and use (for example Frances 2013; Greenberg 2013), furthers a default medicalising discourse for counsellors and counsellor education. Discourse, for us, refers to understanding and communicating by systematically coherent meanings, extending to a logic that governs consistent language use and what is to follow from that use (Dean 2013; Foucault 2008). In a world of diverse understandings and ways of communicating, critical questions should be raised about what is obscured or excluded if any discourse becomes a profession's default discourse. Such a default discourse could furnish what Hook (2007) referred to as a disciplinary technology, especially when its understandings translate to expected counselling practices. Despite a pluralistic tradition, counsellors are concerned about medicalising tendencies of DSM discourse and its associated evidence-based practices (Cooper and McLeod 2011; Hansen 2007).

Enabling DSM-5 (APA 2013) to become a default discourse is its purported legitimacy as a scientifically developed and institutionally accepted language, despite its use for research purposes recently being deemed unacceptable by the USA's NIMH (Insel 2013). For example, at the American Counseling Association's Knowledge Center, DSM-5 is referred to as 'the standard classification of mental disorders used by mental health professionals in the United States and contains a listing of diagnostic criteria for every psychiatric disorder recognized by the U.S. healthcare system'. Further, for licensure in the USA, many counsellors must be competent in using DSM-5 diagnoses (National Board of Certified Counselors 2014).

In such a medicalising zeitgeist, new curricular developments in counsellor education have been occurring, influencing counsellor education, though not without tensions. Tensions occur when no singular discourse (such as medicalisation) finalises meanings and practices. Counsellor education can be seen as an ongoing and contested professional project with different influential parties shaping its development. We share Cooper and McLeod's (2011) view that counselling and counsellor education are better off if differences are not reduced to a single overarching approach to counselling, such as that which could be enabled by the diagnose-and-treat, medicalising discourse of DSM-5 (APA 2013). Using Adele Clarke's (2005) situational analysis, we show different influences or tensions shaping how counsellor education is developing. Specifically, we analyse relevant textbooks, relevant research, course syllabi and programme website information to highlight tensions that pertain to counsellor education.

Counsellor education's postmodern situation

Why counsellor education would experience tensions as a professional project is something that needs explaining. Part of the issue is with how a medicalising approach can seem at odds with other approaches that are focused on meanings, relationships, social justice, spirituality and so on. Counsellors do not perform conversational equivalents of surgical procedures, nor will their assessments of clients' concerns offer the assurances of medicine's X-rays or blood tests. Instead, we see counsellors as engaged in meaning-making with clients (Strong 2003). Counselling is also an interpretive, as opposed to an information transmission-reception, activity. The crux of our concern is over whether counsellors should 'apply' medicalised forms of knowledge in ways that are akin to Hook's (2007) 'discursive technologies', in predetermined understandings of human concerns and interventions to address them.

Our concern is not merely about academic arguments to be resolved in the ivory tower (for some challenging research questions, see Lacasse 2014). Thanks to the Internet and other media, DSM-5's diagnoses are now part of what Lionel Trilling referred to as the 'slang of our culture' (cited in Illouz 2008: 10). Clients present themselves to counsellors as already diagnosed, often fashioning identities that are based on these medicalised understandings and what needs to be done accordingly (Charland 2004; McLaughlin 2012). Look closer at how counselling is now funded, administered, rationed and regulated as a healthcare practice (Grohol 2013; Johnson 1995). DSM-5 diagnoses, treated using evidence-based methods, are becoming the expected norm when funding counselling services (Strong et al. 2012). Responsive counsellor educators are increasingly having to reconcile preferred pedagogies and orientations to this default discourse of DSM-5 and evidence-based practice. Irrespective of what students might have learnt in their graduate counsellor education, a medicalising (diagnose-and-treat) logic awaits them in practicum settings and internships, and the jobs that they hope to step into after graduation.

Counsellors and counsellor educators have sometimes felt like dumb professional colleagues to their counterparts in clinical psychology, where the discourse of research and practice is often highly medicalised around psychiatric diagnoses and 'treatment plans' (Ogunfowora and Drapeau 2008; Seligman 2004). However, applying psychologically derived knowledge to human endeavours such as counselling has been suspect for some time (Sampson 1981) for the faith put in reified and concretised scientific metaphors (Soyland 1994; Whitehead 1997). While psychological and medically oriented researchers and therapists persist with correct diagnoses and proven treatments, a warm and supportive therapeutic alliance persists as the most important aspect of helping clients to make desired changes (Duncan et al. 2009).

Finally, a postmodern era has emerged for some counsellors (for example Paré 2013), replacing an era where expertly applied psychological knowledge was seen as the primary ethical basis of good counselling.

Postmodern counselling draws from social constructionist insights that suggest that meaning and action are products of our relational processes (Anderson 1997; Gergen 2009). A collaborative, generative and deconstructive approach is advocated by postmoderns – one customised around preferred and actionable meanings within the clients' resources and circumstances. These approaches eschew standardised ways of naming and addressing clients' concerns, and they lack an expert 'evidence base' that is reassuring to counsellor educators who are expected to show scientific support for their curricular decisions (Larner 2004). However, new notions of counselling expertise are emerging, based less on adherence to diagnostic and treatment protocols than on aligning counsellors' resourcefulness with the preferences and resourcefulness of clients in pursuing client-preferred outcomes (Tracey et al. 2014). Regardless, considerable interest, inside and outside counsellor education programmes, has been shown towards the postmodern approaches to counselling (Sharf 2012).

The kinds of tension or difference that we have been describing over what should be taught in a counsellor education curriculum are consistent with our view of postmodernity. Modern science was to universally resolve such tensions or differences; postmoderns deal with them in situated ways. The tensions that we have been describing are arguably dominated by the contested classification system of DSM-5 (Frances 2013; Greenberg 2013) and expected evidence-based interventions to treat its disorders (Strong and Busch 2013). Equipped with the insights of linguistic and poststructural philosophy, fortified by feminist and postcolonial critiques of exclusion and dominance, and sensitised by sociocultural and dialogical understandings of relational processes, postmoderns approach professional projects, such as curriculum development, as ongoing negotiations of meanings and practices. In the postmodern situation we have been describing – counsellor education – negotiations of difference are evident in the documents through which counsellor educators articulate their views of what being a good counsellor entails. Our interest is in making evident the medicalised tensions that are associated with using DSM-5 and to show their influence on the discourses of contemporary counsellor education.

Mapping curricular tensions

> I personally see no space outside of politics of some kind. Things can be more or less implicitly or explicitly engaged.
> (Adele Clarke in Clarke and Keller 2014)

Adele Clarke's (2005; Clarke and Keller 2014) situational analysis is a research method that is well suited to representing the kinds of tensions that we have been describing. The tensions of cultural and professional projects, such as curriculum development, follow from different discourse communities that she terms 'social worlds', vying to influence what gets developed, and extending to how that development will occur. For Clarke, such politics as those shaping counsellor education are inescapable, and they make for what she terms a 'situation'. Situations are reflexively shaped by the politics and negotiations which sustain and transform them. Though scientists and professionals aim to be above such politics, the aforementioned DSM-5 controversies show how counselling and other disciplines that influence it have been negotiating before and after DSM-5's publication (for example Grohol 2013; Lacasse 2014). Such tensions and negotiations highlight vital, engaged and ongoing human differences in play.

Mapping such identifiable tensions and negotiations is the methodological and analytic challenge for situation analysts. Thus we turn to publicly accessible documents to show medicalising tensions that we see influencing contemporary counsellor education. In situational analysis the primary means for showing such tensions is to map them, to highlight the actors (human and non-human) that are reflexively engaged in influencing the situation – in this case, counsellor education. We begin with what Clarke (2005) describes as a social world/arenas map.

Who has something at stake in counsellor education?

Figure 15.1 depicts key people and institutions that have something 'at stake' (Potter 1996) in how counsellor education develops. For example, academics in this situation (for example counsellor educators or psychologists) might see stakes involved in particular kinds of knowledge that are at odds with, or irrelevant to, accrediting bodies, practicum sites or clients. Thus, counselling programme graduates who are trained according to such knowledge would be ill-prepared for their professional responsibilities. If practicum sites need students who can diagnose clients' concerns using DSM-5, and students receive no such training, issues could arise for the students and their counsellor education programmes. The interests of the people or institutions shown in the figure are being negotiated as part of the curriculum-development process. We can support our claims with textual data that are articulated in publicly accessible documents such as those found on counsellor education programmes, course syllabi and professional organisation websites.

246 Critiques of Training and Learning

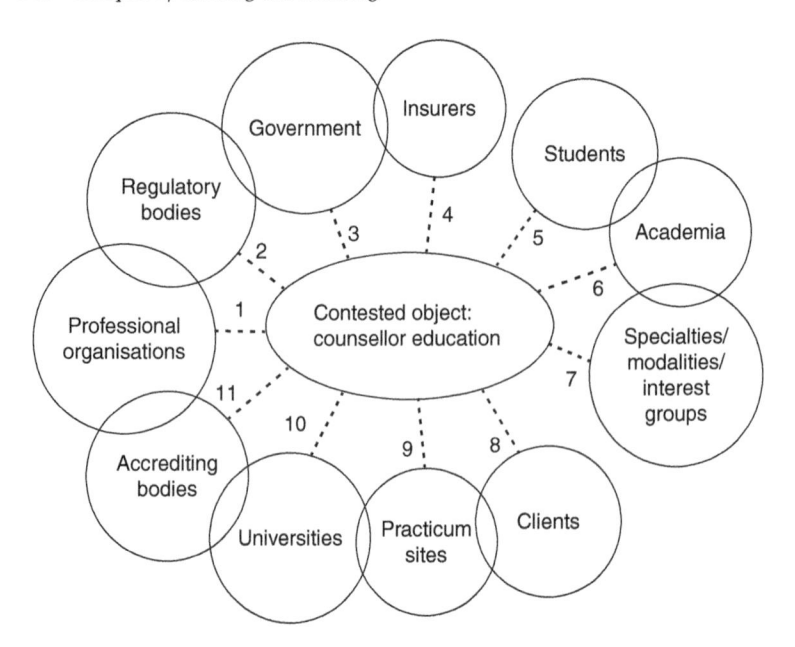

Figure 15.1 Who has something at stake in counsellor education?

Staying with Figure 15.1, readers will note that there are numbers associated with each 'stakeholder'. Each number flags for us a body of textual data that we identified as being associated with that 'stakeholder' regarding medicalising tensions in counsellor education. To illustrate the world of 'Regulatory bodies', in the Canadian province of Ontario, psychotherapy is regulated by the Health Professions Regulatory Advisory Council (HPRAC) because the term 'counselling', itself, has been appropriated by the province's psychologists. The HPRAC (2006) used medical language to position psychotherapy as a healthcare service: 'prior to engaging in psychotherapy with a patient, all therapists need to formulate the case and develop an appropriate treatment plan' (p. 222). Counselling, on the other hand, was framed as the provision of information, advice or encouragement regarding emotional, social or spiritual matters, and it was specifically not regulated as a healthcare practice. Some might claim here that attention to such distinctions in language use is a kind of semantic splitting of hairs. However, very real consequences, such as getting paid or professionally reprimanded, follow from expectations that counsellors adhere to these regulatory statements or requirements. Counsellor education programmes ostensibly prepare graduates (as counsellors and/or psychotherapists?) to meet such changing and sometimes ambiguous requirements. To illustrate further, reimbursement for counselling services is often administered by third-party insurers. In the Financial Services Commission of Ontario (FSCO) guidelines for reimbursing professional services (by master's- and doctoral-level practitioners) following motor vehicle accidents are stated in a section headed 'Assessment and clinical diagnosis before treatment'. The FSCO stipulates: 'In all psychological treatment contexts, assessment must precede treatment. It is essential that the psychologist determine sufficient information about the patient's condition and situation in order to prescribe treatment' (2001: 6). Such requirements may seem unrelated to counsellor education programmes until one recognises that student practica sometimes occur in sites where such requirements must be met.

Our aim with the social worlds/arenas map of Figure 15.1 has been to answer Clarke's (2005) question, 'What are the salient social worlds operating "here?" ' (p. 110), 'here' being the broader arena of counsellor education. The social world of clients is different from that of regulatory boards, or that of insurers, yet we claim that each 'world' has something at stake in how counsellor education reflects their interests. The medical language of DSM-5, and the 'treatments' that follow from its use, takes on particular salience within each of these social worlds. Collectively, across these different social worlds depicted in Figure 15.1, one finds medicalising tensions associated with DSM-5's prominence that influences counsellor education. We next turn to how such tensions are becoming evident in counselling textbooks.

What do the textbooks say?

Textbooks distil the knowledge and recommendations of a profession, such as counselling. We examined common counselling textbooks for knowledge and recommendations that illustrate medicalising tensions that we associated with the use of DSM-5 and evidence-based practice. Ten counselling textbooks were selected because they were (1) recommended by faculty members at the University of Calgary as key books for training future counsellors; (2) included in different syllabi across Canadian counselling programmes; and (3) accessible at the University of Calgary's Taylor Digital Family Library. For more examples illustrating medicalising tensions drawn from those ten counselling textbooks, see Appendix 15.1.

Of particular interest to us in analysing the textbooks were 'contradictions' in how knowledge was portrayed or in how practices were recommended. Such contradictions, for us, speak of what we have been describing as discursive tensions, not authorial inconsistencies. We see such 'contradictions' as evidence of authors (intentionally or otherwise) trying to satisfy the stakeholders of the different kinds of social worlds that are depicted in Figure 15.1. For example, in Gerald Corey's 2009 edition of his popular textbook, *Theory and Practice of Counseling and Psychotherapy*, readers can find these two statements:

> It is through our own genuineness and our aliveness that we can significantly touch our clients. (p. 17)

> Although assessment and treatment occur together, a formal assessment takes place prior to treatment to determine behaviours that are targets of change. (p. 239)

These quotations show Corey initially writing from his personal view, and in a later chapter describing medicalised expectations (i.e. 'treatment') for counsellors using CBT. The differences between quotations are striking, relating to possible differences between Corey's preferred style and that needed to represent an approach that is different from his style. Turning to another prominent textbook, *An Introduction to Counselling* (McLeod 2009), one finds this pair of statements:

> Counselling is not focused on symptom reduction, but on enabling the person to live their life in a way that is most meaningful and satisfying to him or her. (p. 7)

> A series of studies have established the effectiveness of Beating the Blues as an intervention for mild and moderate levels of depression. (p. 560)

Our aim with such analyses, again, is to not advocate for consistency but to point out that the content of such counselling textbooks exemplifies tensions that are associated with medicalising discourse involved in using DSM-5 and evidence-based interventions (Chwalisz 2003; Feltham 2005; House and Bohart 2010). After informing students that counselling is not focused on symptom reduction, McLeod later returns to discuss an intervention that reduces symptoms of depression. Communications of this kind are ubiquitous (Illouz 2008), and terms like 'depression' have become part of everyday parlance, further publicising a 'diagnose and treat' logic that is associated with DSM-5. We could continue with other examples, further juxtaposing non-medicalising and medicalising discourses in textbooks of counselling. Regardless, since the American Psychological Association's *Report of the 2005 Presidential Task Force on Evidence-Based Practice* (Levant 2005), and developments leading to DSM-5's recent publication, counselling textbooks increasingly use medicalising discourse alongside other discourses of practice. Counselling textbooks adopt more medicalising discourse now than before, and, whether by straightforward advocacy or by default, this merits critical reflection. Readers can trace such discursive developments over the 5th to 9th editions of Wedding's collaboration with Corsini on *Current Psychotherapies* (2010, particularly in the chapter Wedding co-authored with Pope, 'Contemporary challenges and controversies').

Mapping the perceptions of students and counsellor educators

For Clarke (2005), messy maps offer researchers a preliminary way of identifying relevant features in a situation of research interest prior to ordering these features according to traceable relations between them. With more data or literature on this topic we would more confidently represent these relations, an aim for the broader project (including later survey and interview data) encompassing this component of our research. Examining student and counsellor educators' perceptions of counsellor education offered us a preliminary means of 'messily' representing salient features of counsellor education. What made features of this literature salient to us were their potential relations to a medicalising discourse of counselling. Appendix 15.2 is our messy map for this focused review of the literature.

Examining this messy map more closely, we identified five rough clusters of features that pertain to perceptions of counsellor education. While features of each cluster could be traced to medicalising associated with DSM-5 in counselling, one in particular – the smallest, most central cluster – directly pertained to medicalising discourse. Specifically, students and educators in our review of the literature sometimes voiced that they wished to be treated on a par with medical colleagues, with their knowledge and skills in using DSM diagnosis being central to that parity. Other clusters and their features were not as easy to associate with DSM-5 or medicalising discourse. For example, in one section focused on professional identity, counselling students and educators sometimes metaphorically and enviously referred to themselves as 'stepchildren' of clinical psychology. This self-identification perhaps alludes to clinical psychology's more established focus on diagnosing and treating psychopathology.

In another cluster, external features, such as programme-accrediting or professional regulating bodies, were seen as shaping counselling practice and education in ways that are deemed medical. This echoes comments identified above when we discussed our social worlds/arenas map. Relations between learning areas or activities identified in another cluster (featuring supervision and competency) and medicalising discourse were more tenuous, though still relevant to our analyses. To illustrate, students and educators practising from a strengths-based approach, such as solution-focused counselling, can experience tensions when reconciling a 'diagnose and treat' approach with a focus on client resourcefulness. Finally, students and educators voiced values and theoretically based preferences that are possibly at odds with a medicalising approach, such as with social constructionist orientations being at odds with the 'realist' medical focus on symptom diagnosis. In mapping and selectively discussing these student and educator perceptions we aimed for an overview of features that they considered to be salient to counsellor education – specifically, features that are possibly related to medicalising that education.

Mapping positions relevant to medicalising education

Important in Clarke's (2005) situational analysis is identifying discursive positions within any 'situation'. Where the earlier social worlds/arenas map depicted relevant influences in the situation of medicalising counsellor education, position maps – the analytic resource we next use – help to identify different discourse positions in the 'situation'. Discourses, in this sense, are not bound to particular people and institutions; people and institutions can take up more than one discourse, as did textbook authors such as McLeod (2010). Thus a student or counsellor educator could understand or act according to a strengths-based discourse in one aspect of counsellor education, while in another aspect they might be expected to communicate a client's concerns to a supervisor on DSM-5 terms. Such variability in discourse positions is not a concern until one considers how dilemmas, such as whether to teach in a strengths-focused over a DSM-5 diagnose-and-treat manner, are addressed and justified. We contend that counsellor education can be seen as a contested curriculum. It is in this contest that discourse positions – given how they are articulated and acted upon – become significant, if not consequential to how a situation such as counsellor education develops.

Appendix 15.3 shows a simplified version of positions that are evident in our analyses of publicly accessible counsellor education programme websites and syllabi across Canada. The programmes that we examined were master's level and housed in varied academic faculties or departments (for example education or health science). Some programmes were housed in counselling psychology departments that also offered doctoral degrees, and a few met accreditation requirements that are set by bodies such as the Canadian Psychological Association (i.e. for counselling psychology) or the Council for Accreditation of Counseling and Related Educational Programmes. The programmes varied in their requirements of medicalised/non-medicalised requirements (for example hours of practica, thesis- or course-based). Thus a heterogeneity across programmes characterises counsellor education in Canada (Bedi et al. 2012).

The simplified positions in Appendix 15.3 are presented in dilemmatic ways to highlight what we mean by medicalising tensions. Seen one way, they reflect polarised positions on arguments for or against medicalising counsellor education in ways that are consistent with a DSM-5 – diagnose and treat – approach. Seen otherwise, we were able to depict how positional statements, which are accessible from Canadian counsellor education websites and syllabi, relate 'more' or 'less' to medicalising discourse across different, contested aspects of counsellor education.

The degree to which psychological knowledge itself was cited as foundational to the learning varied within these programmes. Some programmes were positioned to be allied with clinical psychology (for example as is newly the case at the University of Toronto; OISE University of Toronto 2014a) or used clinical language that is associated with DSM-5 diagnoses. This contrasted with other university programmes (such as those of Acadia University 2011b; Memorial University of Newfoundland 2014; University of New Brunswick 2014), which articulated their mandate as being focused on training counsellors to facilitate education, vocational guidance and personal development. McGill (2011) indicated clearly that graduates were discouraged from working in medical settings while emphasising the 'clinical skills' of their graduates.

Turning to positions that were evident regarding relational practice in counselling, the differences became more distinguishable. While practising from a collaborative or conversationally focused approach need not be at odds with technical proficiency, programme wording could be as different as what is shown by the following two quotes:

> The guiding belief of the programme is that a compassionate response to those in need is best provided by individuals who possess an

integrated sense of who they are and what they know in order to deliver effective service to others.

(University of Western Ontario 2011: 3)

Our students are trained to work with *mental health issues* as clinicians and as researchers and to understand the relationship between clinical practice and scientific research and how each is informed by the other.

(emphasis added, OISE University of Toronto 2014b: 2)

Programmes differently balanced language that focused on relations with clients or language that was clinically and scientifically oriented in ways that we associate with medicalising. Some programmes, such as that at the University of Alberta (2013), used the language of 'patients' in places, alongside the language of 'clients'.

A particularly notable contrast in positions articulated across these programme websites related to how clients' concerns or aspirations were represented. While most programmes described students and graduates as helping clients to address developmental concerns, problems in daily living, relationship difficulties or the 'enhancement of human potential' (Acadia University 2011a: 3), others more directly cited diagnosing psychopathology (DSM-5 disorders) as preparation for clinical work.

Our distinctions were developed through conversations over an extended period during which we reviewed textual data from these different websites and syllabi. We aimed to show how medicalised language, such as 'clinical', 'treatment' and 'patient', featured on these websites. We also considered the ambiguous language of 'mental health' while reflecting on the language of evidence-based practice and medicalisation (Chwalisz 2003), since such an approach was imported from medicine into the psychology and counselling professions (Levant 2005). Instead of semantic precision, we wanted to highlight how discursive tensions may be influencing counsellor education, as they are articulated on programme websites and in syllabi.

Discussion

The basic psychology of legislating language is that it allows us to believe we can control our destiny. When language appears no longer to be something we can discipline, we suspect that wider anarchy is nigh.

(Hitchings 2011: 254)

Approaching counsellor education as a 'situation', to study curricular tensions that are associated with medicalisation, has helped us to show a particular kind of professional language or meaning-making at work. The curriculum offerings and developments in counsellor education are contested or negotiated, with many influences being evident. DSM-5 offers a language for standardising and medicalising counsellor education, particularly when expected evidence-based interventions accompany its use. Such standardising and medicalising would help counselling and counsellor education to better align with other health professions. However, this medicalising approach has not been advanced without criticism (Frances 2013; Mozdzierz et al. 2011). While partly taken up by counsellors and counsellor educators (for example Seligman 2004), it has also been resisted by others whose ideas, values and practices seem to be incompatible with the particular science and assumptions that inform a medicalised approach. Such a standardising direction and approach has offended and mobilised the field's pluralists (for example Cooper and McLeod 2011). Examining how medicalisation plays out, or is negotiated, in counsellor education exemplifies socially constructed processes and meanings.

More is at stake in this situation, however, than what counsellors might learn in their textbooks, lectures and supervised experiences. Counsellors are important service providers to clients facing diverse human concerns, not all of which are translatable to diagnosed disorders inside them. As Illouz (2008) and deVos (2012) have highlighted, medicalised and psychologised knowledge now circulate in the culture at large. People have become increasingly vigilant in using such knowledge, self-applying it with consequences that we have yet to fully understand (Charland 2004; McLaughlin 2012). The stakes in this situation become clearer if one asks what is left out of counselling dialogues that accept medicalisation as their focus.

The range of what is meaningful to discuss in counselling narrows considerably when these conversations are limited to symptoms and their treatment. As practitioners drawing from social constructionist approaches to meaning, where meanings are not singular, we are also attentive to the reflexive possibilities of dialogues with clients (Lock and Strong 2012). Counsellor education focused on symptoms, treatments and singular meanings concern us. Our concern relates to the kind of linguistic legislating to which this section's opening quote referred. We 'mapped' (Clarke 2005) relevant influences (and tensions between them) to draw attention to how contemporary counsellor education is linguistically articulated in key documents such as textbooks, graduate programme details and research. The next generation of counsellors is being educated in ways that are reflective of the influences that we have mapped, though specifics will vary for each counselling student, counsellor educator and graduate programme.

Expected use of DSM-5 and evidence-based practice is on the rise for funded counselling services in the USA (Grohol 2013). Counsellor educators have also raised concerns about aligning themselves with this medicalising direction in practice (for example Hansen 2007; House and Bohart 2010). While our examination of diverse educational documents shows that medicalising language is present (in courses such as assessment, ethics and practica), DSM-5 is not (yet?) the default language of counsellor education; counsellor education retains much of its pluralism.

Appendix 15.1: Examples of tensions between non-medicalised vs. medicalised discourses in counselling textbooks

Non-medicalised discourse	Medicalised discourse
'The counsellor does not diagnose or label you, but does his or her best to listen to you and work with you to find the best ways to understand and resolve your problem.' (McLeod 2010: 1)	'One of the major challenges for any counsellor is when a client appears to suffer from a deeply ingrained self-destructive pattern of relating to other people. A person with this kind of difficulty is often described as having "personality disorder".' (McLeod 2010: 259)
'Counselling is not focused on symptom reduction, but on enabling the person to live their life in a way that is most meaningful and satisfying to him or her.' (McLeod 2010: 7)	'A series of studies have established the effectiveness of *Beating the Blues* as an intervention for mild and moderate levels of depression.' (McLeod 2010: 560)
'Even though counselors do not tend to be experts in psychopathology, they do have knowledge of mental disorders and know when to refer individuals who need more in-depth treatment.' (Neukrug 2012: 5)	'part of me didn't want to do it, because I really didn't believe in making a diagnosis. I had to use this book called the Diagnostic and Statistical Manual-II (DSM-II) that had descriptions of the various emotional disorders. It soon became my bible.' (Neukrug 2012: 322)

'Rarely does a counseling theory prescribe what *specific* goals of counseling should be. Since there is much room for alternative viewpoints on such matters as normal human functioning, how people change, and what is a desirable outcome, different theories have emerged to reflect these various viewpoints.' (Hackney and Cormier 1996: 5)

'Counseling involves a basic acceptance of the client's perceptions and feelings, regardless of outside evaluative standards.' (Hackney and Cormier 1996: 8)

'The effectiveness of counselling depends on many factors, but among the most important is for the counselor and client to be able to understand and relate to each other.' (Gladding and Newsome 2010: 68)

'Counselling psychology advocates an interactive alternative. Rather than expecting clients to submit compliantly to treatment prescribed by professionals, it emphasizes the subjective experience of clients and the need of helpers to engage with them as collaborators, seeking to understand their inner worlds and constructions of reality.' (Strawbridge and Woolfe 2010: 10)

'The medical model relies upon diagnosis; that is, the ability to define and describe illness or disease in the organic body and psychopathology of the mind. Reference is usually made to the Diagnostic and Statistical Manual (DSM) of the USA (American Psychiatric Association 1980).' (Hammersley 2010: 633)

'Counseling strategies constitute the plan within which most therapeutic work and change take place.' (Hackney and Cormier 1996: 141)

'Two general functions that clinical mental health counselors need to conduct skillfully are assessment and diagnosis.' (Gladding and Newsome 2010: 165)

'Of particular importance to counselors of the 21st century is the need to select counseling interventions based on outcome research. Counselors need to select *evidence-based interventions*...' (Gladding and Newsome 2010: 16)

'Clinical mental health counselors are expected to be skilled in biopsychosocial case conceptualization and treatment planning.' (Gladding and Newsome 2010: 130)

'Because anxiety is also a symptom of other mental disorders, counselors need to know how to diagnose anxiety accurately.' (Gladding and Newsome 2010: 184)

(Continued)

Non-medicalised discourse	Medicalised discourse
'The centrality of this humanistic value system offers one answer to the question of how counselling psychology differs from medical and other psychological approaches... As the focus shifts away from the applications of specific treatments, what we do *to* clients, to how we are *with* clients, the emphasis becomes one of *being-in-relation* rather than *doing*.' (Strawbridge and Woolfe 2010: 11)	'The research evidence so far suggests that brief interventions can be extremely effective when used appropriately, and computerized packages, such as those in health centres, can be useful.' (Sanders 2010: 126)
'If we become merely technical experts and leave our own reactions, values, and self out of our work, the result is likely to be sterile counseling.' (Corey 2009: 17)	'Although assessment and treatment occur together, a formal assessment takes place prior to treatment to determine behaviours that are targets of change.' (Corey 2009: 239)
'From my perspective, the counselor's role is to create a climate in which clients can examine their thoughts, feelings, and actions and eventually arrive at solutions that are best for them.' (Corey 2009: 23)	'DSM provides the diagnostic system used for communicating among professionals. It is applied as a way of organizing clients' behaviours.' (Kress and Eriksen 2011: 258)
'The counseling profession typically emphasizes growth and development, multiculturalism, and contextual thinking, all of which stand in opposition to the illness and remediation worldview traditionally implied in doing "diagnosis and treatment planning".' (Kress and Eriksen 2011: 255)	'counselors do need diagnostic capacities for a number of reasons. For one, were counselors to give up diagnosis, they would be disadvantaged financially. Third-party payers will most likely continue their requirements that counselors diagnose in order to be reimbursed for providing mental health services. Further, *Diagnostic and Statistic Manual of Mental Disorders* (DSM; APA 2000) labels have some professional advantages.' (Kress and Eriksen 2011: 255)
'The counseling model is more generally egalitarian. The counselor is viewed as client's fellow traveler on the road of life...' (Hutchinson 2012: 12)	'The implications for counselors of a developmental approach to assessment are obvious. We need to structure our interventions, our activity, and the things we say and do with our clients...' (Hutchinson 2012: 156)

Appendix 15.2: Messy Mapping the Perceptions of Students and Counsellor Educators

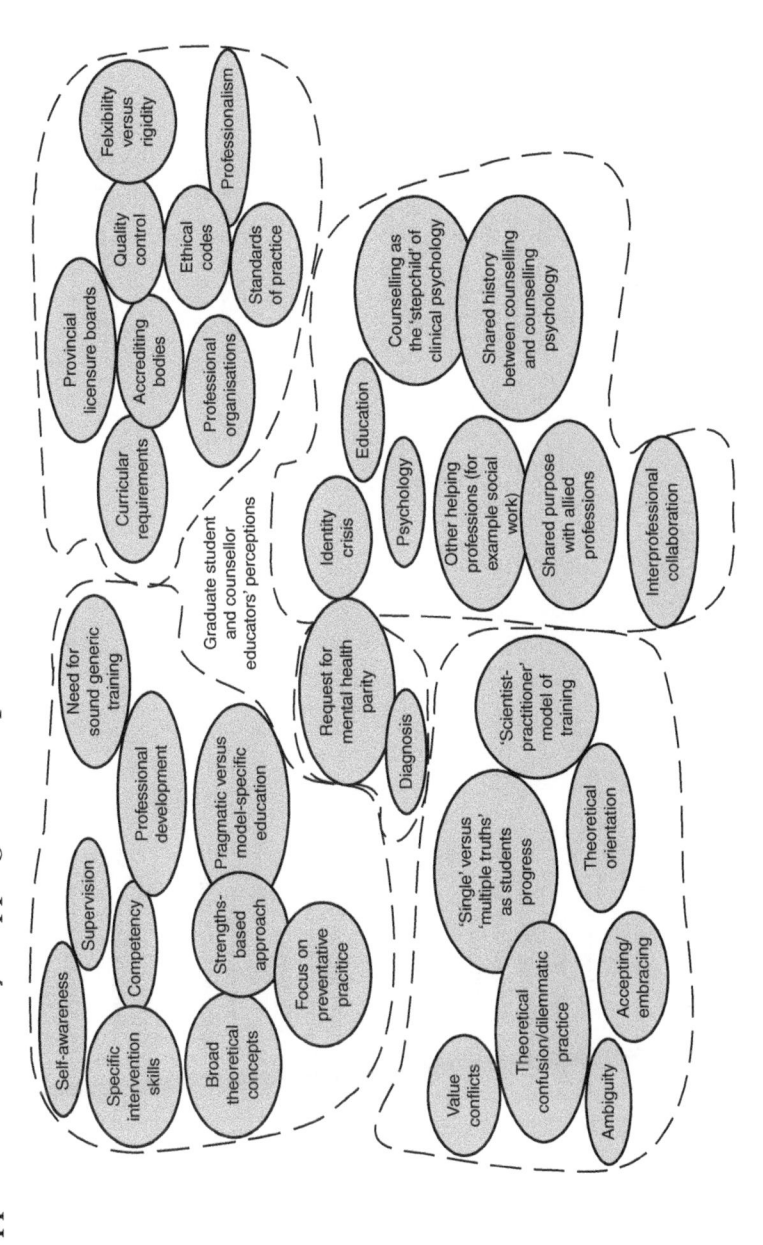

Appendix 15.3: Simplified Positional Map: Medicalising Tensions in Counsellor Education

Less medicalised		More medicalised
Counselling is distinct from "clinical" approaches	<--------------->	Counselling psychology is closely related to clinical psychology
Problems are socially constructed, grounded in meaning-making	<--------------->	Realist/objectivist view of problems, which must be correctly assessed
Counselling as a conversational or relational practice	<--------------->	Counselling as a (mental) health profession
Individually tailored and responsive counselling dialogues	<--------------->	Standardized and replicable methods
Focus on mutual relational processes	<--------------->	Focus on counsellor's actions or skills
Counsellors work with problems of living	<--------------->	Counsellors work with mental illness
Counsellors enhance human growth/potential		

References

Acadia University (2011a) Graduate programmes: Master of education in counselling. http://education.acadiau.ca/graduate-programmes.html.

Acadia University (2011b) Programme description. http://education.acadiau.ca/med-counselling/articles/programme-description.3602.html.

American Psychiatric Association (2013) *Diagnostic and Statistical Manual of Mental Disorders* 5th ed. Washington, DC: American Psychiatric Association.

Anderson, H. (1997) *Conversation, Language, and Possibilities*. New York: Basic Books.

Bedi, R.P., Klubben, L.M. and Barker, G.T. (2012) 'Counselling vs. clinical: A comparison of psychology doctoral programmes in Canada', *Canadian Psychology*, 53(3): 238–253.

Charland, L.C. (2004) 'A madness for identity: Psychiatric labels, consumer autonomy, and the perils of the internet', *Philosophy, Psychiatry & Psychology*, 11, 335–349.

Chwalisz, K. (2003) 'Evidence-based practice: A framework for twenty-first century scientist-practitioner training', *The Counseling Psychologist*, 31:5, 497–528.

Clarke, A.E. (2005) *Situational Analysis: Grounded Theory after the Postmodern Turn*. Thousand Oaks: Sage.

Clarke, A.E. and Keller, R. (2014) 'Engaging complexities: Working against simplification as an agenda for qualitative research today. Adele Clarke in conversation with Reiner Keller' [137 paragraphs], *Forum Qualitative Sozialforschung/Forum: Qualitative Social Research*, 15:2, Art. 1. http://nbnresolving.de/urn:nbn:de:0114-fqs140212.

Cooper, M. and McLeod, J. (2011) *Pluralistic Counselling and Psychotherapy*. Thousand Oaks: Sage.

Dean, M. (2013) *The Signature of Power: Sovereignty, Governmentality, and Biopolitics*. Los Angeles: Sage.

De Cicco, M. (2007) Communication strategy plan with regard to the CCA name change. http://www.ccpa-accp.ca/_documents/CommunicationStrategy.pdf.

de Vos, J. (2012) *Psychologisation in Times of Globalisation*. New York: Routledge.

Duncan, B., Miller, S., Wampold, B. and Hubble, M. (eds.) (2009) *The Heart and Soul of Change* 2nd ed. Washington, DC: American Psychological Association Press.

Eriksen, K. and Kress, V.E. (2006) 'The DSM and the professional counseling identity: Bridging the gap', *Journal of Mental Health Counseling*, 28, 202–217.

Feltham, C. (2005) 'Evidence-based psychotherapy and counselling in the UK: Critique and alternatives', *Journal of Contemporary Psychotherapy*, 35, 131–143.

Financial Services Commission of Ontario (31 March 2001) *Psychology Assessment and Treatment Guidelines*. https://www.fsco.gov.on.ca/en/auto/autobulletins/archives/Documents/a-05_01-2.pdf.

Foucault, M. (2008) *The Government of Self and Others: Lectures at the College de France 1982–1983* trans. Burchell, G. New York: Palgrave Macmillan.

Frances, A. (2013) *Saving Normal: An Insider's Revolt against Out-of-Control Psychiatric Diagnosis, DSM-5, Big Pharma, and the Medicalisation of Ordinary Life*. New York: William Morrow.

Gergen, K.J. (2009) *Relational Being: Beyond Self and Community*. New York: Oxford University Press.

Greenberg, G. (2013) *The Book of Woe: The DSM and the Unmaking of Psychiatry.* New York: Penguin Books.

Grohol, J. (2013) *Final Rules for U.S. Mental Health Parity Released: No Surprises But Also No Silver Bullet.* Blog posting, 9 November 2013. http://psychcentral.com/blog/archives/2013/11/09/final-rules-for-u-s-mental-health-parity-released-no-surprises-but-also-no-silver-bullet/.

Hansen, J.T. (2007) 'Should counseling be considered a health care profession? Critical thoughts on the transition to a health care ideology', *Journal of Counseling and Development,* 85:3, 286–293.

Health Professions Regulation Advisory Council (27 April 2006) *Regulation of Health Professions in Ontario: New Directions.* http://www.health.gov.on.ca/en/common/ministry/publications/reports/new_directions/new_directions.pdf.

Hitchings, H. (2011) *The Language Wars: A History of Proper English.* London: John Murray.

Hook, D. (2007) *Foucault, Psychology, and the Analytics of Power.* New York: Palgrave Macmillan.

House, R. and Bohart, A.C. (2010) 'Empirically supported/validated treatments as modernist ideology: Alternative perspectives on research and practice', in R. House (ed.) *In, against, and beyond Therapy: Critical Essays towards a 'postprofessional' Era.* Ross-on-Wye: PCCS Books, pp. 252–268.

Illouz, E. (2008) *Saving the Soul: Therapy, Emotions, and the Culture of Self-Help.* Berkeley: University of California Press.

Insel, T. (29 April 2013) Transforming diagnosis. Blog entry at the National Institute of Mental Health. http://www.nimh.nih.gov/about/director/2013/transforming-diagnosis.shtml.

Johnson, L. (1995) *Psychotherapy in the Age of Accountability.* New York: W.W. Norton.

Lacasse, J.R. (2014) 'After DSM-5: A critical mental health research agenda for the 21st century', *Research on Social Work Practice,* 24:1, 5–10.

Larner, G. (2004) 'Family therapy and the politics of evidence', *Journal of Family Therapy,* 26:1, 17–39.

Levant, R.F. (2005) *Report of the 2005 Presidential Task Force on Evidence-Based Practice.* American Psychological Association. http://www.apa.org/practice/resources/evidence/evidence-based-report.pdf.

Lock, A. and Strong, T. (eds.) (2012) *Discursive Perspectives on Therapeutic Practice.* New York: Oxford University Press.

McGill University (May 2011) *Graduate Students' Handbook.* http://www.mcgill.ca/files/edu-ecp/CounsellingHandbook2011.pdf.

McLaughlin, K. (2012) *Surviving Identity: Vulnerability and the Psychology of Recognition.* London: Routledge.

McLeod, J. (2009) *An Introduction to Counselling.* New York: McGraw Hill.

Memorial University of Newfoundland (2014) *Counselling Psychology.* http://www.mun.ca/edu/grad/counselling.php.

Mozdzierz, G.J., Peluso, P.R. and Lisiecki, J. (2011) 'Evidence based psychological practices and therapist training: At the crossroads', *Journal of Humanistic Psychology,* 51:4, 439–464.

National Board of Certified Counselors (April 2014) *How Is the DSM-5 Affecting NBCC's Examinations?* http://www.nbcc.org/Assets/DSM5_Update_April_2014.pdf.

Ogunfowora, B. and Drapeau, M. (2008) 'Comparing counselling and clinical Psychology practitioners: Similarities and differences on theoretical orientations revisited', *International Journal for the Advancement of Counselling*, 30:2, 93–103.

OISE University of Toronto (July 16 2014a) *Counselling & Clinical Psychology*. http://www.oise.utoronto.ca/aphd/Prospective_Students/Programmes/Counselling_Clinical_Psychology/index.html.

OISE University of Toronto (16 July 2014b) *Master of Arts – Clinical & Counselling Psychology*. http://www.oise.utoronto.ca/aphd/Prospective_Students/Programmes/Counselling_Clinical_Psychology/MA.html.

Paré, D. (2013) *The Practice of Collaborative Counseling & Psychotherapy: Developing Skills in Culturally Mindful Helping*. Los Angeles: Sage.

Potter, J. (1996) *Representing Reality*. Thousand Oaks: Sage.

Sampson, E.E. (1981) 'Cognitive psychology as ideology', *American Psychologist*, 36, 730–743.

Seligman, L. (2004) *Diagnosis and Treatment Planning in Counseling* 3rd ed. New York: Springer.

Sharf, R.S. (2012) *Theories of Psychotherapy and Counseling: Concepts and Cases* 5th ed. Belmont: Brooks/Cole.

Soyland, A.J. (1994) *Psychology as Metaphor*. London: Sage.

Strong, T. (2003) 'Getting curious about meaning-making in counselling', *British Journal of Guidance and Counselling*, 31, 259–273.

Strong, T. and Busch, R. (2013) 'DSM-V and evidence-based family therapy?', *Australian and New Zealand Journal of Family Therapy*, 34:2, 90–103.

Strong, T., Gaete Silva, J., Sametband, I, French, J. and Eeson, J. (2012) 'Counsellors respond to the DSM-IV-TR', *Canadian Journal of Counselling and Psychotherapy*, 46:2, 85–106.

Tracey, T.J.G., Wampold, B.E., Lichtenberg, J.W. and Goodyear, R.K. (2014) 'Expertise in psychotherapy: An elusive goal?', *American Psychologist*, 69, 218–229.

University of Alberta (1 August 2013) *Counselling Psychology Student Handbook*. http://www.edpsychology.ualberta.ca/en/GraduateProgrammes/~/media/edpsych/Documents/GraduateProgrammes/CounsellingPsychology/Counselling_Handbook_August_2013.pdf.

University of New Brunswick (10 July 2014) *Counselling*. http://www.unb.ca/fredericton/education/graduate/mastereducation/concentrations/counselling/.

University of Western Ontario (2011) *Graduate Handbook: Counselling Psychology Programme*. http://www.edu.uwo.ca/graduate education/documents/professional/CounsellinghandbookJune11.pdf.

Wedding, D. and Corsini, R.J. (2010) *Current Psychotherapies* 9th ed. Belmont: Brooks/Cole.

Whitehead, A.N. (1997) *Science and the Modern World*. New York: Free Press (original published in 1925).

References for textbooks

Brown, S.D. and Lent, R.W. (eds.) (2008) *Handbook of Counseling Psychology* 4th ed. Hoboken: John Wiley and Sons.

Corey, G. (2009) *Theory and Practice of Counseling and Psychotherapy* 8th ed. Belmont: Brooks/Cole.

Gladding, S.T. and Newsome, D.W. (2010) *Clinical Mental Health Counseling in Community and Agency Settings* 3rd ed. New Jersey: Pearson Education Inc.

Hackney, H.L. and Cormier, L.S. (1996) *The Professional Counselor. A Process Guide to Helping*. Needham Heights: Allyin and Bacon.

Hammersley, D. (2010) 'The interface between psychopharmacological and psychotherapeutic approaches', in R. Woolfe, S. Strawbridge, B. Douglas and W. Dryden (eds.) *Handbook of Counselling Psychology* 3rd ed. Thousand Oaks: Sage, pp. 630–652.

Hutchinson, D. (2012) *The Essential Counselor. Process, Skills, and Techniques* 2nd ed. Thousand Oaks: Sage.

Kress, V.E. and Eriksen, K. (2011) 'Teaching the diagnosis and treatment planning course', in G. McAuliffe and K. Eriksen (eds.) *Handbook of Counselor Preparation. Constructivist, Developmental, and Experiential Approaches*. Thousand Oaks: Sage, pp. 255–275.

McLeod, J. (2010) *An Introduction to Counselling*. New York: McGraw Hill.

Neukrug, E. (2012) *The World of the Counselor. An Introduction to the Counselling Profession*. Belmont: Brooks/Cole.

Sanders, S. (2010) 'Cognitive and behavioural approaches', in R. Woolfe, S. Strawbridge, B. Douglas and W. Dryden (eds.) *Handbook of Counselling Psychology* 3rd ed. Thousand Oaks: Sage, pp. 105–129.

Strawbridge, S. and Woolfe, R. (2010) 'Counselling psychology: Origins, developments and challenges', in R. Woolfe, S. Strawbridge, B. Douglas and W. Dryden (eds.) *Handbook of Counselling Psychology* 3rd ed. Thousand Oaks: Sage, pp. 3–22.

Wedding, D. and Pope, K. S. (2010) 'Contemporary challenges and controversies', in R. J. Corsini and D. Wedding (eds.) *Current Psychotherapies* 9th ed. Belmont: Brooks/Cole, pp. 568–603.

References for messy map

Alves, S. and Gazzola, N. (2011) 'Professional identity: A qualitative inquiry of experienced counsellors', *Canadian Journal of Counselling & Psychotherapy*, 45:3, 189–207.

Calley, N.G. and Hawley, L.D. (2008) 'The professional identity of counsellor educators', *The Clinical Supervisor*, 27:1, 3–16.

Chang, J. (2011) 'An interpretive account of counsellor development', *Canadian Journal of Counselling & Psychotherapy*, 45:4, 406–428.

Dickson, G.L. and Jepsen, D.A. (2007) 'Multicultural training experiences as predictors of multicultural competencies: Students' perspectives', *Counselor Education and Supervision*, 47:2, 76–95.

Fernando, D.M. and Hulse-Killacky, D. (2005) 'The relationship of supervisory styles to satisfaction with supervision and the perceived self-efficacy of master's-level counselling students', *Counselor Education and Supervision*, 44:4, 293–304.

Furr, S.R. and Carroll, J.J. (2003) 'Critical incidents in student counsellor development', *Journal of Counseling & Development*, 81:4, 483–489.

Gale, A. and Austin, B. (2003) 'Professionalism's challenges to professional counselors' collective identity', *Journal of Counseling & Development*, 81:1, 3–10.

Gaubatz, M.D. and Vera, E.M. (2006) 'Trainee competence in master's-level counseling programmes: A comparison of counselor educators' and students' views', *Counselor Education and Supervision*, 46:1, 32–43.

Howard, E.E., Inman, A.G. and Altman, A.N. (2006) 'Critical incidents among novice counselor trainees', *Counselor Education and Supervision*, 46:2, 88–102.

Leong, F.T.L. and Leach, M.M. (2007) 'Internationalising counseling psychology in the United States: A SWOT analysis', *Applied Psychology*, 56:1, 165–181.

Rak, C.F., MacCluskie, K.C., Toman, S.M., Patterson, L.E. and Culotta, S. (2003) 'The process of development among counsellor interns: Qualitative and quantitative perspectives', *Canadian Journal of Counselling & Psychotherapy*, 37:2, 135–150.

Woodside, M., Oberman, A.H., Cole, K.G. and Carruth, E.K. (2007) 'Learning to be a counselor: A prepracticum point of view', *Counselor Education & Supervision*, 47:1, 14–28.

16
Systemic Means to Subversive Ends: Maintaining the Therapeutic Space as a Unique Encounter

Jay Watts

Psychotherapy has become a marketplace for an increasing number of approaches – over 400 at last count – with wildly different perspectives on what it means to suffer, and whether an approach focused on cure is possible and advisable (Cooper and McLeod 2010). Within this marketplace, CBT has become the dominant approach, as has an ideology that revolves around notions of 'illness', 'cure', 'regulation' and 'evidence base'. This is challenging for the critical practitioner; maintaining space for alternative, subversive approaches is problematic when most believe therapeutic techniques can be decided prior to the unique encounter between a psychotherapist and patient (for example Loewenthal 2011). This chapter has a simple aim: to argue that rather than be slave to such changes we can, and must, develop and train new generations to maintain spaces in the public arena for multiple approaches to storying distress and treatment. To this end I will demonstrate how systemic techniques, influenced by post-Foucauldian theory, were incorporated into a doctoral training programme that was subject to increasing pressure to become mainstream. Such 'critical competencies' allowed trainees to situate themselves in an alternative story of the future of psychotherapy – one where we ally closely with the psychiatric survivor movement, and use ourselves as sites to question norms whenever we come across them, be that on social media or in a team meeting. I aim to show that techniques for playful subversion of mainstream ideas outside the consulting room can maintain room for a practice-driven psychotherapy, and empower trainees to feel that they can influence what happens next.

Let us start with the dominant grim story that can be heard wherever critical practitioners congregate.

The dominant story

Most practitioners working in mainstream services are feeling bleak about the future of psychotherapy right now (for example Quality Psychotherapy Services in the NHS 2013). One reason for this is the rise of what Power (1999) has labelled 'the Audit Society'. His book (of the same name) showed how techniques which have their origin in accounting firms have been transferred to public services. What has become more commonly known as the 'audit culture' rests on the unspoken assumption that making people's activities visible is both possible and a good thing – as if the goal for every patient was the same and could be measured. Within the psy professions, this audit culture has taken the form of the 'social movement of evidence based medicine' (EBM; Pope 2003). The most emblematic example of EBM and the move to 'regulation', 'audit' and 'evidence base' is the UK's NICE guidelines (NICE 2006) which are positioned as the best treatment guidelines for a number of conditions and diagnoses. Though relatively recent, these have had a constitutive effect in the restructuring of service provision (Flynn 2002), and have rewarded professions and professionals who comply.

The NICE guidelines operate by placing 'evidence' in a hierarchical position in relation to professional opinion. The move to privilege 'evidence' can be read as an attempt to delocate judgement at a time when trust in the authorities is at an all-time low (Power 1999). It is important, then, to see how they are constructed as objective. The personal investment and lenses of the members of the Guideline Development Group who write the guidelines, for example, are cleansed from a charge of subjectivity by the 'declaration of interests' at the front of each document. This type of 'discursive move' can also be seen in the surface recognition of the problematic construct validity of the conditions that are covered in the NICE guidelines, such as 'bipolar disorder' and 'depression'. By stating a critical objection or an interest briefly, without citations or details of critical alternatives (Moncrieff and Timimi 2013), the dominant argument can be constructed as 'common sense'.

Yet the assumptions in such documents are hardly common sense if looked at in any detail. Consider the archetypal diagnosis of psychiatry, 'schizophrenia'. As Bentall sums up, and as even the NIMH acknowledges (2013), schizophrenia 'consists of no particular symptoms, has no particular outcome, and responds to no particular treatment. No wonder research revealed that it has no particular cause' (Bentall 1988). Or consider the privileging of RCT design as the 'gold star' of the evidence base (Slade and Priebe 2001). RCTs have no reliable construct to study, do not effectively follow basic principles of 'double blinding', are subject to publication bias and use participants who cannot be generalised to real ones in routine care who do not tend to have distinct problems (Goldenberg 2006; Guy et al. 2011; Slade and Priebe 2001). RCT design becomes even more problematic in the field of psychotherapy, where the goal of a work is not predecided or predecidable (Guy et al. 2011), where there is no clear distinction between therapeutic modalities (Guy et al. 2011), where 'researcher allegiance' to a model and transmodality factors explains the variance in outcome between different therapies (Luborsky et al. 2002) and where branded therapies which are compared with one another are at best an umbrella term for a number of different techniques which will not be used on everyone, and which stem from wildly different and contradictory epistemological groups (for example Herbert et al. 2013; Richardson 2006).

Yet any protest of the mystical, unconscious, unpredictable nature of the psychotherapeutic encounter (for example Van Deurzen 1997) is storied as old-fashioned and non-progressive, as if a personal insult to the governmental push of finance into EBM-fluent services such as IAPT. Unable to work within such discourse, critical psychotherapists are leaving the NHS in their droves (for example Quality Psychotherapy Services in the NHS, 2013). However, the problems outlined are not unique to the NHS. The voluntary sector, private sector and academia are also affected by the backcloth of audit culture, and the branding of therapies and the problems that this encourages. This backcloth constructs common sense around mental health and illness; it influences how people approach funders, who gets funding, who gets tenured academic positions, how private therapists advertise themselves and how the public medicalise their suffering (Cookson et al. 2001).

As the worker, the skills that they have and the techniques that they might teach to new generations come under the eye of surveillance and regulation (Butcher 2002), the tacit nature of psychotherapeutic knowledge becomes more and more impossible. Tacit knowledge does not lie in a person to be explained but is accrued through a 'practice of doing', through an 'indwelling' that allows us to 'know more than we can tell' (Polanyi 1966: 8). This clashes with the increasingly professionalised therapist who has to comply with performance-measurement systems while maintaining some autonomy (Power 1999). Maintaining this autonomy becomes more and more difficult as treatment-adherence measures are introduced, CORE measurement scales are used to assess how many of one's patients meet certain expectations of getting better, and one's proficiency in 'core competencies' decontextualised from the writer's politics and vested interests become the norm (for example UCL core competencies: UCL 2011; Skills for Health core competencies: Skills for Health 2011). Compliance with these measures affect not just opportunities for continuing professional development and promotion but a chance of keeping one's job or, if more junior, gaining a placement that will allow one to finish a psychotherapeutic qualification. Pressure to show 'performance', 'governance' and 'information-sharing' are balanced by a 'rhetoric of support' involving ongoing training, new jobs, continuing professional development and a focus on supervision, which make it difficult to protest as one is storied as getting more (Nettleton et al. 2008).

Academia is no longer a safe place for critical psychotherapists who are subject to a demand to score well in the Research Excellence Framework (REF; Times Higher Education 2013). The REF is a relatively new way for academic departments to be rated according, predominantly, to how many publications their academics get into 'high-impact' journals. The journals which have the highest impact tend to be those that publish articles based on diagnostic criteria and use the perceived 'gold standard' research design, RCTs. Such studies solidify and naturalise 'Big Pharma' diagnoses and claim the distinctiveness of different therapies. The easily demonised managers and politicians are subject to the impossible demands of the system that they have helped to create. Thus there is constant pressure for things to be 'new', 'improving' and 'innovative'.

The fascination and lust for this can be seen in the public's thirst for neuroscience. The latest collection from the uber-cool designer Christopher Kane, for example, consists of images from functional magnetic resonance imaging scans pasted across shirts, skirts and dresses and now literally in *Vogue*. If the new was genuinely innovative and appealing, this might be of interest. However, the history of innovation in psychiatry is littered with discoveries which prove to be less effective than they initially seem to be, and it has been persuasively argued that there has been no real progress across psychotherapy, pharmacotherapy and service design in the past 30 years (Priebe et al. 2013). If we take the example of the Improving Access to Psychological Therapies Programme, it's implementation tends to lead to an increase in demand at more complex levels of service provision as the treatment is not good enough (Cairns 2013). Managers, commissioners and politicians, unable to acknowledge a fundamental lack in what could ever be achieved, and with jobs existing because of their perceived competence in 'risk', 'innovation' and 'cure', are forced into a complex and generally unconscious game of smoke and mirrors which burns out staff in record numbers.

Public discourse can often reinforce this emphasis on 'illness', 'cure' and 'disorder', with mainstream stigma campaigns insisting that mental distress is 'an illness like any other' (Link and Phelan 2013). This biomedical insistence is partly precisely because mental distress is a 'contested illness' that is not readily associated with a discernible biomedical abnormality (Barker 2008; Brown 2007), and thus is not taken as seriously as physical illness. The desire to convince the Other that mental distress is an illness is partially because of the serious lack of a rhetoric of suffering, such that to doubt the validity of mental illness is often taken as an attack on the legitimacy of someone's distress. This lack of available discourses on distress links to the history of increasing individualism and the emergence of the psy complex (LaFrance 2007) during the twentieth century. The psychotherapist-fuelled self-help culture, which emerged in the 1970s, has been especially pernicious in its implication that anyone can get over anything, placing responsibility for not doing so with the individual (Rimke 2000). Lacking a culturally sanctioned discourse of how symptoms can be manifestations of familial and cultural problems (Lai 2004), claiming an uber-medicalised, diagnosable mental illness is one of the only ways to speak legitimately without blame, and get what Parsons (1951) originally called a 'certificate of exemption' from the horrors of day-to-day life. This quest from the public for the legitimitisation of psychic distress through medicalisation fulfils the governmental drive for consumer satisfaction. It also masks the government's responsibility for the social factors – from poverty to racism – which are so clearly linked to mental distress (Marmot 2012).

Is this tale of doom and gloom the only way to construct the current moment?

An alternative story

The rise of the audit culture, and EBM as a manifestation of that, can be read as an attempt to protect power for those in authority within a culture where the traditional arbiters of truth – the police, television, doctors, politicians, journalists, judges – no longer enjoy the same level of trust. This is not just related to the succession of recent scandals; rather, the societal move has resulted from a wider, postmodern focus on moral pluralism, and a horizontalisation of power (Haraway 1996).[1] Though notions of 'lack of insight' can still shut down this voice within the confines of a particular psychiatric care system (Harper

1994), identity politics (Sampson 1993), and the wider cultural focus on the rights and responsibilities of the consumer (Salzer 1997), have radically changed who gets to speak about what. The best example of how these cultural shifts benefit our work is the rise of the psychiatric survivor voice, from the initial 'fish manifesto' (Crossley 1999) to 'Mad Pride' (Mad Pride 2001), the 'recovery movement' (Romme et al. 2011) and service-user forums in cyberspace. The exponential rise in social media means that psychiatric survivors and critical thinkers have access to more people than was ever imaginable. If a community mental health team treats you badly and you blog about it, it might well go viral. Knowledge presented as fact is now subject to surveillance and scrutiny by critical thinkers in cyberspace. Consider @neurobollocks (2013). He has thousands of followers and trouble reports and commentary that come out dazzled by fMRI technology. Crucially, @neurobollocks critiques from both a critical and a mainstream perspective, which means that his tweets are read and responded to by those in dominant groupings. Also of note is the playful and irreverent nature of his chosen moniker, which allows access to those who are less interested in 'science'. It is, perhaps, no coincidence too that of all the newspaper articles against the new DSM-5, it was the playful parody of DSM-5 as a Borgesian Dystopian Masterpiece that went viral (Kriss 2013).

All of us have the opportunity to write, link and connect with people whom cultural forces might have blocked us from contacting even a couple of years ago. For example, editors of the psychiatric stalwarts *The Lancet* and *The British Journal of Psychiatry* routinely get into long debates with service users on Twitter. This is not for show; behind the safety of the computer screen, users feel able to challenge and critique in a way that power dynamics might stifle in embodied discussion (Watts 2014). As an example of this, one prominent professor was recently on the flagship BBC radio programme *Start the Week* arguing that psychology is a science, against a philosopher of mind. Though he stuck to his argument, after the discussion continued on twitter he changed his position. This can lead to very real material changes.

Recently, critical tweeters have joined to campaign against the 'Psycho' Halloween costume that the supermarket chain ASDA was selling (BBC 2013). This led to the removal of the item, and a public apology. Lastly, critical thinkers do not need to gain grants or academic postings to gain the money for such activities. The cash-starved trainee can use the social media app Kickstarter to get tens of thousands of pounds of donations to film an idea (for example Entrepreneur 2013), while the app Meetup can be used to organise a philosophy meeting at the local pub. Conrad may have written blistering academic papers on the sociology of mental illness (Conrad and Barker 2010), but I would bet – at more than 0.5 million viewers – Eleanor Longden's TED talk about being admitted to psychiatric hospital as a voice-hearing 18-year-old has changed the world more (TED 2013).

How can we incorporate some of these activities into our training programmes? Can we use them to challenge ideas of EBM which threaten psychotherapy as a subversive site?

Power and language

As I hope to have shown, psychotherapy has been placed in a vertical, and vertiginous, relation to various discourses such as 'evidence', 'performance' and 'skills'. This vertically inferior position is relatively new to the profession but is one that is known to most psychiatric patients, whose subjectivity and individuality have long been crushed by discourses such as that of the 'insightless patient who cannot be believed' or the 'axe wielding schizophrenic' (Watts 2005). To be able to breathe, to be able to manoeuvre, to be able to influence, it is crucial to have skills to subvert the mainstream discourse, and to create sites where different thinking and feeling is possible. To theorise this, I turn to social constructionist and systemic principles around discourse (for example Gergen 1999).

Discourse communities are 'groups of people who share common ideologies, and common ways of speaking about things' (Little et al. 2003: 73). Bakhtin (1981: 263) argued that 'discourse communities' such as psychiatry create an especially 'monoglossic' way of speaking, which insists on the power of the 'authoritative word' and which 'demands that we acknowledge it, that we make it our own; it binds us, quite independent of any power it might have to persuade us internally (Bakhtin 1981: 342). This monoglossic discourse of fixed meaning is in opposition to 'heteroglossia', where 'a multiplicity of social voices and a wide variety of their links and interrelationships' (Bakhtin 1981: 236) are used, allowing 'counter stories' of resistance to emerge (Nelson 2001). Stories we tell ourselves and that we are caught within from outside are constitutive of what we feel, and what 'subject positions' (Harré 2002) we are allowed to take up in 'joint action'. For example, if one is storied as insightless and thus irrational, any communication that one makes is subject to being discarded and not heard. Thus the positions that we hold and are given discursively 'ascribe rights and duties to think and act in certain ways work as constraints on human thought and action' (Harré 2002: 611).

Social constructionism is interesting on paper but it is in using its principles within action that it comes alive. One school of therapeutic thinking that has done this is systemic psychotherapy, a progression of family therapy incorporating postmodern thinking (Jones 1994). This approach uses the core systemic principles of 'hypothesizing', 'circular questioning' and 'curiosity' (after Cecchin 1987) to provoke heteroglossic discourse at an individual and familial level. Interest in unpicking the discursive realities in which people are located is supplemented by a concern with the relationship between discourse and material realities (Ussher 2002). For example, the habit of patients being excluded from a prediscussion of their case during ward rounds would be troubled from a systemic perspective, with attention to what discourses make this material act appear to be justifiable.

Systemic psychotherapy with individuals and their families has some similarities with the linguistic focus of other talking therapies (Donovan 2003). My aim in this chapter is not to present it as another, better therapy for such work. Rather, my intention is to use its principles to deconstruct the type of discourse which prevents a patient from reaching a psychotherapist in the first place, or which has had such an influence on the psychotherapist's ideas of what they should do therein that the patient's unique experience and words are lost. There is strong evidence that systemic principles can be used to influence psy organisations, and the wider 'discursive backcloth' (Wetherell 1998: 404) from which and through which it gets decided who can do what. The shining example is the Open Dialogue approach, which was developed in Scandinavia to change cultures around first-episode psychosis. This approach emphasises the need for discursive challenging within the 'micropoetics' of organisations (Seikkula and Olson 2003), such as within team meetings, information leaflets and public communications. Usefully, Open Dialogue has an unparalleled evidence base – changing the culture of meetings and speech around first admission greatly improves the prognosis after 18 months (Seikkula et al. 2006). This is generalisable to the English context, for research shows implementation of even a colossus such as the NICE guidelines is subject to social and political influences at the micro- as well as the macrolevel (Spyridonidis and Calnan 2011).

A critical training in mainstreamed times

To show how this might work in practice, I will outline some ways in which systemic thinking was added to a doctoral training programme in counselling psychology just prior to a first Health and Care Professions Council (HCPC) accreditation, after years of pressure to mainstream the curriculum. The compression of regulation and institutional politics meant that this had to be achieved through 'code switching' (Auer 2002): switching between two language systems, in this case that of 'meeting the need of the consumer'/'NICE regulations as desired by HCPC' (broadly EBM) and 'a critical, subverting perspective' (broadly post-Foucauldian). Critical 'core competencies' were legitimatised by being added to multiple modules and ratified through university committees. As they were added to multiple modules, they were more difficult to get rid of than a standalone critical module would have been. In addition, alternative evidence of the effectiveness of critical thinking was collected: high ratings on module feedback with qualitative feedback stressing the value of a critical approach; stories and posters of the community projects that trainees had carried out; and so on. To pass the training, trainees needed to show competencies in critical thinking, engagement and practice, alongside knowledge of mainstream discourses in different forms of assessments. These included essays and case reports; group experiential exercises and supervisions; and placements assessments. In addition, trainees had to complete a community project in small groups or individually during their second year. Thus systems were put in place such that the HCPC and the British Psychological Society as regulators would have to be informed and investigate if the critical elements of the programme were removed.

What core competencies were developed, and how?

Towards heteroglossia

One of the main aims was to teach skills to slow down groups that were reaching a conclusion too early – to facilitate a 'tolerance of uncertainty' (Seikkula and Olson 2003). Expanding discursive possibilities relies on listening outside what is being meant to be said. Thus the trainee works to draw out hesitations, interruptions and alternatives which threaten to leak out but do not quite, just as they would in an individual session. This allows other voices to emerge, from within the individual or within a group. Thus, in a family meeting, a silenced patient might be bought in by 'positively connoting' (Jones 1994) what a dominant member of the group is saying, using 'curiosity' to unpick where it comes from, and then passing the baton to the service user by saying: 'I wonder what your thoughts are on this.' Similarly, in a meeting about how a service is to be reconfigured to privilege CBT as a treatment, one might joke about pesky service users insisting on saying that its the relationship that matters, and using that discursive move as a springboard to a wider conversation about the evidence base for integrative therapies.

Such training often consisted of practical exercises. As an example, before going on placement in a particular area, or with a particular group or treatment modality, trainees were asked to write the main discourses on a large piece of paper. These were then troubled using the deconstructionist questions shown in Table 16.1.

Trainees were then asked to build up a list of 'rhetorical devices' that are used in argument (Harris 2002), both from the literature and from everyday observations. The classic example of this is Mary Boyle's work on the power of 'simple assertion' ('Of course, Schizophrenia exists' – Boyle (2002), a parallel to which might be the assertion 'Of course its better to have IAPT rather than nothing'). Trainees were then asked to counter these discourses both from within EBM and from a critical perspective. The 'thickened discourse' and territory that the trainees then had (White and Epston 1990) allowed them to think and act outside the monoglossic discourse. They were then encouraged to wear these knowledges lightly, so as to develop skills in the timing of when to 'code switch' between different forms of knowledge so as to be 'the difference that makes a difference' (Bateson 1972: 459) – that is, to introduce more new ways of talking and thinking without being so different from the culture that one is part of that one is thrown out, psychically or physically.

Table 16.1 Sample deconstructionist questions

What coherent ways of speaking surround a word for example 'randomised control trial', 'schizophrenia', 'trauma', 'patient', 'evidence'?
Who is empowered to develop these?
What evidence of resistance to dominant discourses is there?
Who is speaking in particular discourses and who is silent?
What power relations are at play (for example between different professionals, service user and carer)?
What rhetorical devices are used to present a particular discourse as true or valid (for example assertion, evoking imagery)?
What subject positions are implied by a particular discourse?
Which actions are encouraged and which discouraged?
What other discourses support the use of particular discourses?
What material methods are used to support particular constructs (for example the exclusion of patients from the beginning of ward rounds)?

Locating speakers

One of the aforementioned problems is the decontextualisation of speakers through an appeal to 'evidence'. Trainees were introduced to the GRRAACCEESS acronym (Gender, Race, Religion, Ability, Age, Class, Culture, Ethnicity, Education, Sexuality and Spirituality; Burnham et al. 2008) to prompt thinking about what differences might be present between people, whether in therapy, a meeting or a wider cultural space. Before and after encounters, trainees were encouraged to link these differences with hypothesised scripts at the level of the individual, family, profession and culture (Pearce 2005). For example, one might hypothesise that a manager has a script 'CBT is evidence based and NICE compliant so is the treatment of choice' which might conflict with a script 'Choice is important' and an individual script 'Some traumas are impossible to get over'. As soon as there is more text – more contexts through which a person thinks and a symptom speaks – there is an opportunity for contradiction and challenge which, if brought in benevolently, can open the way for something new. These approaches were used, then, not to impose a new truth on a setting but to prime trainees' 'third ear' (Reik 1948) to the bits that miss the dominant story, to skill them to knit a text with more open 'subject positions' for psychotherapists and patients alike.

The systemic principle of 'curiosity' was used to expand trainees' knowledge of differences. Thus a trainee working with a female Eritrean patient might be encouraged to explore the history of the formation of Eritrea, and gendered experience therein, to be primed to the traces of such histories in the discourse of the patient. This was especially important for trainees who held identities of the dominant group, or where a specific struggle was echoed in the identities of two or more speakers (for example a civil war). This listening for what may pulsate at the borders of speech and the sayable opens up what is hearable. Crucially, it was not just used with patients but in group-speak about policy and guidelines. Accordingly, trainees were encouraged to locate members of the guideline development groups for the NICE guidelines and DSM-5, as well as the authors of influential papers, those chairing committees and user forums and so on, to show the subjectivity implicit within subjectivity implicit within policy and guidelines.

Attention also focused on the contexts from which and through which trainees think and speak. In addition to reflective groups and personal therapies, trainees were involved in groups to discuss their 'transference to authority' and 'transference to knowledge' to explore how this affected how they positioned themselves within bureaucratic groups and the psychocultural discourse around psy. The intent here was to encourage trainees to take up multiple positions within groups, and to see these as important sites of influence, indirectly affecting the culture that patients inhabit.

Challenging mindsets

Changing mindsets is at least as influenced by emotions and stories as rational argument is by EBM, or indeed post-positivist critique. Consider the classic example of the Ken Loach movie *Cathy Come Home*. This story changed homelessness policy through its evocativeness far more than all of the academic statistics on homelessness (Donaldson 2006). To this end, trainees were encouraged to read and have access to as many stories as possible, from the dialectic behaviour therapy founder Marsha Linehan's account of her incarcerations (*New York Times* 2011) to Rufus May's record of his need to disengage from psychiatric services to start a recovery (*Independent* 2006) to psychiatrist Sonia Johnson's telling of how she would not take antipsychotic medication after a first or even second episode of psychosis given the evidence base (Johnson 2011). If and when these popped into trainees' heads in group settings, they were invited to speak about them without triple thinking why.

Trainees were encouraged not to glorify their own training and profession. The aim here was to disturb the tendency to divide the world into 'goodies' who understand critical theory and 'baddies' who maintain the status quo (Steiner 1987), while recognising that groups hold different power and privilege. Constructing a 'straw dog' may help with one day's fight but it rarely leads to culture change and the long-term horizontalisation of power relations. To this end, having some information about the histories and politics of different professions can facilitate what Minuchin and Fishman (1981) have called 'joining' the system, to then be able to differ from it. Table 16.2 shows an example of work on this within a seminar.

Trainees were roused to continue their learning about how language gets opened up and shut down outside the consulting room – for example, keeping an ear out for how this works in favourite films, and bringing in clips to show this in action. Lastly, trainees were encouraged to own their own personalised positions, should they so wish, and use these in psy arenas and wider psychocultural spaces. Thus, linking to the importance of emotions and stories in producing change, an account of a personal experience of lack of hope or trauma can allow

276 *Critiques of Training and Learning*

Table 16.2 'Situating professionals' exercise

The week before a class, trainees are assigned roles (patient, psychiatrist, psychotherapist, manager, social worker, etc.) in small groups. They are asked to find out a little of the histories of the professions they are role-playing. Thus the trainee role-playing the psychiatrist might have found out that the profession is looked down on within medicine (for example Feifel et al. 1999) and so is always trying to claim itself as a science. Or the trainee playing a social worker might have found out how close the social worker was to psychoanalysis, family therapy and sociology in the 1970s (for example Casement 1992), and how crushed that profession is under the obsession with 'risk' (for example Parton 2008). Or the psychiatric nurse might have found out about the Project 2000 move to shift nursing from a vocation to a profession (for example Elder et al. 2009). Or the psychotherapist might read about our profession's building of the self-help movement and psy complex that have 'infuse[d] and shape[d] the personal investments of individuals' (Rose 1998).

In class, one trainee is asked to role-play a patient trying to speak of 'suffering' during a ward round. The trainee playing the psychiatrist is asked to try to restory suffering as a 'symptom'. The social worker and psychotherapist role-players have their attempts to say something different shut down. Or alternatively, they might choose to underline the medical discourse in an alliance with the psychiatrist. The small groups role-play organically, and then feed back as individuals to the wider group.

The group facilitator focuses on bringing out not just power/knowledge relations but also the psychodynamics around anxiety (after Menzies-Lyth 1960).

people to connect outside the roles and titles that they hold. Accessing a personal experience often helped to deconstruct a 'them and us' dichotomy within a professional team, and between professional and patient (*Independent* 2010).

Connecting with critical allies

Such alliance-building is crucial. Counselling psychology and psychotherapy courses appear to have engaged less with the survivor movement than some of the state-funded trainings, perhaps because the requirement for personal therapy and analysis means that all trainees can story themselves as service users. Yet there is a great difference between someone who has had their own, chosen, privately funded psychotherapy and someone who has been subject to injected medication, restraint and forced incarceration (though a number of trainees will have had these experiences too). Trainees were required to access radical psychiatric spaces, whether that meant attending a Mad Pride gig, campaigning against Atos (Campaigning against the government appointed Work Capability Assessment agency Atos Healthcare) or writing a piece for *Asylum* magazine.

This contact served the triple purpose of linking trainees with the survivor movement, which is not without its excitements and power basis, as well as having one's practice subject to the gaze of those who have experienced the psychiatric system at its worst, and forging recognition of the relative social power that psychotherapists have, even today. These encounters often inculcated a sense of responsibility to open up and speak out more in monoglossic spaces, though scary – be that the *Daily Mail* comments section or a team meeting – for if one has met the victims, can silence be so justified? Trainees were encouraged to find out about critical groups within the area in which they work, such as Hearing Voices Groups, Philosophy in Pubs groups or civil liberties groups. This was a part of joining with the local community, visiting the sink estates that white, middle-class professionals would not normally go to, asking advice from the local imam or pastor about how to make more inclusive services and so on.

Lastly, trainees were asked to think about what the local blocks to an inclusive service were, be that a 'low-cost psychotherapy service' that charges £30 per session, an information leaflet about psychosis that fails to attend to culturally specific fears or a family interventions service that closes at 5.00 pm. Trainees then created a community project of their own, choosing across the span of a year. As part of the induction session for this, they were asked to reassess how they wished to change the world when they were little, or first embarking on their psy career. This all sounds terribly serious, but the frame was much more one of play and empowerment rather than prescription. The aim throughout was to give a sense of what might be possible, and to story psychotherapy as a profession that has an influence outside the consulting room, as well as within.

Conclusion

There are thanatonic and triumphant stories that critical psychotherapists can tell about the present moment. We now have a choice. Either we see ourselves as trapped, submerged and excluded by the EBM culture of the time, and retreat to private practice or the few remaining critical pockets within academia, or we recognise the extraordinary subversive work that is going on in the survivor movement and cyberspace, and use systemic skills to draw these into the space of everyday psy interactions both within organisations and within the wider psychocultural sphere.

If we choose the latter, we can produce spaces that can incorporate multiple stories on 'evidence', 'illness' and the other signifiers that otherwise threaten to colonise us.

Note

1. The manner in which the psy professions have lapped up the audit culture through the idea of 'evidence' can be storied as a way of side-stepping the considerable post-positivist critiques of psychiatry (for example Feyerabend 1975; Hanson 1961; Kuhn 1970), such as post-Foucauldianism (Rose 2006), social constructionism (for example Gergen 1999), phenomenology (for example Spiegelberg 1972) and feminism (Ussher 2002).

References

Auer, P. (2002) *Code-Switching in Conversation: Language, Interaction and Identity*. London: Routledge.
Bakhtin, M.M.M. (1981) *The Dialogic Imagination: Four Essays* No. 1. Texas: University of Texas Press.
Barker, K.K. (2008) 'Electronic support groups, patient-consumers, and medicalisation: The case of contested illness', *Journal of Health and Social Behavior*, 49:1, 20–36.
Bateson, G. (1972) *Steps to an Ecology of Mind: A Revolutionary Approach to Man's Understanding of Himself*. New York: Ballantine.
BBC (2013) 'Asda and Tesco withdraw Halloween patient outfits'. http://m.bbc.co.uk/news/uk-24278768. Accessed 10 November 2013.
Bentall, R.P., Jackson, H.F. and Pilgrim, D. (1988) 'Abandoning the concept of "Schizophrenia": Some implications of validity arguments for psychological research into psychotic phenomena', *British Journal of Clinical Psychology*, 27:4, 303–324.
Boyle, M. (2002) 'It's all done with smoke and mirrors. Or, how to create the illusion of a schizophrenic brain disease', *Clinical Psychology*, 12:9, 16.
Brown, P. (2007) *Toxic Exposures: Contested Illnesses and the Environmental Health Movement*. Columbia: Columbia University Press.
Burnham, J., Alvis Palma, D. and Whitehouse, L. (2008) 'Learning as a context for differences and differences as a context for learning', *Journal of Family Therapy*, 30:4, 529–542.
Butcher, T. (2002) *Delivering Welfare*. Buckingham: Open University Press.
Cairns, M. (2013) 'Patients who come back: Clinical characteristics and service outcome for patients re-referred to an IAPT service', *Counselling and Psychotherapy Research*, 11(1), 1–8.
Casement, P. (1992) *Learning from the Patient*. New York: Guilford Press.
Cecchin, G. (1987) 'Hypothesizing, circularity, and neutrality revisited: An invitation to curiosity', *Family Process*, 26:4, 405–413.
Conrad, P. and Barker, K.K. (2010) 'The social construction of illness: Key insights and policy implications', *Journal of Health and Social Behavior*, 51:1 suppl., S67–S79.

Cookson, R., McDaid, D. and Maynard, A. (2001) 'Wrong SIGN, NICE mess: Is national guidance distorting allocation of resources?', *British Medical Journal*, 323:7315, 743.

Cooper, M. and McLeod, J. (2010) 'Pluralism: Towards a new paradigm for therapy', *Therapy Today*, 21, 9.

Crossley, N. (1999) 'Fish, field, habitus and madness: The first wave mental health users movement in Great Britain', *The British Journal of Sociology*, 50:4, 647–670.

Donaldson, D. (2006) 'Cathy come home, the legacy', David Donnison on homelessness and poverty, 40 years on from Ken Loach's film. http://tinyurl.com/pf9oayx. Accessed 20 November 2013.

Donovan, M. (2003) 'Mind the gap: The need for a generic bridge between psychoanalytic and systemic approaches', *Journal of Family Therapy*, 25:2, 115–135.

Elder, R., Evans, K. and Nizette, D. (eds.) (2009) *Psychiatric and Mental Health Nursing*. Sydney: Elsevier Australia.

Entrepreneur (2013) '5 signs your product is perfect for kickstarter'. http://www.entrepreneur.com/article/230061. Accessed 20 November.

Feifel, D., Moutier, C.Y. and Swerdlow, N.R. (1999) 'Attitudes toward psychiatry as a prospective career among students entering medical school', *American Journal of Psychiatry*, 156:9, 1397–1402.

Feyerabend, P. (1975) *Against Method: Outline of an Anarchistic Theory of Knowledge*. London: Verso Books.

Flynn, R. (2002) 'Clinical governance and governmentality', *Health, Risk & Society*, 4:2, 155–173.

Gergen, K.J. (1999) *An Invitation to Social Construction*. Cleveland: Sage.

Goldenberg, M.J. (2006) 'On evidence and evidence-based medicine: Lessons from the philosophy of science', *Social Science & Medicine*, 62:11, 2621–2632.

Guy, A., Thomas, R., Stephenson, S. and Loewenthal, D. (2011) *NICE under Scrutiny: The Impact of the National Institute for Health and Clinical Excellence Guidelines on the Provision of Psychotherapy in the UK*. UKCP Research Unit, Research Centre for Therapeutic Education Roehampton University.

Hanson, N.R. (1961) *Patterns of Discovery*. Cambridge: Cambridge University Press.

Haraway, D. (1996) 'Modest witness: Feminist diffractions in science studies', in P. Galison and D. Stump (eds.) *The Disunity of Science: Boundaries, Contexts, and Power*. Stanford: Stanford University Press, 428–442.

Harper, D.J. (1994) 'The professional construction of "Paranoia" and the discursive use of diagnostic criteria', *British Journal of Medical Psychology*, 67:2, 131–143.

Harré, R. (2002) 'Public sources of the personal mind social constructionism in context', *Theory & Psychology*, 12:5, 611–623.

Harris, R. (2002) *A Handbook of Rhetorical Devices*. Salt Lake City: Virtual Salt.

Herbert, J.D., Gaudiano, B.A. and Forman, E.M. (2013) 'The importance of theory in cognitive behavior therapy: A perspective of contextual behavioral science', *Behavior Therapy*, 44:4, 580–591.

Independent (2006) Dr Rufus May: One man and a bed. http://www.independent.co.uk/news/people/profiles/dr-rufus-may-one-man-and-a-bed-410698.html. Accessed 20 November 2013.

Independent (2010) Rufus May: We must all learn how to care for one another. http://www.independent.co.uk/voices/commentators/rufus-may-we-must-all-learn-how-to-care-for-one-another-2096373.html. Accessed 20 November 2013.

Johnson, S. (2011) *Early Intervention. Alternative within and beyond Psychiatry.* Soteria Network Conference. Derby, 11 November 2011.

Jones, E. (1994) *Family Systems Therapy.* London: Wiley.

Kriss, S. (2013) 'Book of Lamentations'. http://thenewinquiry.com/essays/book-of-lamentations/. Accessed 20 November 2013.

Kuhn, T.S. (1970) *The Structure of Scientific Revolutions.* London: Chicago Press.

LaFrance, M.N. (2007) 'A bitter pill: A discursive analysis of women's medicalised accounts of depression', *Journal of Health Psychology,* 12:1, 127–140.

Lai, D.W. (2004) 'Impact of culture on depressive symptoms of elderly Chinese immigrants', *Canadian Journal of Psychiatry,* 49:12, 820–827.

Link, B.G. and Phelan, J.C. (2013) 'Labeling and stigma', in C.S. Aneshensel, J.C. Phelan and A. Bierman (eds.) *Handbook of the Sociology of Mental Health.* New York: Springer, 525–541.

Little, M., Jordens, C.F. and Sayers, E.J. (2003) 'Discourse communities and the discourse of experience', *Health,* 7:1, 73–86.

Loewenthal, D. (2011) *Post-Existentialism and the Psychological Therapies: Towards a Therapy without Foundations.* London: Karnac.

Luborsky, L., Rosenthal, R., Diguer, L., Andrusyna, T.P., Berman, J.S., Levitt, J.T. and Krause, E.D. (2002) 'The dodo bird verdict is alive and well – mostly', *Clinical Psychology: Science and Practice,* 9:1, 2–12.

Mad Pride (2001) *Mad Pride: A Celebration of Mad Culture.* London: Handsell Publications.

Marmot, M. (2012) 'Health inequalities and mental life', *Advances in Psychiatric Treatment,* 18:5, 320–322.

Menzies-Lyth, I.E.P. (1960) *The Functioning of Social Systems as a Defence against Anxiety.* Tavistock Pamphlet No. 3. London: Tavistock Publications.

Minuchin, S. and Fishman, H.C. (1981) *Family Therapy Techniques.* Harvard: Harvard University Press.

Moncrieff, J. and Timimi, S. (2013) 'The social and cultural construction of psychiatric knowledge: An analysis of NICE guidelines on depression and ADHD', *Anthropology & Medicine,* 20:1, 59–71.

National Institute for Mental Health (2013) 'Director's blog: Getting serious about mental illnesses'. http://www.nimh.nih.gov/about/director/2013/getting-serious-about-mental-illnesses.shtml. Accessed 1 November 2013.

Nelson, H.L. (2001) *Damaged Identities, Narrative Repair.* Cornell: Cornell University Press.

Nettleton, S., Burrows, R. and Watt, I. (2008) 'Regulating medical bodies? The consequences of the "Modernisation" of the NHS and the disembodiment of clinical knowledge', *Sociology of Health & Illness,* 30:3, 333–348.

@Neurobollocks (2013) 'Twitter Account Description'. https://twitter.com/neurobollocks. Accessed 20 November.

New York Times (2011) Expert on mental illness reveals her own fight. http://www.nytimes.com/2011/06/23/health/23lives.html?_r=0. Accessed 20 November 2013.

NICE (2006) 'Methods for development of NICE public health guidance', National Institute for Health and Clinical Excellence. London. http://www.nice.org.uk. Accessed 20 November 2013.

Parsons, T. (1951) 'Illness and the role of the physician: A sociological perspective', *American Journal of Orthopsychiatry*, 21:3, 452–460.

Parton, N. (2008) 'Changes in the form of knowledge in social work: From the "Social" to the "Informational"?', *British Journal of Social Work*, 38:2, 253–269.

Pearce, W.B. (2005) 'The coordinated management of meaning', in W. Gudykunst (ed.) *Theorizing about Intercultural Communication*. Thousand Oaks, CA: Sage, 35–54.

Polanyi, M. (1966) 'The logic of tacit inference', *Philosophy*, 41:155, 1–18.

Pope, C. (2003) 'Resisting evidence: The study of evidence-based medicine as a contemporary social movement', *Health*, 7:3, 267–282.

Power, M. (1999) *The Audit Society: Rituals of Verification*. Oxford: Oxford University Press.

Priebe, S., Burns, T. and Craig, T.K. (2013) 'The future of academic psychiatry may be social', *The British Journal of Psychiatry*, 202:5, 319–320.

Quality Psychotherapy Services in the NHS (2013) http://www.psychotherapy.org.uk/hres/Summary%20findings%20from%20NHS%20survey.pdf. Accessed 20 November 2013.

Reik, T. (1948) *Listening with the Third Ear: The Inner Experience of a Psychoanalyst*. London: Palgrave Macmillan.

Richardson, P. (2006) 'Evidence-based practice and the psychodynamic psychotherapies', in C. Mace, S. Moorey and B. Roberts (eds.) *Evidence in the Psychological Therapies: A Critical Guidance for Practitioners*. London: Routledge, 154–170.

Rimke, H.M. (2000) 'Governing citizens through self-help literature', *Cultural Studies*, 14:1, 61–78.

Romme, M., Escher, S., Dillon, J., Corstens, D. and Morris, M. (2011) 'Living with Voices: 50 Stories of Recovery', *Tijdschrift voor Psychiatrie*, 53:7, 439–440.

Rose, N. (1998) *Inventing Our Selves: Psychology, Power, and Personhood*. Cambridge: Cambridge University Press.

Rose, N. (2006) 'Disorders without borders? The expanding scope of psychiatric practice', *BioSocieties*, 1:4, 465–484.

Salzer, M.S. (1997) 'Consumer empowerment in mental health organizations: Concept, benefits, and impediments', *Administration and Policy in Mental Health and Mental Health Services Research*, 24:5, 425–434.

Sampson, E.E. (1993) 'Identity politics: Challenges to psychology's understanding', *American Psychologist*, 48:12, 1219.

Seikkula, J., Aaltonen, J., Alakare, B., Haarakangas, K., Keränen, J. and Lehtinen, K. (2006) 'Five-year experience of first-episode nonaffective psychosis in open-dialogue approach: Treatment principles, follow-up outcomes, and two case studies', *Psychotherapy Research*, 16:2, 214–228.

Seikkula, J. and Olson, M.E. (2003) 'The open dialogue approach to acute psychosis: It's poetics and micropolitics', *Family Process*, 42:3, 403–418.

Skills for Health (2011) 'Digest of NOS for psychological therapies'. http://tinyurl.com/pqhlwp2. Accessed 20 November 2013.

Slade, M. and Priebe, S. (2001) 'Are randomized controlled trials the only gold that glitters?', *The British Journal of Psychiatry*, 179:4, 286–287.

Spiegelberg, H. (1972) *Phenomenology in Psychology and Psychiatry: A Historical Introduction*. Evanston, IL: Northwestern University Press.

Spyridonidis, D. and Calnan, M. (2011) 'Opening the black box: A study of the process of NICE guidelines implementation', *Health Policy*, 102:2, 117–125.

Steiner, J. (1987) 'The interplay between pathological organizations and the paranoid-schizoid and depressive positions', *International Journal of Psychoanalysis*, 68:1, 69–80.

TED (2013) 'The Voices in My Head'. http://www.youtube.com/watch?v=syjEN3peCJw. Accessed 20 November 2013.

Times Higher Education (2013) 'REF more burdensome than RAE, pro V-CS states'. http://www.timeshighereducation.co.uk/news/ref-more-burdensome-than-rae-pro-v-cs-state/2009371.article. Accessed 12 November 2013.

UCL (2011) 'Competence frameworks for the delivery and supervision of psychological therapies'. http://www.ucl.ac.uk/clinical-psychology/CORE/competence_frameworks.htm. Accessed 1 November 2013.

Ussher, J. (2002) *Body Talk: The Material and Discursive Regulation of Sexuality, Madness and Reproduction*. London: Routledge.

Van Deurzen, E. (1997) *Everyday Mysteries: Existential Dimensions of Psychotherapy*. London: Routledge.

Watts, J. (2005) *Doing Care, Doing Schizophrenia: An Investigation of How the Notion of the Carer Affects Family-Talk about Psychotic Distress*. London: DPsy, University of East London.

Watts, J. (2014) 'Digital narcissism in the consulting room', in C. Bainbridge and C. Yates (eds.) *Media and the Inner World: Psycho-Cultural Approaches to Emotion, Media and Popular Culture*. London: Palgrave Macmillan, 168–182.

Wetherell, M. (1998) 'Positioning and interpretative repertoires: Conversation analysis and post-structuralism in dialogue', *Discourse & Society*, 9:3, 387–412.

White, M. and Epston, D. (1990) *Narrative Means to Therapeutic Ends*. New York: W.W. Norton and Company.

Part VII

Is There an Unfortunate Need for Critical Psychotherapy, Psychoanalysis and Counselling?

17
Psychotherapy, Psychoanalysis and Counselling for Oppressors and Oppressed: Sex, Violence and Ideology in Practice?

Del Loewenthal

Talking therapies, the state and neoliberalism

There was the idea in the talking therapies that patients/clients could explore what they found to be problematic in being clear about themselves. It was often also the case that what needed to be spoken about was taboo within the particular culture that they came from. State-involved changes in the cultural practice of the talking therapies increases the possibility that patients/clients cannot speak about what is not usually permissible, and that talking therapists will be less likely to be trained to hear what is usually not said.

This collection has been provided as a way of assessing the usefulness of the word 'critical' as a prefix for psychotherapy, psychoanalysis and counselling. In so doing, through the book what has primarily, but not exclusively, been explored is the extent to which such critical approaches can resist and provide an alternative to what is increasingly being offered through the state, which in turn can also be seen to regulate normality within the neoliberalism of late capitalism. There is a further question as to whether our authors are really just the pigs on Animal Farm, who have been unable to secure enough power in the current status quo and/or have not really worked through issues with their mums and dads. In part to further explore such questions, the contributors have been asked to write briefly what they would regard as the most critical argument against what they have written in their chapter. (The initial responses to this request varied from what appeared to be some minutes of a meeting, to you 'don't ask for much/my heart's not in it', to 'no probs', to incredulity, to requests for numerous clarifications and attempts at refusal – so perhaps our contributors are human.) Hence, as has been mentioned, for each of the chapters there is an abstract, a self-critique and brief biographical details which are given separately before Part I. It is, of course, up to readers to take what for them are the salient points. I will now, however, provide my thoughts about these chapters before returning to questions of whether current and future practitioners should and will take on such critical perspectives.

What can we learn from critical psychiatry and critical psychology?

In Chapter 2, 'The medical model: What is it, where did it come from and how long has it got?', Hugh Middleton warns the talking therapies about being caught up in an inappropriate medical model. He quotes from the paper by Bracken et al. (2012): 'There is no conclusive science supporting claims that any of the psycho-pharmaceuticals work as claimed, and when they do help, it is as likely as not that "help" is the result of complex phenomena not indistinguishable from placebo.' From the same source he also quotes, which is of vital importance to the psychological therapies, 'Useful outcomes of a psychological therapy are primarily the result of a helpful relationship, rather than the result of any identifiable psychotherapeutic technique.' He further questions whether the need for psychological therapists to demonstrate that their practices are evidence based is always really necessary. Hugh concludes that it is striking that the psychiatric establishment has not contested these conclusions; that there is now a call for medical, psychiatric and nursing students to be trained first in sociology and anthropology; and that there is a shift towards more patient-centred approaches. To briefly comment on this, the psychological therapies seem to have always had to fight to be independent of the medical model, though for some the attraction of the status and the idea that one could diagnose and treat is compelling – but I consider this to be wrong. Students of the talking therapies should also be educated regarding cultural practices and the inter-relationships with politics, economics and technologies. They could at least be given an introduction to the sociology of health. Regarding Hugh's welcoming the shift towards more patient-centred approaches, this is vital, though there are dangers here that this will be confused with overprivileging on the one hand person-centred approaches, and the far greater danger of consumerism on the other. I think what would be helpful is if future talking therapy students were to consider changing notions of what is taken as evidence/proof/research as also cultural practices. Surely the idea that randomised controlled trials are of any use in objectively generalising about the talking therapies is an absurdity – could one really change one variable and keep everything else constant? The same criticisms are also true regarding the increasing time students that are wasting doing what is currently called research, whether quantitative or qualitative. Hugh also cites Foucault's identification of the seemingly intractable problem of our reactions to such aspects as deviance and distress. However, this should not take away from the argument that the talking therapies should be able to provide a confidential space for exploration with someone who is able to hear it. My concern is that such possibilities are decreasing.

With regard to psychology, Ian Parker reminds us in Chapter 3, 'Towards critical psychotherapy and counselling: What can we learn from critical psychology (and political economy)?', that psychotherapy and counselling are often seen as alternatives to mainstream psychology. In my own case, as someone who also established a doctoral programme in counselling psychology, I cannot see where what is currently taught in many countries as psychology is of much use to the talking therapies. Rather, it produces well-intentioned, often bright people with a professionalisation to often cover up personal and academic insecurities. Ian warns us about various dangers in psychology, which critical psychology has attempted to expose. But perhaps we should not go down these so-called psychological paths in the first place? Although, as he emphasises, as talking therapists we need to be critical of ourselves (including the question as to whether we should or can be 'relentlessly critical'), and able to consider how our work is part of capitalism and the operations of the capitalist state. This chapter gives further credence that, following Chapter 2, talking therapists, including counselling psychologists, need to be educated not only in sociology and anthropology but also in political economy.

In Chapter 4, 'The neurobiological turn in therapeutic treatment: Salvation or devastation?', Kenneth J. Gergen concludes in some ways similar to Hugh Middleton, stating: 'Psychiatrists are essentially using a disease model of diagnosis, and prescribing medication with virtually no basis for either the diagnostic categories or evidence of neurobiological malfunction. The side-effects of these prescriptions – both biological and psychological – along with the disinterest in terminating prescription are injurious to clients.' This again is extraordinarily damning about what we are allowing to happen, whether we be psychiatrists, talking therapists or members of the public. However, not only has there always been the danger that the disease model is attractive to some psychological therapists, including some psychoanalysts and counselling psychologists, but what Kenneth importantly points out in this chapter is for us not to get seduced by the neurobiological turn. In my experience there are many now across most of the modalities in the talking therapies who hope that neuroscience et al. will somehow provide an answer. This is despite those directly involved in neuroscience not making such claims. For Kenneth, these brain-based explanations wrongly remove the complexity of our work.

Users' perspectives

While I think we need to be very concerned about the consumerist movement taking away from the therapeutic relationship, it can nevertheless reduce what can be seen as the unnecessary verbal abuse that the power place of the therapist can so easily overindulge in. One study that attempts to explore the experiences of those who have received a treatment for 'schizophrenia' is provided by Tom Cotton and myself in Chapter 5, 'Personal versus medical meanings in breakdown, treatment and recovery from "schizophrenia"'. Here we argue that the mainstream treatment of 'schizophrenia' is dominated by a medical model and modernist discourse, focusing on symptom management. Tom in his research found that personal meaning was central to participants' understanding and recovery. Therapy-as-symptom-management was seen by these 'users' as an obstacle to restoring personal meaning and hence to recovery. It would appear that if people who are feeling wretched can have others to talk to, where they can explore personal meaning, then there is far less need for medication and, surely if this is available elsewhere, psychological therapists.

Critiques coming more from outside

When I was a student we all seemed to talk about alienation. Nowadays perhaps we are so alienated that we can no longer even do this. In Chapter 6, 'Critical theory and psychotherapy', Anastasios Gaitanidis examines some of the claims of the Frankfurt School, which might be seen as one of the originators of the notion of critical theory, though interestingly it does not appear very present in some of the critical works mentioned in Chapter 1, including critical psychiatry. Anastasios describes how therapeutic success comes to be seen as adaptation to society, rather than through critical theory how mental distress can result from 'the very structure of the existing social order'. For me, this attempt by the talking therapies to normalise clients and patients at the expense of the social/economic/political context is what psychological therapists, as evidenced by the content of their training programmes, are instructed to do. There's a concern that the talking therapies are increasingly becoming agents of the overall political status quo, though some may still retain the potential subversiveness with regard to their client's/patient's immediate social relations. What also comes out from Chapter 6 is the potential evilness in all of us. Do talking therapists increasingly deny this both in themselves and in their patients/clients?

Another important question is how critical can we be of our values as talking therapists? For example, to what extent do we implicitly see our clients'/patients' success in terms of being able to have enduring, intimate relationships? Mari Ruti and Adrian Cocking in Chapter 7, 'When love is not all we want: Queers, singles and the therapeutic use of relationality', wish to alert us 'to the possibility that their propensity to assume that close relational bonds are essential to "the good life" may feel alienating to some patients'. What seems particularly important is the extent to which we can question our own values as talking therapists through what might be different perspectives, such as in queer theory and feminism, and again the extent to which our training and continuing professional development are able to open up such questions for us regardless of where we are coming from in terms of our own personal sexual practices and so on. (For further discussion of this, see Clark and Loewenthal 2015).

Perhaps Lois Holzman more than most looks to how one might create 'practical-critical psychotherapy and counselling approaches'. In Chapter 8, 'Relating to people as revolutionaries', she describes the group approach of social therapy that she and others have evolved over many years as a way to engage the alienation and authoritarian commodification of contemporary life (as, for example, discussed in Chapter 6) by relating to people (with the help of Marx and Vygotsky) as revolutionaries. What Lois very much hopes to be writing about is an approach designed to affect our very being and not just for writing and talking about.

Significantly, what seems to be happening in the UK and elsewhere is that the increasing attention given by governments to the psychological therapies is changing the very nature of our work. As mentioned in Chapter 1, one commentator has said: 'we seem to be going from cottage industry to factory production' (Parry et al. 2010). Following what we have been saying regarding alienation, Michael Rustin in Chapter 9, 'Work in contemporary capitalism', addresses how we have moved from potentially enjoying the intrinsic rewards of work to, through capitalism, hoping to enjoy the extrinsic rewards that the money for our labour can buy. He explores this change by considering what we might learn from Marx, Ruskin and Morris. He concludes by asking whether in our neoliberalist world there can be space for a renewal of interest in the quality of our working lives. I do think that previously working as a talking therapist provided the possibility of a better quality of working life. There is also the danger, as Ian Parker writes in Chapter 3, that as therapists we see the ultimate goal for our clients/patients to also be therapists. But even where this is not the case, perhaps encouraging too many people to have time to consider getting closer to their desires and the place of work in itself can be a threat to the existing social order. So returning to a place where most of the work of talking therapists and their clients'/patients' is more about intrinsic rather than extrinsic rewards may not be allowed.

Critiques coming more from inside

One question raised is to what extent the contributors to this book can be critical of themselves. As mentioned, all of the authors have been asked to be critical of what they have written so that the reader can see what our contributors publicly state, and in so doing what might be their blind spots. Examples of how they might be challenged are given in Chapter 10, 'Everything you always wanted to know about therapy (but were afraid to ask): Fragments of a critical psychotherapy'. Here, Andrew Samuels, who has perhaps written and been involved with politics and the talking therapies more than most, criticises what may be a different form of romantic notion to that referred to in Chapter 9. He questions such propositions as whether we can be free and independent professionals, whether the therapy relationship is just between two people and, again, whether the talking therapies are vocations, not jobs. Andrew thought-provokingly concludes that our role should be that of the trickster where we disobey 'normal' rules and conventional behaviour.

When I first trained as a counsellor, thinking was regarded as intellectualisation and a defence against feelings. Colin Feltham in Chapter 11, 'Critical priorities for the psychotherapy and counselling community', usefully explores the place of thinking and theorising in psychotherapy and counselling, including suspicions about such thinking. He suggests that we prioritise an exploration of aetiologies of distress and question the credibility and inevitability of our 500 or more differently named models. He further questions how we explore outcome; whether our professional mess is beyond reform; that training courses turn out far more practitioners than there are employment openings; whether most therapy constitutes a conservative, collusive, anti-revolutionary quietism; and whether we should also be social activists and be engaged, for example, in ecotherapy. Colin concludes with what is perhaps potentially the most stinging criticism of this book: 'I am afraid that most of us are merely talking rarified jargon to ourselves in our critical coteries and narcissistically expecting to be taken seriously'. What I do think we could have had more of in this volume, and might be the basis of a future book, is for contributors to primarily write case studies of critical psychotherapy, psychoanalysis and counselling in action.

In a different way from Chapter 7, Chris Oakley's Chapter 12, 'The Deleuzian project', examines aspects of how Deleuze and Guattari attempt to challenge Freud's family romance and some of what can be seen as Lacan's totalising moves. This account of schizoanalysis not only aims to open up psychoanalytic dogma but also includes aspects of our sexual desire and its interweaving with capitalism, all of which we seem to deny. It is some time now since Deleuze and Guattari wrote *Anti-Oedipus* (2004), which even on those trainings which consider continental philosophy has rarely seen the light of day, perhaps further showing how our theorising successfully reflects our political and sexual denial.

Steven Groarke in Chapter 13, 'Psychoanalysis and the event of resistance', starts by asking the question: Does psychoanalysis matter politically? Interestingly, he considers the Freudian interpretation of resistance 'as a critical and political resource' that goes beyond the treatment of the patient's internal resistances. He argues that the political significance of psychoanalysis depends on the historical together with the personal meaning of resistance. In employing Derrida's distinction between 'resistance-*to*-psychoanalysis' and 'resistances-*of*-psychoanalysis', he argues that the courage and conviction that accompany speaking out against the consensus are integral to the analytic experience and form part of the historical event of resistance (which can, for example, be seen in the context of anti-psychiatry). Steven argues that resistance is a matter of living well in the face of the Other's death; and of particular interest for critical psychotherapy, psychoanalysis and counselling is his point that state regulation need not 'exhaust the theoretical or institutional capacity of psychoanalysis, but rather give new capacities for resistance'.

In Paul Moloney's Chapter 14, 'Psychology, psychotherapy – coming to our senses?', he argues that psychotherapy, psychoanalysis and counselling are more part of the problem than the solution to our individual problems. (There was a strong case for starting this book with his chapter.) He considers that it is only when the talking therapies stop helping to shape the existing power structures of our world, together with our more honestly recognising their limitations and finding more thoughtful approaches to researching them, that our lives may change for the better.

What has become increasingly clear from these chapters is that in order to be thoughtful we need help from outside theories of psychotherapy, psychoanalysis and counselling. This is perhaps partly a truism in that in order to explore any dimension we need an additional dimension. However, if we see the talking therapies primarily as cultural practices then in a different way all of the modality theories also come from outside and can be seen as an attempt at legitimisation along with the accepted research methods of the moment. As mentioned in Chapter 1, surely the nature of knowledge in the talking therapies is such that when you are in it, it's different (for example Polanyi 1966; Wittgenstein 1998; Loewenthal 2011; Heaton 2013).

Critiques of training and learning

A further conclusion from these chapters is the importance of the 'what and how' of training and continuing professional development in the talking therapies. It has been suggested that we need to have anthropology, sociology and political economy as part of our basic training. Two chapters in this book looked at aspects of this education and training. The first, Chapter 15, was from Tom Strong and colleagues entitled 'Contesting the curriculum: Counsellor education in a postmodern and medicalising era'. Here they recount, and usefully warn us of the North American experience, where DSM-5 has become the language of the helping professions, threatening the traditional conversational approach of counsellors and the pluralism of their approach, which until recently had in some ways been strengthened by postmodernism's legitimising multiplicity of meanings. Of particular use to them, and, I hope, to all of us, in analysing these medicalising tensions that attempt to shape counsellor education is their use of Adele Clarke's situational analysis.

Then, in Chapter 16, 'Systemic means to subversive ends: Maintaining the therapeutic space as a unique encounter', Jay Watts provides a useful case study of an attempt to keep open a training programme for counselling psychologists. Here again we are shown how 'an ideology that privileges notions of "illness", "cure" and "evidence-based treatments"' can be problematic. Importantly, Jay gives examples of how we combat this through such new developments as what is going on in the survivor movement and cyberspace. For her, and, I hope, for all of us, 'we can produce spaces that may incorporate multiple stories on "evidence", "illness" and the other signifiers that otherwise threaten to colonise us'.

So is there an unfortunate need for critical psychotherapy, psychoanalysis and counselling?

It would appear best if we don't have the notion of 'critical' pscyhotherapy, psychoanalysis and counselling but, instead, existing and future practitioners attempt to stay open to such ideas as are in this book. If, however, this cannot be maintained as mainstream psychotherapy, psychoanalysis and counselling, there is a case for using the word 'radical'. The main problem here is that such a term is one that most practitioners will not wish to be associated with, as argued by Double (2006). We are therefore left with the probable better cul-de-sac in neoliberal capitalism of 'critical' psychotherapy, psychoanalysis and counselling, which all academics can appear to be legitimately interested in and which will influence, I hope, at least some practitioners – but not in a way that will change the world.

At the start of this book I wrote of David Cooper's idea of anti-psychiatry. Since then we have moved from 'radical' to now 'critical'. Yet as we have seen, even the term 'critical' tends often to ignore the Frankfurt School's critical theory that it would appear to come from. What happened in 1943 when the Frankfurt School went to Columbia University, USA, to escape fascism is perhaps salutary and seen by some as a retreat from Marxism. Here, as reflected in Adorno and Horkheimer's *Dialectic of Enlightenment* (1994/1997), politics was replaced by philosophy, and capitalism by modernity. They did, however, write that through the Enlightenment we had descended into modern barbarism and that God had not been replaced by science; rather, in our alienation we have been consumed by the 'candy floss culture' (also referred to as 'white trash'), the only alternative being isolation (see Winship 2013).

Perhaps what we also need to include or reinstate on our psychotherapy, psychoanalysis and counselling reading lists are the works of Erich

Fromm and Herbert Marcuse. Marcuse in *Eros and Civilisation* (1955) argued that we are caught by our internal forces of both repression and external capitalism, and that the resolution of either is inherently interlinked. Subsequently in *One Dimensional Man* (1964), he explored how capitalism had by then successfully suppressed radicalism. Rather than religion being the opium of the masses, now the mass media, technology and consumption were how people through a false economy of need experienced cultural (also termed 'surplus') repression. Here we are only allowed to think in ways that will reproduce existing systems of inequality and critique as opposition. Hence, with so many people now needing psychotherapy, psychoanalysis and counselling, this is minimised through primacy being given to consumption. As Winship (2013), to whom I owe much of these accounts of Marcuse and Fromm, shows us, for those such as Marcuse the important thing was consciousness-raising rather than the psychoanalytic idea of the unconscious becoming conscious. But what possibility of combining both? It was indeed Marcuse who was invited as top of the bill at the Dialectics of Liberation conference, famously held at The Roundhouse in London, with Laing, Cooper, Ginsberg, Bateson, Carmichael et al., where therapy, rather than just being the insight of personal knowledge, was for just a moment intertwined with what was seen as the revolutionary energy of the 'oppressed'.

The Frankfurt School had been interested in psychoanalysis. Adorno, with the encouragement of Horkheimer, went into psychoanalysis with Karl Landauer, leading to Horkheimer approving the establishment of a psychoanalytic department led by Landauer (a student of Freud).

Again, as reported by Winship (2013), it was Fromm, however, who particularly brought together psychoanalysis and politics. In Fromm's *Fear of Freedom* (1965 [1941]) he attempted to show how patriarchy and Freud's (1913) notion of the creation of order underpinned the social order of pre-war Germany and hence Hitler coming to the fore. (Though, in contrast, Adorno and Horkheimer (1997 [1944]) focused more on narcissism and identification as primarily submerging the individual.) With *The Sane Society* (1955), Fromm returned to the relationship between psychoanalysis and Marxism whereby 'the productive activity of everybody in his work, stimulates the unfolding reason and enables man to give expression to his inner needs in collective acts and rituals' (1955: 276).

By now Fromm had lost interest in capitalism and what he saw as the celebration of individual sovereignty in the USA. Instead he thought that psychotherapy should be concerned with the false consciousness of the politically alienated patient such that the analyst needed to be politically educated to able to do this. He also put forward the idea that the analyst should now be proactive but also in a way that privileged Marx over Freud (which perhaps Lois Holzman in Chapter 8 comes closest to in this volume).

A conclusion from this book is that three very difficult personal and collective courses of action may be required if we are able to significantly change our practices. The first is to continue to remind ourselves and others, as stated in Chapter 1, of Plato's plea that while the scientific and technical are important, they should always come second to the resources of the human soul (Cushman 2002). Second, we must remember that the human soul in all of us is capable of good and evil, and we need to be aware of those theories that side-step realising how we make and are capable of making others wretched. Third, we should not forget not only that will we through the powers that be, in our current case of neoliberalist capitalism, be seduced or otherwise forced away from really opening up to our clients/patients and ourselves, but that we will individually wish to escape, through denial, unsavoury aspects of ourselves. Yet the assumption remains that the more we can stay open to all of this and work it through, the greater ours and others' potency and potentiality.

There is much in this book to support the idea that the state is using psychotherapy, psychoanalysis and counselling as a form of social control. While it can be argued that oppressing oppresses the oppressor, perhaps it is particularly pertinent that in some ways surely both oppressors and oppressed wish to be oppressed. Both Marx and Nietzsche in different ways have suggested that religion enables people to stop thinking. However, with the demise of religion and our fast-developing alienated states of being (facilitated by the state), we also individually welcome this 'opportunity'. The therapies on offer provide either a way of directly taking one's mind off what worries one (CBT) or a way that reflects back that we are the person that we would like to think of ourselves as; or, to a decreasing extent, approaches that do neither. Yet perhaps it is almost too difficult to find a therapy which would allow one not only to see the good in people but also to not deny our sexuality and violence, and a place to consider our part in the political set-up. This would enable us to consider what we are subject to and what we subject others to, including those who are close and not so close to us.

Perhaps much of this book has already been covered by Paul Ricoeur (1970), as referred to in Chapter 1. Rather than wrongly regarding too much as the natural order of things, we actually see, through Marx and others, how capitalism affects our wellbeing, through Nietzsche how morality is manmade, and through Freud the secrets of our sexuality. All three give us the potential to free ourselves, not completely but from some of that which we didn't even know we were subject to. It is, of course, understandable that attempts are made to dismiss Marx, Nietzsche and Freud, again both from the forces in society and from those in the individual. Similarly, Leiter (2004) has argued the English-speaking world has fallen to what he calls moralising interpreters of Marxian and Freudian thought. Also, Nietzsche has been transformed by moralising interpreters from being engaged in an attack on morality to being concerned with questions of truth and knowledge. I am not suggesting that we shouldn't be critical of them either (we need to be suspicious of their suspicion but not automatically dismissive of them). In order to work effectively as talking therapists, don't we need to keep open for ourselves and others, even if we disagree with Marx, Freud and Nietzsche and their likes, what they were seeking to unmask?

Also clearer to me is that the talking therapies are cultural practices and the way that they are researched are cultural practices. This book has not dwelt as much as some might think on questions such as the inappropriateness of forcing an empirical research method from another cultural tradition onto psychotherapy, psychoanalysis and counselling. Indeed, for Ricoeur (1970), the hermeneutics of suspicion are in opposition to scientific understanding such that, for example, psychoanalysis should not be attempted to be located within the causal discourse of natural sciences. Personally, my dismissiveness is partly due, despite an early interest in research, to considering RCTs not as the gold standard but as scientifically absurd when working with such multivariable situations as the talking therapies. Also clearer to me is that qualitative research is not much of an answer. It may help an individual researcher but it cannot usually be generalised and, indeed, shouldn't be. However, led by psychologists, the idea of the practitioner researcher (McLeod 1999) means that, increasingly, trainees are worse than wasting their time with regard to preparing for their practice. Would it not be better, for example, for such students to consider social, economic and technological contexts, or even literary studies, rather than learning about statistics, a bit of biology and so forth? However, from the point of view of the state, to take people who want to help others and instead fill their minds with such substandard technical thinking can be seen as another form of social control. What is now happening is that the work of the talking therapist is increasingly becoming detrimental to the therapists' own lives as well (see for example Rizq 2013).

I have focused more on the role of the state and less on the inappropriateness of the medical model. I have, though, had personal experience of being grateful – for example, after a considerable time of being part of providing 24 hours' cover for someone without medication – that a psychiatric ward and medication was there, and was successfully and usefully used briefly. Nevertheless, the way in which medication is generally indiscriminately dished out, and rarely – if at all – tested in medical trials other than over an eight-week period (Whitaker 2010), could be regarded as verging on the criminal, as could much of the training of psychiatrists and psychologists who would often seem to be reduced from people who want to help others to relatively thoughtless technicians who are caught up in state-endorsed frameworks.

In concluding this chapter, what emerge for me are two key forces. The first is from the individual who, through what some would call denial, wants to avoid staying with uncomfortable thoughts, fantasies and dreams. The second force is from those in power who do not want those whom they manage to understand how this is done. With regard to the first force, Freud did try to tell us that regarding sexuality we are all polymorphous and perverse. Yet the fashion of what it is acceptable to talk about in terms of sexuality, in any culture at any one time, varies considerably (see Chapter 7). Just look at the changes between and within cultures with regard to homosexuality. Currently, sexuality and children is an even more difficult topic to speak about. Yet how, for example, can parents be so intimate with their children without such issues potentially being there? The consulting room, if a therapist and their supervisor are able to hear it, can ordinarily include, for example, dreams parents speak of often with overwhelming shame and guilt, concerning their children.

Similarly, what of violence? Our television programmes and video games are replete with killings – there is even no need to switch on private browsing to watch them (see Chapter 12 on the money shot). Certainly our path leaves the possibility that any of us could have potentially devised the Holocaust (see Chapter 6) and have at least dreamt of 'just obeying orders'. Yet how many psychotherapists, psychoanalysts and counsellors (and their supervisors) are able to consider such sexuality and violence within themselves? And if they can't, how can they leave open the possibility of a client/patient speaking of such? Even if significant figures in the field open up such possibilities of exploring one's own demons, they soon become sanitised, as Lacan attempted to point out has happened with Freud. Didn't something similar happen to Rogers, who became systematised by Egan (1997) and others, restricting almost to death his ideas such as in *Freedom to Learn* (1969). Of course, there are what Freud would call resistances that can become too great. For example, in working with trainees in a group setting, it became too difficult for the majority of participants to hear a female student describe how erotic she found the touch of a baby's skin. Similarly, in another group, a large man spoke of how he enjoyed fighting and how wonderful it was when somebody shouted at him 'Stop that thief!', and he tackled someone even larger than himself running off with a bicycle. Yet most of the rest of the group couldn't let him describe his pleasure in overcoming the thief, and soon after the man left the group. Another such instance occurred when someone in an analytic group felt that no one really wanted to listen to her concerns about a suspected paedophile in her family.

So if it's not a false assumption that through the talking therapies we can become clearer as to who we are and there will therefore be less chance of us acting it out, this taking place seems very unlikely if the patient/client cannot speak of it because the therapist has not had their own personal therapist or supervisor who could stay with the darker side of things. As Zizek (2009) argues, the physical violence that we see is often generated by the systemic violence that sustains our political and economic systems. He concludes that doing nothing is often the most violent course of action that we can take.

While most talking therapists think that they should be able to work with issues of sex and violence, even though this may not always be the case, when it comes to ideologies and the political, most in my experience feel that this is not for them. Yet when are our consulting rooms not replete with the economic and social affecting our clients/patients? Recently, four young prisoners asked to see me for individual therapy:

Frank: I met a girl when I was 14/15. She was a proper girlfriend, eventually we split up and I couldn't deal with it. I self-harmed more and so we moved to a council house in another area. I used to wake up every day and no one was in the house other than my little brother, and I got wound up and cut myself deep, really bad. Went to hospital and hostel and then foster family. I thought I could not trust another girl again.

Dan: My friend recently got shot. It's like when you see people in the news, whose son or daughter has gone missing. It's the area where you are living – this is why I want to try and leave the country'.

Mickey: I'd love to live out of London, somewhere like Yorkshire.

DL: But you wanted to work in London?

Mickey: I'm able to drive throughout the night every day... there are times when I haven't had sleep for days, so long as I'm able to pop pills, ecstasy etc.

Jake: I've never loved anyone so much as my daughter... my mum brought me over from Africa when I was 14. I never knew who my father was. My mum said I couldn't go to school because she had lost my passport. Her bag was stolen. So when I was 15, I left home and I could only afford to stay with friends who involved me in crime and would've been thrown out if I hadn't gone along with them. My partner is a good woman, she is staying in a hostel. I don't know where we'll stay when I leave prison. I do need to fight back otherwise I'm a victim allowing other people to put a knife in your back.

So does one hear that these situations are to do with social, economic contexts or the individual client's responsibility? Jake showed me the many knife wounds that he had from living on the streets and he knew that on release the only way he could provide an income for his daughter was to return to crime, for while he would have to sign on and would be able to stay in the UK, he would not be allowed to work. How should one respond as a talking therapist? Not get involved? Give Jake the telephone number of the Council for the Welfare of Immigrants? Phone them for him? Rouse probation? Seek to change the law? Perhaps most difficult is to hear and stay with the despair (Gee and Loewenthal 2013), and what might or might not emerge from it. Importantly, with the increasing experience of alienation, aren't more and more of us in our neoliberalist world in a despair, like these prisoners, that we dare not attempt to work through for fear of being even more in despair?

Perhaps one of the difficulties, as mentioned earlier, is that once we leave the notion of radical then at best we might take part in a sceptical tradition which, while importantly questioning dogmas and so on, seems usually to omit those economic and social contexts which can lead to emotional deprivation and distress. Again as mentioned previously, when those such as Freud and Rogers do point out what others don't want to consider, it gets lost – sanitised again. Indeed, didn't this also happen to some of the founders of psychology? Didn't Wilhelm Wundt (1904) write of the importance of marrying the empirical with the cultural historical? Where is this in the training of psychologists? What got translated, at least for the British and Americans, focused on laboratory experiments. Again, how many psychology students know much, if anything, about the empirical radicalism of William James (1912)? So those young people who are interested in helping others by becoming psychologists end up learning about statistics. Importantly, now psychotherapy, psychoanalysis and counselling, which were seen by some as offering a different form of psychology, are now moving into state-endorsed programmes where anything really potentially alive has any remaining jagged corners rounded off. Shouldn't all of these people who want to help others at least, as has been argued, also be learning about economics and sociology? In an age of evidence-based practice, couldn't we at least explore a few different forms of, for example, capitalism, Marxism and socialism, and some advantages and disadvantages of each, particularly in terms of our relations with each other? At the very least, students might do a module on literature, or even the soaps, if they want to think about people.

We are, of course, in a society which is increasingly alienated (see Chapter 9) where possibly it wouldn't suit everybody if through the talking therapies people were to get closer to their desires, let alone feel less wretched. Our work as talking therapists is speedily moving to a place where we will experience our alienation in less beneficial ways. Of course, there is also the danger that therapists and their clients/patients become more of a social elite, being able to more successfully manipulate their relations with others. Also, just look at what happens in relations among therapists and between our therapeutic groupings to know that therapy need not be a panacea necessarily enabling a more humane future for all. Yet if we are to have the hope of a better life, not just for ourselves but for those around us, then isn't the notion of ideology crucial? Don't we need to look at our personal and economic relations with those around us, as well as those out of sight in other countries?

One of the reviewers of the proposal for this book stated: 'the proposed engagement of psychotherapy, psychoanalysis and counselling with critical theory (such as Marxist, feminist and Foucauldian scholarship) is rare in itself and when married to the broadness of the disciplines covered will make it an almost unique text'. I hope that this has been achieved to at least some extent for both our academic and our practitioner readers.

To conclude, unless psychotherapy, psychoanalysis and counselling can be critical in practice, moving towards including a consideration of the strengths and limitations of capitalism for the individual's wellbeing, and in so doing considering other perspectives, including Marxism (which doesn't necessarily say one has to end up a Marxist), as an important oppositional critique (or as Marcuse would say, the dialectic), then we will become too stagnant. So perhaps critical psychotherapy, psychoanalysis and counselling are a way in which capitalism will allow us (as previously with 'modernism' and 'postmodernism') to become a little bit alive so long as it's not too much.

References

Adorno, T. and Horkheimer, M. (1997 [1944]) *The Dialectic of Enlightenment*. London: Verso.

Bracken, P., Thomas, P., Timimi, S., Asen, E., Behr, G., Beuster, C., Bhunnoo, S., Browne, I., Chhina, N. Double, D., Downer, S., Evans, C., Fernando, S., Garland, M.R., Hopkins, W., Huws, R., Johnson, B., Martindale, B., Middleton, H., Moldavsky, D., Moncrieff, J., Mullins, S., Nelki, J., Pizzo, M., Rodger, J., Smyth, M., Summerfield, D., Wallace, J. and Yeomans, D. (2012) 'Psychiatry beyond the current paradigm', *British Journal of Psychiatry*, 201, 430–434.

Clark, D. and Loewenthal, D. (2015) 'The counselling psychology of sex, sexualities and gender', in C. Richards and M. Barker (eds.) *The Palgrave Handbook of the Psychology of Sexuality and Gender*. Basingstoke: Palgrave Macmillan.

Cushman, R. (2002) *Therapeia: Plato's Conception of Philosophy*. New Brunswick and London: Transaction Publishers.

Deleuze, G. and Guattari, F. (2004) *Anti-Oedipus: Capitalism and Schizophrenia*. London and New York: Continuum Books.

Double, D.B. (ed.) (2006) *Critical Psychiatry: The Limits of Madness*. Basingstoke: Palgrave Macmillan.

Egan, G.E. (1997) *The Skilled Helper: A Problem-Management Approach to Helping* 6th ed. London: Brooks Cole.

Freud, S. (1913) *Totem and Taboo: Some Points of Agreement between the Mental Life of Savages and Neurotics* (1913 [1912–1913]), The Standard Edition of the Complete Psychological Works of Sigmund Freud, Volume XIII, (1913–1914): Totem and Taboo and Other Works, vii–162.

Fromm, E. (1955) *The Sane Society*. Greenwich: Fawcett Premier Books.

Fromm, E. (1965 [1941]) *The Fear of Freedom*. New York: Avon Books.

Gee, J. and Loewenthal, D. (2013) 'Working with despair: A phenomenological investigation', *Psychology and Psychotherapy: Theory, Research and Practice*, 86:2, 229–243.

Heaton, J.M. (2013) *The Talking Cure: Wittgenstein on Language as Bewitchment and Clarity*. Basingstoke: Palgrave Macmillan.

James, W. (1912) *Essays in Radical Empiricism*, edited by R. Barton Perry. New York: Longmans, Green.

Leiter, B. (2004) *The Hermeneutics of Suspicion: Recovering Marx, Neitszche and Freud U of Texas Law*. Public Law Research Paper no. 72. Available at: SSRN: http://ssrn.com/abstract=691002.

Loewenthal, D. (2011) *Post-Existentialism and the Psychological Therapies: Towards a Therapy without Foundations*. London: Karnac.
Marcuse, H. (1955) *Eros and Civilisation*. Boston: Beacon Press.
Marcuse, H. (1964) *One Dimensional Man*. Boston: Beacon Press.
McLeod, J. (1999) *Practitioner Research in Counselling*. London: Sage.
Parry, G., Blackmore, C., Beecroft, C. and Booth, A. (2010) *A Systematic Review of the Efficacy and Clinical Effectiveness of Group Analysis and Analytic/ Dynamic Group Psychotherapy*. www.academia.edu/2723418/A_systematic_review_of _the_efficacy_and_clinical_effectiveness_of_group_analysis_and_analytic_ and_dynamic_group_psychotherapy. Accessed 17 August 2014.
Polanyi, M. (1966). *The Tacit Dimension*. Garden City: Doubleday and Co.
Ricoeur, P. (1970) *Freud and Philosophy: An Essay on Interpretation* trans. Savage, D. New Haven, CT: Yale University Press.
Rizq, R. (2013) 'IAPT and thoughtcrime: Language, bureaucracy and the evidence-based regime', *Counselling Psychology Review*, 28:4, 111–115.
Rogers, C.R. (1969) *Freedom to Learn (Studies of the Person)*. New York: Charles Merrill.
Whitaker, R. (2010) *Anatomy of an Epidemic: Magic Bullets, Psychiatric Drugs, and the Astonishing Rise of Mental Illness in America*. New York: Broadway Books.
Winship, G. (2013) 'A genealogy of therapeutic community ideas: The influence of the Frankfurt School with a particular focus on Herbert Marcuse and Erich Fromm', *Therapeutic Communities: The International Journal of Therapeutic Communities*, 34:2/3, 60–70.
Wittgenstein, L. (1998) *Culture and Value* 2nd ed. trans. Winch, P. Georg Henrik (ed.) von Wright in collaboration with Heikki Nyman, revised by Alois Pichler. Oxford: Blackwell.
Wundt, W. (1904 [1874]) *Principles of Physiological Psychology* trans. Tichener, E.B. London: Allen.
Zizek, S. (2009) *Violence*. London: Profile Books Ltd.

Index

Locators followed by n refer to notes.

Adams, M., 183
Adorno, T.W., xix, 6, 95–6, 100–5, 293–4
Minima Moralia, 100
see also Frankfurt School
Ahmed, S., 110–11
Albee, G., 233
alienation, xix, 13, 36, 134, 288–90, 300
Alliance for Counselling and Psychotherapy, 18, 159
American Counseling Association (ACA), 242
American Psychological Association (APA), 248
Anti-Oedipus: Capitalism and Schizophrenia, 189–90, 194, 291
anti-psychiatry, 14, 41, 70, 182, 201
see also Cooper, D.; Laing, R.D.
anxiety, 171
Arendt, H., 138
Aristotle, 9, 138, 143–4
Armstrong, D., 146
Aschaffenburg, G., 201
Asylum Magazine, 277
Attention Deficit Hyperactivity Disorder (ADHD), 59, 63, 66
audit culture, 5, 7, 10, 12, 265, 268
austerity programmes, 149

Beckett, S., 103, 172, 183, 202
Benjamin, W., xix, 95–6, 98–9, 100–1, 103, 105
see also Frankfurt School
Bentall, R., 15, 265–6
Berlant, L., xxi, 111
Beyond the Current Paradigm, xiii, 37–8
Bikini Kill, 193
Binswanger, L., 78

bio-medical model, 15, 54, 232, 268
and psychiatry, 15, 232
see also medical model
bipolar disorder, 62, 265
Blair, T., 149
Bloch, E., 212
Bollas, C., 88
Boss, M., 78
Boyle, M., 273
Bracken, P., 15, 79, 89, 286
Braverman, H., 150
British Association for Counselling and Psychotherapy (BACP), 49, 175, 177, 185
British Journal of Psychiatry, 269
British Psychoanalytic Council, 49
British Psychological Society (BPS), 272
Butler, J., 112

Canadian Counseling and Psychotherapy Association, 241
Canadian Psychological Association, 251
capital governance, xxxvii
capitalism, xiii, xxiv, xxxviii, 15, 18, 46, 48, 50–1, 112–15, 122, 139, 143–4, 146, 150, 186, 195–6, 198, 217, 227–8, 285, 287, 290–1, 293–6, 300
and class, 46
and social disadvantage, 228
and the state, 50
Caygill, H., 205–6
Cayne, J., 16
Chondros, K., xxxii–iii
Clarke, A., 242, 245–7, 249, 292
messy maps, 247, 249
situational analysis, 242, 245, 292
Clarkson, P., 167
Clinique de la Borde, 190, 194, 201

Cobb, M., xxi, 108, 118–19
Cocking, A., xx, 9, 289
Cognitive Behavioural Therapy (CBT), 4, 85, 164, 167, 171, 178–9, 183, 232, 248, 264, 272–3, 274
confidentiality, 5
Cooper, D., 6, 14, 16, 201, 293
see also anti-psychiatry
core competencies, 267, 272
Corey, G., 248
Cotton, T., xvii, 13, 16, 29, 78, 288
Council for Accreditation of Counseling and Related Educational Programmes, 251
counselling, *see* talking therapies
counsellor education, xxxiii–xxxv, 241–54, 292
and medicalising discourse, 241–2, 245, 248, 249, 252–3, 292
and postmodernism, 242
textbooks, 247–50, 253
see also training
Craib, I., 13
critical thinking, 175–8

Daily Mail, 277
Davies, J., 16
Dean, T., 116
Deleuze, G., xxviii–ix, 189–93, 195–7, 218, 291
see also Guattari, F.
DePaulo, B., 118–19
depression, 58, 61, 64–5, 171, 248, 265
Derrida, J., xxx, 6–8, 200–4, 206–10, 213, 215–16, 219, 291
Resistances de la psychanalyse, 200, 218
resistance-to-psychoanalysis, 201, 205, 291
resistances-of-psychoanalysis, 201, 291
desire, 192–5
erotic pleasure, 193
orgasm, 193–6
sexual pleasure, 193
see also sexual desire
diagnosis, *see* psychiatric diagnosis

Diagnostic and Statistical Manual of Mental Disorders(DSM), xxxiii–iv, 16, 61, 66, 80, 83, 136, 171, 241–5, 248–51, 254, 269, 292
DSM-III, 36
DSM-5, xxxiii–iv, xxxvi, 38, 62, 171, 241–5, 247–51, 254, 269, 292
and illness categories, 61
and social values, 61
Dillon, J., 80
dodo-bird verdict, 29
Donzelot, J., xxx, 216
Dosse, F., 190
Double, D., 14, 293
Dylan, B., 172

ecotherapy, 183
Eliot, T.S., 172
Epstein, W., xxxvi, 230
ethical codes, 162
see also talking therapies
Etzioni, A., 8
European Journal of Psychotherapy and Counselling, 6, 12
European Psychoanalytic Federation, 206
evidence-based medicine, 265–6, 267, 271–2, 274, 276
evidence-based practice, 5, 37, 242–3
evidence-based treatments, xxxv, 248, 293

Fanon, F., 201
Feltham, C., xxvi, 13, 18, 175, 183, 290
feminism, xiv, xiii, 15, 244, 289
Fort Bragg Demonstration Project, 225
Foucault, M., xiii, xiv, xxx, 5, 30, 33, 36, 38–9, 44, 113–14, 190–2, 197, 203–4, 208, 218, 264, 287
and alienation, 36
Frankfurt School, xix, 6, 13, 95, 288, 293
Freud, S., xxvii, 8–9, 30, 53, 88, 96, 183, 193, 195, 200, 202–4, 211, 214–15, 217–18, 222, 291, 294–9
Civilisation and its Discontents, 96, 211
Nachträglichkeit, 98, 100

repetition compulsion, 99, 214
resistance, 200
Thoughts for the Times on War and Death, 99
see also psychoanalysis
Fromm, E., 294
Frosh, S., 19

Gadamer, H-G., 8
Gaitanidis, A., 16, 288
gay rights, 115
Genet, J., 214
Gergen, K.J., xv, 14, 287–8
globalisation, 149
Gramsci, A., 113–14
Green, A., 191, 212, 216
Groarke, S., xxix, 7, 291
Guattari, F., xxviii–ix, 189–92, 194–8, 201, 291
Three Billion Perverts on the Stand, 194
see also Deleuze, G.

Habermas, J., 60, 202
Halberstam, J., 122
Hare-Mustin, R., 122
Harper, E., 190
Health and Care Professions Council (HCPC), 18, 46, 159, 272
Health Professions Regulatory Advisory Council (HPRAC), 246
Hearing Voices Network, xxxvi, 70, 78, 80, 89
see also Psychiatric Survivor Movement
Heaton, J., 6
Hegel, G., 46, 100, 153–4n, 206
Heidegger, M., 78, 80–1, 88, 89–90, 99, 102–4, 175, 208
Being and Time, 79
Heteronormativity, 108, 117, 163
Hinshelwood, R.D., 19
Hiroshima, 95
Hitler, A., 191, 294
Holland, E., 198
Holocaust, the, 95, 97, 297
Holzman, L., xxii, 7, 289, 295
homonormativity, 117

Honneth, A., 202
Horkheimer, M., 6, 293–4
Horney, K., 58
Hoshmand, L., 13
House, R., 15, 21
Huxley, A., xxxiv

Improving Access to Psychological Therapies (IAPT), 11, 165, 266, 273
Ingleby, D., 14
International Statistical Classification of Diseases and Related Health Problems, 10th Revision: Chapter V: Mental and Behavioural Disorders (ICD), 136

James, W., 300
Johnson, Sonia, 275
Johnson, Sue, 119–21
Johnstone, L., 15
Jones, J., 145
Joyce, J., 98, 103, 183, 202
Jung, C.G., 166–7

Kafka, F., 101–2
Kane, C., 267
Kant, I., 176, 205
Kessler, M., 233
Kipnis, L., 109, 112–14, 120
Kirsch, I., 171
Kleinman, A., 14
Kraepelin, E., 81

labour, 50, 130, 233
  and alienation, 10, 47, 141
  and economic growth, 151
  extrinsic value of, 142, 144–8, 150, 290
  intrinsic value of, 140, 142, 144–8, 150
  psychotherapeutic, 50
Labour (political party), 145
  New Labour, 149
Lacan, J., xxviii, xxx, 189, 191–2, 196, 207, 209, 211–12, 216, 218, 297
Ecrits, 191

Laing, R.D., 6, 14, 80–1, 89–90, 190, 199, 201
  see also anti-psychiatry
Landauer, K., 294
Layard, R., 11, 154n
Leiter, B., 296
leucotomy, 34
Levinas, E., 6, 8, 207–9
LGBTQ movement, 115–16
Linehan, M., 275
Loach, K., 275
Locke, J., 139
Loewenthal, D., xi, xxxvi, 13, 15, 20, 264, 288
Longden, E., 270
Lotringer, S., 125
Lukács, G., xxxviii
Luther King Jr., M., 125
Lyotard, J-F., 195

Marcuse, H., 113–14, 202, 207, 211–13, 294, 301
marriage, 111–16, 119, 121
Martin, E., 59
Marxism, xiii, xiv, xxxvii, 18, 51, 133, 202, 212, 293–4, 300, 301
Marx, K., xiv, xxii-v, 8, 46, 48, 97–8, 125, 128–9, 130, 134, 139, 141, 153n, 202, 289–90, 295–6
  Economic and Political Manuscripts, 128, 141
  The German Ideology, 128
Masson, J., 178
May, R., 275
McLeod, J., 248, 250
measurement scales, 226
  Beck Depression Inventory, 223
  Clinical Outcomes in Routine Evaluation (CORE), 267
medicalisation, xxxiv, 241–5, 247, 249–50, 252–3
  of training and education, 242, 245, 247, 249, 253
medical model, xii–iii, 59–60, 126, 288, 297
  see also biomedical model
medication, 67, 287–8, 296
  see also psychopharmacology
mental health legislation, 30

'mental illness', 30, 33, 37, 54, 57–61, 68–9
  cultural constitution of, 59
  cultural meaning of, 68
  messy maps, 247, 249
  see also Clarke, A.
Middleton, H., xii, 15, 286–7
Moloney, P., xxx, 21, 292
Monbiot, G., 9–10
Moncrieff, J., 15
'money shot', 196, 297
Moon, L., 122
Morris, W., xxiv, 139, 141, 290
Mussolini, B., 191

National Health Service (NHS), xxxvi, 35, 49, 160, 171, 179, 265
  mental health services, 34–5
National Institute for Health and Care Excellence (NICE), xvii, 11, 85, 172, 224, 265, 271–2, 274
  Guideline Development Groups, 265
National Institute for Mental Health (NIMH), 224, 242, 265
neoliberalism, 3, 6–9, 48, 115, 122, 140, 152, 285, 293, 295
  and capitalism, xxxvii
neurobiology, xvi, 54, 57–61, 66, 70
  cultural effects, 57, 65
  and human suffering, 57–8
neuroscience, 61, 225, 267, 288
Newnes, C., 13
New Public Management, xxxvi, 7, 9, 12, 18, 20, 186
Nietzsche, F., 18, 96, 192, 295–6
  On the Genealogy of Morals, 96

Oakley, C., xxviii, 7, 291
Obsessive Compulsive Disorder (OCD), 63
Oedipus, 192, 195–6
Open Dialogue, 271
Orange, D., 8
orgasm, 193–6
Oury, J., 201
outcome research, 223

Parker, I., xiii, 7, 15–16, 287, 290
  Discourse Unit, 16
Parnet, C., 190
Peguy, C., 161
person-centred therapy, 20, 35, 166
  see also Rogers, C. R.
pharmaceutical industry, 56, 67, 71
Philadelphia Association, 6, 15, 190
Phillips, A., 190
Pinel, P., 30
Plato, 138, 295
political economy, xxxvi, xiv, 45, 47, 128, 287
postmodernism, xxxiv, 8, 15, 68, 128, 242–4, 268, 292
  and training, 242, 292
power, 135, 229
  and authority, 135
Professional Standards Authority for Health and Social Care, 46
Prozac, 56
psychiatric diagnosis, xvii, xxxiii, 13, 37, 54, 56, 58–9, 64, 71, 182, 243–4, 250, 252, 267, 287–8
  diagnostic criteria, 37
  disease model, 287–8
Psychiatric Survivor Movement, xxxv, 4, 70, 269, 276
  Autistic Advocacy, 70
  Hearing Voices Network, xxxvi, 70, 78, 89
  Mad Pride, 276
  Mind Freedom, 70
  peer support, 78, 87
  social media, 269
psychiatry
  biomedical research, 36
  critical psychiatry, 3, 79, 182
  democratic psychiatry, 41
  United Kingdom Critical Psychiatry Network, xiii, 15, 29
Psychoanalysis, xxvii, xxix, xxx, 4, 13, 18–19, 49, 85, 108, 110, 153n, 162–3, 168, 176, 191, 193–4, 198, 200–5, 208–19, 291–2, 294, 296
  As alternative to politics, 217
  and politics, 200, 202, 205, 212
  see also Freud, S.

psychology
  clinical, 243
  clinical, 4, 176–7, 287
  counselling, 42
  critical, xiv, 3, 15, 41–5, 51, 135, 182, 185
  discursive, 15
  ego, 216
  evolutionary, 177–8
  Marxist, 126
  Queer, 118
  radical, 41, 51
psychopharmacology, xvi, 30, 36, 53–6, 58, 60, 64, 66–8, 198
  cultural effects of, 57
  see also medication
psychosis, 89, 198
Psychotherapists and Counsellors for Social Responsibility, 18, 160
psychotherapy, *see* talking therapies
psy Complex, 268

Quality Assurance Agency (QAA), 185
Queer theory, xx, xxi, 108, 110, 115–16, 289

Randomised Controlled Trials (RCTs), xxxi, xxxvi, 11, 171, 230, 266–7, 296
Reich, W., 18
relationality, xxi, 108, 110, 117, 121
  and singles, 108, 110, 117–20
Research Centre for Therapeutic Education (RCTE), 15, 18
Research Excellence Framework (REF), 267
Ricardo, D., 139
Ricouer, P., 8, 295–6
  hermeneutics of suspicion, 8
Rizq, R., 16
Rogers, C. R., xxvii, 12, 166, 297, 299
  see also person-centred therapy
Romme, M., 80
Ross, K.H., xxxii
Royal College of Psychiatrists, xiv, 29, 38, 48
Ruskin, J., xxiv, 139, 141, 290
Rustin, M., xxiii, 7, 146, 290
Ruti, M., xx, 9, 289

Samuels, A., xxv, 5, 17–19, 159, 160, 290
Sartre, J-P., 212
Scanlon, H., 145
schizoanalysis, xxix, 197
schizophrenia, xvii, 62–3, 77, 78, 197–8, 288
  breakdown, xvii, 82
  personal meaning, xvii, 77, 89, 288
  psychotherapy, 84–7, 89
  recovery, xvii, 78, 87
  treatment, 82–4
Searles, H., 145
service users, 4, 15, 20
Sesma-Vazquez, M., xxxiii
sexual desire, xxxvii, 195, 291
sexuality, xxxvii, 22, 297
shock therapy, 34
sick role, 31–9
  limitations of, 32
  'mental illness', 33
Sinaikin, P., 55
situational analysis, 242, 245, 292
  see also Clarke, A.
Sklar, J., 205–6
Smail, D., xxxi, 19, 230
Smith, A., 139–42
social constructionism, 271
social therapy, xxii–iii, 125–30, 132–4, 136, 289
statutory regulation, xiii, xxxvii, 3–5, 45–6, 159, 162, 178, 291
Strong, T., xxxii, 12, 292
Stuart Mill, J., 139, 143
systemic therapy, 271
Szasz, T., 6, 36

talking therapies
  aetiologies of distress, 180
  and capitalism, 18, 287
  and class, 48
  as commercial industry, 227
  competing models, 180
  as cultural practices, 286, 292, 296
  and ethical codes, 162
  and gender, 48–9, 181
  legitimisation of power structures, 3
  and meaning making, 68, 71, 243, 253, 288

  nature of psychotherapeutic knowledge, 266
  outcomes, 37–8, 181, 225
  and political economy, 47, 51
  and politics, 18, 20, 169–70, 289
  psychotherapy, 104–6, 108, 110, 164, 173, 180
  and race and culture, 13, 163–4, 169
  relationship, xxvi, 68, 164–9, 226, 290
  research, 13, 179, 223
  and social control, 9
  and the state, xii, 45
  supervision, 162
  as symptom management, xvii, 248
  as vocation, 161, 170, 290
Tavistock Institute, 145
Thatcher, M., 145, 168
Thomas, P., 14–15
Totton, N., 19, 169
training, xxxv, 5, 7–8, 11, 176–7, 182, 231, 273, 275–6, 292
  academic institutions, 177, 266
  critical thinking, 176–7
  employment, 182, 186, 291
  QAA benchmarks, 185
  training standards, 177
  university based training, 11–13, 177
  see also counsellor education
Tudor, K., 18, 20, 21
Tuke, H.S., 30

United Kingdom Council for Psychotherapy (UKCP), 49, 160
United Kingdom Critical Psychiatry Network, *see* psychiatry
Universities Psychotherapy and Counselling Association (UPCA), 6

Verhaeghe, P., 9
Vlulence, xxxvii, 22, 297–8
Vygotsky, L., xxii, 125, 128, 130–4, 289

Watts, J., xxxv, 12, 292
Whitaker, R., xxxiv, 14, 58

Williams, L., 196
Williams, R., 144
Wilson, H., 144–5
Winnicott, D.W., 207, 210–12
Winship, G., 294

Wittgenstein, L., 132, 231
Wundt, W., 299

Zizek, S., 19, 195, 298
Zoloft, 56

Printed and bound by CPI Group (UK) Ltd, Croydon, CR0 4YY